To Don from Gilbert Nov 28, 98

The Loire produces 3 or 4
great Staple Wines that should
be the core of your inventory,

Sancerre   Pouilly Fumé
        almost the same - next to each
        other on a gorgeous part of
        the river

Muscadet   The Best White
    wine value in the World
    Drunk only within 2 years -
    Flinty - crappy dry - "
    drunk on hot days and
        with sea food —

We must broach this beautiful
    wines year after year —
No Dongs - Fabulous

JACQUELINE FRIEDRICH

AN OWL BOOK
HENRY HOLT AND COMPANY
NEW YORK

A

Wine and Food

Guide to the

LOIRE

Henry Holt and Company, Inc.
Publishers since 1866
115 West 18th Street
New York, New York 10011

Henry Holt® is a registered trademark
of Henry Holt and Company, Inc.

Library of Congress Cataloging-in-Publication Data
Friedrich, Jacqueline.
A wine and food guide to the Loire /
Jacqueline Friedrich.
p.   cm.
Includes bibliographical references and index.
1. Wine and wine making—France—Loire River Valley.   I. Title.
TP553.F75   1996   95-44727
641.2'2'09445—dc20   CIP

ISBN 0-8050-5782-X

Henry Holt books are available for special promotions and
premiums. For details contact: Director, Special Markets.

First published in hardcover in 1996 by
Henry Holt and Company, Inc.

First Owl Books Edition 1998

Designed by Kate Nichols
Maps designed by Jeffrey L. Ward

Printed in the United States of America
All first editions are printed on acid-free paper.∞

1   3   5   7   9   10   8   6   4   2

Several passages in this book have previously appeared in *The Wine
Spectator*; a handful of others appeared in *Travel & Leisure*, the *Los
Angeles Times*, and *Fine Wine Folio*.

CONTENTS

ACKNOWLEDGMENTS

Many people helped me survive my seven-year Loire odyssey. Among them, I would like to thank:

The two other charter members of "the old broad network"—Anne Mendelson (the only food writer I know whose prose reads like Jane Austen's) and my wonderful, idealistic editor, Beth Crossman.

Peter M. F. Sichel, who almost literally adopted the book and its author after having been asked to evaluate the manuscript by Holt—all the more moving as Peter has always been one of the people I most respect in wine.

Joyce Canel, who dotted my *i*'s, crossed my *t*'s, added accents, and brought groceries when deadlines kept me housebound.

Dave Stare, who came to the aid of a mathematically challenged wine writer faced with conversion tables.

Jim Gordon, my editor at *The Wine Spectator*, who, well aware of my likely transgressions, offered sage, sensible advice, and whose article assignments permitted me to update my research and test-fly my opinions.

Jean-François Dubreuil for Mouchamps, Noah, epic-tasting expeditions, and general hilariousness; Guy Bossard for his saintly patience and generosity; Auguste Blanchet, of Nantes's Chambre d'Agriculture, and Pascal Cellier, the director of the Anjou office of the Institut National des Appellations d'Origine (INAO), for their willingness to share their passion and their expertise; Michel Desroches and Jean-Jacques Thomas for being the world's least pretentious sommeliers as well as endlessly rewarding tasting buddies. Charles Joguet for super wines, meals, stories, and excursions and for having been the first to "get it."

Also: Régis and Lucette Abellard, Michel Augereau, Coco Baillargeant, Nono Baillargeau, Jean Baumard, Annie Bossard, Léon Boullault, everyone at the Château du Cléray (especially Philippe Aubron), Bernard Caron, Yves Chidaine, Didier Dagueneau, Philip di Belardino, Pierre Doucet, Martine Dubreuil, Colette Guilbaud, Anna Hennessey, Jérôme and Sylvie Huan, Michel and Réjane Humeau, Theo Kazamias, Joseph Landron, Monique Lansade, Michel Malinge, the Morgats, Paul Pauvert, Jean-Yves and Christiane Péron, Gérard Ryngel, Bernard Thevenet, the Nantes bureau of the INAO, and Olivier Couteaux in the Tours office.

Finally, four men who retired from "the vine" while I was writing this book, all from Anjou and each a source of inspiration for the quality revolution going on in that region today:

Jacques Boivin, who once closed an improvised but brilliant tasting on the theme of noble rot with three different *cuvées* of his father's extraordinary 1947 Château de Fesles Bonnezeaux, noting: "I was only ten years old when it was made but I participated from my heart in its vinification."

François Roussier, the gentle dean of Savennières, who, when I despaired of being able to taste mature versions, unearthed samples from the 1950s which had been bottled by the restaurant Le Vert d'Eau. (Roussier's lissome cabernets supplied yearly proof that Anjou could make beautiful reds as well as majestic whites.)

Dominique Jaudeau, elegant even in overalls, his voice made gravelly by cigarillos, which he drew on reflectively one crisp fall night near the end of the '89 harvest as we sipped a glowing, aristocratic '75 Layon-Chaume from brandy snifters.

And James Gauthier, who was there, too, that night. Not a winemaker but a bureaucrat who was about to retire from his job at the INAO, Gauthier's love for the vine is singularly unbureaucratic. On another night, in another cellar, we ended a day-long tasting with an exquisite 1921 Coteaux du Saumur, a sweet Chenin Blanc. James tasted. He shook his head. After more than forty years in wine, he was once again moved to tears, and said, "To think that a cluster of grapes could make this."

Amen.

PREFACE

The idea for this book followed a four-day stay in Touraine in June 1988. Like many outsiders who one day end up living in the Loire, I had previously written off the region as too grand, too bland, and too pretty, with its soft light and pink clouds and seemingly endless supply of must-see Renaissance châteaux. My interest in Loire wines hadn't gone much further than the tasty "petit Chinons" I habitually drank in the wine bistros of Paris. I simply didn't like Chenin Blanc as a grape variety. Or so I thought.

In four days I changed my mind completely. Not only did my thirst grow for the mouth-watering little Chinons, but I found the "serious" versions made by vignerons like Charles Joguet and Bernard Baudry exhilarating. The Vouvrays I tasted were revelations—gorgeous wines, some of the longest-lived and most complex whites in the world. A convert, I railed—glass of Gaston Huet's 1947 Vouvray in hand—against those who had given the Chenin Blanc grape a bad name by pushing it to overproduction and making from its juices flat, insipid wines.

I was hooked. And Touraine represented just a handful of the Loire's sixty-odd appellations. Once home in New York, I tacked the region's official wine map on my wall and found myself obsessively studying its circuitous path from Muscadet country in the west, through Anjou, Saumur, and Touraine (the heart of the Loire Valley), to Sancerre and Pouilly-sur-Loire in the east. The map stops there. The Loire does not. As the river swings south to its source in Ardèche, its upper reaches encompass four little-known appellations: Saint-Pourçain, the Côtes d'Auvergne, the Côte Roannaise, and the Côtes du Forez. (These enticed me, too. As a lover of gastronomic footnotes, I have a soft spot for quirky, personalized country wines.)

I began my research in July 1989, spent most of 1990 traveling along the Loire, and have been living in Touraine since 1991. Over the past six years I have met, interviewed, and tasted with more than six hundred winemakers (actually, I lost count after six hundred); sat on dozens of wine juries, including those for the *Guide Hachette;* attended scores of wine fairs and salons. I discovered wines I'd never heard of and rediscovered wines I thought I knew. And I became convinced that the Loire was France's last great unexplored viticultural region, with a broader diversity of wines—and a greater ensemble of utterly charming ones—than any I could think of.

It must be said that the Loire itself is, in large measure, responsible for its own obscurity: Much of the wines it produced prior to the 1980s were not worthy of acclaim. But the revolution in quality—which is far from over—has made the Loire one of the most exciting wine regions in France.

Even the French are unaware of the gems now being made in the Loire. I delight in provoking them to rethink appellations they took for granted—at the dinner table as well as in articles I've written for French magazines, and on TV and radio broadcasts. (Despite my accent, which I'm assured is "charming," I am often invited by FR3, one of France's major TV stations, to be its commentator on Loire wines.)

Not surprisingly, most of these are completely unknown to American wine-lovers. The Loire's several popular appellations are usually represented in the United States by characterless versions from big *négociant* houses. Frequently they round out the "cheap white" section of restaurant wine lists and liquor shop shelves.

Yet some of France's most food-friendly wines come from the Loire. I love substituting Muscadet or Cour-Cheverny for Pinot Grigio with Italian antipasti, or pairing Jasnières with risotto with wild mushrooms, or Sancerre rouge with mildly spiced jambalaya, or Chinon with freshwater fish in red-wine sauce.

Some of France's best winemaking occurs in the Loire, too, though few Americans are aware of it. Connoisseurs who seek out Jobard's Meursault and Clape's Cornas would be hard-pressed to name the best Saumur-Champigny or the quintessential Coteaux de l'Aubance. Tasting a fine-grained red from the Foucault brothers, or a limpid, honey-lemon sweet white from Victor Lebreton, however, is as gratifying as uncorking a wonderful Côte d'Or or an epic Rhône.

Indeed, the most dynamic young vignerons from the Rhône and Burgundy spend their vacations visiting their counterparts in the Loire—as do sommeliers and wine-bar and wine-shop owners, not to mention the wine press from Paris, London, Brussels, and Tokyo. And when I think of the wines and the winemakers—the Joguets, the Baudrys, the Huets, the Foucaults, the Lebretons, and so forth, I understand why I constantly feel compelled to visit yet another winery.

"Astonish me," Cocteau's imperative, is an aesthetic principle that has always resonated with me. Well, the Loire astonished me and it continues to astonish me. Every time I go to a tasting, my "to do" list gets longer: I discover one more fanatical newcomer, a ho-hum estate that has taken a heartening new direction, a group of vignerons who have imposed on themselves tougher standards, or a maniacal perfectionist who has turned a long-held winemaking assumption on its head.

What I hope to do in this book is to introduce you to *my* Loire: to a landscape I've come to love for its infinite nuances; to a river which, for me, has been a constant—and constantly engaging—traveling companion; and to a cuisine which I find both refined and soulful. I'd like to share with you my excitement about and my belief in its wines and its winemakers. In short, I'd like you to meet the Loire that has not ceased to astonish me.

I

The Loire

The Loire is France's royal river. The last wild river in Europe and the longest river in France, the Loire is a grand boulevard stretching 630 miles from its source on desolate Mont Gerbier de Jonc in Ardèche, through château country, to the Atlantic. The Loire has the evocative power of the Mississippi or the Danube. And many are the French authors who have said that, more than Paris, the Loire is the true heart of France, evoking for visitors the cradle of the language, the birth of the nation, its literature, and its history.

The Loire has always been a natural frontier. It divided southerners who spoke the *langue d'oc* from those who lived north of the river and spoke the *langue d'oïl*, which ultimately became the *langue française*. It was a barrier to invaders—even the Germans had to make their way around its tributaries. And until the advent of railroads it was the most important commercial axis in France. Great cities grew along its route: Nantes, Angers, Tours, Orléans, Roanne, Saint-Etienne, and Puy-en-Velay.

Much of French history was played out along its banks. In the fourth century Saint Martin, the most famous saint of the Gauls (it was he who divided his cloak with a beggar) founded the first monastery in France in Poitou. In 732 Charles Martel halted the Saracen armies' northernmost advance outside of Poitiers. Anjou was the seat of the Plantagenets;

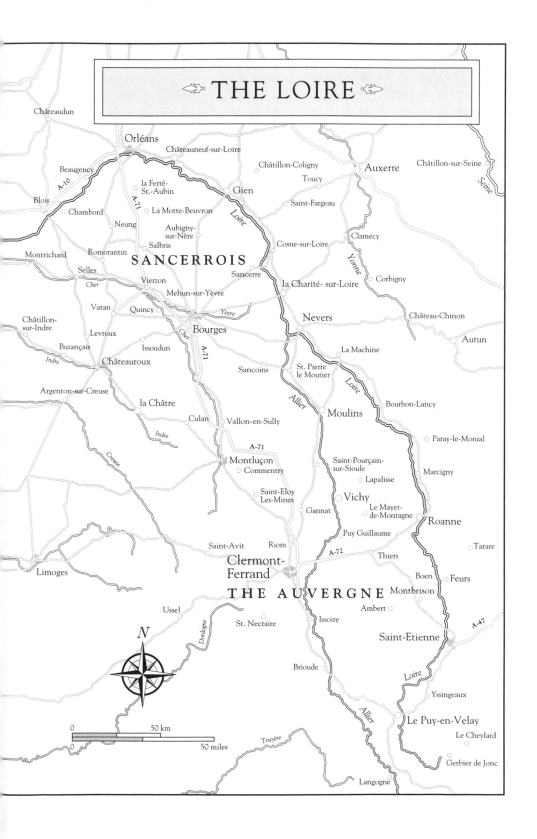

Eleanor of Aquitaine, Henri II, and Richard the Lionhearted are buried there in Fontevraud Abbey. Modern France is said to date from 1429, when, in the medieval château of Chinon, Joan of Arc persuaded the future Charles VII to accept the crown and take arms against the English. The Edict of Nantes, issued by Henri IV in 1598, guaranteed religious freedom to Protestants. The battlefields of France's barbarous and bloody counterrevolution, called the Vendée Wars, spread from Anjou to the Atlantic, leaving still visible scars on the land—razed churches, defaced religious sculptures, and windmills whose blades were lopped off to prevent communication among the rebels.

Many of France's most famous writers lived in and wrote about the Loire. François Rabelais, the great humanist, father of the novel, and author of *Gargantua and Pantagruel,* was born outside of Chinon and set much of the action in his books there. Gargantua drank in its wine cellars; Panurge sought "the truth" in the clear waters of the town's Caves Painctes; and the Picrochole War was fought on its surrounding hills, between the "kingdoms" of Seuilly and Lerné, in reality two farming villages.

Honoré de Balzac, the nineteenth-century author of *The Human Comedy,* a penetrating and often scathing view of French society, evoked the haunting, green Indre valley and the village of Saché (where he hid from creditors) in *Le Lys dans la Vallée.* The poet Joachim du Bellay wrote of the *douceur Angevine* (the mildness, or sweetness, or tenderness of Anjou); Ronsard, of the *douceurs* of Touraine and the Vendômois. The Loire was also home to Abelard, René Descartes, George Sand, and Alain-Fournier, who eulogized the brooding forests and ponds of Sologne in *Le Grand Meaulnes.*

The historian Jules Michelet wrote of the Loire as a dangerously unpredictable river, describing its "capricious and perfidious indolence." Deceptively languid, it is anything but benign. When it overflows, the river inundates the countryside. Talk of damming it, however, always misfires: The Loire is the last wild river in Europe and even the people likely to be hurt by it are against taming it. (Because of its volume, the Loire is also the most "nuclearized" river in Europe; France's first plant was built in Avoine, outside of Chinon.)

The Loire Valley, which runs from Orléans, about eighty miles southwest of Paris, west to Champtoceaux, near the mouth of the river, competes only with Paris and the Riviera as the most popular tourist destination in France. Indeed, for many, the Loire Valley is the countryside they conjure when they close their eyes and think "France." The sky is always soft, often a fragile blue; its light is moist and delicate, even in the dead of winter. The landscape is a tapestry of forests, farmland, and rivers, linking such Renaissance masterpieces as the châteaux of Chambord, Blois, Chenonceau, Amboise, and Azay-le-Rideau and the medieval château of Chinon.

There is another Loire, less grand, less imposing, wilder and more endearing. This is the Loire of back roads, of small Romanesque churches with great frescoes and chatty guardians; the Loire of wizened old women who still lead their goats to pasture and milk them by hand; the Loire of quiet villages, of shady river bends, of farms and vineyards, and now and then a minor castle in the distance, on a hill, beyond a line of trees.

We are in the garden of France. The climate is mild, and the people are, too. Nowhere in the world does daily life seem as agreeable as it does here. As one vintner said, "The Loire is paradise on a weekday."

This is the Loire of our wine route, and it extends far beyond the Loire Valley. Its circuit encompasses sixty-odd appellations and a dizzying diversity of wines, from the Côtes du Forez, whose vines begin north of the fields of green lentils above Puy-en-Velay, to the Fiefs Vendéens, whose vines grow within Frisbee-tossing distance of the Atlantic Ocean. Along our route are pungent Sancerres and creamy Pouilly-Fumés; luscious Vouvrays; succulent Chinons and Saumur-Champignys; opulent Coteaux du Layon; Coulée de Serrant, placed among the world's five best white wines by Curnonsky, Prince of Gastronomes; and Muscadet, as bracing as sea air.

For all their diversity, however, the wines of the Loire share stylistic threads. At the northern limits of viticulture, Loire wines tend to be lighter, nervier than wines from the Rhône or Bordeaux. Relatively low in alcohol, they have in common a gaiety, freshness, and fragrance born of exuberant fruit and bright acidity. They are wines that fit today's streamlined cooking and lifestyle without sacrificing personality. Artisanal, handcrafted wines, they are vivid without being heavy.

In an average year the Loire's roughly 73,000 hectares of vines produce an average of three million hectoliters of appellation—Appellations d'Origine Contrôleés (AOC) and Vin Délimité de Qualité Supérieure (VDQS)—wine plus another one million of Vin de Pays and *vin de table*. Ninety percent of it is made between Nantes and Blois. Aside from a small block between Tours and Saumur where the appellations Chinon, Bourgueil, and Saumur-Champigny are located, the Loire is white wine country. Its major white grapes are Chenin Blanc, Melon de Bourgogne (Muscadet), and Sauvignon Blanc; most of its reds and rosés are based on Cabernet Franc. Each of these grapes is cultivated in other parts of the world, but the Loire established the benchmarks.

Of the four principal grapes, only Sauvignon Blanc is regularly treated as star material beyond the confines of the Loire. To understand that Chenin Blanc can make some of the world's most thrilling, complex, long-lived whites, you must taste the versions from Anjou and Touraine. To comprehend the exciting nuances of Cabernet Franc you must sample wines from Cravant, Benais, and Parnay. To appreciate the fascinating way in which Melon expresses subtle distinctions of the sites and soils on which it grows, you must put a lacy Saint-Fiacre beside a robust Vallet.

Finally, for the wine traveler, I recall with what delight bordering on delirium I passed my first months in the Loire. No other wine region in France welcomes visitors with such warmth or simplicity. Tastings always last hours longer than anticipated, and the vintages tasted are likely to extend well beyond a visitor's birth year.

SOME LOIRE WINE HISTORY

From its source in Ardèche, the Loire rolls north to Orléans, then sweeps west to Nantes before emptying into the Atlantic. Its basin encompasses 20 percent of France. The river and its tributaries (including the Allier, the Cher, the Indre, and the Vienne) touch fourteen departments (loosely, the French administrative equivalent of our states) and about ten ancient provinces, from Auvergne to Brittany.

Vines have been cultivated since Roman times, when local wines slaked the thirst of occupying troops. Viticulture flourished with the spread of Christianity as wine was needed to celebrate the Mass. Subject always to vagaries—wars, invasions, plagues—vines were planted, wiped out, abandoned, and replanted, for the most part by religious orders and local seigneurs. The monks of Vertou, for example, were largely responsible for the development and restoration of Nantais vineyards in the eleventh century, after the barbarian invasion. They also built a dam on the Sèvre which made the river navigable and permitted the transport of local wines to Nantes. The good brothers of Saint-Nicolas-d'Angers cleared, planted, and cultivated the slopes of Savennières; the monks of Saint-Florent prepared the hillsides outside of Saumur for vines; and the order of Saint-Lézin introduced the Pineau d'Aunis grape to the Sarthe. In 1089 Baudry, the abbot of Bourgueil, planted Cabernet Franc in its vineyards. In the fourth century Saint Martin ordered the planting of vines in Vouvray near his Marmoutier monastery outside Tours. The monks of Saint-Satur planted the hillsides of

Sancerre; the Benedictines of La Charité-sur-Loire cultivated those of Pouilly; and the vineyards of Reuilly were intimately linked to a priory in that commune.

Throughout the Middle Ages, vines stretched along rivers extending as far north as La Flèche, Château-Gontier, and Segré and as far west as Guérande. They surrounded the cities of Nantes, Angers, Saumur, Tours, and Orléans. Documents reflect the high esteem enjoyed by wines from Ris, near Vichy, as well as those from Issoudun in the Indre.

Wines from the Loire traveled abroad as early as the twelfth century. Indeed, only Bordeaux shipped more wine by sea than the Loire. The best— or the best situated for shipment— often graced royal tables, inspiring poets, philosophers, and kings. Pierre Bréjoux notes that Apollonius, in the sixth century, sang of an Angers which "Bacchus had showered with his gifts." Writing in 1605 the great agricultural expert Olivier de Serres declared that Anjou was so "well endowed with fine white wines and clairets that it seemed good father Noah had chosen it as the land in which to make his masterpiece and to teach his science to its inhabitants." In the sixteenth century, Rabelais, Joachim du Bellay, and Ronsard wrote of the Touraine's *vins de taffetas* (taffeta wines). Three centuries later its vintages inspired Balzac and de Vigny.

As Bréjoux notes in *Les Vins de Loire* (1956), the movement of the French court along the royal river gave rise to and then ensured the renown of the wines of these provinces. In 1148 Louis VII wrote from the Crusades to order his favorite wine, an Orléanais. The Plantagenets (1154 to 1485) popularized Anjou's *crus* among English nobility. In the thirteenth century Bishop Guillaume d'Auvergne, who prided himself on drinking only the best, served Anjou wines when he received the king. François Ier is credited with having planted the obscure Romorantin grape. Henri IV is reputed to have said of the wines of a village near Sancerre, "Chavignol is the best wine I have drunk. If all the people of my kingdom were to drink it, there would be no more religious wars." He also maintained a vineyard in Vouvray to supply his table. Louis XII favored a long-since-forgotten Blésois *cru*, Le Galipeau. Philippe le Bel was a particular admirer of the wines of Saint-Pourçain and his enthusiasm made them a must among the nobility. Saint-Pourçain also furnished the papal cellars in Avignon; it was poured at the most sacred ceremonies or when the pope received princes or great gentlemen.

A significant factor in the success of many Loire wines was the access to markets afforded by the river and its tributaries. From the Middle Ages until the end of the nineteenth century, the Loire was one of France's most important commercial arteries. Wine was one of the principal commodities carried by ships plying the river.

Here we must separate the Loire into two blocks: west and east. Wines from Blois to Brittany were shipped mostly to Nantes, a sheltered harbor near the mouth of the Loire which linked France with the West Indies, England, and Holland; those from Orléans to Pouilly and Saint-Pourçain went to Paris. The exigencies of those two different markets determined the development of the vineyards in both blocks as well as the styles of wine made.

West of Blois the story is one of taxes. Wine was a cash cow. Taxes levied on its transport rebuilt Saumur after the Hundred Years' War, for example, and filled the coffers of local satraps as well as those of the medieval corporation Les Marchands Fréquentants la Rivière de Loire, a guild of boatmen who used the tax they themselves imposed and collected to maintain the river and its levees and to keep river traffic flowing. In his *Vins d'Anjou* (1925) Dr. Maisonneuve describes the taxes of the sixteenth century as fearsome, listing fourteen for a trip from Angers to Nantes. (Reading this, one is not surprised that taxes were one of the flash points sparking the French Revolution.)

The most onerous tax—and the one that would have the most impact on western Loire wines—was the one collected at Ingrandes, at the border of Anjou and the ancient duchy of Brittany. Until the Revolution, wines entering Brittany for export via Nantes paid heavy duties as they passed the customs office at Ingrandes. Breton wines were exempt. Wines from Anjou or Touraine, inevitably more expensive than the wines of Nantes, had to be worth the inflated price. Thus, only the best wines from Anjou and Touraine were sent down the Loire for export. These were *vins pour la mer* (wines for the sea). Lesser wines were *vins pour Paris* (wines for Paris).

Historians of the vine, such as Dr. Guyot and Roger Dion, believe that this tax, more than incremental changes in climate, explains the abrupt switch from a noble grape variety upstream of Ingrandes, where Chenin Blanc predominates, to a common one downstream, where Gros Plant (Folle Blanche) takes over.

From the beginning of the seventeenth century the Dutch were the kings of European maritime commerce. The principal buyers of Nantais, Anjou, and Touraine wine for the two hundred years preceding phylloxera, they exploited this tax-induced price disparity. They encouraged vintners upstream of Ingrandes to make fine sweet whites, thus ensuring Chenin's primacy, and they won over Nantais producers by paying a lot more for Folle Blanche than its growers were used to getting.

Eager to oblige, the Nantais ripped up red vines, replanted Folle Blanche, and extended the vineyards onto rich agricultural soils for abundant yields. Quite literally, they were making wine to burn. The Dutch, who were largely responsible for the proliferation of Folle Blanche along France's Atlantic front, made distillation part of the normal harvest cycle in the Nantais as they had done from Charente to the Adour. Their clients wanted strong sweet whites. And the Folle Blanche–based *eau-de-vie* was used to "ameliorate" wines of all quality; it beefed up thin, weak ones and, Roger Dion notes, gave the best *"une certaine chaleur qui flattait le goût du consommateur septentrional"* (a certain heat which pleased the taste of consumers in the north). It also became the "cordial" of sailors, who then popularized the beverage in ports of call.

Legislators, meanwhile, feared wheat shortages as well as the ire of Angevins who found themselves priced out of the brandy export market. They imposed export fees on Breton *eau-de-vie* and prohibited further vineyard extensions. But planting continued. Until phylloxera, Folle Blanche covered two-thirds of the Nantais. The vine blanketed the Atlantic seaboard, from the Rhuis Peninsula to the Pyrenees.

The Dutch also moved viticulture from Nantes and Angers to the countryside, to Vallet, for example, and the Coteaux du Layon. They erected warehouses along the Loire and its tributaries in Les-Ponts-de-Cé, Chalonnes, and Rochefort, and they lobbied for the canalization of the Layon.

Neither the port of Nantes nor Dutch merchants influenced viticulture east of Blois, however. From Orléans to Saint-Pourçain, vignerons looked to Paris. In the Middle Ages wines traveled to Orléans and from there to the capital—as well as to England, Normandy, and Flanders. In 1642 the opening of the Canal de Briare linked the Loire and the Loing, giving more direct access to Paris. Wines from Menetou-Salon, and those from Quincy, traveled to Bourges.

Historians surmise that during the Middle Ages the region's wines were white. In the beginning of the fifteenth century Pinot Noir (called Noirien or Morillon) appeared; by the seventeenth century it covered Sancerre's vineyards, while numerous white varieties continued to flourish in Pouilly and Quincy. Those cited include Pinot Gris, Chardonnay, and "Muscat Gennetin" (believed to be Sauvignon Blanc).

Degradation of many of the region's vineyards started in 1577 after the Paris Parliament issued a law forbidding wine merchants, *bistrotiers*, and tavern-keepers from buying wine within eighty-eight kilometers of the city. The first vineyard area beyond that zone was the Orléanais. Growers from Orléans, Blois, Montrichard, Saint-Aignan, and Sologne responded by replacing Pinot Noir, Chardonnay, and the like with the higher-yielding Pinot Meunier, Gamay, and worse —Teinturier and Gouais. After the Revolution and through the nineteenth century, property continued to change hands, vineyard plantings were extended, and yields continued to rise. The vineyards of Pouilly, which at the end of the nineteenth century included at least a dozen varieties, were largely given over to Chasselas. The grape existed in the area and was much sought after by Paris fruit merchants who came to the region looking for table grapes, for which they were willing to pay higher prices than they paid for wine.

At about the time that Paris fruiterers were buying up the Chasselas crop in Pouilly, the vine louse phylloxera was eating its way through the French vineyards, entering those of the Loire a bit before 1880. Reconstitution took place in the interstices of the two World Wars, accompanied by an exodus of the young from the countryside. The setting up of the appellations, begun in 1936, resumed in the 1950s, along with the evolution of specialized farming and the founding of cooperatives. Schools of viticulture and enology were created and nearly every aspect of viticulture was mechanized. These upheavals revolutionized the production of wine in France, with stunning impact on the Loire. Before considering some of these developments, which are, in essence, man-made, I'd like to examine Mother Nature's contribution to Loire viticulture by looking at its climate, its soils, and its choice of grapes. (Because the vineyards of Auvergne are so distant—in every respect—from those of the rest of the Loire, they will not be discussed here.)

THE CLIMATE

Weather forecasters in France use the Loire to demarcate climatic regions, describing tendencies for all areas north of the river, then those to the south. The river, too, marks the northern limit of viticulture, which is generally described as running along the right bank of the Loir, approaching the Loire downstream of Angers. Balmy ocean air, sucked up the corridor of the Loire and its tributaries, brings a tempering maritime influence far into the continent. As we move east, however, the ocean's influence becomes more attenuated, the climate more continental. Indeed, in climatic terms, the Loire can be divided into two distinct blocks, the same as above: from Nantes to Blois, and from Orléans to Pouilly.

The French sum up the climate of the western Loire in two words, *doux* (mild) and *humide* (damp). Summers and winters are clement; brutally hot days are as infrequent as snow. Magnolias, cedars, fig trees, and parasol pines flourish as in Provence; Nantais truck gardens send vegetables to market all year. Spring comes early, however, making frosts—like those of 1945, 1991, and 1994—the perennial nightmare of the vigneron. Luminous and warm autumns permit the Angevin and the Tourangeau vigneron to wait—sometimes until mid-November—to pick late-ripening Chenin for their lush *moelleux*. In the Nantais, however, autumns can be abrupt, bringing stiff winds and torrential rain. By the end of September the Muscadet harvest had better be in.

Aside from several notable exceptions, the region's greatest vineyards are located on the left banks of the Loir (a river running from the Ile-de-France to Anjou) and the Loire, often where it meets a tributary, as in the Sèvre-et-Maine and the Coteaux du Layon. Here the vine finds numerous accommodating sites—particularly on the south-facing hillsides which are sunnier than the cold, wet plains, and often sheltered from ocean storms and winds by various reliefs. The most dramatic example is the Coteaux du Layon, which is protected from inclement weather by the Mauges mountains at the border of the Maine-et-Loire and the Loire-Atlantique.

As we travel east of Blois the ocean's influence diminishes. By the time we arrive in the Sancerrois, the climate is as much "continental" as it is oceanic. Its harsh winters and hot summers approach the extremes of Burgundy. The butte of Humbligny, the highest point in the Paris Basin, traps rainfall before it reaches Sancerre and Pouilly, which are, as a result, relatively dry. Spring frosts and hail, however, are constant threats, seriously diminishing, even annihilating, entire crops. The best vineyards are on hillsides and ancient alluvial terraces.

It is often said, and it is true, that the notion of vintage is critical in the Loire because of the great fluctuations of rainfall and sunlight from year to year. In general, however, grapes have no problem reaching maturity—though in the cooler climate of the Loire, maturity, for grapes like Cabernet Franc and Sauvignon Blanc, usually hovers around 10.5 to 12 percent potential alcohol (the degree reached when the sugar has been converted into alcohol by fermentation). In great vintages like '89 and '90, these varieties easily reach 13.5 and 14, and higher. And Chenin Blanc shoots off refractometers, attaining 23 to 30 percent potential alcohol.

THE SOILS

The Loire begins its journey to the sea in the Massif Central and flows into the ocean in the Massif Armoricain. As it loops its way north and west it crosses a third landmass, the Paris Basin, created in the Secondary era when the sea invaded a huge bowl bounded in the west by the Saumurois and the east by Sancerre-Pouilly. When the ocean retreated it left behind a soft, chalky deposit known as tuffeau or tufa.

The soils of Anjou and the Nantais are Massif Armoricain soils, laid down in the Primary era. The shallow topsoils of the Nantais range from sand or pebbles to gneiss and granite; its subsoils consist of decomposed rock with varying percentages of clay, silica, and schist. Anjou's obdurate blue-black soils, while primarily schist, are striated with sandstone, silica, granite, and volcanic rocks such as quartz and phthanite as well as the slate which provides the Loire's emblematic roofing material.

The Paris Basin meets the Massif Armoricain south of Angers, near Gennes and Les-Ponts-de-Cé, marking the beginning of the Saumurois. Saumur and Touraine rest on a tuffeau base. As the rivers dug their beds in the tuffeau, they molded the gentle slopes; well-exposed, well-drained hills, generally from 50 to 120 meters high, which just happened to be perfect for vines. (And the tuffeau cliffs, quarried for châteaux, bridges, and homes, left deep, cool cellars, perfect for wine storage.)

After crossing the marshes and forests of Sologne we reach Sancerre and Pouilly, the southeastern rim of the Paris Basin. The best soils, chalk on tender Kimmeridgian marl, resemble those of Chablis. This type of soil, which makes the region's finest, most complex wines, is often found on slopes whose bases are layered with compact chalk.

Within each zone the variations are infinite. Some soils are streaked with silex, for example; others with quartz. Some have greater percentages of clay, others are sandier, and so forth. This is why a Muscadet from the commune of Vallet seems more robust than a lacy Saint-Fiacre; or why a Layon from Saint-Lambert seems blander than one from Chaume; or a Chinon from the sandy riverbanks of Savigny more of a quaffer than a structured, tannic bottle from the slopes of Beaumont; or why Sancerre from the silex-rich soils of Ménétréol is flintier and harder than one from the pebbly, calcareous slopes of Bué. In short, the Loire presents distinctions of soils and exposition to fascinate wine-lovers forever. The choice of grapes further enriches the palette.

THE GRAPES

A land of passage, the Loire benefited from a multitude of influences in viticulture as in other realms. Its vineyards have accommodated the Verdelho of Madeira, the Furmint of Hungary, and hybrids from America, as well as grapes from all parts of France, including vinifera crosses like Arbouriou and Egiodola. Its most important grapes are either indigenous or hail from the southwest, notably the Bordelais, or from Burgundy. The four key varietals are Chenin Blanc, Cabernet Franc, Melon de Bourgogne (better known as Muscadet), and Sauvignon Blanc. (When speaking of Chenin and Sauvignon, the French do not add the word *Blanc*. I hereinafter adopt that usage.)

Chenin, also known as Pineau de la Loire, is the king of the Loire. Cultivated in Anjou since at least 845, it takes its name from the Clos du Mont-Chenin in Touraine. A robust variety, Chenin is the principal white wine grape of Anjou, Touraine, and the Sarthe, producing about 500,000 hectoliters yearly, more than a quarter of the Loire's white wine. It is the sole grape permitted for their greatest wines—Savennières, Coteaux du Layon (including its *crus*, Bonnezeaux and Quarts-de-Chaume), Coteaux de l'Aubance, Anjou-Coteaux de la Loire, Coteaux de Saumur, Vouvray, Montlouis, and Jasnières—as well as the base of much of the Loire's sparkling wine.

A true marriage of varietal, soil, and climate, Chenin's primacy is an exciting illustration of how grape, *terroir*, and man can conspire to make exceptional wine. Nowhere else does Chenin succeed so brilliantly. Perhaps no other varietal could achieve the stature Chenin does in the marginal climate and on the particular soils of the Loire. Yet its importance seems a contradiction: The vine flowers early, making it vulnerable to the Loire's not infrequent spring frosts. It ripens fairly late, usually in mid-October, a gamble in a zone marking the limit of boreal and meridional climates. But autumns in Anjou and Touraine are often long and sunny. And Chenin's best vineyards are situated on south-facing hills whose well-drained soils permit the grape to reach the end of its vegetative cycle.

Before I came to the Loire I thought I simply didn't like Chenin. Jug Chenins from California—where the grape was pushed to yield 130 hectoliters per hectare—were flabby; *négociant* Vouvrays were oversulfured, oversugared, dirty, and sharp. After tasting my way through Vouvray, the Layon, Aubance, and Savennières, however, I've got a cellar full of Loire Chenin. It has become my desert island white.

Its best producers say, and I agree, that Chenin is a difficult wine for new-comers but an exciting one for connoisseurs. It is, perhaps, unique in that its sole purpose is to be exceptional. It is hard to make and hard to understand; in mediocre vintages it can be painfully acid; when poorly made— or simply in a dumb stage— it can smell vulgar and raunchy (when Chenin flaunts its negative aspects, locals say it *chenasses*); and it always needs bottle age. To really taste Chenin, you need to give it time. Most important, it doesn't *do* mediocrity well. Either it's nasty or it's extraordinary. The banal ones may be pleasant enough drinking, but they have lots of competition. "Good" is not where Chenin shines. (Sauvignon, on the other hand, can make top-notch "good" wines.) If Chenin is not destined to make an out-of-this-world wine, there is no reason to plant it. Never standard, never monotonous, it expresses each nuance of climate, of soil, of winemaking.

The keys to making great Chenin are good land, low yields, and harvest by *tris*, successive passes through the vineyard in order to pick the best clus-ters at the best stage of their development.

In the Loire, Chenin is elaborated in a number of different styles. The three types of sparkling wine are *pétillant*, *mousseux*, and *Crémant de Loire*, made by the *méthode champenoise*. Still wines come in a range of sweet-nesses: sec (dry or slightly off-dry); demi-sec (literally "half-dry" but more accurately half-sweet); *moelleux* (fully sweet); and *doux* or *liquoreux* (pro-foundly sweet, almost syrupy). In the Coteaux du Layon (including Bon-nezeaux and Quarts-de-Chaume) and the Coteaux de l'Aubance, *doux* and *liquoreux* are sometimes called Séléction de Grains Nobles (SGN or GN).

The INAO does not specify the amount of residual sugar required for each level of wine. The European Economic Community (EEC), however, defines terms used on labels as follows: sec, up to 4 grams residual sugar (with the possibility of up to 9 grams depending on the wine's acidity); demi-sec, from 4 to 12 grams; *moelleux*, from 12 to 45 grams; anything above 45 grams is *doux* or *liquoreux*. In my experience, however, vintners in Anjou and Touraine appear to respect these laws about as much as they do speed limits: Many are the secs or *sec-tendres* (a category not recognized by the EEC) with 5 grams or more of residual sugar, and *moelleux* on a label can often bring a wine with well over 50 grams.

Botrytis, the noble rot that makes Sauternes so luscious, is not all that fre-quent in the Loire, where there is less fog than in Bordeaux. (Though a mid-morning visitor to the Corniche Angevine often sees mists rising off the Loire Valley.) Some vintages ('90 is a notable example) yield heavily botrytized grapes; others, including years like '89, find very little noble rot; rather the grapes are picked at "normal overripeness" or they shrivel like raisins and are called *passerillés*. This concentrates the sugars and results in little loss of acid, producing classic Chenins—lush, textured, balanced, fresh, and vivacious.

Soils account for the dramatic difference between the great Chenins of Touraine and those of Anjou, starting with the sheer weight of the wine. Next to a Layon, Vouvray seems austere, fine-boned, lace rather than velvet. It is less alcoholic, but that doesn't say it all. A Layon will taste and feel thicker, more unctuous; Vouvray, more restrained, svelter. It is as if the wine reveals the different effort made by the vine to thrive on the Loire's different soils; the structure and texture of the wines mirror now the obdurate black soils of Anjou, now the porous creamy stone of Vouvray. A Layon vine, forcing its roots through schist, makes a fleshy, muscular, as well as alcoholic Chenin. On chalk—easier for a vine's roots to penetrate and for the sun to heat—Chenin is ethereal.

Young Chenin is a charmer—floral, honeyed, with scents of quince, pineapple, peach, and apricot. It passes rather quickly from nubile youth into an ornery adolescence, which can last a decade. After that it begins to reveal its endless complexity and lip-smacking succulence. In a good cellar it is immortal. I've sampled many '76s, '59s, '47s; even as far back as the 1890s. The wine just keeps getting better. Rabelais was right on the money when he had a character in *Gargantua* exclaim, "It's a wine of taffeta, well woven and of good yarn." Indeed, the flavors seem to shimmer, like light on taffeta, offering layer after layer of honey, lemon, herbs, toast, menthol, and more. The wine, which seems to become drier over time, is constantly appetizing. You feel you never get to the bottom of it. Simultaneously taut and luscious, austere and voluptuous, it teases you. It gives you the impression of being sweet and then persuades you that it is utterly dry.

One of my favorite descriptions of aged Chenin comes from Robert Denis, a winemaker in Azay-le-Rideau, where orchards abut vines. "In an old Chenin you often find flowering linden blossom followed by an infusion of mint and ripe hay," he said as we tasted his sumptuous '67. "When I was a boy and harvested hay I'd put my arms around a bale and stick my nose into it. That's the aroma I mean. Then you get pear blossoms and apple blossoms. Often the flavors blend in, but sometimes they seem compartmentalized so that you have the image of an entire countryside passing before you." There were tears in his eyes.

Cabernet Franc is the queen of the Loire. It reigns in Chinon, Bourgueil and Saint-Nicolas-de-Bourgueil, in Saumur-Champigny, and in Anjou. Though its dominance wanes as we move east, Cabernet Franc also plays an important role in many of the Touraines—either alone or blended—as well as in reds from the Orléanais, Haut-Poitou, Fiefs Vendéens, and various Vins de Pays. It is also the base of many dry and off-dry rosés, including Cabernet d'Anjou. Overall it represents 46 percent of the Loire's red-grape acreage.

A relatively late ripener, Cabernet Franc is a hardy grape and resistant to rot, which enables it to take advantage of the Loire's Indian summers. Planted in Anjou and Touraine sometime in the Middle Ages, it arrived by way of Bordeaux, where it is still widely cultivated, particularly in Saint-Emilion, where it dominates the blend of the great Cheval Blanc. Cabernet Sauvignon, which ripens somewhat later than Cabernet Franc, is the red grape of Bordeaux's Médoc and Graves districts. It is also planted in the Loire. With the exception of Anjou, however, its role is of minor importance here. When locals say "Cabernet" they mean "Franc."

(In the Loire, Cabernet Franc is often called Breton, a name many ascribe to the grape's port of entry to the vineyards of the Loire; others claim the name came from Richelieu's Abbé Breton, who, according to this theory, first cultivated the grape in its vineyards. But Rabelais, a reliable chronicler of all things gastronomic, spoke of the "good wine of breton which does not grow in Brittany but in this good land of Véron" [part of the Chinon appellation] nearly two hundred years before the Abbé's arrival.)

Cabernet Franc is favored for its concentrated berry flavors, its supple texture, its finesse, its gentle tannins, and its lively acidity, all of which account for the fact that it charms when young and beguiles when aged. On the gravelly riverbanks of Bourgueil and Chinon, Cabernet Franc makes a buoyant red, a cross between a juicy Beaujolais and a young claret, a perfect *vin de soif* (thirst-quenching wine). Champignys have, for the past decade, been among the most fashionable red wines of Paris. They, as well as reds from the hillsides of Chinon, Bourgueil, and Saint-Nicolas-de-Bourgueil, have the effortless elegance characteristic of grapes grown on tuffeau, the soft, porous stone of the Loire's châteaux. Anjous tend to be chunkier, chewier, more "masculine"—foursquare reds issued from schisty soils.

A young Breton sometimes tastes bell-peppery but is more often downright jammy and surging with fruit flavors—strawberry, raspberry, *cassis*, plum, and cherry. A Breton ages beautifully, too —though not like a Bordeaux, a Burgundy, or a Rhône. It passes through a secondary phase when it fairly reeks of musk and hung game. Then, instead of flowering, it seems to shed its baby fat, to be constantly refining itself, becoming translucent, a distillation of scents and nuances— of cranberry, cinnamon, and *crème de cassis;*

prune, licorice, and sandalwood; dried flowers, dried fruit, ripe hay, mint, bark, truffles, and ash—all the while retaining its vigor and mouth-watering freshness. I often think of old Bretons as the embodiment of memory—not of a specific memory, but of memory itself. I have an image of an old handkerchief made of fine cloth softened after years of being folded into purses, still carrying whiffs of many exquisite perfumes, mingled, muted, and fugitive.

Melon de Bourgogne, with more than 750,000 hectoliters yearly, is the Loire's second most important white varietal. It became the principal grape of the Nantais, along with Gros Plant, when growers sought winter-hardy vines to replace those destroyed by the devastating freezes of 1709. Banned from its native Burgundy in 1567, it was probably imported to the Nantais in the seventeenth century, where by 1635 it had become Muscadet. When vineyards were once again reconstituted after phylloxera, Muscadet eclipsed Gros Plant; it was richer and less acidic, and it ripened by mid-September, before the fall equinox brought rain and cold weather.

Muscadet is naturally low in acid. Contrary to its gum-curling reputation (which likely stems from wines without sufficient fruit or alcohol to balance even trace levels of acid), it must be picked early to retain its freshness.

Another surprise is that Muscadet is not as easy to understand as one thinks: It is subtle, not flashy; its flavors are low-key—lemon and bitter almond. It doesn't have the instantly identifiable green-bean aromas of Sauvignon or the exotic litchi perfumes of Gewürztraminer. It lets its site speak. According to Léon Boullault of the Domaine des Dorices in Vallet, the "Capital of Muscadet": "Muscadet is not a grape where you're looking for varietal character. With Muscadet, you're looking for a wine of the *terroir*, not of the grape; and above all, a grand finesse."

The Southwest disputes with the Loire the origins of Sauvignon, the principal white grape of Sancerre, Pouilly-Fumé, Menetou-Salon, Reuilly, Quincy, and Coteaux du Giennois. It is the most successful generic white Touraine, particularly around Oisly and Soings as well as in Haut-Poitou. It is also a popular varietal for the Loire's numerous Vins de Pays and part of the palette in the Fiefs Vendéens and Saint-Pourçain.

Most authorities say that the grape came to the Loire via Bordeaux, where it is blended with Sémillon, making a suave dry white as well as Sauternes. But if it originated in the Loire, it disappeared for quite a while, returning in force only in the 1920s—at about the time that paid vacations and car travel took Parisians past the vineyards of Sancerre and Pouilly on their way to beaches where sun, surf, and seafood created an unquenchable thirst for dry white wines.

Once Sauvignon took hold in the Loire, however, it forged a style that would be imitated from Napa to New Zealand—a fruity, instantly recognizable, zingy white, with a fullness of body that approaches Chardonnay.

Unlike Chenin, Sauvignon is an easy wine to like and an easy one to understand. Immediately appealing, it is usually the first grape debutant tasters can distinguish blind. Its characteristic aromas are green bean, asparagus, grass, grapefruit, cat's pee, and so forth. In the Loire's cool climate, Sauvignon has typically made a nervy, aggressive wine, and its admirers came to love just that pugnacity—so bracing in a wine bar, so perfect with a tangy goat cheese.

There's a new Loire Sauvignon, however. I'm not referring here to the high-yield, bordering-on-fraud Sauvignon of which the Loire, alas, has far too many. I'm talking about an ambitious Sauvignon that takes its inspiration from Burgundy, replacing aggressive herbaceousness with subtler fruit, creamier texture, and depth of flavor. The new Sauvignon is harvested later, vinified more slowly, at cooler temperatures — often with aromatic yeasts— and it is, for people who thought they knew Sauvignon, derailing. Reminiscent of Pinot Gris from Alsace, its aromas include apricot, peach, Muscat, fig, and—if it has fermented in new oak—anise, vanilla, and toast. It's sumptuous and it's classy, terrific as a first-course wine in, say, Taillevent or the Four Seasons.

Where Sauvignon will never equal Chenin, however, is that it really doesn't age in a way that's compelling. It can't sound the depths of complexity and nuance that Chenin does. It has given the best of what it's got to give five years after the harvest. I've tasted old ones, very old ones, and have been impressed that they were still alive—charmed even—but I was not convinced that they had gained anything in the process. That shouldn't diminish their popularity. When they're good, they're delicious enough to consume happily while contemplating the Chenins aging quietly in the cellar.

A footnote to the Sauvignon story is the recent foray into late-harvest versions. Inspired by the spectacular ripenesses of the drought years of '89 and '90, a number of vintners in Sancerre, Pouilly, the Coteaux du Giennois, and Reuilly made off-dry and *moelleux* versions. Some were rather stunning, most were rather vulgar. At least at this stage, sweet Sauvignon does not seem to be the wave of the future. But the grape does: At 300,000 hectoliters yearly, it has replaced Gros Plant as the Loire's third most important white varietal.

Gros Plant came to the Loire from the Southwest. The Folle Blanche of Charente, it is a rude grape that other regions have seen fit to rename Picpoule (lip stinger), Enragéat, Plant Enragé, no doubt in honor of its vigor (Folle Blanche easily yields 100 to 160 hectoliters a hectare) as well as its corrosive acidity. In the Nantais, Gros Plant seems a feckless kind of grape. As one frustrated producer observed, "It ripens poorly, and when it ripens, it often rots. Either it's healthy and unripe, or it's ripe and rotten. From time to time it has good maturity, but finally," he concludes, "it's not very interesting."

Gros Plant's presence in the Nantais vineyard has less to do with the viticultural niceties of soil and climate than it does with the economics of being downstream of Ingrandes, and thus exempt from the tax on wine imposed at the border of the ancient duchy of Brittany. Until phylloxera, Gros Plant covered two-thirds of the Nantais. Then it nearly disappeared until resuscitated by VDQS status in 1954, after which it most likely replaced hybrids. The sharp, acid wine it makes is often recommended by doctors as a diuretic. At 200,000 hectoliters yearly, Gros Plant du Pays Nantais is the largest VDQS in France. The grape is often used as well as a base for the region's sparkling wines, and has been trucked in great quantity to Germany for use in sparkling Sekts.

Among the Loire's other white grapes are the well-traveled Chardonnay; Chasselas, primarily a popular table grape; and several obscure grapes, each unique to a zone of production: Romorantin in Cour-Cheverny, Tressallier in Saint-Pourçain. Arbois, or Menu Pineau (a cousin of Chenin), grows in Touraine but is quickly disappearing. Fié is a mutation of Sauvignon Blanc. Pinot Gris, called Malvoisie in parts of the Loire, is used to make whites and rosés.

In red grapes, Grolleau, discovered in Touraine in the nineteenth century, follows Cabernet as the most widespread. It is the workhorse of the Loire, a heavy yielder used as the base of Anjou's erstwhile cash cow, the off-dry Rosé d'Anjou or de Saumur. Grolleau (or Groslot) Gris, a mutation of Grolleau, makes a copper-tinged wine—its ripe berries are a coppery purple—which drinks like a cross between a rosé and a white wine. Their principal areas of cultivation are Vendée, the Pays de Retz, and Anjou.

Grolleau, whose acreage is rapidly declining, can make savory dry rosés and delightful, tart, kirsch-scented reds. Naturally low in alcohol (between

7 and 10 percent), the reds are usually sold in plastic jugs called cubitainers or in bulk to local *boules* clubs. Producers describe them as *vins de chasse* (hunt wines), *vins de cave* (wine-cellar wines), or *vins de casse-croûte—casse-croûte* being the Loire equivalent of a coffee break, usually consisting of red wine, *rillettes*, *boudin noir*, and *andouillettes*. Though these contexts don't exist in America, they nicely evoke the setting for a good Grolleau rouge, a chillable wine bar red you'd be happy to have along at a barbecue.

Gamay Noir à Jus Blanc is the third most important red grape in the Loire, currently producing 400,000 hectoliters yearly, 25 percent of the Loire's reds and rosés. Principally grown east of Tours and in Auvergne, it also makes delightful reds in Anjou. But throughout the Loire the Beaujolais grape seems to rediscover its innocence. Succulent and flavorful, it recalls the Beaujolais I adored before Beaujolais became so industrialized. Some wineries turn out *primeur* versions, but the best are the regular bottlings. With surging fruit flavors, fine structure (light but firm), and a mineral backdrop, these Gamays are anything but generic. (When I speak of Gamay, unless otherwise indicated, I mean Gamay Noir à Jus Blanc.)

Pinot Noir traveled from Burgundy to Sancerre, Saint-Pourçain, Orléans, and Joué-les-Tours in the Middle Ages. Today it represents a mere 4 percent of Loire plantings. Blended with Pinot Meunier and Pinot Gris in Noble Joué, it makes a delightful rosé; in the Coteaux du Giennois, it can make a light red of substance and charm. The very best red Sancerres are, of course, more serious. They are not Chambertin but they are wonderful, medium-bodied reds expressing everything Pinot nuts like me love about that grape. Pinot Meunier, called Gris Meunier, is now often blended with Pinot Noir in the Orléanais, though I prefer each bottled pure.

Cot, or Malbec, is permitted in a number of Loire appellations but is used extensively only in Touraine, where it may be bottled pure or form part of a blend with Gamay and Cabernet. Cot has been cultivated in the Loire since the beginning of the nineteenth century. It was not extensively replanted after phylloxera because both its fruit set and its yields are uneven, and its image suffered after the grape was used to freshen up cheap *négociant* blends. Lately it has been enjoying a comeback, however. It is a grape winemakers love, as do their private clients who make regular pilgrimages to Touraine's cellars to taste what they buy. When not pushed to overproduction, Cot can make juicy, characterful reds with plenty of alcohol and seductive kirsch flavors—the kind of red that hunters (of which the Loire has plenty) like to drink with game (of which the Loire also has plenty).

Finally, there is Pineau d'Aunis, the most ancient indigenous grape, also called Chenin Noir. Named after its place of origin, the Prieuré d'Aunis in the commune of Dampierre (now part of the Saumur-Champigny appellation), it is a fragile grape with unreliable yields. Its cultivation has been largely abandoned except in the Coteaux du Loir and Touraine, where it makes peppery, characterful, light reds and rosés. Perhaps its greatest claim to fame is that it gave birth to Chenin Blanc.

LES VIGNERONS

We now return to man, the fourth and most variable factor in winemaking. And since World War II, man has done nothing if not vary in his role as vigneron.

Over the past thirty years, the typical *domaine* has been evolving from polyculture—a hectare of vines plus cereal crops, a horse, poultry, perhaps goats and goat cheese—to specialized farming: A family winery now has from eight to fifteen hectares of vines. Recently created schools such as the Château de Briacé in the Nantais, Montreuil-Bellay in Anjou, and the Lycée Viticole d'Amboise in Touraine are training a new generation of Loire winemaker. Cellars are cleaner and vintners are upgrading equipment and continuing to experiment, working with local enologists, either government-sponsored technicians or private consultants such as Jean-Luc Chaigneau (in the Nantais) and Didier Coutenceau (in Anjou). They may still sell part of their crop in bulk to *négociants,* to local cafés and *boules* clubs, as well as to customers who drive up to the cellar door with a trunkful of cubitainers ready to be filled. But increasingly, they bottle their production themselves.

There are still vignerons who make wine "the old-fashioned way"—putting the crushed grapes in an old barrel and tasting at Christmas. But vinification is becoming more rational. A number of trends can be discerned. Old casks can be good, neutral receptacles, allowing very gradual aeration of the wine. They continue to be used for fermentation and aging (though conscientious vignerons are eliminating the chestnut barrels which give the wines a bitter edge). Easier to clean tanks, however, made of stainless steel, cement, or fiberglass are also common now. And an increasing number of young vintners experiment with *barriques,* oak barrels with a 225-liter capacity. (Fermenting and/or aging wine in new oak adds flavors in the vanilla and toast range as well as tannin. Secondhand barrels, which have been used for one or two wines, add some, but fewer, of these components.)

Oppressive heat at harvest was rare in the Loire; usually the reverse was true. Thus, many vignerons had some system, however crude, for heating the must, but not for chilling. After the brutally hot '89 and '90 harvests, many invested in equipment to keep fermentations cool. Many are investing, too, in machine harvesters—which, to my mind, is regrettable, if understandable.

In white wine production, many vintners extract bolder aromas and thicker textures by leaving the grape skins in contact with the juice for several hours—or for as long as two days—rather than pressing and separating them immediately. They prefer cool, leisurely fermentations—18 to 20 degrees Centigrade—which favor the production of fruit rather than alcohol. Whites are often bottled by the spring following the harvest (without going through malolactic fermentation) to preserve their fresh fruitiness, though a particular procedure such as barrel aging or keeping the wine on its lees may demand more time.

Chenin, particularly the sweet version, presents several distinct issues. In the best appellations, harvest by *tri* is required under INAO legislation. Although some vignerons kept the faith during the bad old days, most picked everything at once, compensating for underripe grapes with sugar. The return to harvest by *tri*, which began in the late 1970s and picked up force in the '80s, is the symbol of the Loire's quality revolution.

In the winery, some vintners work with aromatic yeasts and skin contact, but *moelleux* made from fine grapes don't need a lot of gimmicks. Where cellars are clean and the harvest is good, it matters little whether fermentation occurs in old barrels, cement, or stainless steel, or costly new *barriques*. Cool fermentations are important, however, to protect the must from oxidation and to maximize fruit, freshness, and aromas over the production of alcohol. Sometimes the wines stop fermenting on their own. More often the winemaker stops the fermentation by adding sulfur when the wine has reached the balance he likes.

There has been a crying need for a finer hand with sulfur. Excesses of it have largely contributed to the bad image Loire Chenins continue to fight. Though enormous progress has been made, the liberal use of sulfur won't disappear completely. While overdoses often went hand in glove with overdoses of sugar, sulfur is, at least, something of a necessary evil. Because *moelleux* have a lot of residual sugar, because they don't go through malolactic fermentation, and because they are bottled early, the conditions are ripe for refermentation in bottle. Thus sulfur. (Botrytis, however, seems to inhibit yeasts, thus reducing the need for sulfur, particularly when the wines are aged for a year before bottling. Within the past couple of years, a number of Loire vintners have drastically reduced the amount of sulfur in their sweet Chenins, particularly in their barrel-fermented SGNs made from grapes affected by noble rot.) Filtration, too, seems an evil necessitated by the threat of refermentation. But taste an unfiltered Layon or Vouvray and, while you'll sympathize fully with the vigneron, you're sure to lament that so much of the wine's opulence stays on the filter pad. That said, it testifies to the immense progress made in Anjou and Touraine that sulfur and filtration are mere quibbles. (Indeed, anyone tasting the dozens, perhaps hundreds, of super '89s and '90s realizes the extent to which the quality revolution has taken hold and trickled down. The happy fact is that there are many fabulous versions to choose from.)

The current red wine dilemma—and here we are really talking Cabernet—is whether to "keep the Loire fruit" or to make a rich, tannic red. Many resolve the matter by offering at least two reds: a quaffer, often from young vines, and a more "serious" one meant for cellaring. For the most part the harvest is destemmed. Containers for fermentation as well as temperatures vary. Vatting lasts from five days for a quaffer to a month for an old-vines *cuvée*, during which time the cap of grape solids is either punched down, pumped over, or stirred up, or a combination of all three, to keep the fermentation going. Punching down, traditionally done by foot or with a *pilon* (pestle), may now be done automatically, if the vigneron can afford an expensive *cuve à pigéage*, a stainless steel tank equipped with a mechanism to break through the solid cap. In regions where consultant Didier Coutenceau's concepts about Loire red hold sway—Anjou in particular—a technique called *brassage à l'air comprimé* is preferred; in this method, a canister introduces purified air into the mass. Malolactic fermentation, haphazard until the late 1960s, has now been mastered. Many of the best vintners age their richest reds in used Bordeaux *barriques*, and an increasing number put the wine in barrel after it has been pressed off its skins but before it has gone through malolactic fermentation.

Clearly the Loire quality revolution proceeds at a different pace from region to region. Those that had fallen the farthest—Muscadet and Anjou—have made the deepest, most widespread, and most fundamental changes. Vouvray, too, lived through bleak years during a slump in the *moelleux* market; its young vignerons are as dynamic as any to the west. The wines of eastern Touraine and the Loir-et-Cher improve with each vintage as the region distances itself from its erstwhile image as a supplier of mass-market plonk.

A number of the Loire's most fashionable wines, however, have been riding for a fall. Included here are Saumur-Champigny, Sancerre, Pouilly, and their Sauvignon satellites—though there has been exciting improvement in some important Sancerre houses within the past couple of years, and Champigny, because of market realities and a tough, idealistic regional INAO chief, may be edging toward higher quality. The Chinonais is the Loire's Sleeping Beauty, for the moment content to loll in Rabelaisian languor. But given the world wine-lake and a consumer market in which people are drinking "less but better," every one of these regions will be forced to evolve as more dynamic regions have already done and are still doing. (Throughout the Loire, yields remain an issue.)

To give the ups-and-downs of the Loire's vinous history a human face, I'd like to introduce you to Vincent Lecointre, a serious vigneron in the Coteaux du Layon who is part of the generation that is reclaiming the hillsides and the legacy of its grandfathers. His family saga, typical of the Layon, speaks for all of the Loire.

Our conversation took place at the end of the '89 harvest. A brooding, gray sky erupted into a tempest of howling winds and rain an hour after the last of Lecointre's grapes had come in. The cellars were noisy with the cleaning of presses and the racket of the labeling line. Lecointre looks and talks like a Jean-Luc Godard student, with a French passion for logic, formulation, and explanation. His great-grandfather created the *domaine* in Champ-sur-Layon in 1900; Vincent succeeded his father upon his retirement in 1988.

"In my grandparents' time Layons were very famous and sold well. But during my parents' time there was a crisis for *moelleux*. So my adolescence coincided with the difficult time in Anjou. I saw only the bad side, none of the good. I didn't want to be a winemaker and got my degree in science. Then, in the mid-seventies, I spent time with friends in the Rhine Valley in Germany. For the first time I saw the vine from the outside and realized what could be done with magnificent *terroir*. So I came back to France and studied viticulture and enology in Macon.

"Before phylloxera, Anjou's vines had been planted on the slopes, and the winemakers loved their wines. When the vineyards were replanted, some chose the hillsides, which was hard and expensive. Others planted on the plains where yields were higher, they chaptalized [added sugar to the must to raise the alcohol level] more, and they could make wines more cheaply, though not as well. Then *moelleux* wines fell out of fashion, and this accelerated the decline. Layons had been drunk as aperitifs. After the war, industrial aperitifs such as Ricard replaced *moelleux*, and consumers sought out dry wines.

"Anjou was left with no great appellations. People forgot the hillside wines. By the sixties most of the vignerons had abandoned their steepest slopes. In 1961 my father abandoned his best parcel, the three-hectare Clos de la Roche Gaudrie in Faye. We still own it, but I don't have the money to plant it.

"My father left it, crying. Everything had to be done by hand, and we couldn't price the wine high enough to pay for this. For ten years he made Coteaux du Layon without earning a cent off it. He did it for love and he made his living off rosés, then dry whites, and now mostly reds.

"New appellations were created. The region was seeking a new identity. But winemakers couldn't sell 'Anjou'; they had to sell their own name. My father went on the road with a little truck and barrels of wine, selling to private clients. In the old days—fifty or so years ago—there were many small *négociants*, one in every village. Often they made wine, too, and they selected wines in the *caves* by quality. After the war they were eaten up by several big *négociant* houses who didn't help this region at all. They had other Loire regions. They didn't select or promote quality. They paid the same whether the wine was bad or good. If my father had sold to those *négociants* he'd never have made a living. The only solution for a winemaker was to take to the road himself.

"My father started with blanc *moelleux* and Cabernet d'Anjou. Then clients wanted dry wines, so winemakers like my father started making a dry Chenin. Enologists from Bordeaux came to help develop the wine. They advised harvesting the grapes when they were scarcely ripe. At this stage Chenin is very hard and acid. So Angevins started adding ameliorating varieties, which is how we came to have Sauvignon and Chardonnay in our vineyards. Then the private clients said they wanted red wines. We already had Cabernet vines. So Anjou rouge was born, sometime in the early seventies, though we'd always made reds for home consumption. But consumers thought all Anjou wines were *doux* so we often dropped the name Anjou, which had become associated only with sweet rosés and bottom-of-the-line wines, the mass-distributed *négociant* wines.

"Now, however, there's a rebirth. We've learned how to vinify dry Chenin. We realize we must pick it very ripe, so that it's less acid, and we use skin contact. So we don't need to add Chardonnay and Sauvignon even though it's permitted by law. And there's a new generation of wine-drinker coming to us, people who belong to wine clubs, people who are tired of confected aperitifs like Ricard and are seeking out wines like Sauternes and Coteaux du Layon.

"Finally, even the Angevin winemaker is rediscovering his land. Everything is in our hands. We've had thirty years of hard times, an experience few viticultural regions have ever had. Now the young vignerons are doing good things, and we can once again see the image of Anjou."

At this critical juncture, life in the Loire brings to mind the ancient Chinese curse "May you live in interesting times." It is radically different from—and more exciting than—the settled image of wine one has of Pauillac, say, or Vosne-Romanée, appellations where the great truths of viticulture and enology seem long ago to have been discerned, encoded, and obeyed, needing only occasional tinkering to allow for the invention of tractors and industrial yeasts. In the Loire, laws are constantly changing: The delimitations of the Layon vineyards are being rewritten, as are those of Saumur-Champigny. Vintners in Sancerre debate a classification by *cru*, while those in Muscadet want to rehaul the entire appellation system. A lawsuit brought by a group of Angevins resulted in the brief nullification of the appellation Anjou-Villages. Yields and alcohol levels are being revised. And in a number of zones, vintners must alter the varietal composition of wines they've made all their lives, to correspond to new regulations set by the INAO.

Naturally, evolution is not smooth. France is not the clean slate that is viticultural Long Island or Oregon. There is history, there are vested interests; oxen are being gored and internal wars fought over the fine points of vineyard practices and vinification.

Take Louis Métaireau, the man who put Muscadet on the map and on France's top wine lists. He ran afoul of the law in 1986 when he decided to pick before the official date to begin harvest had been declared, in order to make the type of high-strung Muscadet he likes. The wines were declassified. Others are accused of making a Meursault of Muscadet, fermenting and aging wines from their oldest vines and their best plots in new oak barrels. They worry that if they submit a bottle to the INAO for the obligatory analysis and tasting, the wine won't be approved for the Muscadet appellation because it is not "typical." Nowhere is it writ that Muscadet may not be fermented and aged in new oak. Nor is "typical" anywhere defined. But a view has taken hold that new oak obliterates the delicacy and freshness that are Muscadet's strongest suits. Ironically, Muscadet was "traditionally" fermented in barrel. And the *barrique Nantaise* remains the reference for fixing

Muscadet's prices, although tanks, both cheaper and easier to clean than barrels, have for the most part superseded wood.

Typicity and tradition have become the two hobgoblins of the Loire. Jean Baumard, one of the Loire's most adept, conscientious vignerons, is constantly maligned for not making Savennières in the "family-style." True—most Savennières are the result of sloppy harvesting and sloppy vinification, characterized by fast, hot fermentations which favor the production of alcohol over fruit. Baumard's sleek, focused wines—the result of harvest in small champagne cases, of healthy grapes put intact into stainless steel tanks and fermented at low temperatures—stick out like orphans. Throughout the Loire, juries in wine competitions often eliminate the best samples because the wines don't fit concepts of what's "traditional" or "typical." An Aubance, for example, the product of numerous passes through the vineyard to get only botrytized grapes, was denied first prize because it was "atypical"; a super Anjou-Villages that had evidently spent some time in new oak was eliminated from consideration as "untraditional." The Anjou-Villages appellation was created in 1987, annulled, revised, and reenacted in 1991; what— or whose—tradition are we talking about?

Granted, many gorgeous Muscadets, Aubances, and Anjou-Villages are made strictly by the book. Law-abiding citizens, they embody the current ideal of typicity as serenely as Thomas Jefferson or Benjamin Franklin or even Walter Cronkite incarnate the ordered liberties of a democratic society. They never raise a ruckus. But appellations as unsettled as these need their Martin Luther Kings, their Václav Havels who challenge us to do and be better. Instead of trying to nail down notions of Muscadet or Aubance or Anjou, embalming them midpoint in their search for themselves, these appellations need a Bill of Rights spacious enough to accommodate a rabble-rousing, early-harvest Muscadet as well as a civilly disobedient oaked Anjou-Villages.

But in this respect the Loire presents a paradigm for all those wine regions that aren't Pauillac or Vosne-Romanée. You find the Middle Ages. You find the Napa Valley. And you find every single stage in between. And while life can be aggravating and confusing, it's thrilling and stimulating for the wine-traveler. Between the morning's croissant and the *andouillettes* of lunch, you can sample the following extremes in just two winery visits: The first stop is at Eusèbe Charrier's Domaine de la Chaume; the second tasting is a short walk across the village square, at Leblanc Père et Fils. (Unlike all other portraits of vignerons in this book, both Charrier and Leblanc are composites, though I admit that any resemblance to vintners living or dead is fully intended.)

That Eusèbe Charrier—or, better, *le père* Charrier—is colorful goes without saying. And he milks his folkloric aspect for all it's worth. If you can resist buying a case of wine from him, you're stronger than I. He's a born storyteller, a true poet with a humorist's mastery of the language, as well as a superb baritone. Stooped and wiry with a malicious gleam to his eye, his perennial props are his beret and his corkscrew made of an old vine stump. He holds court in a dirt cellar with ancient oak and chestnut barrels. Grimy walls are covered with diplomas, awards, and girlie calendars from the 1950s. The small tasting glasses have broken stems.

Le père Charrier has seven hectares of vines and is only now beginning to realize that yields of 150 hectoliters per hectare are not something to brag about. But that's understandable. When the *domaine* also included cereal, poultry, and goats, high yields were enviable, particularly after you'd lost the previous year's crop to spring frosts. Where vinification is concerned, *le père* Charrier lets nature takes its course—aided by sulfur, sugar, and filter pads, not to mention a bit of excess '92.

Rough, rustic, and alcoholic, Charrier's wines lack neither charm nor personality, and they bespeak a certain truth—the truth of wine in that time and in that place. They empty quite naturally into the carafes of local cafés and *boules* clubs, the blending tanks of Loire-Atlantique *négociant* houses, or the plastic cubitainers of vacationers. As his production sells out, *le père* Charrier sees no reason to change. His grandson, however, has other ideas, similar to those of Marc Leblanc, his classmate at the Lycée Viticole de Montreuil-Bellay.

Leblanc, a twenty-five-year-old graduate of Montreuil-Bellay, is taking over his father's thirteen hectares. He wants to make Great Wine. He has apprenticed in Burgundy and California and plans to work the next harvest in Australia. He has built an aluminum siding winery and filled it with temperature-controlled stainless steel tanks and a couple of used *barriques* from Château d'Yquem and Figeac.

Leblanc, who wears Lacoste shirts and Top-Siders, conducts businesslike tastings. Working with local enologists he experiments with trellising systems, dates of harvest, skin contact, and yeast selections. He thins clusters in June and again in August, if necessary. Not only can he discuss the fine points of punching down, pumping over, and *brassage*, he can let you taste his various experiments with each of these methods, side by side.

You may not be charmed by Leblanc's wines but you will find them delicious. They are impeccable. Clean and fruity, they evidence a mastery of the craft while still expressing the particular characteristics of Leblanc's land and his vines.

Leblanc is phasing out the "cubi" business—and fills out the appropriate tax forms for the few such sales he continues to accept—and now bottles 80 percent of his production. His wines are in the finest local restaurants as well as some ambitious wine bars in Paris. Fauchon is a client. Current best-sellers are his '93 Vieilles Vignes *cuvée*, which won a gold medal in Paris, and the '90 Les Rascasses, from a south-facing slope so steep it can only be worked by hand. Those two wines sell for 150ff, ten times the price of a bottle chez Charrier.

I love that the Loire encompasses both the Charriers and the Leblancs of the wine world—and everyone in between. Despite its image as being *négociant*-dominated, the Loire is indisputably the region of the vigneron. True, *négociants* account for 80 percent of the wine sold in the Nantais, 60 percent in Touraine, and 50 percent in the Maine-et-Loire. But those numbers don't tell the whole story. The *négociant* share of Muscadet has declined 10 percent in the past decade, for example. While sales by vignerons amount to only 20 percent, one-fifth of Muscadet's average harvest of 750,000 hectoliters is more than the volume of entire appellations like Saumur-Champigny. In Anjou, *négociants* dominate the rosé market but leave the region's noblest wines—its Layons, Aubances, Savennières, Champignys, and Brissacs—to be sold by the man who made them. Sixty percent of Sancerre is sold by its vignerons, and the wines of La Sarthe, as well as those of Auvergne, are sold entirely by the *domaine*, as they have always been.

WINES OF MEMORY
AND SENTIMENT

Not all appellations are created equal. The noblest—the Layons, the Vouvrays, the Chinons, the Sancerres, and so forth—are the focus of this book. But they are supported by an array of simpler wines—VDQS, Vins de Pays (500,000 hectoliters yearly), and *vins de table* (500,000 hectoliters yearly). Many are obscure, unknown to 99.9 percent of wine-drinkers. Have you ever tried a Cabernet from Mareuil, for example, a rosé from Corent, or a Romorantin from Cour-Cheverny? I'd like to take a moment here to put these wines in context as well as to discuss yet another chapter in the life of the Loire—the era of hybrids.

It is a fine Indian summer Sunday in Vendée, and the menfolk of Mouchamps are warming up for lunch by making the rounds of one another's wine cellars. First stop: Petit Pierre's *cave*, a mess of old barrels, recycled soda bottles, and stemless glasses, dug into the cliffside under the town square. As the devout climb the hill to church, Petit Pierre waits at the door for the usual suspects to arrive.

Henri Martin, photographer-journalist-poet-historian, unpacks "breakfast" with the bravura of a three-star maître d'hôtel, proffering first a basket of wild figs from the island of Noirmoutier. After it elicits the appropriate "Ah!"s comes a crate of Breton oysters. Next a box of giant prawns, then— Ladies and Gentlemen!—a raw-milk, hand-ladled, farmhouse Camembert.

Meanwhile, Gros Pierre shuffles in, wearing house slippers so comfortable that he couldn't bear taking them off and changing into socially acceptable street shoes. Referring to the well-worn, tartan plaid slippers, he sighs, "*Je ne dois pas sortir dedans mais je ne peux pas me retirer.*" ("It's not proper to go out in them, but I can't bring myself to withdraw" is as close English gets to the double entendre that occurs naturally in French and that, just as naturally, was mined for every last sexual nuance, later, in another cellar.)

Dédé Bécuit leans against a barrel, unusually glum. A pack of hounds, having nothing else to hunt in the drought, scattered his hens into the hills. But Jean-François Dubreuil, the baby of the bunch and its unofficial revel master, is in high spirits. Even on a normal day Dubreuil tends toward ebullience, crusading for unsung wines and obscure appellations from his stylish liquor shop in Nantes. Matrons who ask him for a nice bottle of Pomerol leave with a case of Mareuil Cabernet. Now he's cackling, sort of, and rubbing his hands gleefully. Things could not be better: He has just seen tufts of chicken feathers along the riverbank; Petit Pierre doesn't realize his fly is open; the figs, the oysters, the prawns, and the cheese are minor masterpieces; and we are about to drink Noah.

Noah is not only obscure, it's illegal. Like absinthe, it is reputed to drive people crazy. Henri's jowls sink into his neck. Visibly nervous, he sips the thin grapey white as if it's LSD and he's waiting for the hallucinations. Jean-François tastes and the aria begins.

"Noah is the flavor of my childhood," says he, in his lilting tenor whose cadence and squeezed nasal twang recall W. C. Fields. "Noah is to me what the madeleine was to Proust. I never drank plain water. When I came home from school, my grandmother would make me something to eat and she'd fill a bucket with water and a liter of Noah. When we went on outings she'd pack a box of sandwiches and a well-sealed jar of water nicely dosed with Noah. I am unable to resist Noah. It is a wine of memory and sentiment."

Noah is a native American grape uniformly vilified by enologists for the "foxy" aroma it inherits from the *Vitis labrusca* side of the family. If you have visited the Finger Lakes during harvest when the scent of freshly crushed Concord (100 percent *labrusca*) fills the air, you know what "foxy" means. Like Concord, Noah might make better juice and jelly than it does wine. But if Noah-induced insanity has ever been diagnosed, its victim was less likely a consumer than one of the bureaucrats driven mad trying to rid the glorious French vignoble of it.

In the nineteenth century the vineyards of France were devastated first by oidium, a vine malady, then by phylloxera, a vine parasite, both of which entered Europe on American vines. By grafting European grapes, which belong to the *Vitis vinifera* family, onto resistant American rootstock, the crisis was solved.

But until the right rootstocks were found and until the French vineyards were reconstituted, numerous ungrafted hybrids such as Noah provided the wine of daily life. And the successive ravages of bad weather, mildew, black rot, and wartime deprivation led to the proliferation of these hardy, resilient grapes throughout France. They were easy to cultivate. They could withstand anything a rude climate inflicted in the way of winter and spring frosts. They needed little care, which seemed a godsend when chemical fertilizers and vine treatments, not to mention manual labor, were scarce.

By 1929 hybrids accounted for 13.5 percent of French wine production. Hybridizers like Maurice Baco and, later, Johannes Seyve-Villard were busy developing thousands of new hybrids which they promoted on radio talk shows as well as on road tours complete with field trips, tastings, lunches, and order forms. Some of the more complex hybrids, with vinifera as part of the parentage (Léon Millot and Chambourcin, for example), made demonstrably superior wines.

In 1935, following an abundant harvest, the French government prohibited what it deemed the six worst hybrids: Noah, Othello (its red-wine counterpart), Isabelle, Clinton, Jacquez, and Herbemont, which, at the time, accounted for more than 3 million hectoliters of wine a year (the equivalent of an average Loire harvest today). Despite official claims that production had dwindled to insignificance, it stayed at 3 million hectoliters throughout World War II. And in the mid-'50s, when Jean-François's granny laced his water with Noah, total acreage of the prohibited grapes had actually grown. Plantings of the more complex hybrids, such as 22A Baco, Ravat, Seyval, Plantet, Chancellor, and Villard Noir continued to grow as well, prompted by the privations of war, including the unavailability of vine treatments and the rationing of wine. (The latter forced many homeowners to give over the backyard garden to vines.)

By the late 1950s, hybrid-based wines accounted for more than 30 percent of all French wine; hybrids covered 402,147 hectares, producing 20 million hectoliters of wine. These rugged vines were particularly widespread in regions bordering the Atlantic, where one cold night in May could wipe out the crop, where September rain could spread rot through a vineyard like measles, where farmers didn't have much time to tend their half a hectare of vines when hay needed to be gathered or there was spading to be done.

In the Loire-Atlantique, hybrids covered close to 17,352 hectares (compared with 11,396 for vinifera); in Vendée, 14,727, representing 90 percent of the grape mix; in the Maine-et-Loire, 12,100. In each of these departments hybrid-based wines accounted for a minimum of 95 percent of the *vin de consommation courante* (table wine). In other Loire departments, hybrids represented anywhere from 60 to 85 percent of the *vin de consommation courante*. (It is important to note that hybrids never threatened to replace the noblest grapes in the noblest appellations of the Loire. Hybrids reigned on marginal lands, those most susceptible to frost, for example, lands later encompassed by a VDQS or by one of the Loire's numerous Vins de Pays, or land which reverted to some other form of agriculture.)

When the war was over, the government got back to the business of wine, creating a slew of new appellations as well as a classification of "recommended," "authorized," and "tolerated" grape varieties by department. And it renewed its efforts to banish the prohibited varieties, hunting down the dirty half-dozen like outlaws. To this end the Minister of Agriculture disseminated a blotter along the lines of a Most Wanted poster [original wording and my English translation appear below].

LE NOAH, L'OTHELLO, L'ISABELLE, LE JACQUEZ, LE CLINTON ET L'HERBEMONT

sont des cépages dont la culture est interdite	are grapes whose cultivation is prohibited
Ils doivent disparaître le 1er décembre 1956	They must disappear by December 1, 1956

ARRACHEZ VOS CEPAGES PROHIBES

Ils vous exposent à des sanctions

Ils donnent du mauvais vin

Ils ne sont plus à la mode: ce sont des reliques du passé.

Profitez de la prime de 135,000 francs par hectare accordée pour les arrachages définitifs des cépages prohibés éffectués avant le 1er Décembre 1956.

RIP UP YOUR PROHIBITED GRAPES

They expose you to sanctions

They make bad wine

They are no longer fashionable; they are relics of the past.

Take advantage of a premium of 135,000 francs per hectare for definitively ripping up your prohibited grapes by December 1, 1956.

—Ministre de l'Agriculture, I.V.C.C.

But Noah and Othello had acquired the allure of Bonnie and Clyde. The new interdiction provoked outright rebellion in eight departments, including the Loire-Atlantique and Vendée (the two had the dubious distinction of having the most acreage of the outlaw grapes) as well as the Maine-et-Loire and the Loir-et-Cher. Growers attacked government inspectors, held them hostage, and set fire to their cars. And in categorizing hybrids as relics of the past that were no longer fashionable, the Minister of Agriculture provoked a violent reaction by the Catholic clergy of western France, who interpreted the blotter as an attack on religion. The Bishop of Angers forbade the distribution of the "tendentious blotter" in his diocese and sent the cartons back to the government.

The end was in sight, however. By the 1960s, hybrids such as Plantet and Seyval were replacing Noah and Othello. And they, in turn, were increasingly replaced by vinifera as stiff EEC regulations put an end to new hybridizing and as chromatographs enabled enologists to detect the presence of hybrids in mass-market blends. Ever more restrictive laws, combined with the creation of scores of new appellations (including the important Vin de Pays category), succeeded in bringing the hybrid chapter to a virtual close. Grape varieties were once again reclassified in the early 1980s, this time divided into two categories, "recommended" and "authorized." With the exception of 22A Baco for Armagnac, no hybrid made the recommended list; Seyval, Ravat 6, Plantet, Chambourcin, and Villard Noir were among the hybrids authorized for the Loire, but Castel, Baco Noir, Oberlin, and Chancellor joined the list of prohibited varieties. And by the end of 1988, any producer seeking an appellation for his wine had to present a declaration of his grape mix. The presence of hybrids, however minuscule, would disqualify his entire production from appellation status.

Petit Pierre and Dédé Bécuit may cultivate their plots of Chambourcin and Léon Millot because they don't seek appellations for any of their wines. In similar settings throughout the Loire, the sturdy Oberlins (now as illegal as Noah), spicy Léon Millots, luscious Ravats, and floral Seyvals I tasted were often better than the Gros Plants, Gamays, and Grolleaus. It made me wonder about this across-the-board varietal obsession.

Folks in Mouchamps — or Champtoceaux or Lerné — don't much care whether the wine's an Oberlin, a Grolleau, or a Chardonnay. Wine is an expression of friendship, not connoisseurship. The context in which these wines are made and shared, more than the grape, transmits the soul, the particularity, of the land. What defines them is good enough growing conditions and spirit that is beyond compare.

And so after our Noah tasting we make two other stops. First we call on the reigning champion of the delectable Vendée version of Pineau de Charente, *trouspinette*, a sweet pink fusion of unfermented grape juice and *eau-de-vie*. Dédé rejoins us, having found all but two hens. Then we're off to Gustave's, at the other end of Mouchamps, to sample his award-winning Léon Millots. But, alas, it's nearly noon. Wives and mothers wait. Roasts wait. On the other hand, André's cellar is staring us in the face. When we emerge several *trouspinettes*, a couple of Bacos, and a Seibel later, Jean-François readies the "cold roast" defense: "There are rules about when you may enter a *cave* but none on when you must leave."

As the kids abandon Mouchamps for the city, its richly textured life becomes folklore. As polyculture evolves into specialized farming, as the toolshed – cum-*cave* grows into a full-fledged winery, the Chardonnays and the Grolleaus of the Nantais, the Gamays of Auvergne become more polished, more "presentable" than, say, Dédé's Castel Noir, an ink-black wine that tastes like berry concentrate. Vinification, too, is more "enlightened" than Dédé's technique of lowering the Castel's potential alcohol from 18 percent to a less lethal 14 percent by hosing the juice down with water.

Vendée continues to host a yearly hybrid competition. Hybrid wines still account for 2 to 3 percent of Loire Valley wine. You can find and taste them by leaving the wine-and-château routes, following instead the back roads through farmlands where the culture of cereal crops replaces that of the vine. In the workers' cafés in small provincial towns, the little house white may be a Seyval; the red, a Chambourcin-Plantet blend. Relics, surely, but they are just as surely the forebears of many of today's VDQS and Vins de Pays — of the Chenin-Chardonnay of Vix, the Cabernet of Thouars, the Pineau d'Aunis of the Vendômois, the Gris Meunier of Orléans, most of which still empty into the carafes of local cafés and cubitainers.

True, there are purists like Philippe Orion, Guy Bossard, and Alain Paulat who, out of sheer obstinacy, make super VDQS and Vins de Pays that transcend the relatively meager "givens" of land or grape. But the Loire's best vineyard land was long ago claimed by its leading AOCs. What was left when VDQS and Vin de Pays zones were carved will never be Saint-Fiacre, Chaume, Sancerre, or Chinon.

The bonhomie of the Sunday morning tasting, the spirit in which these wines were born, remains the spirit in which they are made and drunk. Like the Grolleau Gris poured at the fisherman's hangout on the Lac de Grand Lieu, they are really good country wines, true wine-bar wines, great beach-barbecue wines. Direct, tasty, and inexpensive, they are at times a bit rustic, often quirky, and anything but anonymous. Above all, they're specific to a time, a place, a way of life. Somewhere a farmer searches for his hens, a widower finds indecent comfort in his slippers, a vigneron pours one last round for his pals, and the MBAs come home every weekend. Even for those of us who didn't grow up in Mouchamps, they are wines of memory and sentiment.

VINTAGES

Vintages '91 to '94 were difficult, to say the least. But '95 promises to be somewhat finer than '88 (which was excellent) though somewhat less spectacular than the superb '89 and '90. Quantity, too, was generous for these two "vintages of the century," which means that '89 and particularly '90 are generally available—if not at the winery, then in restaurants.

1995: The best vintage since 1990. July and August were hot, dry, and sunny. September brought rain, cool weather, and strong winds. The grapes were relatively ripe and very healthy before the rain, however, and low-ish yields (thanks, in part, to spring frosts) combined with low temperatures and drying winds prevented serious outbreaks of rot. October was dry and sunny, one of the warmest on record. Harvest continued until the end of November when the last *tris* of Chenin were brought in. While it's too early to make firm pronouncements, it's safe to predict a wealth of extremely good wines from Muscadet to Auvergne as well as a significant number of masterpieces, particularly from the top Cabernet and Chenin appellations. (In these zones, in particular, it may be important to know who picked after the rain.) The reds promise to be deeply colored, fleshy wines with generous fruit. Vouvray and Montlouis should produce classic Chenins in the sec and demi-sec range as well as some lovely *moelleux*. Angevins once again pushed the envelope. Anjou's INAO chief, Pascal Cellier, reports 1,800 declarations of intent to make Grains Nobles. The average potential alcohol of Claude Papin's harvest in Layon, for example, was 30 percent. In Sologne, probable alcohols of 14 percent in his Sauvignon Blanc permitted Henry Marionnet to make his first M de Marionnet since 1990.

1994: It would be difficult to imagine a more heartbreaking vintage. Spring frosts, once again, reduced the crop. Though the damage wasn't nearly as extensive as in '91, some growers may well have wished it had been come September. June, July, and most of August were hot and humid. Growers talked of another '89 or '90. Then came the rains of September— biblical rains that just didn't let up until harvest was essentially over. Rot spread through the vineyards like wildfire. On top of this, there was hail damage in parts of Muscadet, Pouilly (in June, August, and September), Bourgueil, and in the broad Touraine appellation. Harvest was desperate—a mix of rotten grapes, ripe grapes, and unripe grapes. In general, the wines are light and diffuse. Some, of course, seem confected. And a taste of stem rot, more or less pronounced, seems nearly unavoidable in wines made from Chenin, Gamay, and Gros Plant. (When the wine is rich, however, the stem rot is barely noticeable. This is the case with a number of the best Gamays and Chenins.)

There were some (relatively) bright spots, notably where there wasn't much frost damage—in Saumur-Champigny, for example, and in Sancerre. In the best Chenin-producing regions of Anjou, some growers produced extremely concentrated Grains Nobles. Generally, these were producers who had very low yields, who waited out the rain, harvesting—by *tri*—in late October. The wines are extraordinary, with a lot of botrytis. Alas, this is usually accompanied by trace amounts of stem rot, too, though the earthiness is buried by the abundance of other flavors.

Of course, there are personal triumphs in each appellation. To cite just a few: Claude Branger and Domaine de la Fruitière in Muscadet; Marc Delaunay in Bourgueil; Clos Neuf des Archambaults in Touraine; Domaine Mardon in Quincy; Didier Dagueneau in Pouilly; and a good number in both Anjou-Saumur and Sancerre.

1993: I like this vintage. The growing season was generally cool and stayed cool during harvest, when it rained. (Not as much as in '94, however.) The cool breezes helped fend off rot. The grapes had been healthy and they stayed healthy, due, in part, to thick skins (which produced deeply colored, tannic Cabernets). Maturity was fair—actually more representative of the Loire than '89 and '90—making '93 a rather "typical" year.

The vintage might, however, turn out to be memorable for its reds. Well-made Chinons, Champignys, and Bourgueils remind me of the '86s (and perhaps the '88s). Like the '86s, they have a hard, steely edge and a noticeable acidity; they need cellaring. But the better ones, the product of low yields, are concentrated, well structured, and built to last. (The Champignys of the Foucault brothers and of Château de Villeneuve, as well as Pierre-Jacques Druet's Bourgueils, are gorgeous.) The red Sancerres are succulent, as are many of the Touraine reds. While some Anjou-Villages I've tasted were too hard, others were full and generous.

There are also firm, classic dry whites throughout the Loire, from Muscadet to Azay-le-Rideau to Reuilly, Sancerre, and Pouilly (despite heavy rain). Two terrific Touraine Sauvignons come to mind: Charles Guerbois's Vinovorax and Domaine des Corbillière's Cuvée Fabel Barbou. In Anjou, some courageous souls with low-yielding vines harvested in mid-November and made wonderful Grains Nobles. Vouvray and Montlouis produced mostly sec and some demi-sec. I'd be skeptical of most '93 *moelleux* from Touraine but have tasted some marvels, notably from Bernard Fouquet. (But here again we are talking about extreme rigor.)

In short, '93 wasn't a great year but it was a more-or-less "correct" and typical Loire year. There are quite a few wonderful wines and many, many good ones to choose from.

1992: The vines responded to the frosts of '91 by rebounding with unprecedented yields. A few producers' cluster thinned but others did not, saying they would simply leave clusters on the vines at harvest. They did just that, but when the vines were giving 200 hectoliters per hectare, you have to stop picking somewhere! The weather wasn't spectacular either. The wines tend to be diffuse in color (reds in particular), structure, and flavor.

There *are* some successes. Guy Bossard, in Muscadet, is one of the few in the Nantais who cluster thinned and he was rewarded with several wonderful *cuvées* of Muscadet (and a damned delicious Gros Plant). Philippe Orion made lovely wines in Vendée. There are many good Anjous (among the top producers such as Mark Angeli and Claude Papin). Marc Delaunay and Jean-Yves Billet made very pretty Bourgueils. Château de la Grille produced a magnificent Chinon; Robert Denis, a near-miraculous demi-sec Azay-le-Rideau; and Michel Gendrier, a savory Romorantin. Huet tops the list in Vouvray, though Foreau, Fouquet, Champalou, Pinon, and Château de Gaudrelle made excellent wines as well. Alain Cailbourdin came out with some marvelous Pouilly. And the Saint-Pourçain co-op turned out a pleasant Ficelle.

1991: Not a vintage many vignerons want to remember. The Saturday night massacre—killer frost the weekend of April 20—wiped out most of the crop. (It was the second year of frost in the Nantais.) There was some second growth but it rained during harvest, so there were rot problems. Many picked earlier than they would have liked, to avoid rot. With the exception of Anjou (where frost caused less damage), it was a small vintage, in both quantity and quality. Some winemakers—notably Guy Bossard in Muscadet, Alphonse Mellot in Sancerre, and Didier Dagueneau in Pouilly-Fumé—made quite lovely wines. In any case, drink up. There are many fine Anjou wines, though they are hardly of the quality of '90, '89, and '88. In Vouvray much of the small amount harvested was used to replenish stocks of sparkling wine.

1990: The third consecutive great vintage. (The quantity is good, too, as is availability.) This was the second drought year in a row. June was cool but July and August were hot—so hot that photosynthesis stopped for a time, delaying the harvest, which, while not as early as that of '89, was early all the same. And the weather was fine — except in the Sancerre area where there was intermittent rain. Ripeness levels were as high as in '89, though yields were much higher in '90. Many winemakers prefer their '90s to their '89s—because they benefited from a year of experience with exceptionally ripe grapes and some had invested in cooling systems. Overall a superb vintage, with some regional variations. In Muscadet, May frost killed off many of the first buds, leading to uneven ripening. But many consider the '90s better than the '89s because they harvested earlier to keep some acidity for a better-balanced and more age-worthy wine. There was more botrytis for the sweet Chenins from Anjou, Touraine, and Sarthe than in '89. These wines are the glories of '90 (as they are of '89)—simply fabulous wines that can age for decades. The Cabernet-based reds are excellent, too, though they tend to be softer, less age-worthy than '89, and should be drunk in the near term (with exceptions like Foucault in Saumur-Champigny and Joguet's Dioterie in Chinon). In Sancerre hail reduced some of the crop but '90 was, overall, excellent, fitting the ripeness profile of the rest of the Loire.

1989: Until 1990, this was the year of the century. Unprecedented heat and drought led to the earliest harvest since 1893. The grapes were phenomenally healthy and ripenesses were extraordinary: Muscadets with probable alcohols of 14 percent; Chenins with more than 22 percent. There were some failures—stuck fermentations and so forth—but most succeeded. In general the wines tend to be more alcoholic and less acid than usual, and therefore somewhat uncharacteristic, but they are fabulous, from Vendée through Auvergne. The Cabernet-based reds will age better than the '90s. Where sweet Chenins are concerned, there was less botrytis than in '90; the grapes, instead, were shriveled (*passerillés*) or just normally overripe. The best appellations can age for decades. Jacques Boivin, of Bonnezeaux's Château de Fesles, observed that each generation had its great vintage: For his grandfather it was '21; for his father, '47; for him, '89. (Then along came '90. . . .)

1988: I like this vintage a lot. It's been eclipsed by '89 and '90, but it produced very classic, elegant Loire wines. Flowering was relatively early, though the advance was lost due to a cool, rainy July. August and September were warm and sunny, however, and the weather was beautiful late in the season when Chenin and Cabernet were harvested. Yields were moderate and the wines have good sugar-to-acid balance. Vintners in Muscadet who feared a repetition of the rains of 1987 may have picked early, when grapes hadn't reached maturity. Those who waited for ripeness, harvesting at the end of September, made good wines that have evolved well. The Cabernet-based reds are classic. I believe they will age better than the '90s. And '88 is my favorite year for Loire Sauvignon because of that classic structure—which I, perhaps alone, prefer to the full-blown '89 and '90s. Finally, '88 Chenins from top producers—Baumard, Claude Papin, Vincent Ogereau, Philippe Foreau, Didier Champalou—will evolve as majestically as the '89s and '90s. Overall, a very-good-to-excellent vintage that will age well. (One caveat: Some grapes were attacked by stem rot, which went undetected until pressing. This left a taste of rot in the affected wines. For the most part, we are talking about Gamay and Gros Plant, but I also noticed it in some Chenins.)

1987: For most of the Loire this was a mediocre year at best, due to heavy rain in late September. In Muscadet, however, where harvest is earlier than the rest of the Loire, it was an excellent vintage, marked by a good rhythm of rain followed by sunshine during the growing season. By mid-September the grapes had achieved probable alcohols of 10 percent, which is high for Muscadet, and the wines tend to be more elegant, finer, and less rich than the '85s and the '89s; good agers. There were also some lovely Chinons and Bourgueils. Most will have peaked by now, though Charles

Joguet's Dioterie and the richer *cuvées* of Bourgueil from Pierre-Jacques Druet are likely to be drinking well.

1986: Where Cabernet-based reds and Sancerre-Pouilly are concerned, this is a vintage I love. The growing season was cool, the harvest relatively late, and the alcohol good, though nowhere near '89 and '90. Early-harvested Muscadets were thin. However, growers like Guy Bossard and Joseph Landron who waited for greater ripeness were able to harvest grapes with much higher sugars and made beautiful wines. In Vouvray it rained in mid-harvest, but those who picked by *tri* had some lovely successes in the demi-sec range. There were similar successes in top houses in the Layon. In Chinon, Bourgueil, and Champigny you can find solid, classic, austere, long-lived wines. They are rather acidic, however, and need cellaring to round off the rough edges and to reveal their underlying richness. The same notes apply to the best Sancerres (reds included) and Pouillys: Fine, structured, and razor sharp, the whites have a nerviness that I prefer to the ripe wines of '90.

1985: A very highly regarded vintage that, Muscadet aside, I don't really love. In Muscadet a fine, sunny growing season resulted in a vintage considered to be one of the best of the '80s; the wines are beautifully balanced, long, dry, and rich. Elsewhere: All the Chenins have been blocked in their evolution; from the Layon to Vouvray, they're just not budging. There's wonderful wine underneath, but it's hard to say when it's going to be revealed. Nearly all of the Cabernets are marked by strong green–bell pepper aromas and flavors—all right as a nuance but not at the level at which they appear in this vintage. White Sancerres and Pouillys, too, are characterized by pronounced herbaceousness. The red Sancerres are much more appealing.

GOOD: '83, '82, '81, '79, '75, '73

MEDIOCRE: '84, '80

PAST GREATS: '76, '71, '69, '64, '59, '55, '53, '49, '47

A NOTE ON LAWS AND YIELDS

Many laws governing the making of wine are in the process of being, or have just been, revised. The changes affect yields, for example, minimum and maximum levels of alcohol, and delimitations of particular zones. Most of the VDQS areas have applied for promotion to AOC; others have been upgraded within the past two years. The granting of the higher status often entails a change in the way many make their wines: Some are now obliged to blend grapes; others, to use a single variety.

Reducing yields is as big an issue in the Loire as it is in most French viticultural regions. I had originally included the legal yields, as they appear in the INAO statue, for each appellation. I changed my mind, however, because it seemed meaningless to specify something that has so little to do with reality—and that seems to change with the phases of the moon.

Let me give you an example: On the books, yields for the appellation Saumur-Champigny are set at 40 hectoliters per hectare. This is called a *rendement de base* (basic yield). In practice, however, the "official" yield is 55 hectoliters per hectare, and I assume that the law on the books will be changed to reflect that. (Though you never know.) The *rendement de base* may be altered according to the vintage, and generally it is augmented.

The law sets a limit for such augmentation, however. In some cases, it is called the *plafond limite de classement* (or PLC), which permits up to 20 percent higher yields, or a *rendement boutoir,* which essentially means the same thing. The producers within a given appellation, along with the INAO, decide what the limit should be for each harvest. Thus every vintage has its own official, legal yield—which has little to do with what's on the books: the ceiling on Saumur-Champigny's yields for 1994 (a year in which spring frost had reduced the size of the crop) was 60 hectoliters per hectare, though many growers surely exceeded that.

II

The Loire Table

Poets, philosophers, and gourmets alike speak of the *douceur* of the Loire's cooking. The Loire is a land of equilibrium. In its temperate climate, where the weather is neither too hot nor too cold, its inhabitants never have to fight nature. That equilibrium and comfort are expressed in its foods. A cuisine balanced to the point of seeming unaccented, so mild it tastes unseasoned, Loire cooking is, above all, reasonable, as prudent as the generations of housewives who created it.

Foods speak of themselves and are best when least is done to them. Nothing more exotic than pike sauced with an emulsion of butter, white wine, and shallots called *beurre blanc*; nothing jazzier than an unctuous potted-pork spread called *rillettes de Tours*; nothing more elaborate than the caramelized apple pie called *tarte Tatin* or a well-aged goat cheese from Sainte-Maure-de-Touraine.

All these dishes originated in the Loire yet none seem inextricably linked to the region in the way that bouillabaisse is to Marseilles and *choucroute* to Alsace. Loire cooking is cooking we seem always to have known and perceived as quintessentially French, just as we seem always to have known and identified as quintessentially French the farmlands, orchards, châteaux, and rivers of the Loire.

A well-fed local matron once said to me that the cooking of the Loire was "the cuisine of everywhere and nowhere," summoning up the image of the Loire as a land of passage: The preferred circuit of kings and their entourages, its foodways were modulated by the need to please all palates. Local cooking was buffeted, too, the theory continues, by numerous influences. Crusaders introduced spices and *damas* plums. Catherine de' Médicis, the wife of Henri II, imported cooks and gardeners (though her influence on French cooking is hotly debated). Seafaring traders brought sugar, coffee, and chocolate. Antonin Carême, installed in the kitchens of the Château of Valençay by Talleyrand, made gastronomy a diplomatic art and concocted dishes like *tournedos Valençay*, in which the beef was garnished with noodle croquettes and posed on a Madeira sauce enriched with mushrooms, sheeps' brains, beef tongue, cockscomb, green olives, and truffles.

However great Carême's influence was on French cuisine, his impact on the cooking of the Loire was negligible. The docility of the Loire's cooking has as much, if not more, to do with the gentleness of its climate and its countryside than with whatever traffic passed along its main thoroughfare. Its gastronomy is seen, above all, in its resources: The dishes of daily life tend to form around a *cuisine de cueillette*—what's at hand and what's in season. In this respect, the poet Ronsard more accurately represented the Loire spirit of eating and drinking well, preferring the "artichokes and salad greens, asparagus, parsnips, and the melons of Touraine" over the "great mounds of royal meats." And perhaps one reason Loire cooking seems so familiar is that the region provides, and has always provided, the rest of the country with so much of its raw material.

Touraine has been called the garden of France (first, perhaps, and most notably, by François Rabelais), but I see no reason not to extend that description to the entire Loire Valley. From the endless fields and greenhouses south of Nantes to the apple and pear orchards stretching from the outskirts of Angers to the limits of Orléans, the valley is a huge market garden punctuated by stone houses with lush hydrangea, quince and cherry trees, and tiny towns with tight streets and simple cafés.

The Nantes market (Marché d'Intérêt National, or MIN) is second only to Rungis in Paris. Nantais truck gardeners produce 80 to 90 percent of France's mâche (lamb's lettuce) and its muguets (or lilies of the valley). The alluvial soils and mild climate here, as well as along the riverbanks between Angers and Saumur, favor the cultivation of fruits such as strawberries, raspberries, and *cassis;* vegetables such as carrots, early leeks, cucumbers, tomatoes, radishes, branch celery, onions, shallots, artichokes, and fava beans; and "gourmet" crops such as fancy salads, fresh herbs such as cilantro, and baby vegetables such as miniature squash and eggplant.

From the island of Noirmoutier come early potatoes that can be peeled with the fingertip and are perfect for sautéing. Vendée cultivates a type of white bean called *mogette*, which, along with cabbage, is the western Loire's traditional garnish to the Sunday roast. The provincial town of Chemillé, on the border of Nantais and Anjou, specializes in medicinal plants like chamomile and tilleul for tisanes (herbal teas). At Chênehutte-les-Tuffeaux, south of Angers, the mushroom caves of the Saumurois begin.

The region, which stretches east through the Chinonais, supplies France with 70 percent of its button mushrooms as well as shitakes and *pleurottes*. The constant temperatures and humid air of the Loire's tuffeau cellars provide the ideal growing environment. And raw material for the compost (sterilized, decayed horse manure and straw) is in steady supply; the Ecole Nationale d'Equitation, Saumur's prestigious riding academy, is minutes away.

From the Loire's forests come a wealth of mushrooms—*bolets, chanterelles, trompettes de la mort,* and *coulemelles*. A large, delicate mushroom often grilled over a wood fire, the *coulemelle* is the subject of a country song that the old folks know and, after many bottles of wine have been emptied, can be coaxed to sing.

Though Bourgueil hosts a garlic and basil festival every year, the former is not a loud presence in Loire cooking and the latter does not seem to be used at all. Sorrel, however, grows everywhere and goes into stuffings, omelets, soups, and sauces.

On the abrupt slopes of Seuilly, the birthplace of Rabelais, the kiwis of nouvelle cuisine are a new crop, and the flatlands around Lémeré are given over to melons. Long, pyramidal dirt tracts signal white asparagus from the borders of Saumur to the limits of Sologne, adding broad patches of umber to a quilt of forests and fields of sunflowers, hay, and corn. Berry leads France's regions in the cultivation of lentils—although the Rolls-Royce of lentils comes from the fields above Puy-en-Velay, at the end of our wine route.

Sea kale, physalis (Cape gooseberry), and root chervil are among the uncommon vegetables being prepared for the market by experts in Angers, thus continuing that city's centuries-old tradition of horticultural research.

Indeed, throughout history the Loire in general, and Anjou in particular, have been centers of horticultural research. They take credit for *chou-fleur d'hiver*, a variety of cauliflower planted in August and harvested in May;

salads like *cornet d'Anjou*; as well as many of the nation's most celebrated varieties of apple, pear, and plum: the *reinette*, the *doyenné de Comice*, and the *reine-claude* (or greengage, named after the wife of François Ier) were developed in its experimental gardens, as were the *cognassier d'Angers*, an early and reliable quince; the apricot *précoce de Saumur*; and the Gaillard melon.

Anjou is France's largest producer of apples to eat out of hand. Non-French varieties like Golden and Red Delicious, Jonathan, Melrose, Idared, and Granny Smith predominate, though local apples like *la reinette du Mans* and *clochard* are often available. Pear varieties include William, Comice, the *beurrés*, *passe-crassane*, and *conférence*. The choice of plums includes *Sainte-Catherine*, *reine-claude*, and mirabelle. (Regrettably, many ancient varieties of both apple and pear seem to have disappeared completely.)

The *gros damas*, "the prune of Tours," which gave rise to many Tourangeau specialties—pork with prunes, stuffed prunes, prunes steeped in *eau-de-vie*—is no longer cultivated either. Hard frosts, the reorganization of farmland into large parcels (to accommodate new machinery), and the demand for wood for furniture making killed off most of the region's walnut trees. Local vinaigrettes usually include walnut oil, however. And enough trees remain so that winter evenings are spent around the fire, cracking autumn's harvest; come spring, the nut meats will be pressed into oil at a nearby mill.

And there seems to be renewed interest in "forgotten fruits and vegetables." In what I hope signals a return to tastier apples, I found the *patte de loup* in a market at the stand of a local grower. Developed near Beaupréau (in western Anjou) in the nineteenth century, it is an apple-lover's apple, crisp and juicy, honeyed but still keen and malic. At a fair for heirloom fruits and vegetables, I bought the evocatively named *cuisse de dame* (lady's thigh) pear and a half-dozen obscure varieties of pumpkin and squash.

Angers researchers reintroduced *crosne* (Chinese or Japanese artichokes) to the market. Groves of truffle oaks have been planted in the Richelieu area in an attempt to re-create an industry that flourished after phylloxera destroyed the region's vines. And in the spring of 1995, Noirmoutier farmers inaugurated the commercialization of the *bonotte* potato (a variety formerly cultivated in home gardens) by offering its first crop at auction in Nantes.

From the coastline of the Nantais to the ponds of Sologne, as well as from the banks of the Loire and its many tributaries, come all manner of fish and shellfish. The number of fishermen constantly declines, however, and the catch changes almost literally with time and tide. Some local fish, such as bream, are no longer popular with clients; others, such as salmon, have become scarce, a casualty of pollution, overfishing, and faster currents caused by digging to deepen the riverbed, as well as by a muddy bottleneck at the estuary, which tosses the migrating fish back into the ocean.

Salmon is called the king of the Loire by local fishermen like Michel Humeau, who likes to recount a tale common to every salmon region: Salmon used to be so abundant in the Loire that seasonal farm laborers added clauses to their contracts specifying that they *not* be fed salmon more than three times a week. Humeau purses his lips voluptuously when describing the attributes of the fish, saying, "Compared with farmed salmon, Loire salmon is like a garden tomato or peach compared with an industrial one."

He's right. Loire salmon is simultaneously gamy and delicate, meaty, *moelleux* (in this context, marrowy), rich, meltingly tender, and unimaginably subtle. Until 1994 it was possible to taste Loire salmon; as of spring 1995, however, a five-year prohibition on fishing them went into effect in order to replenish stocks. But salmon is so firmly anchored in the foodways of the Loire that it is featured on local menus and at special family meals at all times, though what is served almost always comes from other climes.

Frogs are still found in parts of Vendée and around the Lac de Grand Lieu, the largest plains lake in France. Most now come from Central Europe, Egypt, and Albania. Pike is still caught by men who fish the inland riverbanks and ponds and streams from Nantes to Sancerre, though demand far outdistances supply. Mullet, bream, and *sandre* (a predatory, perchlike fish introduced into Loire waters after World War II) are relatively abundant. Shad fishing is now strictly regulated. The Loire was once a major shad region, however, and a local saying goes, "When the sorrel starts to grow in the gardens, the shad will be coming."

Charles Barrier, chef-owner of Restaurant Barrier in Tours, underscores the wisdom of this, adding, "Our ancestors always understood the correlation between vegetables and other foods. Salmon and shad mount the Loire in sorrel and asparagus season. They were served with sorrel sauce and garnished with asparagus. Salmon and pike were served with *beurre blanc*. In theory, *beurre blanc* should only be made in July, during the season for gray shallots."

Considered one of the fathers of modern French gastronomy, Barrier notes that salmon with sorrel sauce was an ancient local recipe in which the entire fish was presented. In the 1970s, the Troisgros brothers turned scallops of salmon napped in sorrel sauce into an illustrious example of nouvelle cuisine.

Perhaps no sauce has become more of a staple of modern chefs, however, than *beurre blanc*, which, according to local mythology, was born in the Nantais a bit over a century ago. Although it seems a natural outgrowth of Nantes's resources, *beurre blanc*'s invention is credited to *la mère* Clémence, a cook at the home of the Marquis de Goulaine, south of Nantes.

Legend has it that Clémence was making a sauce Béarnaise but left out the herbs and the egg yolks. But voilà! Her botched Béarnaise became *beurre blanc*. No suicide à la Vatel for *la bonne mère*. She left the château to open a restaurant on the banks of the Loire. A hundred years later the city of Nantes celebrated the centennial of her invention; Restaurant Clémence, under different ownership, still whisks up *beurre blanc* today; and the sauce is part of the repertory of cooks the world over.

As with any legend, the details vary depending on the source. Some say Clémence bungled her hollandaise, not her Béarnaise. Others claim she was a short-order cook whose clientele was largely made up of sailors. *Beurre blanc*, this theory goes, was the result of Clémence's attempts to invigorate a bland but locally popular emulsion of butter and vinegar. Purists, of course, continue to debate the recipe's essentials: the type of shallots, for example (the pungent gray ones are preferred); wine or vinegar, or both; and the pros and cons of cream (it holds the sauce). But every self-respecting western Loire housewife makes *beurre blanc*. Réjane Humeau, Michel's wife, is like many; she was taught to make *beurre blanc* by her mother-in-law, "the first thing after I was married."

Her recipe: "In a heavy casserole, cut, very fine, two good tablespoons of shallots. Add wine vinegar to really cover the shallots. Reduce the vinegar over a low flame. When it's almost dry, add a bit of white wine (less than the vinegar). Reduce again. Add very cold butter by pieces—big nuts each time. (Sunday we were eight and I put in a pound and a half of butter.) Turn the butter in the shallots. Cook over a very low flame to make sure it doesn't boil. Add a little pepper."

Local fish are also panfried or cooked in court bouillon and served with butter or in cream, wine, and mushroom sauces. Carp and shad are often stuffed with mushrooms or sorrel, bread, shallots, and white wine. Eel is regularly fished and, with the exception of elvers, regularly eaten. It is fried—as are tiny smelt-sized fish called *ablettes* and *gardons* that make up the *fritures* served in cafés lining the river—or grilled, or smoked, or used for pâtés. Both eel and lamprey are made into red-wine stews called matelotes or, if made with white wine, *bouilletures*. Eel grilled *à la Berrichonne* is prepared with vinegar, walnut oil, and herbs.

Elvers, or baby eels called *civelles* or *pibales*, sometimes find their way to Nantais tables, but most are exported to Spain. The catch accounts for almost 90 percent of the year's income of the fishermen who ply the Loire's estuary near the port of Paimboeuf.

Poultry and cattle raising are big business throughout the Loire. The most prestigious local bird is the Challans duck, a domesticated wild duck "ameliorated" over the centuries. Also called the *canard de marais* (marsh duck) and the *canard de Nantes*, it thrives in the marshlands of the Vendée littoral, in a thirty-by-fifteen-kilometer zone north of the town of Challans. Rich and gamy with firm, dark, tasty flesh, this is the duck served at La Tour d'Argent in Paris. Challans ducks, the region's farmhouse capons and chickens, as well as free-range birds from Loué (a bit north of the wine route), have Labels Rouge (government-recognized seals of quality, though not appellations). Next in line for distinct labels are the *geline de Touraine*, a rustic but succulent black hen, and the Parthenaise cow, considered the Loire Basin breed. The fine-boned *geline* was nearly extinct and the Parthenaise was fast disappearing less than a decade ago when local producers revived consumer interest in them.

Beef recipes do not loom large in the Loire, aside from the ever popular *tête de veau*, pot-au-feu, and *grillades* (barbecues). In chèvre-producing regions, kid is spit-roasted with new garlic and spring onions. Whatever game has been hunted—boar, doe, stag, hare, duck—ends up in wine-laced stews, blood-thickened stews called *civets*, or terrines. Partridge is frequently cooked with cabbage; pheasant may be stuffed with chestnuts or stuffed into cabbage.

Chicken is often simply roasted; if not, it appears in some sort of stew. There is surprising support for the opinion that coq au vin originated in Auvergne, at the end of our wine route. There, it was (and is) prepared with Chanturgue, a robust local red. Loire Valley chefs remain faithful to wines from Chinon and Bourgueil, however, maintaining they hold their color better than other reds in cooking. In Berry, chicken is cooked *en barbouille*, a blood-thickened red-wine stew. *Fricassée de poulet à l'Angevine* is made with local white wine, local cream, and local mushrooms.

The farm animal most eaten throughout the Loire is the pig, often called *Monsieur*. Pork has always been a cornerstone of the country diet. Until quite recently every farm killed a pig or two a year. And the west-central Loire—Anjou-Maine and Touraine—created a style of charcuterie now found on every supermarket shelf. The most famous is *rillettes*, a delicious, rough-textured hash of pork conserved in its fat.

Documented as early as the eleventh century, *rillettes* are described—with evident relish—by Honoré de Balzac as a "(brown confiture) [that] formed the principal element of a Tourangeau midafternoon snack." In *Les Heures Peintes pour Anne de Bretagne*, a fifteenth-century Tourangeau artist selected the slaughter of the pig to illustrate the month of December, depicting among other things stoneware pots set out to be filled with *rillettes*. To see how such charcuterie was made on the farm—and how every last mouthful of the pig was used—I visited Mme. Marie Turpault in the hamlet of Cornu in Anjou.

Born in 1903, Mme. Turpault moved to her current home in 1923 and ever since has harvested its grapes and wheat, and tended its hens, cows, rabbits, and pigs. While she no longer churns her own butter or grinds her own flour, Mme. Turpault is nearly as self-sufficient today as she was fifty years ago. Germain, her bachelor son, kills a pig a year and Mme. Turpault carves out cutlets, conserves the thigh in salt, puts it in a burlap sack, and stuffs it up the chimney, where it will dry over the fire. From other morsels she prepares *boudins, andouilles,* and other sausages. Each pig also provides about thirty pounds of scraps and fatty parts which Mme. Turpault puts in a cast-iron kettle with water and salt to cook over the fire for five or six hours to make *rillettes*. They are meaty and good.

As farming became increasingly specialized after World War II, charcuterie was ever more exclusively the business of the professional, from industrial firms to artisans. This trend was reinforced by EEC laws regarding everything from feed to slaughter to the size of buildings, methods of transformation, modes of sale, and hygiene, hygiene, hygiene. While industrial *rillettes* seem to get fattier by the year, the artisanal versions (especially from wine towns, like Rochefort, Bourgueil, Vernou, and Vouvray) remain relatively authentic. The two classic varieties are the fine, burnished *rillettes de Tours* and the chunkier, paler *rillettes du Mans*.

Rillons, or *grillons*, an equally ancient Tourangeau specialty, are large cubes of pork, salted and cooked for two hours until golden. Anjou's *rillauds* are cubes of breast meat of pork, each about 5 centimeters (2 to 2½ inches) and between 100 to 200 grams (3½ to 7 ounces), which have been salted for twenty-four hours and then cooked slowly in water, lard, and salt for an hour or more until fork-tender.

Anjou claims that its *gogue* is one of the first pork dishes ever cooked. The Charcutier's Code specifies that *gogue* be made with 15 to 20 percent each of blood and diced fat and lean pork and up to 60 percent onions stuffed into a casing and simmered for four hours. More elaborate versions add Chinese cabbage, leeks, and spring onions. Spicy and dense, with the bloody richness of *boudin noir, gogue* is eaten cold, or is grilled or sautéed and served with potatoes.

Vendée's *fressure*, another antiquity making tasty use of "variety cuts," was among the dishes Rabelais's Gastrolatres offered to their god Manduce. Made of head, heart, and lungs cooked with stale bread and onions and thickened with blood, it looks like a terrine when cold. I have eaten it hot, like a hash. Vendée ham (raw, like Bayonne) is rubbed with *eau-de-vie*, spices and herbs, and local salt (preferably from Noirmoutier), grilled and served with *mogettes*. Modern *grillades* in the Nantais usually include *saucisses au Muscadet*, the local version of sausages made with white wine. And Easter in Berry or Poitou will surely bring *pâté de Pâques*, a terrine of pork and veal and hard-boiled eggs, traditionally enclosed in a pastry crust. With the exception of Auvergne's distinctive charcuterie (which will, along with its great cow's-milk cheeses, be discussed in the Auvergne chapter, as the region's cooking can hardly be considered Ligerian), the Loire's charcuterie is moist and mild, a perfect reflection of the moist, mild climate in which it developed. The same may be said of its cheeses.

Dairy is a major industry in the Loire. In Anjou and the Nantais, this means milk and butter. Much of the butter sold under the Poitou-Charentes appellation comes from Vendée. And cooking from this region is more butter-based than that of the rest of the Loire. (As sea salt is a local industry—salt marshes stretch from the Guérande Peninsula to the Vendée coast—Nantais butter is usually salted or lightly salted, *demi-sel*.) There is not much of a cheese tradition here, however, beyond *crémet* (fresh cheese molded with cream and egg whites, eaten with cream and sugar or fruit) and Curé Nantais (or Fromage du Pays Nantais, dit du Curé). Supposedly named for the Vendée cleric who "invented" it in the nineteenth century, this is a squarish, washed-rind, cow's-milk cheese, loud in both aroma and flavor. The industrial cow's-milk cheese Port Salut, formerly an artisanal cheese made by the Trappist monks of Entrammes, comes from the Laval area, slightly north of the wine route.

Cheesemaking extends across Touraine, Poitou, and Berry. Both cow's-milk and sheep's-milk cheeses exist, but this is basically goat-cheese country: Poitou-Charentes leads French chèvre production.

Loire chèvres may be fresh and yogurty—to be eaten mixed with chopped chives, onions, and garlic; with herbs; or with fresh fruit and sugar. They can be firm and creamy, or Camembert-like, or hard as rocks. They may be shaped like logs, pyramids, bricks, disks, or drums—most of which forms date from the nineteenth century. Some have no name, others have brand names, and others fall within one of the appellations or labels made from Chinon to Pouilly. They are perhaps France's best-known chèvres: the log-shaped Sainte-Maure; the Eiffel Tower–shaped Pouligny-Saint-Pierre; the flat disk Selles-sur-Cher; the truncated pyramid Valençay or Levroux; the small, cylindrical Chabichou de Poitou; and the small drum Crottin de Chavignol, from the Sancerrois.

Fossils found near Vouvray indicate that goats inhabited Touraine prior to recorded history. Cheesemaking, it is said, became part of daily life during the Arab occupation. The Saracens brought their herds with them, and legend has it that their women taught the craft to the inhabitants.

In the days of mixed farming, chèvre was made by wives who tended small herds. With a little effort you can still find such cheeses. One night I went to a farm in Panzoult, near Chinon, in search of a hauntingly delicate chèvre I'd tasted at a friend's house. As I entered the barn the last rays of sunlight outlined a man leaning against a pile of hay, languidly smoking a cigarette while his wife milked her goats by hand. She sold me my cheese—which was aging on a basket hanging from a pulley in a cool shed—and lingered to chat about her grandson who was taking over the family vineyards.

In truth, these rustic cheeses are not invariably the hauntingly delicate embodiments of our cheese fantasies. They range from exquisite to flawed, when they might be bitter or raunchy. Most agree that the qualitative differences between chèvres have been leveled as goat-cheesemaking has become more "professional": Glorious cheeses are hard to come by, but outright failures are rare, too; increasingly, chèvres range from bland to very good—a few are excellent.

Since 1975 the production of goat cheese has been almost entirely transformed. As specialized farming replaces polyculture, the widow with three goats is quickly becoming an endangered species. Today's average goat farm is run by a couple with sixty to eighty milkers and thirty hectares of land on which to grow clover, hay, and barley to feed their herd. (Some goats pasture, but the trend is to keep them penned and feed them crops raised on the farm or locally. This goes by the Orwellian term *zero pasturage*.)

All appellation cheeses are pure, whole goat's milk; the best are raw milk, though many industrial chèvres are made from pasteurized milk. Depending on the appellation, the curds may be frozen. The cheese must have a minimum of 45 percent fat. The goats are milked twice a day. Rennet is added, and the milk is left to curdle for a day or more at mild temperatures of about 20 degrees Celsius. When the curds form a flanlike mass, the cheese

is ladled into molds to drain. Then it is unmolded and salted. In some appellations the salt is mixed with ash to encourage development of the mold.
(Once, ordinary wood ash from the hearth was used; now most is produced
industrially from powdered charcoal mixed with salt. Many believe that this
coating prevents the interior of the cheese from ripening; rather, it stays
white and mild.) Chèvres age for different periods of time according to the
appellation as well as the cheesemaker. Most farmers sell all or part of their
milk or fresh cheese to cooperatives or to the cheese merchants and dairies
that dominate the business.

There are thousands of goat-cheese producers in the Loire, and although
everyone uses the classic forms, not everyone within a given zone seeks the
official label. The appellations are relatively new and require inspections
and investments, which can be onerous for artisanal producers. And
admirable though the appellation system is in theory, it is often manipulated
dishonorably—to wit, politically.

Big dairies and major *affineurs* (cheese ripeners) often head committees
and guilds that have much to say about the criteria for appellation cheeses.
That the laws regulating production of such cheeses permit pasteurization
and the use of frozen curds or powdered milk, for example, is clearly a sop to
industry—which wants, among other things, shelf life and continuity of
product in the busy holiday season when fresh goat's milk is in very short
supply. (While many goats have been de-seasoned—spreading out the
birthing cycle so chèvre can be made all year—this is not enough to satisfy
end-of-year demand.) Their vote is also key when selecting which cheeses
will be granted the appellation, as well as which will represent it in national
food fairs. Big dairies don't relish competition, particularly in the form of
individual cheeses that only call attention to the banality of their own versions. If they, or like-minded technocrats, sit on juries determining who gets
into an appellation or who wins a competition, the homogenized, often pasteurized, versions win; authentic, handcrafted versions are excluded. And if
the EEC adopts proposed regulations imposing draconian requirements in
terms of hygiene and the minimum size of workspace, the laws would force
some of the acknowledged best producers of farmhouse cheese—of all
types—out of business.

Each cheese has its own story, however. And despite the odds, a growing
number of producers age part or all of their output to sell at the farm and at
markets. (If the couple does everything themselves—from milking to
cheesemaking, aging and marketing—the pair can earn as decent a living as
a French bureaucrat, though they work a helluva lot harder!) While the best

dairies have progressed within the past decade—some even work with raw milk—the cheeses are still bland when compared with a good farmhouse chèvre.

When aged, the *croûte* (crust or rind) of a chèvre is mottled with a blue-white-gray mold. It should be evenly and attractively spread, not thick and wrinkly. One expert appropriately described the mold as the *pourriture noble*, or noble rot, of goat cheese. (Many supermarket chèvres have an artificially induced, downy white mold.)

The cut of the cheese should be forthright, as flawless as china; the texture unctuous and smooth, not granular. The cheese itself is creamy white; the flavor forthright, too, milky, lightly pungent, at times grassy, fruity, nutty, or smoky, with a good balance between salt and acid. When a chèvre is very dry, cut off the crust and suck the cheese like a candy; it should melt in your mouth. However dry they become, though, Loire chèvres remain *moelleux* (in this context, "mellow"). Happily, there are still spectacular cheeses to be found. And despite the de-seasoning of goats, it is still true that the best chèvres are made from Easter to All Saints' Day.

The Loire's most significant contributions to French baked goods come from either end of the valley: Nantes is the home of the country's biggest and most famous cookie companies, LU and BN; and Lamotte-Beuvron, a whistle-stop in Sologne, is the reputed birthplace of *tarte Tatin*.

A major sugar and spice port, surrounded by wheat fields and dairy farms, Nantes might have been expected to have developed a tradition of biscuitry—the dry cakes provided sustenance for sailors and were popular among the homebound population as well. Similarly, *tarte Tatin*, an apple pie that is baked upside down and then served right-side up, would seem a natural outgrowth of an apple- and grain-growing region. Yet, in a saga as fanciful as the la mère Clémence story, its creation is traced to the turn of the century and credited to Stephanie and Caroline Tatin, the owners of Hôtel Tatin across from the train station of Lamotte-Beuvron.

Some say that Caroline forgot to line her pan with dough before adding the apples and then improvised, laying the dough across the bed of fruit. The current owners of Hôtel Tatin say that this was deliberate. The sisters were behind schedule and rather than lack dessert, Caroline placed sliced apples (presumably Orléans *reinettes*) in a buttered *tourtière* over a bed of sugar, heated them until they were well caramelized, then lay on the dough, placed the pie in a hot oven for half an hour, and unmolded it to the delectation of all present.

A fruit tart worthy of similar celebrity is Anjou's *pâté de prunes*, a buttery two-crusted pie made with greengage plums. Single-crust fruit tarts have always been made throughout the Loire, as have dessert fritters such as Anjou's *bottereaux*, Vendée's *foutimassons*, and Berry's *rousseroles*. Often made for holidays, the fritters are scented with *eau-de-vie* or orange-blossom water, as is the *brioche Vendéenne*, a fifteenth-century bread, a lightened version of which has become a popular supermarket loaf. Poitou's *tourteau fromagé*, a mushroom-shaped cheesecake with a distinctive blackened dome, is also sold throughout France.

Most regions have some variation on the *fouace* or *fouasse*, an ancient bread whose name derives from *panis focacius*, or focaccia, dough cooked in a hearth. By the Middle Ages, *fouace* had come to mean a deluxe bread. Today it is often an aromatized, rustic brioche, although the word sometimes applies to plain, flat loaves. The Nantes version is a slightly sweet, dry cake shaped like a five-pointed star. *Fouée* is made from bits of leftover dough which puff as they cook, leaving hollow centers like pita. The *fouée* is often filled with chèvre or *rillettes*. The *fouace*, now eaten at breakfast or tea, was traditionally linked with the harvest and new wine.

Roasted chestnuts are the classic accompaniment of *bernache*, the fermenting grape must, the arrival of which is more genuinely anticipated in local cafés than Nouveau Beaujolais. A surprisingly durable, pan-Loire dish—also wine-related and also the pretext for festivity—is sugary red-wine soup, sometimes thickened with bread, called *routie*, *mijet*, *miot*, or *le trempé*, depending on the region. Local red wine is also poured over strawberries. Pears are often stewed in wine or they are sautéed and stuffed into crêpes and laced with Cointreau.

Cointreau was created in Angers at the end of the nineteenth century, as was Giffard's Menthe-Pastille. (The city's tradition of liqueur production dates back to the Middle Ages.) The Château of Chambord lends its name to a deluxe liqueur produced nearby. *Eau-de-vie* is made all along the Loire, as are regional oddities like Kamok, the coffee-based liqueur of Vendée, and an assortment of sweet, fortified wines such as *vin de pêche*, *vin d'épine*, and *vin de guigne*, made by macerating leaves of fruit trees, the spring shoots of wild sloe, or cherry pits in a brew of wine, alcohol, and sugar. Tasty and potent aperitifs, they were made exclusively in the home until quite recently when a wine cooperative east of Tours took out a patent on Vin d'Epine and began marketing it.

The commercialization of this rustic aperitif, as well as the resurgence of *fouaces* and *fouées*, are further evidence of the renewed interest in old local recipes. Restaurants now offer *beuchelles*, an ancient Tourangeau stew of sweetbreads and cockscombs in a mushroom cream sauce; *carpe à la Chambord*, a return-from-the-hunt recipe from François Ier's day; and the luxurious nineteenth-century hare stew *lièvre à la royale*. At fairs, I've tasted a Cholet specialty I'd seen on many old family menus of tongue in a piquant caper sauce, and *caberillons*, duck thighs which have been grilled, marinated with herbs and Cabernet d'Anjou, then sautéed in oil and lard. Nantais charcutiers are again making *pâté de casse*, so called because it is baked in earthenware terrines. The practice of preserving apples and pears by long baking, flattening, and drying has been revived by artisans near Saumur and Tours. They reconstitute their *pommes* or *poires tapées* (flattened apples or pears) as local grandmothers did, in red wine infused with spices.

The surprising truth is that however much the Loire's foodways have been undermined by modern life, its most popular dishes are pretty much the same ones Rabelais enumerated in the sixteenth century. As you travel from Nantes to Pouilly, you get the impression of a great sweep of Loire cooking which, taken as a whole, resembles the cooking of other wine-and-agriculture regions situated on the banks of rivers—from the matelotes of freshwater fish and the game and poultry in wine-based or blood-thickened stews to the fruit tarts and mild, fresh cheeses. The regions within the Loire *do* change, but so incrementally that the modifications sneak up on you: Suddenly the landscape is different, and so is the food. You are as unlikely to find *rillettes* on a typical Sancerrois menu as you are to find a *galette de pommes de terre* in Nantes.

Since Ligerians like nothing better than eating what they have always eaten, I found I could delimit Loire regions by the dishes served me when invited for a meal. It was *beurre blanc* from Nantes to the Coteaux du Layon—until I reached the *matelotes d'anguille* of Saumur-Champigny and Chinon. *Civet de lièvre* and *coq en barbouille* took over in Berry and Sologne, *potée* in Auvergne. In Nantes, everything was cooked and served with butter; in Berry and Auvergne, potatoes replaced the *mogettes* of Vendée. In Vouvray a meal began with *rillettes*—unless it happened to be white asparagus season, when the fat spears were served tepid with a walnut oil vinaigrette or a hollandaise sauce.

When I think of Loire cooking I think of a cave in Auvergne where Saint-Nectaire cheeses age on mats of rye straw and where a four-month-old version, complex as a great wine, brought tears to my eyes. I think of the Dollet family, the last *fouasse* makers of La Haie-Fouassière, baking their breads literally in the shadow of the futuristic LU factory. And of Martin-

Pouret, the last artisanal vinegar maker of Orléans, a city that was once a capital of production.

I think of the lentil farmers on the high plateaus above Puy-en-Velay, near the source of the Loire, and of truck gardeners just south of Nantes. Of a summer afternoon when I entered a garage where the air smelled of mint and thyme. Seven women, four generations, sat in a circle under a shaft of sunlight, snipping and bunching chives. I think of farmers from Saumur to Sologne bent over long, low furrows to pluck asparagus before it sees daylight and turns green. And of their wives, peeling piles of spears over sheets of the *Nouvelle République*.

In June, when the weather turns hot and heavy, I think of the snails you pluck from the garden that taste of the sorrel they fed on. And of the snails you find days later hiding under the armchair or fastened to the front door.

I think of women at market stands, sanding and scraping eels, and of the fishermen who love the hard, good life of the Loire and who, after a day on the river, make the rounds of one another's wine cellars, returning late, but never too late for the catch of the day, lightly fried, glistening with butter.

I think, hungrily, of a lunch, after a hot August morning spent on the Loire with Michel Humeau. We sat on the terrace of his house overlooking his four kilometers of fishing rights on a little harbor called La Patache, upstream of Nantes.

His wife, Réjane, served us local melon, *sandre* (fished by Michel), a roast, salad, berries from the garden, and a moonshine cognac before we returned to work emptying eel traps. And I often dream of that *sandre* poached in court bouillon and napped with one of the best sauces I have ever eaten.

"It's just *poisson à la crème*," laughed Mme. Humeau, gently amused at my enthusiasm—not to mention my appetite. "You cut an onion very fine. Melt in a good nut of butter, the size of a hen's egg. Then chop four or five medium button mushrooms until you almost can't see them. When the onion is almost transparent, add the mushrooms and the juice of half a lemon. Cook for ten to fifteen minutes. When ready to serve, make a *beurre manié* using a big nut of softened butter with a coffee spoon of flour. Add it to the mixture, stir well, and add a *pot* of crème fraîche and some pepper. Cook long enough for the flour to mix in. This sauce holds better than *beurre blanc*."

Local fish, local butter, local mushrooms. On another visit we feasted on matelote of eel, a beast for which I'd developed a particular affection after that backbreaking afternoon pulling up and emptying thirty eel traps. (The haul was about sixty eels—around eight kilos—including a monster more than three feet long.) Cooked like a civet, the eel marinates overnight with coarse red wine, onion, and a bouquet garni. The marinade is reduced for several hours and the slices of eel are browned, then set to simmer over a low flame with the reduced marinade for four to five hours. Finally, the matelote is thickened with blood drained from the eel. Some regions add prunes or currants; some, hard-boiled eggs and croutons fried in walnut oil.

When I think of eels, I think of a pre-dinner walk with Auguste Blanchet, the second son of a Pays-de-Retz farmer who left the seminary for the Chambre d'Agriculture to return to the land he would have preferred to till. He wanted to show me the heart of the Pays-de-Retz, the western reach of the Nantais—and the Loire.

We drove through marshlands given over to game-bird preserves and along canals lined with trees and long grasses. Hunters silently stalked the open fields. Now and then a gunshot muffled by mist broke a quiet as absolute as I could imagine the world ever being.

It was yet another face of the Loire, which, in spirit, joined the Loire of vines and cellars. Beyond the Loire of châteaux and nuclear power plants, there is the Loire of people whose fierce, loving bond with nature struck an unsettling chord of self-reproach in this city dweller, so removed from the sounds, smells, and rhythms of the land.

The sun was setting. It was that time of day the French call *entre chien et loup* because your eyes play tricks on you and you can't distinguish a dog from a wolf. But Auguste had no trouble identifying the birds that rose from the dark water into the darkening sky. He pointed out herons, a flock of coots, an egret, a teal, before taking "*l'Américaine*" to his home for a meal that was pure tradition. The main course was a mallard he'd hunted. The first course was eel grilled over vine cuttings.

"I didn't catch an eel this week and my usual source didn't either," Auguste said, smiling slyly, "so I went to La Patache and bought one from your friend Humeau."

It was the monster I had pulled from the Loire several weeks earlier. How delicious it was, rich, meaty, and fine. And all the more marvelous as I had fished it, and a friend, unaware of the coincidence, had bought it to offer a foreigner a true taste of the Loire.

III

The Wine Route:
A User's Guide

AN OVERVIEW OF OUR
ITINERARY

D ividing the Loire into five subregions, I start at the mouth of the
river in the Nantais and Vendée. Then we move east to Anjou and
Saumur with a visit to Thouars as well. Next we travel to Touraine
where we'll also taste the wines of Haut-Poitou, Jasnières, the Coteaux du
Loir, the Vendômois, Cheverny, and Valençay. Then it's on to the Sancerrois and the Vignobles du Centre, including Châteaumeillant, Coteaux du
Giennois, and the Orléanais. Finally, we track the river to its source and
pick up wine regions that seem to have little to do with the Loire: Saint-
Pourçain, Côtes du Forez, Côtes d'Auvergne, and the Côte Roannaise.

When deciding where to place the more far-flung appellations, I have
followed local custom or official groupings. It isn't always easy. The Côte
Roannaise, for example, has much more in common with Beaujolais than
with any appellation in the Loire Valley; indeed, it works with government-
sponsored enologists and labs in the Lyonnais. But it is situated on the Loire
and is included in the Loire appellations. The Côtes d'Auvergne, too, is
grouped with the vineyards of the Loire though it is very far from the

river—as well as from anything remotely Ligerian. Cheverny, Valençay, and the Vendômois could have been grouped with the Vignobles du Centre rather than Touraine, but as producers in the first two abut Touraine and make wines under that broad appellation, it seemed sensible to include them in that chapter; as the Vendômois abuts Jasnières, which is due north of Tours, it, too, belongs in Touraine.

I broke with the custom of including the wines of Orléans in Touraine. I place them with the Vignobles du Centre for reasons of geography, history, and the use of Pinot Noir.

When selecting gastronomic specialties, I've followed the viticultural regions. Thus, I don't really discuss oysters in the Nantais, Loué chicken in Anjou and the Sarthe, Pithiviers in the Sancerrois, Cantal in Auvergne, and so forth. And goat cheeses such as Valençay and Selles-sur-Cher are really Berrichon (and therefore logically belong to the Vignobles du Centre), but since they overlap the Touraine appellation wine zone, they are included within that chapter.

PRODUCER RATINGS
AND TASTING NOTES

Not every producer I interviewed in the course of my research is included here. And for reasons of length, many who are included are mentioned only in an annotated list. Brief as that entry may be, it was based, in more than 90 percent of cases, on a meeting and at least one tasting—though in most cases, many more.

In longer reviews, I have tried to give an idea of the style of wine a producer makes, year after year. (I've also tried to limit the number of wines described, again for reasons of length.) Where discussions of specific vintages or *cuvées* serve no compelling purpose—because everything is recommended—I have limited myself (or tried) to a discussion of the way the producer works and the style of his wines. Most, by the way, qualify as "boutique" wineries, making five thousand cases yearly, sometimes less.

I have rated the producers within each appellation. My classifications are as follows:

Outstanding: These producers are among France's "artist-vintners." They make the best and most exciting wines in their respective appellations and in the Loire, every year. Often the conscience or the benchmark of their appellations, they are the ones who, because of their rigor and/or creativity, pushed the region further in the direction of quality. They are exigent in the vineyards and in the cellar. Yields are low; many practice either organic or biodynamic viticulture (although this was not a criterion); vinification is painstaking, based on reflection—and sometimes on divine madness. There is often a touch of genius in the wines. These vintners are usually the innovators—the first to have bottled by vineyard or by soil type, the ones who waited to harvest until December to make Grains Nobles or who dreamed up special *cuvées*. It's not just fancy packaging: You can taste the difference. The wines are extraordinary. To be in this category, a producer's entire line must be of extremely high quality, even if not every bottling attains the level of the best *cuvées*.

Leaders: In French, these wineries are referred to as *locomotives*. Many are grower-*négociants* and all have high-profile estates. Most participate in major tastings and wine fairs. They are frequently written about by the wine press and their wines are well distributed. The wines, in each case, range from highly recommended to outstanding, depending on the *domaine*.

Excellent: These producers are first-rate. Their wines are classic. Often very close qualitatively to those in "Outstanding," they sometimes—in certain years and with certain *cuvées*—outshine them. There are artist-vintners here, too, as well as innovators. Why don't they qualify for "Outstanding"? It varies from winery to winery. Some will surely move up. In other cases, it's a question of cutbacks due to financial hardship, or of young vines, or of too great a discrepancy between the top *cuvées* and the generic bottlings. Some producers are ever-so-slightly less exigent; still others simply lack that spark of genius. The wines—and the winemakers—are usually more "rational" than their confreres in "Outstanding." But they are true ambassadors for their respective appellations, year after year. Their wines are, in a word, excellent.

To Watch: Newcomers—or newish, serious vintners who haven't yet found their voice—who I expect to evolve into "Outstanding" or "Excellent."

Highly Recommended: Reliably good producers who make very good wines, these *domaines*, generally, are the best representatives of a "typical" winery within an appellation. They do not go to the extremes of those in "Outstanding" or "Excellent"—in yields and other viticultural practices or experiments—and their wines tend to be less concentrated, less complex, less age-worthy (where that is a consideration). Because of this, they are more subject to the vagaries of vintage. So taste first in difficult years. But on the whole, the wines are very good; sometimes more.

Recommended: In most years, these vintners produce wines that make for pleasant drinking, and are fairly accurate representatives of the good middle ground of their appellations.

Floating Categories: In the text, these categories follow the above classifications and may change from appellation to appellation:

- *Other:* This means I have a strong, specific opinion that precludes a recommendation, cf. Coulée de Serrant.
- *By the Glass:* Producers whose wines would be interesting to taste in a wine bar—though you might not want to commit yourself to a whole bottle.
- *Tasted in Passing with Pleasure:* Winemakers I feel I don't know sufficiently but whose wines I've enjoyed—either because of high quality or an interesting quirkiness—and would like to know better.
- *Tasted and Considered:* Average or below average; a category I use for high-profile estates, producers with wide distribution, or frequent award winners.
- *In Transition:* Generally a major winery with a recent change of ownership and personnel.
- In certain appellations I include an annotated list of producers under a specific rubric. Examples include large Muscadet grower-*négociant* houses; excellent Anjou estates making very good rosés; promising young Vouvray producers.

Note: The listings always start with a producer's name, followed by a village or commune. Where producers make wine in a number of appellations, the village or commune appears only in the producer's principal zone of production. Subsequent listings give the name of the producer, followed by the major appellation in parentheses. For example, Domaine Ogereau, located in Saint-Lambert-du-Lattay, is an outstanding producer of Coteaux du Layon. In the Layon listings it appears: *Domaine Ogereau*, Saint-Lambert-du-Lattay. When I rate the *domaine's* generic Anjou, it is listed as *Domaine Ogereau* (Layon). Also, when a producer has attended a school of viticulture or enology, I include a reference to the school in parentheses, e.g., Victor Lebreton (Montreuil-Bellay).

Prices are what you would pay at the winery. They are given in francs, which, at the time of this writing, are five to the dollar.

WINESPEAK

The aromas and flavors of wine fall into nine or ten recognized groups. (These have been classified by enologists such as Emile Peynaud in his *Goût du Vin*.) The groups include fairly easy associative leaps like flowers (violets, roses), fruits (berries, apples, lemon, fig), vegetables (bell peppers, green beans), and spices (cinnamon, clove, pepper). Also included are less familiar comparative categories such as animal (visceral, musk, game), balsam (pine, cedar, eucalyptus, mint), wood (vanilla, coconut), roasted scents (toast, coffee, crème brûlée, leather), chemical/fermentation (yeasts, hard candy), and off-odors (rotten egg, garlic, onion).

Some words or associations will be more meaningful than others to a given taster. I would like to define several descriptions I often use, as well as some words that may seem strange or off-putting.

Pits: Many fruity red wines have a flavor reminiscent of cherry pits. It's quite focused and succulent—mixing the flavor of the fruit with that of bitter almond. You may recognize the taste from *eaux-de-vie* or liqueurs, or sauces made with them, as pits of various fruits often macerate with the pulp in the production of fruit brandies.

Cat's Pee: Ever since I began tasting wine seriously I have felt that many Sauvignon Blancs had an aroma of cat's pee. As revolting as this sounds, it is not a disagreeable scent in a wine. It's a pungent, vegetal aroma with a bit of something feral in it. If you've ever had a close relationship with a cat, you'll probably agree that the image is apt.

Petrol: Sounds unappetizing, too, but this aroma and flavor is typical in many fine Rieslings (from Germany and Alsace) as well as Loire Chenins and Sauvignon Blancs.

Quinine, herbal tea or *tisane*, and medicinal herbs such as chamomile, linden blossom (*tilleul*), verbena (*verveine*): I adore these nuances in a wine (and in other beverages, e.g., Schweppes Bitter Lemon, Campari). They are slightly bitter but extremely appetizing.

Goût de terroir: The concept of *terroir* unites the specifics of a vineyard site—its soils, subsoils, exposition, the opening of the countryside. When a wine seems to express this specificity, this uniqueness, it has a *goût de terroir*, or it is *terroirté*. This is a stamp of identity and an aspect of complexity. It is something I look for in wine. (Note, however, that some wine experts use the term pejoratively, to describe an earthy wine.)

Stem Rot: In several vintages ('94 and '88, for example) certain grape varieties—notably Chenin Blanc, Gamay, and Gros Plant—were attacked by stem rot. Often the winemaker is not aware that it exists until the grapes have been crushed (or so I'm told). To me, stem rot recalls the humid, earthy smell of Long Island potato fields after an August rain. It may be quite pronounced or it may be barely noticeable. In the latter instance, particularly if a wine is rich and complex (as is the case with many '94 Layons), you may not perceive the taste at all.

PRACTICAL TIPS

In the appendices of the book, I've included:

Wining, Dining, and Touring: This section includes restaurants, hotels and bed-and-breakfasts, shops, fairs, and major sights for each region, followed by a recommended itinerary of winery visits.

Glossary: There are three brief sections. The first lists useful French terms, such as *stage* and AOC, as well as words often used in the Loire, e.g., *douceur*, Ligerian. The second is devoted to wine; the third, to cheese. Suggested temperatures for serving Loire wines are briefly described.

Conversion Tables: I generally use French terms: Celsius, hectoliters, hectares, and so forth. The brief conversion table translates these into American weights and measures.

IV

The Nantais

As the Loire passes Ingrandes at the Anjou border, loops under the city of Nantes, and opens into an estuary between the fishing port of Paimboeuf and the industrial banks of Saint-Nazaire before flowing into the Atlantic, its course describes the northwest limits of the vineyards of France.

You sense the ocean here. The sky has a high, wide, going-out-to-sea luminosity. A perpetual haze, gritty and incandescent, seems to leach the pastel palette of the inland Loire, leaving halftones of ochre and green.

Vines radiate south, southeast, and southwest of Nantes, on the gentle slopes and plateaus of the foothills of the Massif Armoricain. Most make Muscadet; the rest fall into one of three VDQS—Gros Plant du Pays Nantais, the Coteaux d'Ancenis, and Fiefs Vendéens—or one of several regional Vins de Pays or they are simply *vin de table*.

THE MUSCADETS

STATUS: *4 AOCs: Muscadet de Sèvre-et-Maine, 1936; Muscadet des Coteaux de la Loire, 1936; Muscadet, 1937; Muscadet Côtes de Grand Lieu, 1994*

TYPES OF WINE: *Still, dry white*

ZONE AND PRODUCTION: *About 750,000 hectoliters yearly (of which 85 percent is Sèvre-et-Maine), from 13,000 hectares. Muscadet Côtes de Grand Lieu applies to about 200 hectares around the Nantes airport and stretching west to the Atlantic. Vines running east to Anjou along the banks of the Loire are Muscadet des Coteaux de la Loire. Muscadet de Sèvre-et-Maine begins south of Nantes and spills southeast to the Vendée border. It takes its name from two rivers running through it.*

GRAPES: *Muscadet (also known as Melon de Bourgogne or Melon)*

SOILS: *A mixture of sand, clay, silica, schist, and gneiss*

PRICE: *10 to 45ff*

BEST VINTAGES: *'95, '93, '90, '89, '87, '85, '82, '79, '76, '69*

In the immense sweep of the Loire few wines promised less than Muscadet and no wine surprised—or chastened— me more. I set off for Nantes with fond memories of an ice-cold Muscadet at a bistro near my Greenwich Village apartment—so brisk, so simple, so satisfying with a plate of steamed mussels, a summer breeze, a curbside table; a slew of not-so-fond recollections of Muscadet as little more than vinous mouthwash; and an afterimage of Muscadet as a monotonal, cheap white, pleasant enough if it wasn't too acid.

When friends with more or less the same view winced at the idea of tasting vintage after vintage in cellar after cellar, I hid similar qualms behind stouthearted vows to find the passionate artisans who made *Serious* Muscadet.

Frankly, I had no specific idea what Serious Muscadet might mean or taste like, but, a hard-core utopian, I assumed the key was "Tradition," which to my mind comprehended low-tech as well as low-yield, perhaps a single vineyard, a passage in wood, as well as honest-to-God *sur lie* bottling. Surely there existed two or three zealots, uncorrupted by commerce, who made the Real Thing, whose handcrafted Muscadets, obscured though they had been by seas of meretricious *négociant* blends, preserved and revealed the Great Truths of the Appellation.

I found Serious Muscadet. But my half-savvy, half-sappy, thoroughly romantic notion of "Tradition" got a much-needed shaking out and reorganizing. Neither esoteric nor a museum piece, Serious Muscadet emerged in force within the past twenty years. It's not a blockbuster Chardonnay to be sure. Usually around 12 percent alcohol, Muscadet is not, by its nature, powerhouse material. But the best can hold its own against many a Pouilly Fumé or Fuissé as well as the sleek whites coming out of Italy. And the very best can make you dream.

Pale, racy, and dry, Muscadet's appeal is its delicacy and the steely vigor it expresses within that context. Its tart lemon tang is offset by savory almond flavors and a Badoit-like taste of minerals. A barely perceptible sparkle lifts the wine across the palate with an exciting, hard, cold tingle, like a mountain stream flowing fast over rocks.

The passionate artisans who make this wine call it "Serious Muscadet," too, but few, if any, resemble my fantasy vigneron—a grandfather, gnarled as his prephylloxera vines, with Aesop-like tales to tell of spring frosts and harvest rains, and wine lore to dispense whose roots descended to Saint Martin of Tours.

As often as not, my zealots would rather analyze market trends as well as the merits of a pneumatic versus a horizontal press. And they understand that a fundamental change in drinking habits dictated overhauling tradition rather than adhering to it: Consumers are drinking less but better wine. They want dry whites but demand a higher quality than Muscadet historically delivered.

Stricter regulations were enacted in the mid-sixties and early seventies. (At roughly the same time, discontent over prices led many small growers to bottle their own wine rather than sell in bulk to *négociants*.) Cellars are being renovated and equipment upgraded. The plonk hasn't disappeared, but its days seem numbered. Even some of the hardest-nosed *négociants* are turning out admirable Muscadets. Along with Muscadet *nouveau*, which debuts at the same time as Beaujolais *primeur*, there are old-vines Muscadets, single-*clos* Muscadets, Muscadets fermented in new oak barrels, Muscadet priced like Sancerre and determined to steal its thunder.

On a deeper level, Muscadet is still very much a work in progress. A new Muscadet appellation was created in 1994 at the same time that an important revision of the law on *sur lie* went into effect. Commissions are studying a system of classification, and a committee of producers has requested the legal lowering of permitted yields. The issue is no longer one of making good, clean, competitive whites. It's a question of defining the Real Thing; a wine ever more specific to the grape, the land, the integrity of the vigneron. Although Muscadet received *appellation contrôlée* status sixty years ago, its Great Truths are being sounded now.

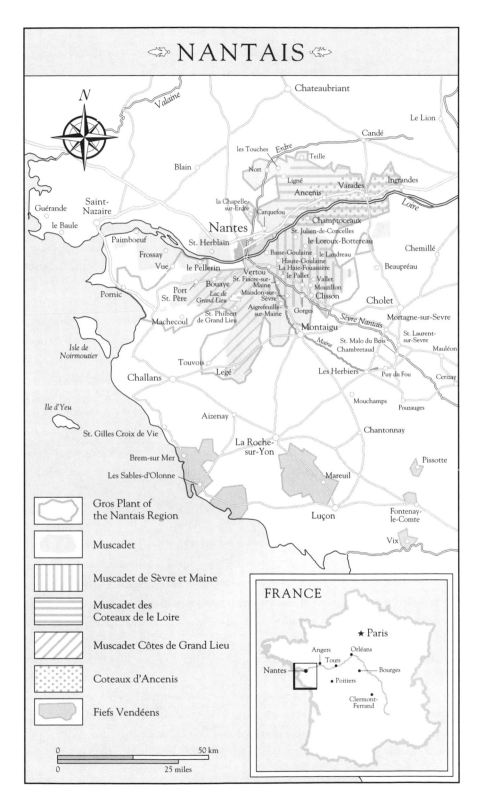

NANTAIS

Gros Plant of the Nantais Region

Muscadet

Muscadet de Sèvre et Maine

Muscadet des Coteaux de le Loire

Muscadet Côtes de Grand Lieu

Coteaux d'Ancenis

Fiefs Vendéens

0   50 km

0   25 miles

FRANCE

★ Paris

Angers   Orléans
Nantes   Tours
          Bourges
      Poitiers

Clermont-
Ferrand

Chateaubriant

Le Lion

Candé

Valaine

les Touches   Erdre   Teille
Blain   Nort   Ingrandes
               Ligné   Varades
la Chapelle-   Ancenis   Loire
sur-Erdre   Carquefou
Guérande   Saint-   Champtoceaux
le Baule   Nazaire   Nantes   St. Julien-de-Concelles
Paimboeuf   St. Herblain   le Loroux-Bottereau   Chemillé
Frossay   Basse-Goulaine   le Landreau
Vue   le Pellerin   Haute-Goulaine   Beaupréau
              Vertou   La Haie-Fouassière
Pornic   Bouaye   St. Fiacre-sur-   le Pallet
         Lac de   Maine   Vallet
Port   Grand Lieu   Maisdon-sur-   Mouzillon
St. Père   Sèvre   Clisson   Cholet
         St. Philbert   Aigrefeuille-
Machecoul   de Grand Lieu   sur-Maine   Gorges
                        Montaigu   Sèvre Nantais   Mortagne-sur-Sevre
Isle de   St. Laurent-
Noirmoutier   Touvois   Maine   St. Malo du Bois   sur-Sevre   Mauléon
                        Chambretaud
Challans   Legé   Les Herbiers   Puy du Fou   Cerizay
Ile d'Yeu
                        Mouchamps
St. Gilles Croix de Vie   Aizenay   Pouzauges
                              Chantonnay
Brem-sur Mer   La Roche-
              sur-Yon   Pissotte
Les Sables-d'Olonne   Mareuil
                                 Fontenay-
                    Luçon   le-Comte
                        Vix

———

Melon is a neutral grape. Its characteristic blandness more readily begets a standardized wine than a distinctive one. Someone once said of Robert Redford, "He looks alike." And in the brave new world of high-tech whites, an impeccable Muscadet is often just another pretty face.

Winemakers, however, test the boundaries of Melon's finite palette with just about every technique known to enology—from skin contact to yeasts cultured from their property, to barrel fermentation, to the length of time the wine stays on its lees.

The shadings are subtle. You have to go out to meet them. Muscadet doesn't pretend to Le Montrachet's epic spectrum of flavors. But the incremental differences between one producer—or *clos* or *cuvée*—and another are definite. The nuances often embody not only a specific method of vinification but a specific soil and a specific vision. It's at this point that we sentimentalists get excited and start babbling about wine-as-art.

The widespread practice of bottling *sur lie* distinguishes the vinification of Nantais wines, Muscadet in particular, among still whites. In theory, *sur lie* Muscadet stays on its lees of vinification until it is bottled. This procedure harks back to the days when families kept a barrel of their best wine for special occasions such as Easter, First Communions, or weddings. When the wine was drawn off its lees for the festivities, growers noticed that it had conserved its freshness, it was rounder, it had a meatier texture, its flavor was more complex, and it had a prickle of carbonic gas, which imparted a bracing thread of bubbles.

Essentially, *sur lie* is a less-is-more approach to winemaking, but by doing little it does a lot. Technically, the lees, or dead yeast cells, sink to the bottom of the wine after alcoholic fermentation. They create amino acids that combine with polysaccharides, adding flavor, fleshiness, and a wonderful rich, marrowy texture. The lees also trap small amounts of carbon dioxide, which add that thrilling sparkle. By preventing oxidation, aging *sur lie* preserves the wine's breezy vitality and somehow seems to underscore the expression of *terroir*.

Under the new INAO regulations, Muscadet may be labeled *sur lie* if it has been bottled directly off its fine lees of vinification. The statute establishes two periods for *sur lie* bottling: the first, between March 1 and June 30 following the harvest; the second, from October 15 to November 30. As Melon responds badly to manipulation, the law further provides that *sur lie* wine may only be bottled in the cellar in which it was made. (*Négociants* are given until 1997 to fully comply with this aspect of the law; it means they will have to buy grapes or must and vinify in their own cellars, or bottle at the particular property—which is what some leading *négociant* houses have been doing for years.)

The amended law represents a significant victory for quality Muscadet in a number of ways. First, it extends the time a wine may rest on its lees, which studies (and my empirical tastings) have shown to be beneficial. (The previous law set June 30 as the only cutoff date.) Next, by specifying fine lees, the law permits an initial racking after fermentation to eliminate the gross lees. (Fine lees are made up primarily of yeast cells; gross lees often include particles of mineral or vegetable matter which have not settled out during a decanting prior to alcoholic fermentation.) Third, the restrictions imposed on *négociants* should work in favor of authenticity.

Nevertheless, there are some producers who feel the law does not go far enough. Léon Boullault, for example, would like to extend the *sur lie* period to two years or more. His '85 and '87 Cuvée Grande Garde, two extraordinary Muscadets that are frequently mistaken for Burgundies in blind tastings, spent eighteen and twenty-seven months respectively on their lees but, in theory, may not include any mention of *sur lie* on the label as the wines were racked off their lees after the cutoff date.

The regulations will probably be revised to include a third bottling date, which would encompass people like Boullault. Muscadet muckety-mucks concede that Boullault's wines benefit from long lees time because of his land. Rich in clay and schist, his vineyards produce full-bodied Muscadets that are both "long to express themselves" and "long-lived." This brings up another burning issue: the appellation itself.

As of 1994, the law specifies four Muscadets: generic Muscadet, Muscadet des Coteaux de la Loire, Muscadet de Sèvre-et-Maine, and, most recently, Muscadet Côtes de Grand Lieu, for the region around Bouaye just past the Nantes airport.

Sèvre-et-Maine was designed to signify the top of the line, but as it represents 85 percent of Muscadet production, the appellation structure resembles—to quote the producers—a pyramid on its head and gives quality-conscious vintners yet another massive image problem: how to tell a fine Muscadet de Sèvre-et-Maine from a fair or a lousy one.

To compensate for the lack of a meaningful hierarchy, winemakers issue more than the usual number of prestige bottlings with highfalutin names:

Pierre Luneau's Le L d'Or, Jean Douillard's Première, and Claude Branger's Excellence are but three. Sauvion and Donatien Bahuaud created special bottlings—Cardinal Richard and Le Master respectively—which are chosen by juries composed of enologists, winemakers, and restaurateurs. And there are small groups of vignerons like Hermine d'Or and Louis Métaireau's Vignerons d'Art who have, in effect, created their own classification system, carefully selecting *cuvées* of participating members whose wines scored higher than 15 out of 20 in blind tastings to obtain the group label.

But many Sèvre-et-Maine winemakers would like something official to separate the wheat from the chaff. Residents of Saint-Fiacre, which is on the confluence of the Sèvre and the Maine, favor a Muscadet-Villages system which would recognize superior communes within the region the way Brouilly and Moulin-à-Vent are distinguished in Beaujolais.

Vintners in other towns object, even if they are located in a commune that would get its own, like Vallet, as they fear that Saint-Fiacre, the smallest of the twenty-three communes in the Sèvre-et-Maine, would become a de facto *grand cru* and that the wines would sell whether they were good or not. They, in turn, favor an official *cru* system, whether that means distinguishing higher-quality wine in yearly tastings or demarcating the best vineyard plots as *premier* and *grand cru*, like Chablis.

Official action is unlikely anytime soon, although a local commission is studying the issue. A growing number of winemakers have begun the winnowing process on their own, however. They offer three or four Muscadets a year—an aperitif version from sandy soils; one or two "serious" Muscadets from older vines on more complex soils; and, following the Burgundian example, a single-*clos* bottling highlighting the characteristics of a specific parcel.

And if the vintners have a say in the matter, their old-vines, single-vineyard Muscadets will be vintage Muscadets, to cellar for five or ten years, even more. They are not the lunatic fringe. Everyone's got '79s, '76s, '69s tucked away.

Not all Muscadets can age. And maybe the best were better when they were young and sassy. But a very good Muscadet from a very good vintage becomes toasty and rather creamy over time, knitting in flavors of beeswax and pine while retaining a thirst-quenching freshness. Some have reminded me of old Champagne, others of mature Vouvray *pétillant* whose sparkle has dwindled to a filament of beads, a memory of effervescence. But the reflection of one winemaker was truer, a closure both poetic and just: As Muscadet ages, it rediscovers its roots in Burgundy.

Sèvre-et-Maine

Muscadet de Sèvre-et-Maine begins south of Nantes and spreads east to the pastures of the Mauges and south to Vendée. Broadly, Le Landreau, in the northeast, is known for tender Muscadets. Usually the first region to harvest, its wines are "early to express themselves." Saint-Fiacre, Maisdon, and La Haie-Fouassière, at the heart of the appellation, reputedly make its most elegant wines. Vallet, the Capital of Muscadet, and neighboring Mouzillon and La Regrippière make full-bodied Muscadets that "need to see their first Easter." Additionally, vineyards in Gorges and Le Pallet are streaked with gabbro, a hard rock that imparts a strong mineral and gunflint component to the wine.

Note: Hermine d'Or is a designation given to selected Muscadets from a group of six excellent winemakers: Guy Bossard (Domaine de l'Ecu); Léon Boullault (Domaine des Dorices); Joseph Landron (Domaine de la Louvetrie); Léon Dollet; Alain Forget; and Joseph Hallereau. Each is described individually.

The group schedules three "must-attend" tastings a year to select its Hermines d'Or. Jean-Luc Chaigneau, an enologist who works with most of the winemakers in the group as well as just about every other leading Nantais producer, presides. The wines are tasted blind and must receive scores of no less than 15 out of 20 to be "*Herminé*." Wines that are *Herminés* receive neck labels with the group's name, a stylized ermine (which represents Brittany), the vintage, and the number of the bottle. This insignia is as near a guarantee of quality as I've found.

⤜ PRODUCER RATINGS ⤛

OUTSTANDING
Domaine de l'Ecu   Louis Métaireau

LEADERS
Chéreau-Carré   Sauvion et Fils (Château du Cléray)

EXCELLENT
Château de la Ragotière   Domaine Chiron
Domaine des Dorices   Domaine de la Fruitière
Domaine de la Haute-Févrie   Domaine de la Louvetrie

Domaine Pierre Luneau-Papin
Domaine la Quilla (Daniel and Gérard Vinet)

HIGHLY RECOMMENDED
André-Michel Brégeon   Léon Dollet
Domaine de la Gautronnière   Domaine de la Tourmaline
Joseph Hallereau

RECOMMENDED
Donatien Bahuaud   Château de Briacé
Marquis de Goulaine

TASTED IN PASSING WITH PLEASURE
Henri Bouchaud (Domaine du Bois-Joly)
Château de la Mercredière
Bruno Cormerais   Domaine Bideau-Giraud
Domaine du Perd-Son-Pain   Xavier Gouraud
Jean-François Guilbaud   Petiteau-Gaubert

LARGER GROWER-NEGOCIANT HOUSES MAKING AVERAGE WINE
Barré Frères   Guilbaud Frères
Marcel Sautejeau   Benjamin Sourice

TASTED AND CONSIDERED
Domaine de l'Oiselinière   Philippe Laure   Pierre Lieubeau

꾸 꾸

OUTSTANDING

Domaine de l'Ecu, Le Landreau: At times I dream of having the power to grant the vineyard of my choice to the winemaker of my choice. Savennières's mythic Coulée de Serrant would go to Guy Bossard, one of the most talented, committed, and self-effacing winemakers I've ever met.

An intense man with dark, Mediterranean good looks and disarmingly courtly manners, Bossard makes gorgeous Muscadet—and thank God for it—but Muscadet has never placed anyone in the Winemakers' Hall of Fame. And truth be told, it may never wholly exploit Bossard's potential.

A fifth-generation winemaker with seventeen hectares of vines in Le Landreau, he's an obsessive perfectionist whose nature forces him to reinvent the wheel at every turn. This can mean "back to the future"—using a horse for the spring plowing of fragile old and young vines. It can mean high-tech—pneumatic press, stainless steel tanks, experiments with skin contact that have been the most considered and finely tuned in Muscadet. And it can mean venturing into realms dismissed as marginal: He has practiced organic viticulture since 1975. He makes his own compost of algae, forest brush, and basalt ("In viticulture, compost is as important and as personal as fermentation is for vinification. Every winemaker has his own touch"). And he slowly but steadily embraces biodynamics, a strict form of organic viticulture. (Bossard is also a nurseryman; vine plants constitute a fourth of his business.) And his Muscadets are always among the most complex, freshest, and best balanced in the region, with a sure and true *goût de terroir*.

His regular Muscadet can be consumed quickly; his Domaine de l'Ecu and Clos de Bazillière should age. The first time I tasted Bossard's '86 Domaine de l'Ecu, an Hermine d'Or selection, I thought, "This is what Leonard Humbrecht would make if he were working in Chablis." The wine was perfumed and rich, with full mineral, pine, and fruit flavors. It combined freshness and grip with toasty, mellow, honeyed notes. His Bazillière was the best '89 Muscadet I tasted, complex and layered with fruit and minerals. His '90s were all fabulous—beautifully structured with incredible freshness and mineral expression. The Bazillière was so *terroirté* it was like an archeological dig. After cluster thinning in '92, he turned out a series of gorgeous Muscadets, as he did, once again, in '93.

Louis Métaireau et ses Vignerons d'Art, **Maisdon-sur-Sèvre:** Not a name that rolls trippingly off the tongue. Pretentious, too. But it makes sense. There would be no Vignerons d'Art without Louis Métaireau. And the very idea of winemaking-as-art in Muscadet is key to the Métaireau crusade, the crusade that put Muscadet on the map and in gourmet magazines and that doubled its prices.

Louis Métaireau: He's controversial. He's abrasive. He's flamboyant. He's Hollywood. He's fur coats and tennis whites and tinted glasses and helicopters. And he came along at just the right time for Muscadet.

As one winemaker said to me, "Hats off to Métaireau. In the sixties we were so depressed. We all wondered if we shouldn't change professions. Métaireau gave us confidence. His exigence made us believe in ourselves and in what we were doing."

With only two hectares of vineyards of his own, Métaireau has established his prominence both by pulling together a group of seven excellent winemakers (plus the twenty-seven-hectare Domaine du Grand Mouton purchased by the group) as well as by his promotional genius. He never misses a chance for theater: He brings in notaries to bear witness to the fact that certain *cuvées* are drawn directly off the lees without the merest suggestion of filtration, and he stumps the gourmet campaign trail like a televangelist.

"We should be the top dry white wine in the world," he intones to an audience of one. "A great Muscadet is lacy. It has multiple fleeting aromas. Fugitive, ephemeral aromas; aromas that are scarcely seizable. And above all, great freshness. We're the only white wine that prepares the palate to discover great things. Other wines may be more perfumed, fruitier, but they don't have the same gaiety."

A Métaireau Muscadet is singular, didactic even. He prefers a "wild, irritating" high-acid Muscadet. He likes acid years, like '84, '86, and '88. His Premier Jour, made from grapes harvested the first day of the '89 vintage, testifies to his preference for early-harvested Muscadet. And he promotes his latest offspring, "10,5," as a "wine for the 21st century" because it is low in alcohol. (The '93, a good Muscadet, was a bit short and, well, lightweight.)

Métaireau's wines may not be for everyone. I find them exciting; they have a studied elegance, a steely structure, and are gorgeously appetizing.

The Vignerons d'Art *cuvées* are selected after four blind tastings held at different times in the wine's development, starting a month after the harvest when the group goes through every *cuvée* of each member—about forty to fifty samples to be whittled down to four *cuvées*. Selected wines are bottled at the vigneron's property and his initials are stamped on the cork.

The three principal bottlings, in ascending order, are Grand Mouton, Cuvée LM, and Number 1. The grapes for Grand Mouton are harvested underripe to capture the wild, musky quality Métaireau likes. Roughly 10 percent is unfiltered. (Here's where Métaireau brings in the notary to witness honest-to-God *sur lie* bottling.) I admired the '94 but it won't make me dream the way '88 or the unfiltered '86 did; the first with scents of flowers and freshly sliced ginger, the second with its steely structure and creamy texture.

Cuvée LM is Métaireau's personal choice, selected from the six best *cuvées* after Number 1. Métaireau is looking for a "wine of *haute cuisine*, for a noble fish prepared by a great chef." The top *cuvée* is Number 1, which Métaireau describes as his *grand sec d'apéritif*, his "wildest" wine. Winning *cuvées* must score 17.5 out of 20.

It's hard to choose between the two in vintages like '88 and the super-ripe '89 and '90. The '89 Number 1, for example, had great grip, great length, and with its flavors of green apples, was the richest, fruitiest, and most mineraly of the '89s—though not necessarily better than LM, which was layered and finely structured; excellent in the hard, lean style; and just full enough to keep it from being severe.

That said, Number 1 emerged my clear favorite in the '93 vintage. It was all the words Métaireau likes to throw around so much—lacy, fugitive, fresh, and loaded with mineral and nut flavors. And then I recall other Number 1's I've loved, like a haunting '87 that finished on a note of tea and melon.

LEADERS

***Chéreau-Carré,* Saint-Fiacre-sur-Maine:**   The Chéreau family has had vineyards in the Muscadet region since 1412. Today, with 120 hectares of vines, it is one of the largest proprietors. It is also an important *négociant* house specializing in Loire wines. The four million bottles it sells yearly are split evenly between purchased wines and wines from Chéreau's six different estates. The house is currently run by Bernard Chéreau *père,* a pillar of the Nantais wine community, and Bernard Chéreau *fils,* a doctor-turned-winemaker.

The finest properties are Château de Chasseloir and Château du Coing. The former, a twenty-five-hectare *domaine* on the banks of the river Maine includes a parcel of century-old vines—the oldest Muscadet vines in the Nantais—vinified separately as Comte Leloup de Chasseloir. Château du Coing is a forty-hectare estate on the confluence of the Sèvre and the Maine. Of the two, Château de Chasseloir wines are considered fatter and more masculine; Coing, which I often prefer, is lighter and more elegant. In the realm of Muscadet, however, both wines are rich and voluminous.

Using selected batches from these estates, Chéreau was one of the first to experiment with new oak fermentation. "When we used new oak in 1985 it was like putting a bomb in the vineyards," Bernard *fils* told me. "Melon can be floral and fresh or it can rival Chablis. If you want to make a great white, you need to look at the methods used for making great whites. I use new oak for structure, richness, and ageability."

These wines are very far from being typical Muscadets. I tend to think new oak—at least at 100 percent—is not ideal for Melon; it overwhelms, at least initially, the delicate fruit and the expression of *terroir.* That is not to say I don't love drinking the wines; I do. The oak has always been well integrated; the wine, mellow and beautiful. But the non-oaked Comte Leloup de Chasseloir can be majestic. I am just beginning to drink my '87s from both properties.

They are all about elegance, breed, and finesse, with firm mineral flavors and gorgeous *sur lie* marrow. I would drink the '93s now, but they'll hold for a couple of years. And the resplendent '89s and '90s will wait until I run out of patience. Elegant, fresh, and succulent, they are wonderful expressions of two definite *grands crus* of Muscadet.

Sauvion et Fils (Château du Cléray), Vallet: "To make a bad Muscadet is very difficult now. The problem is standardization," Jean-Ernest Sauvion said to me as we tasted through a dozen different '88s. "We want consumers to understand that there is no *one* Muscadet. Every village, every winemaker, every plot of land makes a different version."

It is this approach to Muscadet that makes Château du Cléray, a family firm run by brothers Jean-Ernest and Yves, the most dynamic *négociant* in the region. Located at the Château du Cléray, a handsome nineteenth-century mansion giving onto a thirty-hectare vineyard, Sauvion currently markets 250,000 cases of Loire wines a year, 76 percent of which is Muscadet in a broad range of styles, from *primeur* and the basic blend called Carte d'Or to numerous estate-bottled Muscadets and Allégorie du Cléray, Muscadet vinified and aged in new oak barrels.

Its Château du Cléray bottling is always a reliable Muscadet. But it is eclipsed by the Découvertes, the Lauréats, and the Cardinal Richard series—each of which illustrates Jean Sauvion's theory that every Muscadet is unique.

Découvertes (Discoveries) are estate-bottled Muscadets from ten to twenty-five small *domaines* whose wines have been selected after a blind tasting by enologists and winemakers. (The growers themselves may participate.) The chosen wines are bottled *sur lie* at the grower's property by Sauvion's mobile bottling line. The grower's name and vineyard plot appear on the label. One favorite in the '93 vintage was Le Balançon, with its pronounced mineral undertow, characteristic of wines from Gorges.

Lauréats (Laureates) are wines that have won gold medals in local wine competitions, such as the Concours of Le Pallet or Saint-Fiacre. Cardinal Richard is the proprietary name Sauvion gives to its top-of-the-line Muscadet bottling. (However, the oak-aged Allégorie now outprices it.) It is a grower's wine that has placed first after several juried tastings, the last of which usually takes place in a major market, far from the quiet banks of the Sèvre—Tokyo, for example—and is accompanied by a great deal of PR hoopla. But the decision to let impartial juries select the wines—and to pay a premium for the winning *cuvées*—signifies a real effort to both encourage and distinguish high-quality Muscadet. (The '93 Cardinal Richard was ultra-classic, lacy and mineral-rich and marrowy.) Indeed, the Découvertes, the Lauréats, and Cardinal Richard are always commendable Muscadets and they give us consumers the opportunity to get to know worthwhile small *domaines* who prefer to avoid the hassle of commercializing their wines themselves.

EXCELLENT

***Château de la Ragotière,* La Regrippière:** Tanned, relaxed, athletic, the Couillaud brothers—Bernard, François, and Michel—seem like California yuppie winemakers. Their collective c.v. includes Briacé, Angoulême, and courses with Professor Harold Olmo at U.C.–Davis. With American gumption, they opened export markets, and plunged into the troubled waters of new oak and Chardonnay. They also make pretty terrific wine.

Their experiments with new oak barrels are impressive, among the best I've tasted. But my favorite wine from this *domaine* is the Muscadet Premier Cru du Château de la Ragotière, which comes in a numbered bottle with a black label. (The normal bottling has a white label.) The '87 was not a huge success, but the '93, '86, and '85 were all finely tuned Muscadets with super structure, texture as silky and marrowy as Vouvray, refreshing *pétillance,* aromas of pine and honey, and long mineral-almond finishes. The '89 showed every sign of developing as nicely, as did '90, a truly sumptuous Muscadet with flavors of minerals, almonds, and peaches.

***Domaine Chiron,* Mouzillon:** Walter Cronkite Muscadets. Everything bespeaks care and intelligence. The cellars are immaculate; the tasting room looks like a cozy inn with its wood beams, big hearth, handblown balthazars, and ancient winepress. The wines, consistently superb, tend not to make headlines. They are well structured and long-lived (due to large amounts of gabbro in his soils, Chiron says). Both the Domaine Muscadet and the single-vineyard Clos des Roches Gaudinières express a family style. They are full-bodied wines with flavors of apples and almonds, supported by a steely structure. The Clos, ampler, more complex, and perfumed, needs cellaring and ages beautifully. The '93, pungent, fruity, and rich, was beautifully textured and finished on a note of melon and minerals. I can't imagine anyone not liking it, or why. A '79 mixed toffee, butterscotch, and mushrooms. It was brisk, complex, and truly appetizing. It recalled a '49 Vouvray *pétillant* I once tasted, its thread of bubbles elusive as a whisper in a dream.

***Domaine des Dorices,* Vallet:** Winemakers I visited repeatedly listed the Domaine des Dorices as one of the best producers. I had also been told that its owner, Léon Boullault, made wine the old-fashioned way. I made an appointment.

The seventy-year-old Boullault bolted out of his cellars to greet me. Retired in theory only, he is well served by his jogging shoes. He never stands still and he never stops talking. He whisked me indoors, up flights of stairs and then down, past presses and vats, discoursing on organic viticulture (he's for), oak casks (he's against), machine-harvesting (he was against, now he uses one), and vineyard variations, before pulling up two chairs in front of a spittoon and a table made from an upturned barrel.

He uncorked a bottle of his '85 Cuvée Grande Garde and poured out two glasses. Here was a Muscadet with all of the flavors I'd come to recognize as classic but unlike any I had tasted. The wine had Muscadet's characteristic blend of lemon, almonds, and minerals. Four years of age added toastiness which was interwoven with honey and pine. Its grip gave it vigor; its *pétillance* made it fresh as a waterfall. It was a sumptuous, complete wine.

The wine was traditional only in the Platonic sense. It was what I imagine those early Muscadets tasted like when they were siphoned off their lees from barrel for weddings. The wine was also visionary and not quite legal: Boullault, a confirmed Royalist, one of the appellation's most impassioned iconoclasts and articulate reformers, had kept the wine on its lees for eighteen months, nearly a year after the INAO's cutoff date.

Boullault works his thirty-seven hectares with sons François (Briacé) and Frederick. They make three *cuvées* of Muscadet. The first, Cuvée Choisie, is the simplest. The next two, the Hermine d'Or selection and the Cuvée Grande Garde, are meant to age.

Boullault's '93 Hermine d'Or resembled those I've tasted from '85 to '92. Structured and marrowy, it had long, persistent flavors of lemon and minerals. In blind tastings the Cuvée Grande Garde is often mistaken for Savennières or Pouilly-Fuissé. It's the wine Boullault keeps on its lees for a year and a half to more than two years. The '87, the last Boullault made, spent twenty-seven months on its lees. It had lavish fruit, a virtual salad of pineapple and citrus, balanced by almonds and minerals and toast. Outstanding.

Domaine de la Fruitière, **Château-Thébaud:** A fine technician as well as a nurseryman, Jean-Joseph Douillard graduated from Briacé and studied at the University of Bordeaux. Domaine de la Fruitière is his excellent base Muscadet. (The '94 is one of the few I'd recommend from the vintage and an excellent Muscadet by any standard.) Next come Bel Abord and Château de la Placière, each single-vineyards. Première and Baron

Noury, Douillard's two top *cuvées*, are selected after tastings with fellow winemakers and sommeliers. Première, made from thirty- to thirty-five-year-old vines, is considered the more restrained and elegant of the two. Baron Noury, essentially a low-yield, old-vines *cuvée* from his Bel Abord vineyard, is richer, riper, and more concentrated. Though Première seems more perfumed, both are top-notch—supple, complex, and generous, with strong mineral backdrops, long finishes, and a surprising, though not unpleasant, saltiness. The richly textured '93 Première had a strong citric-mineral core. Absolutely lovely.

Domaine de la Haute-Févrie, **Maisdon-sur-Sèvre:** Claude Branger is not out to revolutionize Muscadet, but he makes some of its best wine— fresh, full-bodied, and long-lived. In 1988 he inaugurated a special bottling, L'Excellence, made from his oldest (sixty-years-plus) vines. When I first encountered it at a tasting I'd organized, its highfalutin name provoked skepticism—which was overcome with one sip. The wine was head and shoulders above most I sampled. It was incredibly rich, with a texture reminiscent of raw silk, and layers of almonds, minerals, apples, and lemon. Branger has made L'Excellence every year since. In '94, it was not only excellent but a miracle, recapturing the freshness, the feel of raw silk, and the undertow of minerals that make the wine so remarkably delicious. Branger's regular Muscadet is also worth seeking out. Textured and toasty, it has captivating notes of pine and Granny Smith apples.

Domaine de la Louvetrie, **La Haie-Fouassière:** Another exciting house. Joseph Landron, a Briacé graduate, bottles his Muscadet by soil type. (He also served on the appellation's *terroir* commission.) The lightest, most floral *cuvée*, Amphibolite, is named after its soils. It is made to be drunk within the year. (Depending on the vintage, Landron makes it *nature*—i.e., without chaptalizing—and in '93 went a step further and did not filter the wine: Classic in every sense, it was full of marrow and minerals, with the soft fullness characteristic of the best early-drinking Muscadet.) Harder, silica-veined orthogneiss soils make Landron's Hermine d'Or and Fief du Breuil bottlings, which need a year of age to shed their angularity and to blossom into ample, finely structured, citrus-scented Muscadets. While I love the broad, tender Hermine d'Or, my favorite is the Fief du Breuil, which comes from thirty-five-year-old vines on a south-facing slope. Four favorites are the sumptuous '93, which is the kind of Serious Muscadet that makes me dream; the sapid '87, with good grip and flavors of toast, lemon, and minerals; the '86, a ringer for an Alsace Pinot Gris; and the '85, which rivals Boullault's Cuvée Grande Garde.

***Domaine Pierre Luneau-Papin,* Le Landreau:** The Luneau family dates its arrival in the region to 1680; Pierre is the thirteenth Pierre Luneau. But he represents Muscadet's vanguard: Few have experimented as assiduously and with as dependably good results as he. A Briacé graduate, Pierre has also studied with Emile Peynaud and Ribéreau-Gayon. His winery is as high-tech and hygienic as any in Napa. He vinifies grapes from his thirty-five hectares *clos* by *clos*, experimental batch by experimental batch—exploring lees contact, skin contact, new oak (subdivided into types of oak as well as different toast levels), even malolactic fermentation.

There are many different *cuvées*, among them two versions of Domaine de la Grange, a young-vines and an old-vines; Le L d'Or, a *cuvée* that has won an important prize; Manoir la Grange, vinified and aged in new oak barrels; Clos des Allées and Les Pierres Blanches, two single-vineyards; and a Muscadet Coteaux de la Loire. The last, from a nine-hectare parcel, is lean and elegant. An excellent evocation of its appellation, its steeliness is in marked contrast with Luneau's Sèvre-et-Maine style, which tends to be tender and feminine.

I always like the supple, individualized Clos des Allées. Le L d'Or is usually the amplest, most nuanced in the lineup. (As Luneau believes in aging Muscadet, it's still possible to taste his impressive '85, '88, and '89.) The '94 L d'Or embodies Luneau's tender style. And the '93, while friskier than Luneau's gorgeous '90s, reprises the thirst-quenching qualities that made both the L d'Or and Manoir la Grange of that great year so delectable, to wit: silky, mellow fruit to lull you, and razor-sharp, crystalline structure to snap you to attention.

***Domaine la Quilla (Daniel and Gérard Vinet),* La Haie-Fouassière:** "We'll sell vintage Muscadet, but it will take time for people to realize it can rival other wines," Gérard Vinet told me. "That's why I like being a Muscadet producer. We're at the bottom of the ladder. We have nothing to lose and all to gain."

This can-do spirit informs everything Vinet does and illustrates why his is one of Muscadet's most dynamic wineries. As of 1991, Vinet had three Muscadets. The simplest is the Domaine la Quilla, an assemblage from the entire property. Light and tender but solidly built, it offers Muscadet's classic mix of minerals, almonds, and lemon, and a smooth, melony finish. Clos de la Houssaie is a single-vineyard wine issued from vines on a slope with pebbly soils and fine expositions. The '94 was tart and firm, quite meaty for the vintage. The '93 was wonderful, with sweet melon and fig notes.

"Le" is a blend of Vinet's best *cuvées,* chosen with other winemakers, enologists, and sommeliers. Floral and gingery in '88, elegant yet packed with flavor in '89 and '90, it was mouth-filling, marrowy, and exciting in '93. Superb. What the appellation is all about.

HIGHLY RECOMMENDED

***André-Michel Brégeon,* Gorges:**   Michel Brégeon is right out there. No glamour, no folklore, no illusions. He's vigneron as blue-collar worker. With his weedy mustache and straggly brown hair, Brégeon looks like he should be playing rock with Crosby, Stills, and Nash. Appropriately, there's bluesy American country music on the radio in his cellar, a cinderblock garage behind a muddy courtyard. The walls are papered with well-deserved awards, but he's not sentimental about them. One of these days he'll retire with no regrets. For now, however, he's clearly proud of his vineyards and justifiably proud of his wines, which are floral, tangy, and firm, with pronounced flavors of almonds and minerals and vivid *pétillance*.

***Léon Dollet,* La Haie-Fouassière:**   A member of both Hermine d'Or and Métaireau's Vignerons d'Art, Dollet makes precise but generous Muscadets with clear, light, high-pitched flavors of citrus and almonds. (One often finds the initials LD on the corks of Métaireau's top *cuvées,* such as LM.)

***Domaine de la Gautronnière,* La Chapelle-Heulin:**   One of the first Nantais winemakers to invest in a pneumatic press, Alain Forget (Briacé) has a dependable track record for producing superior Muscadets on three levels: a fruity, drink-me-up White Label and a low-yield, old-vines Black Label, which, when it's a year old, often becomes Forget's Hermine d'Or selection.

I like every wine I've tasted from Forget, and I can trust his labels; the wines get progressively richer. His White Label is solid and fruity, to drink right away; the Black Label is more layered, more structured, made for aging. The '90 was supple and full, with penetrating mineral-almond flavors and overriding scents of apple *eau-de-vie*. Discreet and rectilinear, the '93 was an austere, elegant blend of citrus and minerals. A white-shoe Muscadet.

***Domaine de la Tourmaline,* Saint-Fiacre-sur-Maine:**   When I arrived in Muscadet country in August 1989, Michel Gadais, who owns Domaine de la Tourmaline, was president of its *syndicat*. A tall, forthright man, with a nut-brown tan and a loud, unmodulated voice, he took me on an orientation tour. Appropriately, the Muscadets he, his son Michel, and his brother Marcel make from their twenty-three hectares of vines in Saint-

Fiacre and La Haie-Fouassière could be ambassadors for the appellation. Taut, super-dry, with riveting mineral flavors and elegance bordering on austerity, they are archetypal and epitomize the "most Muscadet of Muscadet" character of Saint-Fiacre's low-yielding hillsides of schist, silex, and granite.

Domaine de la Perrière, from their father's vineyards, is a bit less *terroirté*; it's more restrained, or, in New York terms, more Midtown. (An experimental *cuvée* of '93, however, neither fined nor filtered, was deliciously singular, all marrow and minerals.) Domaine de la Tourmaline, the majority of Gadais's production, is stonier, more stoic and rectilinear, with a mineral finish reminiscent of Badoit. I don't think I've ever tasted a more persuasive example of what we wine-lovers mean when we say "bone dry."

Joseph Hallereau, Vallet: A compulsive tinkerer, Hallereau makes everything from *sur lie* Muscadet to a range of sparkling wines to a portlike *vin cuit*. He counts among his clients the Royal Court of Denmark, the royal family of Belgium, and the Nantes Parliament. All his wines ferment in old wood barrels. As he vinifies *clos* by *clos,* Hallereau often has as many as thirty-five different *cuvées* of Muscadet. No matter. The family style is warm and chewy, with flavors of apples, toast, and lemon. Many wines have long, savory, almost salty finishes. The best also taste of freshly sliced ginger. They're mellow, personalized, doggedly authentic, with rough-hewn, warts-and-all allure.

RECOMMENDED

Donatien Bahuaud, La Chapelle-Heulin: Legend has it that the very first Muscadet vine, imported from Burgundy, was planted in 1740 at the Château de la Cassemichère. While that story is somewhat shaky, there is no denying the important role of Cassemichère in the *proliferation* of Muscadet. The château is the home of Donatien Bahuaud, one of the largest *négociant*-grower houses in the Loire. Under its eponymous founder, the firm was key in postwar promotion of Muscadet, expanding its largely regional market to Paris and the United States.

Roughly 25 percent of the firm's business is Muscadet. All wine is purchased except those from Château de la Cassemichère. The top bottling is the much-imitated Le Master de Donatien, a wine selected by a jury of enologists, sommeliers, and wine writers in a blind tasting. Typically, fifty different *cuvées* (from fifty different winemakers) are chosen. Each is bottled at the grower's property three weeks after the tasting. Some are better than others, however, and you are likely to find quite a bit of variation within a given vintage. They are always good Muscadets, but I have always preferred the Château de la Cassemichère. Partially vinified in old barrels, it is a mouth-filling Muscadet with a suggestion of old oak, loads of minerals, and lively *pétillance*. Bahuaud offers eight other Muscadets, including the sassy Fringant.

Château de Briacé, Le Landreau: Created in 1957, Briacé's Ecole d'Agriculture deserves much credit for having trained the current generation of Nantais winemakers and for having furthered Muscadet's revolution in quality. The school's vineyards give students hands-on experience, and the wines are exactly what you'd expect from a respectable teaching institution: competent, reliable, middle-of-the-road, and, above all, textbook.

Marquis de Goulaine, Haute-Goulaine: "We are the oldest winegrowing family in the world," Robert, the eleventh Marquis de Goulaine, let drop as matter-of-factly as if he were telling me he preferred barrels to cement tanks for vinification. We happened to be strolling across the immense courtyard of his Renaissance château, a classified historic monument. It was neither the time nor the place to cross-examine this uncommonly obliging man whose title, after all, comes from Henri IV and whose family tree credibly embraces the eighteenth-century philosopher Helvétius and Mary, Queen of Scots.

His press bio is more circumspect on the wine issue: "The Goulaine family, having owned all the territory without practically any interruption well over a thousand years, are most certainly the oldest family in Europe holding vineyard property under their name."

"The territory" is, loosely, the Sèvre-et-Maine. The Goulaines founded most of its parishes, built its churches, and created the villages of Haute- and Basse-Goulaine. Although the family sold the property a year before the Revolution, an ancestor managed to repurchase two *domaines*— Goulaine and La Grange—in 1858. In 1957 Robert, whose branch inherited the latter, bought Goulaine from an uncle. He sold La Grange (retaining his interest in its vineyards and cellars) to finance Goulaine's restoration.

Robert de Goulaine's categorical statements seem less the product of a boastful nature than a romantic one. Courteous, quixotic, and eager, he pursues the esoteric, the unpossessable—butterflies, for example. (His collection of rare species is a tourist attraction.) He has just completed a book on his favorite wines—ethereal and rare ones like Hungary's sweet Tokays, La Tâche, Yquem. Goulaine makes and sells Muscadet and Gros Plant, as well as Chardonnay, a Vin de Pays, 25,000 to 30,000 cases a year. There are several bottlings of Muscadet. By far the best is Cuvée du Millé-naire, a blend of fifty-year-old vines from Goulaine's four-hectare *clos* La Tâche as well as wine purchased from several growers. It is a very good Muscadet.

TASTED IN PASSING WITH PLEASURE

Henri Bouchaud (Domaine du Bois-Joly), **Le Pallet:** Classically styled Muscadets that often win awards.

Château de la Mercredière, **Vallet:** Fresh, creamy, rich Muscadets from the sunny slopes of Vallet. Medal-winning wines have special labels but the non–award-winning Muscadets are tasty, too.

Bruno Cormerais, **Saint-Lumine-de-Clisson:** Nice balance. Nice structure. Nice flavors. Nice finish. Nice Muscadet. You can count on it.

Domaine Bideau-Giraud, **La Haie-Fouassière:** From twenty-three hectares of vines come three *cuvées* of good *sur lie* Muscadet. Look for the barrel-fermented Sélection Daniel Bideau, made from the *domaine's* best vines. The oak pleasantly seasons the classic mix of minerals, lemon, and almonds and may account for the intriguing smoke and maple syrup under-tones I have found in the wine.

Domaine du Perd-Son-Pain, **Saint-Fiacre:** Roger Visonneau is a seri-ous young man who looks like one of Chekhov's perpetual students. His Muscadets aren't perfect now but seem headed in the right direction. They are stony and tart and delicately flavored.

Xavier Gouraud, **Le-Pin-Mouzillon:** Good land, good winemaking, good sense, and good Muscadet.

Jean-François Guilbaud, **Maisdon-sur-Sèvre:** Louis Métaireau's son-in-law sells high-quality estate-bottled Muscadet from several small *domaines*—chiefly his own father's La Bretonnerie.

Petiteau-Gaubert, **Vallet:** A twenty-four-hectare family *domaine* making attractive, well-structured Muscadets with good pineapple-grapefruit juiciness, steely grip, and persistent flavors of minerals and bitter almonds.

LARGE GROWER-NEGOCIANT HOUSES MAKING AVERAGE WINE

Barré Frères, **Gorges:** Look for the La Bretesche bottling.

Guilbaud Frères, **Mouzillon:** Look for Domaine de la Moutonnière, Clos du Pont.

Marcel Sautejeau, **Le Pallet:** Truly boring Muscadets.

Benjamin Sourice, **Gesté:** Adequate, if unexceptional.

TASTED AND CONSIDERED

Domaine de l'Oiselinière, **Gorges:** Surprisingly bland Muscadets from a singular, gabbro-streaked *terroir.*

Philippe Laure, **Vallet:** These wines often win medals but I've never admired them.

Pierre Lieubeau (Château de la Bourdinière), **Château-Thébaud:** Soft, herbaceous Muscadets made by the book.

Muscadet des Coteaux de la Loire

The steeply sloped banks of the Loire east of Nantes are said to be the oldest vineyards in the Nantais. As towns like Saint-Géréon become bedroom communities, however, only a thin band from Le Cellier to Saint-Florent-le-Vieil remains.

Growers say their Muscadets are drier and more individual than those of the Sèvre-et-Maine. I found them sharper and leaner. I think we're saying the same thing.

❧ PRODUCER RATINGS ❧

LEADERS
Jacques Guindon   Les Vignerons de la Noëlle

EXCELLENT
Domaine Pierre Luneau-Papin

❧ ❧

LEADERS

***Jacques Guindon*, Saint-Géréon:** Firm, accurate, and light, the Guindon Muscadets are excellent examples of the dry, lean style characteristic of this appellation.

***Les Vignerons de la Noëlle*, Ancenis:** The only co-op in the Nantais, Les Vignerons de la Noëlle is the vinous branch of a huge agricultural cooperative that also makes cider and cheese and raises poultry. The co-op purchases grapes from two hundred growers who are paid by quality—maturity and health of grapes. More than half of the wine produced is Muscadet, Sèvre-et-Maine, and Coteaux de la Loire. These are good, middle-of-the-road Muscadets. I invariably found the Coteaux de la Loire harder, leaner, and drier, though quite appealing. My favorite, however, is an estate-bottled Sèvre-et-Maine, the Domaine les Hautes Noëlles (the name similarity is a coincidence), a supple, medium-bodied Muscadet with hints of ash, almonds, and minerals and a long finish.

EXCELLENT

Pierre Luneau-Papin   (*See* Sèvre-et-Maine)

Muscadet Côtes de Grand Lieu

Created in 1994, the latest subregion of Muscadet covers nineteen communes, stretching west from the Nantes airport to the sea.

Serge Batard, a grower in Saint-Léger-des-Vignes, at the heart of the new appellation, compares his Muscadets to those of the Sèvre-et-Maine thus: "We're closer to the sea. It's windier, wetter, and cooler here, but our winters are milder. Only Le Landreau harvests ahead of us. Our soils in Saint-Léger have more clay, so the wine evolves more slowly and often has a bitterness. And the tradition of winemaking developed later here. Now we're getting interesting things."

❧ PRODUCER RATINGS ❧

LEADER
Domaine des Herbauges

TO WATCH
Domaine les Hautes Noëlles

HIGHLY RECOMMENDED
Domaine les Coins

❧ ❧

LEADER

Domaine des Herbauges, **Bouaye:** When giving directions to his winery, Luc Choblet is likely to guide you by the parasol pine on the horizon somewhere between the Nantes airport and the town of Bouaye, where he lives. "It's a Mediterranean tree," he says, "proof of the mildness of our climate."

This type of comment usually segues to the Sèvre-et-Maine comparison. But the best proof that the western hinterlands of the Nantais can rival the vineyards to the east is in the drinking. And the Muscadet habitually trotted out for the test is Luc Choblet's solid Domaine des Herbauges.

He offers a fresh, crisp, mineral, generic Muscadet and two single-vineyard bottlings, Clos de la Senaigerie, a structured and perfumed Muscadet (from a *clos* that is always the first to ripen), and Clos de la Fine, a plot with more clay in its soils, which makes an elegant Muscadet, less marked by its *terroir*.

TO WATCH

Domaine les Hautes Noëlles, **Saint-Léger-des-Vignes:** Intense and articulate, Serge Batard takes his inspiration from Burgundian producers like Coche-Dury and enologists like Denis Dubourdieu, whose names and theories he weaves into discussions of Muscadet.

Perhaps his discourse would have been less surprising had I first encountered Batard in his tony wineshop. But when I drove up Batard's driveway to the barn-cum-winery, I hardly expected an impassioned lecture on skin contact and oak barrels.

Our conversation started like a million other interviews. Batard learned from his father, who retired in 1988. He cultivates what will ultimately reach about seventeen hectares of vines, twelve of which are Muscadet. He bottles 60 percent of his production and sells the rest in bulk. Then I asked about oak—as I heard he fermented his Muscadet in new barrels—and he answered in the roundabout way people do when they can't reduce an idea to a sound bite.

"In eighty-two I opened my shop, La Société de Tastevin. But I knew I'd come back to the vines. Selling wine was a preparation. I learned how to market. I got to taste a lot. I learned to have an open mind. The conventional wisdom about Muscadet is that it's fresh, *pétillant*, nervy, elegant. Okay, it's not very aromatic. And it's light. But it doesn't have to be thin. It's more interesting to taste a wine with aromas, a palate, and volume than a wine that only has carbonic gas. I love white Burgundies. I thought, Melon is from Burgundy, why not try? So I followed the techniques of Coche-Dury. I fermented the wine in oak barrels. The fermentation lasted three weeks. It was never tumultuous. The temperatures didn't get higher than twenty degrees Celsius. The wine stays in barrel until December. Then I start stirring up the lees in order to have a better dilution of the aromatic substances and to fix the color."

Batard's experiments have changed over the years, as he seeks the right balance. He now works with both new and used barrels and usually puts a small percentage of the wine through malolactic fermentation: "The malic aspect of Muscadet doesn't work well with the vanilla aspect of oak, so I wanted some lactic acid to marry with the wood." His '87s, '88s, and '89s all had things to recommend them but seemed works in progress. His '90s displayed more mastery of the craft. The regular Muscadet was a classic in the clean, lemon-almond mode. The barrel-fermented bottling was sapid and creamy; the oak was pronounced, but there was plenty of fruit and good structure. The '94, however, was a bit like the tail (in this case oak) wagging the dog (Muscadet).

Is the oak masking the grape and the *terroir*? Maybe. But my misgivings fade when I recall how Batard explained that, for him, oak was not the be-all-and-end-all. "The future of Muscadet is better expression of *terroir*, a diversification of Muscadet," he told me. "To express the *terroir* you can't be simplistic. Experiments aren't always good but you always learn something. Sometimes you have to go too far to find the right place. I want to see what Muscadet can give, and I don't know the answer yet."

HIGHLY RECOMMENDED

Domaine les Coins, Courcoué: Crisp, clean, taut, and lean, Jean-Claude Malidain's Muscadets are great choices for chilling down and drinking with summer foods in summer settings. Malidain fits the image of easygoing vigneron, too. Elfin, with a big smile and a bigger, permanently purple-veined Pinocchio-as-vigneron nose, the Briacé graduate prefers his Vins de Pays and his Gros Plant to his more prestigious Muscadet. (So do I.)

Muscadet

The simple Muscadet appellation covers the entire zone. In practice, however, it is used by those growers not within one of the three subappellations. Notably:

Château de la Preuille, Saint-Hilaire-de-Loulay: Just across the line separating the Loire-Atlantique from Vendée, this *domaine* misses the Sèvre-et-Maine appellation by a hair. It's generic Muscadet, even though its soils resemble those of Clisson and Aigrefeuille, the Sèvre-et-Maine villages to the north. What's more, the wine's every bit as good. Philippe and Christian Dumortier put a lot of effort into making it that way. The grapes are hand-harvested in small stainless steel cases and fermented, without the addition of yeasts, in thermoregulated stainless steel tanks. The top *cuvée,* misleadingly labeled Premier Cru Classé, Cru Exceptioné (*sic*), is a lovely Muscadet, ample, textured, with classic flavors.

TASTED IN PASSING WITH PLEASURE

Domaine de Haut-Bourg: Nicely structured Muscadets.
Michel Figureau: Rough-and-ready, old-world Muscadet, it's almondy, rich, and a tad oxidized.

GROS PLANT DU PAYS NANTAIS

STATUS: *VDQS 1954*
TYPES OF WINE: *Dry white*
ZONE AND PRODUCTION: *Roughly 200,000 hectoliters, on 2,700 hectares throughout and beyond the Muscadet region*

GRAPES: *Gros Plant (Folle Blanche)*
PRICE: *10 to 13ff*
BEST VINTAGES: '90

Gros Plant is a wine few vintners will let you taste. A wine promoted as a doctor-recommended diuretic. A wine with the dubious distinction of having stunned the Comte de Lur Saluce speechless. "But! That's amazing!" was all the Châtelain d'Yquem could sputter after his first swallow of the raspy white.

The Marquis de Goulaine, more habituated to Gros Plant's biting acidity, gets down to the wine's skin-and-bones essence: "Gros Plant is thin, straightforward, brisk, and clean. Like an old gentleman."

Not a ringing endorsement—particularly from one of Gros Plant's leading producers and the former president of its *syndicat*. But even that doesn't go far enough: It sanitizes Gros Plant. Gros Plant is a rude wine made from a rude grape. The low-alcohol, high-acid wines it produces are ideal for distillation, which explains why it created a noble niche for itself as the base of Cognac and Armagnac. It also explains why your average Gros Plant du Pays Nantais tastes like Muscadet on a diet. (The law sets Gros Plant's maximum alcohol level at 11 percent; Muscadet's at 12 percent.) Without much stuffing to balance it, Gros Plant's acidity stands out in ever broader relief. Then there's the question of rot.

My first sustained contact with Gros Plant was the '88 vintage. Its vines, attacked by stem rot which went undetected until crushing, yielded a wine with a true *goût de terroir*—potato fields after an August rain.

Of course there are passionate artisans who make serious-ish Gros Plant. These are bracing, sinewy wines with the tart, green juiciness of Granny Smith apples. Bottling *sur lie* plumps them up a bit and adds a zippy effervescence. The very best can be gripping and vigorous, with fine mineral undertones. They are almost too good to be Gros Plant, though never as good as the Muscadet from the same winemaker.

At heart Gros Plant is a lowlife. It's a funky, cult wine trapped in a mass-market body—it should be *Eraserhead* not *Rocky III*. As the largest VDQS in France, Gros Plant's importance is way out of sync with its intrinsic value. Its vines cover the entire Nantais vineyard area, extending as far west as the Atlantic Ocean and south of the Lac de Grand Lieu. The 200,000 hectoliters it produces a year alone account for half the volume of VDQS wines. There is just too much for it to be allowed to be its scabrous self. But it has always made money for the Nantais. (Much of it has been trucked to Germany for use as the base of the sparkling wine Sekt.) On the eve of united Europe and its problematic wine-lake, Gros Plant *has* an appellation, so there's too much of it to allow it to go gentle into that good night.

In response to Muscadet growers who would like to see Gros Plant eliminated from their zone, as well as to those who are replacing it with Chardonnay (a Vin de Pays in the Nantais), local bureaucrats say, "In the lean years, when Muscadet was not doing well on the market, the sheer volume of Gros Plant made ends meet." (To which a local saying, "Gros Plant is my bread, Muscadet is my wine," bears witness.) And moral suasion enters the picture: "Everyone makes Chardonnay. We're the only ones making Gros Plant. It's traditional."

Consequently, the Institut Technique de la Vigne et du Vin (ITV) has the thankless task of denaturing Gros Plant, creating a clean, low-acid version in the name of tradition. The experiments are many, tortuous, costly, and thus far, unsuccessful. "Maybe it's for the best if Chardonnay replaces it," a technician admitted. "It's not at all clear that we'll be able to adapt Gros Plant to modern palates."

I suspect the best thing for Gros Plant is that there be less of it, but that what there is be the real thing—in all its down-and-dirty glory.

Tastes change. Boredom with bland, yuppie, high-tech Chardonnay knockoffs could trigger a kind of *nostalgie de la boue* for Gros Plant. Primal, explicit, and keen, it's perfect for nature's other tasty obscenities—the lewd milkiness of oysters, the borderline porn of mussels, the raunchy meatiness of eels, particularly the way you eat them in Richelieu, a provincial town in southern Touraine. On market days you buy eels hot and oily off the grill, you go to a café and you get a carafe of some fast-and-cheap little white. Nothing fits that bill better than a smutty Gros Plant with its "You talkin' to me?" edginess. In this context our antihero takes on a Proustian luster that Prince Chardonnay could never inspire. And should Gros Plant become an endangered species, I suspect I'll devote weeks on end rooting out the rawest, most ornery versions.

Each of the producers rated below is described more fully in one of the Muscadet sections. Unless otherwise specified, the Gros Plants discussed here were bottled *sur lie*. Additionally, many Nantais producers use Gros Plant as the base for their sparkling wines. I have included recommendations for sparkling wines made from a base of Gros Plant in this section.

❧ PRODUCER RATINGS ❧

EXCELLENT
Domaine Chiron   Domaine de l'Ecu

HIGHLY RECOMMENDED
André-Michel Brégeon   Domaine les Coins   Xavier Gouraud
Joseph Hallereau   Marquis de Goulaine

RECOMMENDED
Château de Briacé   Domaine des Herbauges

❧ ❧

EXCELLENT

Michel Chiron (Sèvre-et-Maine): Vinified in old wood barrels and bottled *sur lie*, Chiron's Gros Plant is absolutely lovely—refreshing, crisp, and appley.

Domaine de l'Ecu (Sèvre-et-Maine): The same obsessive care that produces gorgeous Muscadets makes atypically elegant Gros Plants and fine Gros Plant–based sparkling wines. Assembling his *mousseux* (a 30 ff *vin de table*), Bossard is as meticulous as a master blender making a 160 ff Champagne: A recent bottling consisted of 35 percent Gros Plant free-run juice with skin contact, 45 percent Gros Plant free-run juice without skin contact, 10 percent Blanc de Noir of Cabernet, and 10 percent Melon, both with and without skin contact. Some *cuvées* spend more than two years aging *sur lie*. They are surprisingly delicious.

HIGHLY RECOMMENDED

André-Michel Brégeon (Sèvre-et-Maine): Characterful Gros Plant, tart, strong, and grapy, with flavors of Granny Smith apples.

Domaine les Coins (Côtes de Grand Lieu): A savvy distiller I know travels from his home, east of Chinon, all the way to Courcoué for Gros Plant from Malidain. It would be hard to imagine a better companion for local seafood platters.

Xavier Gouraud (Sèvre-et-Maine): Good Gros Plant, tart, lemony, and extremely dry.

Joseph Hallereau (Sèvre-et-Maine): Barrel-fermented Gros Plant, bottled *sur lie*, full of minerals and almonds.

Marquis de Goulaine (Sèvre-et-Maine): Not a true believer in *sur lie* Muscadet, Goulaine doesn't like *sur lie* Gros Plant at all. "The lees dominate," he claims, "and instead of being clean, dry, skin and bones, it gets rounder and looks like a cheap Muscadet. But if a client wants Gros Plant *sur lie*, we make it." All of the *domaine*'s Gros Plants I tasted were bottled *sur lie*. They are good, less aggressively acid than most.

RECOMMENDED

Château de Briacé (Sèvre-et-Maine): If you want an accurate image of the beast, taste here. Even the '88 was good.

Domaine des Herbauges (Côtes de Grand Lieu). Choblet doesn't much like Gros Plant, but he does right by it in vinification. It's bland, but it's clean, round, and citric.

COTEAUX D'ANCENIS

STATUS: *VDQS 1954*
TYPES OF WINE: *Dry and off-dry whites, dry reds, and rosés*
ZONE AND PRODUCTION: *243 hectares, basically the same turf as Muscadet des Coteaux de la Loire, making 16,421 hectoliters. Reds and rosés are 90 percent of production.*
GRAPES: *Whites—Chenin Blanc, Pinot Gris (called Malvoisie). Reds and rosés—Gamay, Cabernet Sauvignon, Cabernet Franc*
PRICE: *12 to 15ff*
BEST VINTAGES: *'95, '90*

Because the appellation Coteaux d'Ancenis applies to a number of types of wine, it is always followed by the name of the grape. The most unusual is Malvoisie, which, according to Pierre Galet, was brought to the region from Burgundy after the Norman invasion. Vinified dry, off-dry, or in exceptional years, *moelleux*, it has attractive floral aromas, at times a honeyed flavor and texture. Often drunk as an aperitif, it is a lovely curiosity. Malvoisie can age a bit; the rest of the appellation's wines should be drunk within the year.

❧ PRODUCER RATINGS ❧

RECOMMENDED

Jacques Guindon

BY THE GLASS

Augustin Athimon   Les Vignerons de la Noëlle

❧ ❧

RECOMMENDED

Jacques Guindon (Coteaux de la Loire): "Malvoisie *liquoreux* is our most personalized wine," says son Pierre. "We started making it by accident, according to my great-grandfather. He said in 1925 our Malvoisie was in a wood press which broke. The wine stopped fermenting and stayed *moelleux*. That's part true and part myth."

When Pierre then told me that 90 percent of the time the Malvoisie grapes ripen enough to make a *moelleux*, I took that to be part true and part myth. In any event, the Guindon Malvoisies are generally off-dry, or demi-sec, about 11 percent alcohol with up to 34 grams of residual sugar. Some lack structure and concentration, but my two favorites suggest the potential of the appellation. The floral '91 was fresh and lovely and long; the plumper '90 was sweet and mellow. The Guindons also make lean Gamays and Cabernets.

BY THE GLASS

Augustin Athimon, **Le Cellier:**   One of the nicest wines I tasted of his was the 1990 Coteaux d'Ancenis Gamay, a light, fruity, wine-bar red.

Les Vignerons de la Noëlle (**Coteaux de la Loire**):   Creditable Coteaux d'Ancenis Gamay.

FIEFS VENDEENS

STATUS: *VDQS 1984*
TYPES OF WINE: *Dry red, rosé, and white*
ZONE AND PRODUCTION: *22,745 hectoliters, on 419 hectares*

GRAPES: *Whites—Sauvignon Blanc, Chenin (50 percent minimum), Chardonnay, Colombard; reds and rosés—Cabernet Franc and Sauvignon, Gamay, Pinot Noir (the last two, 50 percent minimum). Melon and Groslot Gris are permitted in certain communes.*
PRICE: *15 to 25ff*
BEST VINTAGES: *'95, '90*

Locals say Vendée is sunnier than Marseilles. As you drive south of Clisson there *is* a Mediterranean feel. The sepia tones of the Loire-Atlantique give way to sun-shocked villages and whitewashed houses with electric blue shutters. Tourism dominates the coast—from the island of Noirmoutier to Les Sables d'Olonne, providing a ready and eager market for the light, quaffing wines made nearby.

The Fiefs Vendéens vineyards, four distinct pockets, were formed by the ocean. Brem-sur-Mer is on the coast itself, its vines stretching to Olonne. Mareuil, Pissotte, and Vix are located on bands formed when the ocean receded, leaving behind flat plains and low hillsides with subsoils of clay, silex, and schist in Mareuil and Pissotte; calcareous soils in Vix. The names of the zones follow "Fiefs Vendéens" on the labels.

Brem is white-wine country; its mainstays are Chenin, here called Franc Blanc, and Grolleau Gris. On its shallow, sandy soils the vines grow low to the ground for protection against sea winds. Mareuil, the largest of the four zones, is located in the center, south of La Roche-sur-Yon. It is known for rich reds.

The INAO encourages blends for wines carrying the Fiefs Vendéens label—partly in recognition of a fickle climate in which not every variety can be depended on to ripen every year, and partly to emphasize the "place" over the grape.

"Our wines are vinified to be light," Xavier Coirier, one of Vendée's leading producers, told me. "Typically, Vendée wines are fresh, fruity, and aromatic. Not keepers. The wines are gay. They're for light, summer meals—salads and grilled seafood—not for big ceremonies."

❧ PRODUCER RATINGS ❧

OUTSTANDING
Philippe Orion

LEADERS
Xavier Coirier   La Ferme des Ardillers

RECOMMENDED
Gentreau Père et Fils   Michon Père et Fils

TASTED AND CONSIDERED
Domaine de la Chaignée

❧ ❧

OUTSTANDING

***Philippe Orion,* Saint-Philbert-du-Pont-Charrault:**   Talk about a tough row to hoe. Orion's winery is not on the beach route. He's glad about that because he's not tempted to make "simple wines for the tourist trade." But he's not in the VDQS either. He has applied for admission, but while the INAO considers, Orion's wines, the best in Vendée, may only be sold as Vin de Pays. (The Fiefs Vendéens' vintners wisely make Orion a de facto member of the appellation. So do I.)

After studying at Montreuil-Bellay, with *stages* in Alsace, Anjou, and Bordeaux, Orion expanded his father's one and a half hectares to fourteen and built new cellars. Clean, well-structured, and flavory, his wines demonstrate what someone with will and guts can do with little equipment, young vines, and land that is far from being the most viticulturally blessed.

Vins de Pays regulations require that Orion bottle by grape variety. In general, his whites and rosés are light, delicate, and sprightly; the reds, warm and generous. I can't resist talking about his '92s. Orion confirms that old saw "There are no bad vintages, only bad vignerons." His Sauvignon was vivacious and fragrant. I served the Cabernet to one of the Touraine's leading sommeliers—who pegged it for a Chinon. Orion's '90 Cab? A blanket of rich, ripe fruit, a user-friendly red with structure and personality.

Orion is also in charge of a new winery, Domaine des Deux Lays, owned by Jean-François Dubreuil and his partner in his wineshop, Yves Mercier. They are justifiably proud of having won a gold medal for their first wine, a '94 rosé.

LEADERS

Xavier Coirier, Pissotte: Vendée couldn't have a better ambassador than Coirier, the only commercial winemaker in Pissotte. He wins all the awards and talks passionately about the region's potential and generously about his colleagues.

His '93 Pissotte white Séléction was creamy and vinous, a nice job. Of two '90 whites, I preferred the ample, fresh Chenin-Chardonnay blend with apple-mineral flavors. The '91 rosé (Gamay with 30 percent Pinot Noir) was zaftig, with lots of strawberry fruit. Reds usually blend Gamay, Pinot, and the two Cabernets. The '90 was supple, with lots of stuffing. The '93, which won a gold medal in Paris, was a friendly wine-bar red, with pleasant Cabernet flavors.

La Ferme des Ardillers, Mareuil: The son of a *négociant*, Jean Mourat earned a degree in enology from the University of Bordeaux. Although he buys grapes to satisfy demand, his chief interest is the wine he and his partner, Jean Larzellier, make. The *domaine*'s white is a pleasant blend of Chenin and Chardonnay; the rosés, made from Pinot Noir and Cabernet, can be buoyant. In the '94 vintage both wines were fragrant summer quaffers and each won a gold medal in Paris, as did Mourat's honorable '94 red, a supple wine with strawberry–bell pepper accents. Mareuil is best known for its reds, and the *domaine* is particularly known for its blends of Cabernet Franc and Sauvignon. Of recent vintages, my favorite was the '91, a lovely wine for the year, light, well structured, with appealing flavors of cherries.

RECOMMENDED

Gentreau Père et Fils, Rosnay: Solid Vendée wines, ideal for local restaurants.

Michon Père et Fils, Brem-sur-Mer: Patrice and sons Eric and Thierry (Montreuil-Bellay) cultivate twenty-seven hectares of vines on the borders of Sables d'Olonne and seem determined to make "serious" Vendée wine. Their cellars are spic-and-span, with stainless steel tanks facing large, burnished casks. And their wines get better every year. I have a weakness for their rosés, particularly the hand-harvested Tête de Cuvée: Blends of Pinot Noir and Gamay, they are firm, strong, and flavory.

TASTED AND CONSIDERED

Domaine de la Chaignée, Vix: Fair-to-middling Vendée wines from the only commercial winery in Vix. (The Merciers' main business is vine plants and they also own vineyards in the Médoc and Burgundy.)

VINS DE PAYS

Interspersed with Muscadet and the VDQS are five Vins de Pays and numerous *vins de table*. The former account for 300,000 to 400,000 hecto-liters of Nantais wine a year. These may be labeled Vin de Pays du Jardin de la France (an appellation that spans ten departments, including the Loire-Atlantique and Vendée); they may take the name of their department (here Loire-Atlantique and Vendée) or use a subregional appellation. Marches de Bretagne covers Vin de Pays made in the Sèvre-et-Maine; Pays de Retz, the western part of the zone, chiefly the Côtes de Grand Lieu area.

In this category you can find juicy Gamays; tasty Cabernets; firm, vinous Grolleau and Grolleau Gris, and nice little Chardonnays.

Chardonnay is proving as irresistible to the Nantais as it has to growers the world over. It now covers more than two hundred hectares and often sells for more than AOC Muscadet. Some twenty to thirty growers in the Pays de Retz have formed a Groupe des Producteurs de Chardonnay de Pays de Retz to market the wine—and they want an appellation. The Vins de Pays I find most interesting, however, are Grolleau and Groslot Gris from the Pays de Retz and Vendée. Nicely textured rosés and *vins gris*, they are fragrant, taut, and appetizing—perfect for casual seaside meals.

❧ PRODUCER RATINGS ❧

OUTSTANDING
Domaine de l'Ecu

EXCELLENT
Domaine de la Ragotière

HIGHLY RECOMMENDED
Donatien Bahuaud   Château de la Preuille

TASTED IN PASSING WITH PLEASURE
Emmanuel Bodet   André-Michel Brégeon   Michel Choblet
Domaine de Chêne
Domaine des Herbauges   Domaine de Treize Vents
Domaine les Coins   Jean-Marc Ferré
Michel Figureau   Joseph Hallereau   Herissé Père et Fils

❧ ❧

OUTSTANDING

Domaine de l'Ecu **(Sèvre-et-Maine):** Guy Bossard's Cabernet Vin du Pays des Marches de Bretagne is the finest Nantais red I've tasted. Most Nantais plant Cabernet vines on land best used for osiers; Bossard's Cabernet grows on a sunny slope and his yields are 30 to 40 percent lower than the norm. (When invited as a guest on a wine talk show in Tours, I brought Bossard's '90 Cabernet; the host took it for a Champigny.)

EXCELLENT

Domaine de la Ragotière **(Sèvre-et-Maine):** The Couillaud brothers lead in Nantais Chardonnay production in every sense. They have given over sixteen of their forty-two hectares to the superstar grape. The results are impressive (the Chardonnays win awards year after year) and a little scary. Importers can't buy enough, and the two top *cuvées* sell for more than their top *cuvée* of Muscadet. The supple Domaine Couillaud seems a cross between Muscadet and Chardonnay with its flavors of apples and minerals. The barrel-fermented Auguste Couillaud is appetizing and original, with strong flavors of expensive new oak.

HIGHLY RECOMMENDED

Donatien Bahuaud (Sèvre-et-Maine): In 1962 the *domaine* released what was, perhaps, the first bottle of Nantais Chardonnay. Today it uses Chardonnay to blend with Chenin for its Blanc de Mer and it makes two pure versions. Le Chouan, the first, is tart with banana and apple notes. Donatien Chardonnay, the prestige bottle, is a creamy, mineral, and appealing light Chardonnay.

Château de la Preuille (Muscadet AOC): The winery's Domaine de Saint-Hilaire Gamay was the nicest expression of the grape I've tasted in the Nantais. Twenty-five-year-old vines, hand-harvested, destemmed, traditional fermentation (no carbonic maceration), no added yeasts, result in supple Gamays with lively acidity and lovely ripe fruit flavors.

TASTED IN PASSING WITH PLEASURE

Emmanuel Bodet, Saint-Aignan: Lean, bell peppery Cabernets.

André-Michel Brégeon (Sèvre-et-Maine): Peppery, medium-bodied Cabernet.

Michel Choblet, Bouaye: Fresh, bracing Grolleau Gris.

Domaine de Chêne, La Chevrolière: My "Memory and Sentiment" Grolleau Gris. At the Rendezvous des Pêcheurs, a fisherman's café near the Lac de Grand Lieu, the coppery, taut wine was supremely refreshing with lake fish in *beurre blanc* and garlicky fried eels.

Domaine des Herbauges (Côtes de Grand Lieu): Bone-dry Grolleau Vin de Pays de Retz with refreshing *sur lie* spritz.

Domaine de Treize Vents, Saint-Philbert-de-Grand-Lieu: Only the Grolleau Gris is recommended here. But taste first.

Domaine les Coins (Côtes de Grand Lieu): Good, taut picnic Grolleau.

Jean-Marc Ferré, Les Moutiers: Smoky Grolleau Gris; jammy, cute little Cabernets.

Michel Figureau, Pont-Saint-Martin: The whole was more than the sum of its parts. The Grolleau was rather rich and quite bubbly—which balanced the rather heavy strawberry jam flavors. But I really enjoyed the wine. His Cabernet, too, interested me despite flavors that made it seem like a failed Amarone. Good fruit, good intentions, but the winemaking resulted in something sweetish with notes of root beer and bark.

Joseph Hallereau (Sèvre-et-Maine): Vinous and strawberry-scented rosé of Gamay.

Herissé Père et Fils, Bourgneuf-en-Retz: More deliciously rough-hewn, quirky Grolleau Gris (rich, tart, and grapefruity, with a clean finish and a kind of *sur lie pétillance*), and lean Cabernets with licorice accents.

THE NANTES TABLE

Beurre blanc, of course, is the Nantais's most famous culinary contribution. The dearth of other distinctive local recipes makes frogs' legs Provençal—sautéed with garlic and parsley—the second most popular "regional" dish. *Canard au Muscadet*, perhaps, ranks third: Little more than roast duck, the pan juices of which have been deglazed with local wine, it was created for the Vallet wine fair about forty years ago. Plain roast duck, served with local peas and carrots, is even more traditional.

Some trace the relative lack of singular Nantais recipes to the city's focus on industrial food production. Nantes's culinary traditions are a continuum of those of the rest of the Loire, however: Its mainstays are *beurre blanc*, matelotes of eel or lamprey, *fritures*, roasts, and wine-laced stews of hare or fowl, in addition to Breton influences like crêpes and cider. It has established its own culinary identity, as well.

The Nantais prepare frogs' legs, for example, better than just about anyone. The frogs are kept alive until cooked, which makes for rare delicacy and succulence—whether *à la Provençale* or with the equally popular *sauce poulette* (egg yolks, lemon, white wine, butter, and herbs). And the best way to show off the fine flavor of Challans ducks (also known as Nantais ducks) is to do as little to them as possible.

It is true, however, that critical aspects of the region's gastronomic history are revealed in Nantes's early and continued importance in French mass food production. As a sheltered harbor near the mouth of the Loire, Nantes's prominence as a port was initially based on sea salt and wine. Between the sixteenth and the eighteenth centuries, the city formed part of a slave-trade triangle with the Antilles and Guinea; sugar, coffee, chocolate, and spices were unloaded on its docks. By 1863 Nantes had become the first city in France for sugar refining and one of its leading manufacturers of candy.

In the early nineteenth century the Nantais began canning albacore tuna and sardines, fished mostly off the Vendée coast. The noted gastronome Grimod de la Reynière devoted an entire chapter of his 1810 *Almanach des Gourmands* to Nantes sardines packed in oil, declaring them almost as good as those fresh from the sea.

The region's wheat and dairy, combined with its trade in sugar, coffee, and chocolate, led to a tradition of biscuitry. As early as the seventeenth century the city developed all types of *pains de mer* (sea breads) to meet sailors' needs.

The industry really took off at the end of the nineteenth century when two cookie giants—Lefèvre-Utile and Biscuiterie Nantaise—were born. In 1896 Louis Lefèvre, whose parents founded the Lefèvre-Utile bakery in Nantes, introduced Petit Beurre. Inspired by the sweet biscuits popular in England in the nineteenth century, Petit Beurre is a rectangular cookie with scalloped edges. Crunchy and lightly sweet, it is made from milk, butter, salt, wheat—all local—and sugar. Two other Lefèvre-Utile (now LU) specialties date from 1905: Paille d'Or (a multiridged wafer filled with raspberry jam) and Beurré Nantais. All three cookies continue to be best-sellers, sharing shelf space with Casse-Croûte and Goûter Fourré (sandwichlike filled cookies) from Biscuiterie Nantaise (now BN).

Sugar refining ceased to be an important Nantais industry—a result of the end of slavery and competition from beet sugar—though Berlingots and the jam-filled *rigolettes Nantaises*, created in the nineteenth century, continue to be made by local confectioners. The region is still home to LU (which has relocated to La Haie-Fouassière), and BN, now owned by General Mills, as well as to another large cookie company, Saint-Michel, in the Pays de Retz, and to a small family firm that, since 1848, has been turning out Petit Mouzillon, a dry, slightly sweet cookie with no fat and no salt— handmade in the heart of the Sèvre-et-Maine.

Saupiquet and Gendreau, both located in Saint-Gilles-Croix-de-Vie, are major canners whose tuna and sardines are found in every supermarket. Other Nantais industrial food titans include Fleury-Michon, the Vendée-based packager of pâtés, sliced ham, and "dinners" ranging from traditional French stews to Moroccan *tagines* and barbecued spareribs; Cassegrain, for canned vegetables; Tipiak, for manioc-based tapioca and the tapioca-like Perles Japon, derived from potatoes.

In fresh foods, much of the butter sold as Poitou-Charentes *Appellation Contrôlée* comes from Vendée. And the fat of the land throughout the Nantais is definitely butter: Everything in the Nantais is cooked and served with it, even cheese. Thanks to the sea salt industry—which stretches from the Guérande Peninsula to Vendée—local butter is usually salted or lightly salted (*demi-sel*). In the Pays de Retz, where cows pasture and beef and dairy are big industry, everything has cream in it—even pot-au-feu and *beurre blanc*.

South of Nantes, around Saint-Julien-des-Concelles and Haute-Goulaine, the landscape is one of fields, plastic tunnels, and greenhouses. Ninety percent of France's mâche and muguets (or lilies of the valley) are grown here, as are leeks, carrots, radishes, cucumbers, tomatoes, branch celery, and all types of lettuce.

Local melon or small radishes (with butter) often open a Nantais meal. The universal garnishes—cabbage, Noirmoutier potatoes, or the white beans called *mogettes* (also spelled *mojettes* and often cooked in earthenware crocks in front of the hearth)—are made or doused with lavish amounts of butter. Leftover *mogettes* on buttered toast is still a popular, if filling, snack.

Add to the Nantais table everything from the coast: mussels, oysters, prawns, shrimp, and sardines. From June to September, baby sardines called *petits* are caught in the morning off ports such as Le Croisic, La Turballe, and Saint-Gilles-Croix-de-Vie and sold on the streets of Nantes in the afternoon. You can eat them raw with bread and butter; marinate them for several minutes in salt, pepper, oil, and vinegar; grill them; or heat them briefly in a pan with butter.

Local pig cookery features *fressure* (the well-seasoned, blood-thickened hash of the less desirable cuts of pork), grilled Vendée ham, *lard Nantais* (pork cutlets cooked with pork rind and offal), and *saucisses au Muscadet*.

Among the region's traditional breads are slightly sweet loaves called *gâches, brioches Vendéennes,* and *fouasses,* each a part of Nantais cookery since the Middle Ages. Both *gâche* and *brioche Vendéenne* were traditionally made around Easter as well as for various family feasts: They were often offered to the bride by the parents of the groom. Aromatized with orange-blossom water, *eau-de-vie,* or rum, they were chewy and slightly dense, their rising interrupted to make a compact cake. While *gâche* remains chewy and compact, the *brioche Vendéenne* has become a soft, airy, tressed loaf. The former has also remained purely local; it can be found mostly along the Vendée coast. The *brioche Vendéenne,* however, has become a popular bread throughout France. Packaged sliced or unsliced, it has been absorbed into the mainstream of industrial French foods.

The Nantais *fouasse* is a plain, hard bread, shaped like a five- or six-point star. Its dough is fragile and the points must be hand-shaped. (The leftovers were made into scallop-edged bars called *guillerets*.) Traditionally made around November 11, the Nantais *fouasse* has always accompanied the new wine. Indeed, winemakers often baked the breads, the better to sell their thin, sharp whites. And one Sèvre-et-Maine village was such a center of *fouasse* production that it appended the name of the bread much the way Burgundians append the name of their most illustrious vineyards, becoming La Haie (or Haye)-Fouassière. (The village church is ornamented with *fouasse*-shaped studs.)

At the turn of the century La Haie-Fouassière had a hundred *fouasse* bakers; today there are none. The last—the Dollet family, whose workshop was literally in the backyard of the LU factory—went out of business in 1993. When Muscadet wasn't selling well, they told me, the *fouasses* helped promote sales. Once Muscadet sales took off, many vintners bought machine harvesters, and the switch from hand to machine harvests dealt a fatal blow to their *fouasse* market.

Some Nantais bakers have resumed making *fouasses*—usually around November 11. In truth, however, they do not complement Muscadet; nor does the Petit Mouzillon cookie, which is now regularly served at wineries and with the *vin d'honneur* at ceremonies. The Nantais' slightly sweet baked goods are all better with tea or coffee; with Kamok, a coffee-flavored liqueur made in the town of Luçon in Vendée, or with a barrel-aged *fine Bretagne*, distilled from Muscadet or Gros Plant. The last, also known as *Eau-de-Vie de Vin des Coteaux de la Loire* (AOC), is a direct descendant of the brandies created by the Dutch when they dominated the port of Nantes.

V

Anjou and Saumur

njou is the most exciting wine region in the Loire. An ancient royal province, it roughly corresponds to the Maine-et-Loire department. Its 15,100 hectares of vines produce approximately 820,000 hectoliters of AOC wine each year, from sparkling to dry to sweet whites, both sweet and dry rosés, and reds. Most are made from three grapes: Chenin Blanc, Cabernet Franc, and Cabernet Sauvignon.

These fall into one of twenty-five appellations. There are two broad regional ones, Anjou and Saumur. Next come subregional zones like Coteaux du Layon and Coteaux du Saumur, then communal ones like Savennières, and finally, several *crus*, such as Coulée de Serrant, Bonnezeaux, and Quarts-de-Chaume.

Although the two are joined administratively, it is common practice to separate the wines of Anjou from those of Saumur. In Anjou the Massif Armoricain meets the Paris Basin, the start of the Saumurois. The schisty soils of the former, basically the northwestern part of the department, make radically different wines from those produced on the tuffeau soils of the latter, the southeastern segment, which have more in common with wines made in neighboring Touraine. I will therefore discuss Saumur separately, with the exception of rosés and sparkling wines, each of which will be taken as a group.

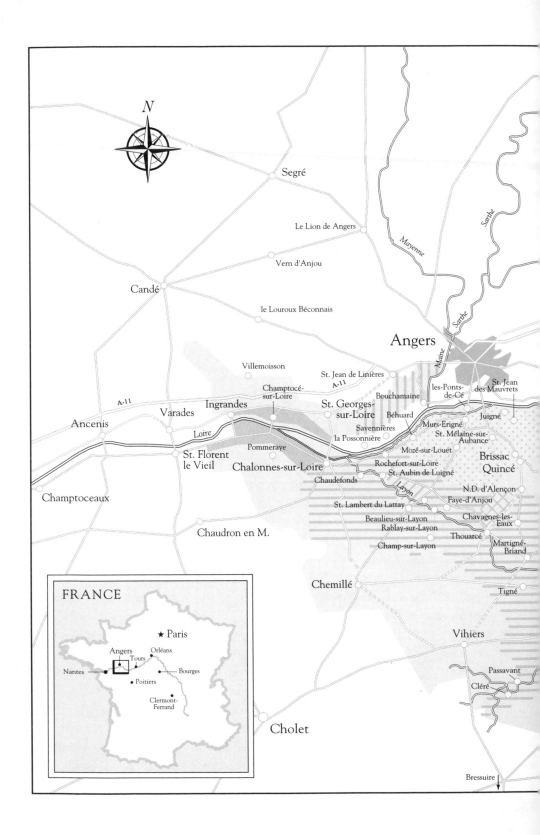

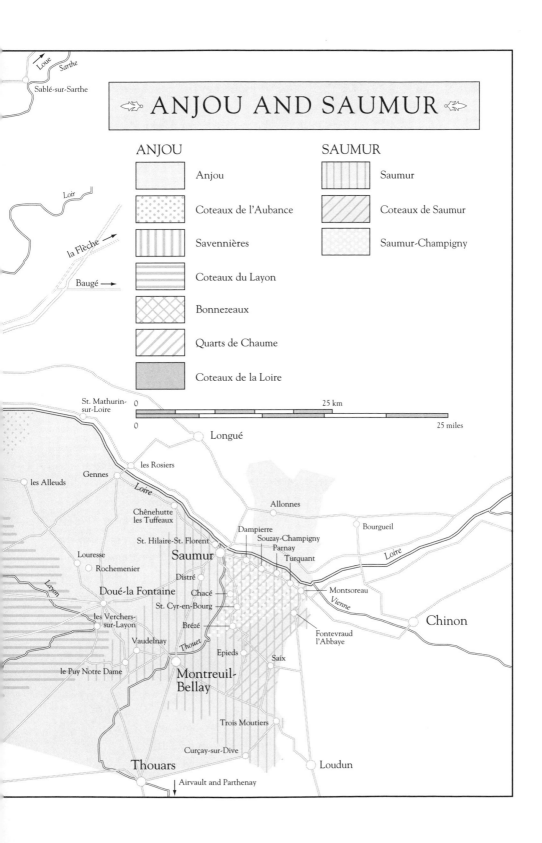

Our Angevin wine route begins just beyond Ingrandes at the Nantais border. It runs east as far as the Loire, and south to the northern communes of the Deux-Sèvres department. For the most part, vines lie southwest of Angers, spread along the banks of the Loire, the Layon, the Aubance, and their tributaries.

Since the story of Anjou is really the story of its great Chenin Blancs, it makes sense to start with these wines. There are four basic appellations.

First, the Coteaux du Layon and its *crus*, Bonnezeaux and Quarts-de-Chaume. These are sometimes demi-sec but usually *moelleux*, or sweet. The profile of generic Layon or Layon-Villages in a middling year might be 12 percent alcohol with from 30 to 45 grams residual sugar; in a very good vintage, 13 to 13.5 percent alcohol with 60 to 75 grams residual sugar, or more, in which case it will most likely be labeled *doux* or *liquoreux*. The *crus* are usually richer.

Next is Savennières, which is sometimes demi-sec but usually sec or *sec-tendre*, with several grams of residual sugar. Then come the Coteaux de l'Aubance and Anjou-Coteaux de la Loire. Like Layon, these may be demi-sec or *moelleux*, though they generally are lower in alcohol and have slightly less residual sugar.

European law permits vintners in Layon, Bonnezeaux, Quarts-de-Chaume, and Aubance to label their *vin liquoreux* as Séléction de Grains Nobles (often abbreviated as SGN or GN). In 1993 vintners in these zones, in conjunction with the local branch of the INAO, wanted to go a step further. Inspired by existing legislation in Alsace, they adopted more stringent standards. Producers must declare their intention to make Grains Nobles before the harvest. Inspectors then visit the vineyard and judge the yields and the condition of the grapes, which must have a potential of 17.5 percent alcohol when picked, or a natural richness of 298 grams of sugar per liter. (If fermentation is stopped at 13 percent alcohol, the finished wine will have about 67 grams of residual sugar.) This is likely to become part of the law governing the making of the above appellations. (And Pascal Cellier, the director of the INAO in Anjou, wants to further amend existing laws to prohibit machine harvesting of grapes for all wines within those appellations, whether Grains Nobles or not.)

In 1994 many producers risked waiting out the bad weather in order to make Grains Nobles, harvesting in late October and into November. A good number of them—particularly those who habitually seek very low yields—made breathtaking wines. Most of these, however, have trace levels of stem rot. That said, the wines are so full of honey, ripe fruit, and other magnificent flavors that you are likely to overlook that vaguely earthy note while savoring all the beautiful ones.

The majority of Angevin producers have vines in one of the great white appellations and make the full range of other whites, rosés, reds, and sparkling Anjous as well.

THE COTEAUX DU LAYON
AND ITS *CRUS*

STATUS: *AOC 1950*

TYPES OF WINE: *Sweet whites*

ZONE AND PRODUCTION: *Roughly 45,000 to 48,000 hectoliters produced on 1,500 hectares (out of a potential of more than 9,000 hectares) in twenty-seven communes. Six villages may attach their names to that of Coteaux du Layon. The hamlet Chaume, in Rochefort-sur-Loire, is another step up. And there are two crus, Bonnezeaux and Quarts-de-Chaume, each entitled to use its name alone on a label. (Much of the Layon's potential vineyard area is planted to other grapes and other crops, and EEC laws inhibit large-scale replanting.)*

GRAPES: *Chenin Blanc*

SOILS: *Primarily schist, the soils are striated with sandstone, silica, granite, and volcanic rocks like quartz and spilite*

PRICE: *35 to 150ff or more for a cru or a special cuvée*

BEST VINTAGES: *'95, some '94s, '90, '89, '88, '85; '76, '75, '71, '69, '59, '55, '49, '47*

No wine-lover can remain unmoved by the vineyards that stretch south and west of Angers. The majestic opening of the countryside, the great rolling hills of vines, announce an important wine region.

This is the Coteaux du Layon. It takes its name from a narrow river which begins in Cléré, at the south of the department, threads its way northeast, then swings northwest to Chalonnes, where it flows into the Loire.

The Layon's schisty soils give the wines a unique and thrilling mineral expression. When young, Layon is a luscious fruit salad, sometimes tasting of pineapple or banana, sometimes apricot, peach, and pear, but always quince, orange, and lemon zests, the whole bound with honey. The texture is unique; at once fine and forceful, it evokes the tensile strength and exquisite delicacy of ballet as well as the durability/fragility of taffeta and silk. Its aromas evolve toward spice, herbal tea, wax, and dried fruit, melding with honey, lemon, and quinine.

I can drink a whole bottle of a wine like this—by myself. Layon producers usually pair it with foie gras. The young ones act a lot like Sauternes with foie gras—the shamelessly opulent partnering the unabashedly luscious. Old Layons are the more compelling partners; with their dry-sweet flavors finishing on notes of quinine and herbal tea, they refresh and excite the palate after each sip.

I think my favorite way to drink old Layons is with absolutely nothing. It's a meditation wine. As one vintner said of his '59, "I would serve it as an aperitif and *only* on the condition that you take your time and talk about it." And those who love these wines as much as I do tend to make a separate course of them, to mark a significant pause between cheese and dessert or, as one friend does on Sunday afternoons, to fill that contemplative time between lunch's coffee and supper.

Once his choice was a '47 Château de Fesles. Its color the topaz of stained-glass windows, it was still fresh and sprightly but infinitely layered with deep, awesome flavors of macaroons, honey, orange zest, smoke, herbal tea, cranberries, and white currants, as well as undertones of chocolate, toffee, cinnamon, and hay. It illustrated perfectly why I think Coteaux du Layon is one of the greatest wines in the world.

Bonnezeaux

STATUS: *AOC 1951*
TYPES OF WINE: *Sweet white*
ZONE AND PRODUCTION: *Roughly 2,044 hectoliters, from about 74 hectares planted, out of a possible 152*
GRAPES: *Chenin Blanc*
SOILS: *Schist, sandstone, and phthanite, with quartz and silex*
PRICE: *20 to 200ff*
BEST VINTAGES: (see *Layon*)

The Bonnezeaux appellation lies about twenty kilometers south of Angers above the commune of Thouarcé. It consists of three south-southwest-facing hills—La Montagne, Fesles, and Beauregard—which overlook the Layon, pitched at 15- to 20-degree angles. The vines are planted on soils composed of schist (the Saint-Georges series), sandstone, and phthanite, with streaks of quartz and silex.

Bonnezeaux was the first Anjou wine to be awarded *cru* status by the INAO, a distinction it owes to persuasive lobbying—and the superb example set—by Jean Boivin.

By law, it must have 230 grams natural sugar, the highest in the Layon. But local vintners don't necessarily think it's the fleshiest. According to Jacques Boivin (Jean's son), Bonnezeaux is different even from its nearest kin, Quarts-de-Chaume. "The two are brothers but not twins," he said. "Bonnezeaux is nervier, Quarts is fatter. A good Bonnezeaux is a vivacious, stand-up wine. It doesn't recline like Mme. Récamier. Quarts is more languorous."

❧ PRODUCER RATINGS ☙

OUTSTANDING
Domaine de la Sansonnière

TO WATCH
Château de Fesles

HIGHLY RECOMMENDED
Domaine du Petit Val

RECOMMENDED
Domaine de Terrebrune   Vignobles Laffourcade

TASTED AND CONSIDERED
Caves de la Loire   Godineau Père et Fils
Rémy Pannier

❧ ☙

OUTSTANDING

***Domaine de la Sansonnière,* Thouarcé:** Mark Angeli, a moonstruck son of Provence and a professional mason, fell in love with *liquoreux* wines and wanted, at all costs, to make them. After studying at La Tour Blanche and working at Château Suduiraut in Sauternes, he scoured France in search of vineyards, finally purchasing land in Anjou, much of it in Bonnezeaux. (He now has roughly ten hectares.)

Angeli practices biodynamic viticulture. He's increasing vine density to more than 11,000 plants per hectare, using selections from his own vines. He does at least five *tris*. (He also manages to harvest grape by grape, thereby disproving conventional wisdom which says it can't be done, due to the compact nature of Chenin's clusters.) His *moelleux* ferment in a mix of new and semi-new *barriques*. He makes a Layon and three *cuvées* of Bonnezeaux.

Angeli was not pleased with his generic Layon in '94. I thought it was gorgeous—bursting with pineapple, honey, peach, and apricot. Angeli's problem with it? He had just taken over that particular vineyard and it's not yet "in biodynamics." Oh, well, I'll drink the wine anytime.

His top '94 Bonnezeaux, Cuvée Mathilde, recalled a Muscat de Beaumes de Venise in its explosion of honey, dried apricot, and tangerine flavors. In '93 and '92 he made nuanced Cuvée Mathildes. In '91 all Angeli's Bonnezeaux went into an excellent Layon. In his debut vintage, '90, he made a handsome Layon from grapes not within Bonnezeaux (45 percent noble rot). The first of three '90 Bonnezeaux was deep, textured, serious. The second—old-vines, 70 percent noble rot—tasted like honey flavored with oak, pineapple, lemon, verbena, and licorice. Cuvée Mathilde spent an additional six months in oak and tasted as rich as maple syrup. The oak, inevitably, was more pronounced but was balanced by bracing flavors of bitter lemon and minerals. Both are dazzling.

TO WATCH

Château de Fesles, Thouarcé: Shock and sorrow greeted news of the sale of this magnificent estate in 1991. With its hard soils of purple schist and its south-facing slopes arching to the Layon, the Château de Fesles was celebrated for producing superb wine as far back as the eleventh century, when its vines were cultivated by the monks of Thouarcé.

More recently, the thirty-three-hectare estate has been synonymous with the Boivins. Jean Boivin, the "Pope of Bonnezeaux," worked for Château d'Yquem and brought to Anjou the concept of harvesting by *tri*. Jacques inherited his father's mastery and turned out exquisite Bonnezeaux that have served as models and inspiration. When, because of inheritance problems, the Boivins sold the historic *domaine* to Gaston Lenôtre, the pastry king of Paris, there rose a collective cry of "Say it ain't so!"

After selling the majority share of his Paris ventures (which included fourteen bakeshops, two restaurants, a cooking school, and catering services), Lenôtre, at age seventy-three, began buying up Anjou's most prestigious properties, beginning with Fesles. He later bought La Roulerie and La Guimonière, both in Coteaux du Layon-Chaume, and the Clos des Varennes in Savennières. And he spent thirty million francs in renovations.

Fesles, where all of Lenôtre's wines are made, now has the most modern and best-equipped cellars in the region. The changes are visible from back roads leading to the winery: High on a hill capping a landscape of vines and dark stone farmhouses are an ensemble of creamy pink modern buildings. A stately rose garden fronts cellars as high-tech, as hygienic, and as efficiently hospitable as any in Napa. The reception/tasting room also houses a confectionery museum. A *pastillage*-trimmed sugar castle and a huge blue pike spun from sugar are displayed under smoked-glass windows which, in turn, look into gleaming cellars. One room is fitted with rows of stainless steel tanks behind a computer panel that regulates fermentation temperatures; in another, the estate's Chenins mature in air-conditioned tranquillity in once-used Yquem barrels.

Day-to-day operations are handled by a team of approximately fourteen people, including a cellar master who is aided by consulting enologist Didier Coutenceau. Lenôtre, who spends eight to ten days a month at Fesles, describes his role as that of Supersalesman, the man who handles important clients, but his imprint is beginning to be perceptible in the wines as vinification techniques such as skin contact for *moelleux* replace those followed by Boivin. Now Lenôtre's white grapes spend twelve to twenty-four hours on their skins before being crushed and placed in stainless steel tanks for fermentation. An increasing percentage ages in *barrique*.

There are three *cuvées* of Fesles: the regular, La Chapelle (a vineyard overlooking the Layon), and the Cuvée Boisée, which spends additional time in oak. All the *moelleux* seem less concentrated and less complex than they had been, however. The standout in Lenôtre's recent lineup of '92s was Roulerie—which was made by its former owner. Gossip has it that Fesles is once again up for sale. Well-placed sources deny that categorically, however. And they are convinced that the *moelleux* will improve, citing a number of factors demonstrating Lenôtre's good faith. Hope springs eternal. The man owns some of the best vineyards in Anjou.

HIGHLY RECOMMENDED

***Domaine du Petit Val,* Chavagnes-les-Eaux:** The wines seem to get better every year. At the time of his retirement in 1988 Vincent Goizil had become one of the pillars of the Bonnezeaux wine community. Son Denis (Montreuil-Bellay) has increased the *tris* at harvest and has purchased new Vosges barrels, and the *domaine*'s Bonnezeaux have progressed from being respectable Layons to exciting expressions of a *grand cru*. There are generally two bottlings; a delicious Domaine and an aristocratic La Montagne, which reveals its nobility in superb vintages—the '90, pure botrytis, was gorgeous and multilayered—as well as in diffuse years like '92 when it was regal and svelte, all refined nuances of honey, fruit, and minerals.

RECOMMENDED

Domaine de Terrebrune, Thouarcé: René Renou, a honcho in the local wine bureaucracy and a partner in this *domaine*, sensed that the evolution of Anjou *moelleux* had not gone unheralded. Two years after presenting a ho-hum '88 at an important tasting, he trotted out a ravishing '90, a special *cuvée*, made from hand-selected grapes. This opulent Bonnezeaux amounts to a fraction of production but shows what the *domaine* can do when it so chooses. Ergo: Look for the special *cuvées*.

Vignobles Laffourcade, Chavagnes-les-Eaux: This big house specializes in Quarts-de-Chaume and Cabernet-based reds. Its Bonnezeaux, however, is sometimes better than its Quarts, though always in the family style. There are often several *cuvées*. These, too, are well within Laffourcade's style: foursquare, commercial *grands crus* for noisy, upscale restaurants.

TASTED AND CONSIDERED

Caves de la Loire, Thouarcé: I wish I liked the wines of this cooperative more than I do. The Bonnezeaux resembles its other wines, lacking focus, concentration, and identity.

Godineau Père et Fils, Faye-d'Anjou: French journalists rave about the Bonnezeaux from this *domaine*. Let's chalk it up to bottle variation. I've never been so lucky. On several occasions I've accompanied friends who buy Bonnezeaux in cubi here. And Mme. Godineau, as tradition requires, opens an old vintage as the checks are being written. I confess I find selling Bonnezeaux in cubi a blasphemy. I also feel this *domaine* could make better wine if it applied more rigorous standards. The Godineaus have great land. The Beauregard and Malabé *cuvées* (in '89 and '90) are distinctive despite the apparent neglect. They should be nobler.

Rémy Pannier, **Saint-Hilaire-Saint-Florent:** The biggest *négociant* in the Loire, selling twenty-five million bottles yearly. Even in '89 it made Bonnezeaux that tasted like sugar water.

Quarts-de-Chaume

STATUS: *AOC 1954*

TYPES OF WINE: *Sweet whites*

ZONE AND PRODUCTION: *Average of 650 hectoliters, made on roughly thirty-four hectares out of a possible forty-eight in the commune of Rochefort, around the hamlet of Chaume*

GRAPES: *Chenin Blanc*

SOILS: *Fragmented schist, sandstone, and pebbles, with shallow topsoils of clay and sand*

PRICE: *100 to 200ff*

BEST VINTAGES: (see *Layon*)

When vintners describe the Quarts-de-Chaume vineyards they extend a hand, palm down, the fingers spread and dipped. The village of Chaume, they say, is at the top of the hand. They stroke the three middle fingers, explaining that these represent the hillsides, the southern versants of which are the vineyards of Quarts-de-Chaume.

The microclimate is unique. Hotter and drier than anywhere else in the Layon, protected from all but the south wind and closer to the river than vines on the plateau above it, vineyards here are more likely to be bathed by fog; the grapes, therefore, are more likely to be attacked by botrytis. Due to erosion, soils vary from the top to the bottom of the slope, creating a complex layering that makes for a more complex wine.

The name derives from an ancient form of sharecropping. The Seigneurs of La Guerche, the owners of Chaume, rented their land to monks of the Abbey of Ronceray in return for a quarter of their crop. The landlord had the right to select which quarter, thus Quarts-de-Chaume.

I'm not sure anyone could distinguish a fine Quarts from a fine Bonnezeaux—at least not all the time. And I find it fascinating that the supposed differences between the two *crus* change depending upon whom you ask. Jacques Boivin claimed Bonnezeaux was the nervier of the two, Quarts the fatter. Jean Baumard says the opposite. Quarts, he says, "distinguishes itself as a wine that's *moelleux* but firm, structured, and nervy. Bonnezeaux is softer, more velvety. Quarts is more like silk. It's tender, airy, vaporous—the expression of a *cru*. Clearly."

Within the past two years the human face of Quarts has changed radically. Three people had dominated the appellation—Jean Baumard, Jacques Lalanne, and Pascal Laffourcade. Baumard has been succeeded by his son. Lalanne sold his estate, though he stays on as director. Laffourcade continues to sell off bits and pieces of his holdings.

⤛ PRODUCER RATINGS ⤜

OUTSTANDING
Domaine des Baumard   Château de Bellerive

TO WATCH
Château Pierre-Bise

RECOMMENDED
Château de Plaisance   Domaine des Maurières
Vignobles Laffourcade

TASTED IN PASSING WITH PLEASURE
Joseph Renou

⤛ ⤜

OUTSTANDING

Domaine des Baumard, **Rochefort-sur-Loire:** Love him or hate him, if you want to have an opinion on Anjou wines you have to come to terms with Jean Baumard. Although I don't agree with everything he does or says, I'm in the "love" camp.

A fastidious man who graduated from both the universities of Dijon and Bordeaux, Baumard's most important vineyards are in Savennières and Quarts-de-Chaume. He is a great technician, and he grows grapes and makes wine *his* way, no matter what the neighbors—or the law—say. He makes some of the best wines in Anjou, but they have often been faulted for being "atypical."

Crystalline structure, razor-sharp definition, and vivacious up-front fruit often separate a newly hatched Baumard Chenin from the rest of the pack. Baumard is fanatical about freshness. To protect Chenin's primary aromas of fruit and spring blossoms, he hand harvests, using small Champagne cases. The grapes are pressed immediately and vinified in stainless steel tanks at 15 to 18 degrees Celsius for as long as possible, developing a richly compact mouth feel and vivid fruit.

A respected enologist aptly described Baumard's Quarts as "a physical wine which also appeals to the intellect." His Quarts are pellucid, definite. His '91 was lacy, with lovely focus; '90 layered on intense flavors of honey, citrus zests, currants, and herbal tea. The elegant '89 mixed fruit and flowers. The '88 offered aromas of incense and blossoms and flavors of zests, honey, and mirabelle. Older vintages reveal that Baumard's Quarts gain from cellaring for fifteen to thirty years. The '62 was a tapestry of dried fruits, the entire honey spectrum, a galaxy of herbal teas and spices, the embodiment of a *grand cru*.

Baumard officially retired in 1993–94, succeeded by his son Florent who had worked beside him for years. But he is still very much in evidence— not only in the style of the *domaine's* recent wines, such as a velvety '93 Quarts with notes of *crème de cassis*, citrus zests, and creamed corn (the last is typical of Baumard's Chenins at a certain stage)—but in the style of other Loire wines as well. Baumard has had an enormous impact on all the wines of Anjou.

Château de Bellerive, Rochefort-sur-Loire: Jacques Lalanne's Quarts is the opposite of Baumard's: brooding and lush, with a kind of throbbing sensuality. Lalanne, who looks like a wiry street cop, ferments his Quarts in old wood barrels for as long as five months. I think that's what makes them so sultry. These are wines that take their own damned time to reveal themselves. And you're never quite sure they're telling you all they know.

In May 1994 Lalanne sold his ten hectares to Serge and Michel Malinge—a sale provoked by inheritance laws and family feuds—but he has stayed on to work the vines and make the wines. And the Malinges, who are new to wine, seem to let Lalanne do exactly as he likes.

Committed to low yields, Lalanne removes clusters in June or July, leaving from two to eight bunches per plant, depending on the age of the vine. At harvest, he passes once every ten to fifteen days. Lots are pressed and vinified separately.

His '94 Quintessence, certainly among the gems of the vintage, was a nuanced blend of honey, herbal tea, and citrus zests, albeit with a whiff of the year's earthiness. His '90 has, curiously, often left me cold, but the '89 expresses that pulsating sensuality along with orange blossoms and honey. The structured '88 seems a fruit compote with blossoms, peaches, maple syrup notes, and a tasty menthol-quinine finish. The '85, with 50 percent noble rot, is a sumptuous blend of honey and quinine, with flashes of ginger, lemon, and menthol. The bottles I'd open tonight, however, are '82, '76, or '75. The last is Quarts personified. It mingles flavors like an old spice box— wax, fig, honey, mint, bitter orange, nutmeg, chamomile, and quinine. Each sip is a discovery.

TO WATCH

Château de Pierre-Bise (Beaulieu-sur-Layon):   Claude Papin took over his father-in-law's estate in time for the super '90 vintage. His first Quarts is richly honeyed, with layers of quinine, herbs, and toast. Since then the Quarts, aged in used *barriques*, have continued to be beautiful; velvet blends of honey, ginger, oak, and medicinal plants like chamomile and verbena.

RECOMMENDED

Château de Plaisance (Rochefort-sur-Loire):   The Rochais family bought a 1.5-hectare parcel of Quarts from Laffourcade. It abuts their vines in Chaume. The '94, fermented in old barrels, won a gold medal in Angers. The most elegant wine in their '94 lineup, it did have a trace of the '94 earthiness.

Domaine des Maurières, Saint-Lambert-du-Lattay: Fair-to-middling Quarts, sometimes better, like the '90, a crowd-pleaser with flashy honey and orange zest flavors.

Vignobles Laffourcade, Chavagnes-les-Eaux: Quarts-de-Chaume is this *domaine*'s flagship wine. Until quite recently, it owned half the appellation; its two key properties were L'Echarderie and La Suronde. Pascal Laffourcade, an interpreter by training, succeeded his father in 1974. He now has vineyards throughout Anjou as well as a *négociant* business. Over the past couple of years, he has been selling off bits of Quarts-de-Chaume, mostly parts of La Suronde. Since 1990 there have also been numerous turnovers in key cellar positions, including winemaker. Throughout all this, however, Laffourcade's policy remains constant. He wants to make Chenins that drink well right away; to wit, good, up-to-date, competitive products. Like others, he has seen the encomiums heaped on the young artist-vintners of Anjou for their Grains Nobles and their special *cuvées*. So he employs techniques like skin contact and barrel aging and puts out four or five versions of Quarts, including an old-vines and a Clos du Paradis. I have always found them commercial, usually banal, but well made and tasty. Don't look for the ultimate Quarts experience. Just a nice, easily fathomable wine from a *grand cru*.

TASTED IN PASSING WITH PLEASURE

Joseph Renou, **Saint-Aubin:** Hervé Renou succeeded his father in 1990, making both Layon-Chaume and Quarts-de-Chaume. I prefer the former. (The '90 was an ambassador for Layon.)

The Coteaux du Layon

STATUS: *AOC 1950*

TYPES OF WINE: *Sweet whites*

ZONE AND PRODUCTION: *Roughly 45,000 hectoliters produced on 1,500 hectares in twenty-seven communes. The six villages that may attach their names to that of Coteaux du Layon are: Beaulieu-sur-Layon (1,244 hectoliters on 52 hectares); Faye-d'Anjou (1,753 hectoliters on 65 hectares); Rablay-sur-Layon (460 hectoliters on 17 hectares); Rochefort-sur-Loire (1,095 hectoliters on 48 hectares); Saint-Aubin-de-Luigné (1,642 hectoliters on 71 hectares); and Saint-Lambert-du-Lattay (1,075 hectoliters on 37 hectares). The hamlet Chaume produces 1,830 hectoliters on 72 hectares.*

GRAPES: *Chenin Blanc*

SOILS: *Primarily schist, with marked variations*

PRICE: (see *Layon and Its Crus*)

BEST VINTAGES: (see *Layon and Its Crus*)

Given the disparity in competence among winemakers, it is too soon to make pronouncements about the style of generic Layons as opposed to Layon-Villages, much less the differences between Beaulieu and neighboring Rochefort, for example. Generally, however, vineyards on the right bank seem to produce Layons more marked by their complex soil structures. These Layons often have strong herbal tea flavors, suggesting chamomile, tilleul, and quinine. This expression seems most pronounced in Chaume as well as in sections of Saint-Aubin, Beaulieu, and Rochefort. Those who prefer blander (though not necessarily less appealing) Layons tend to like versions from Rablay, Saint-Lambert, or generic Layon, particularly those made near Tigné, Martigné-Briand, and Passavant. Many of these are left-bank Layons. The soils here are younger and include sand and gravel washed off the steep slopes of the right bank.

❧ PRODUCER RATINGS ☙

OUTSTANDING
Château Pierre-Bise   Château Soucherie
Domaine Ogereau   Domaine Philippe Delesvaux

EXCELLENT
Domaine des Baumard   Domaine des Forges

TO WATCH
Château de la Genaiserie   Domaine Cady
Domaine de l'Echalier   Domaine de Juchepie
Domaine Jo Pithon

HIGHLY RECOMMENDED
Château du Breuil   Château de Passavant
Château de Plaisance   Château des Rochettes
Domaine de Brizé   Domaine des Closserons   Domaine du Petit Val
Domaine de la Pierre Blanche   Sechet-Carret   Vignobles Touchais

RECOMMENDED
Patrick Baudoin   Michel Blouin   Château Montbenault
Château de Montgueret   Domaine Banchereau   Domaine Grosset
Domaine Touche Noire

TASTED AND CONSIDERED
Domaine Gaudart   Domaine Jean-Louis Robin
Domaine Leduc-Frouin   Domaine de la Motte
Domaine des Maurières   Domaine du Sauveroy

IN TRANSITION
Château de la Guimonière   Domaine de la Roulerie

❧ ☙

OUTSTANDING

Château Pierre-Bise, Beaulieu-sur-Layon: Want to learn about *terroir*? Claude Papin will teach you. Layon Geology 101 begins at the tasting bar on which sits a marble tray covered with rocks, each representing a different soil type—a chunk of *pierre bise* or spilite (the volcanic rock that gives the *domaine* its name), a nugget of *carbonifère* from Chaume, and so forth.

Papin cultivates thirty-five hectares of vines belonging to his family and, as of the '92 vintage, those of the Clos de Coulaine in Savennières. He makes many different Layon-Beaulieus as well as Chaume and Quarts-de-Chaume. All are finely tuned, concentrated blends of fruit and minerals. So Geology 102 picks up with my four favorite Pierre-Bise soil types:

L'Anclaie's schist and feldspar produce subtly perfumed wines. I love the '88's fine, nuanced interplay of honey, bitter orange, and menthol. The '90 is on the list at a bistro in Tours and I am singlehandedly draining the stock.

Les Soucheries, on a composite of several types of carboniferous soil, produces fresh, fruity wines with menthol accents. The gingery, Schweppes-y '88 is Papin's favorite for its voluptuousness on the palate. The '90, a limpid, bright wine, offered graceful honey, mineral, and mint flavors. The '92 is velvety and impressive; '93, regal, deep, and harmonious.

Chaume's complicated mix of soils makes floral, vivacious wines with flavors of quince, green apples, honey, and long mineral finishes. The most powerful of his '88 lineup, it was highly perfumed, a fine mix of honey, quince, quinine, pineapple, and apple sauce, with a long *eau-de-vie* finish. There were two *cuvées* of 1990: The first, Les Tétuères, evoked honey, linden blossoms, and quinine, and had an eternal mineral finish. (In '92 Les Tétuères was magnificent, rich, balanced, and specific.) L'Ouche, more botrytized, was a velvety wine that spread layers of grapefruit and honey over the palate.

Les Rouannières, on spilite, may make the most distinctive of Papin's Layons. Less voluminous, less fruity, it is tightly knit, fleshy with a markedly bitter (as in quinine) flavor. The '88 was flowery, with notes of quince and honey. The finish was an explosion of minerals and bark. An exciting wine. The '90 and the intensely botrytized '92 were splendid, epic tisane statements. There were two *cuvées* of '93 Rouannières. Both were divine. But one, the Grains Nobles, was celestial.

In truth, distinguishing between these wines is like counting how many angels there are on the head of a pin. They're all wonderful.

Château Soucherie, Beaulieu-sur-Layon: "The good times are coming back," said Pierre-Yves Tijou, referring to the days when Chaume sold like Yquem. And Tijou looks primed for a "Lifestyles" feature. Branches of the family tree embrace the aristocracy of Anjou—the Boivins, the Touchais. His wife is beautiful. His tasting cellar is an impeccable series of dramatically lit white stone arches and decorative barrels. His handsome nineteenth-century English-style house has a forty-kilometer panorama of the Layon Valley, of crisscrossing slopes folding against each other, of church steeples beyond the tree line, of morning fog above the Layon River. And the fiftyish Tijou, who looks more like a well-heeled dentist than a vigneron, has a solid track record of making fine Layons.

Tijou inherited thirty-odd hectares of vines (and has added to that with purchases in Savennières) and makes the full line of Anjou appellations. He usually offers five different Layons.

His *domaine* bottling, a Coteaux du Layon–Beaulieu, is always a good representative of the appellation and occasionally exceptional (e.g., a special *cuvée* of '87). My favorite Tijou Layons are his Chaume, his Vieilles Vignes, and some of the *lieux dits*, like Les Mouchis, that he bottles and never talks about or puts on price lists. (The '90 Les Mouchis, with airy floral and apricot scents, had pellucid chamomile-quinine flavors.)

The '88 Chaume was an elegant, persuasive wine. The '90 had floral aromas and lush, tight structure. Vieilles Vignes, made from grapes planted just after phylloxera, may be Tijou's most distinctive wine. The stunning, heavily botrytized '88 was as plush as velvet and as tight and shimmery as taffeta. Limpid, elegant, it was a glowing composite of honey, orange zest, mint, apricots, and pineapple and a long finish of lemon and honey. The sumptuous '89 was all pear and menthol, quinine and butterscotch. The '90 had deep apricot scents and lush fruit.

Domaine Ogereau, Saint-Lambert-du-Lattay: When I visited during the '89 harvest, Vincent Ogereau's cellar looked like an experimental lab, bubbling with microvinifications. In one corner, part of the first *tri* of Coteaux du Layon–Saint-Lambert was fermenting in new oak barrels. The rest of that *tri* had been divided in three to try out different approaches to skin contact. Ogereau bottled three different *cuvées* of Layon that year— each a gorgeous, nuanced wine. The top *cuvée* was a ringer for Sauternes. Still in barrel in early 1991, it was an orgy of honey, toast, vanilla, lemon zest, and coffee.

Ogereau is the fourth-generation winemaker to work those eighteen hectares in and around Saint-Lambert—to which he recently added another two. And as the above scene might suggest, he is one of the Young Turks changing Anjou. After studying at the Lycée d'Agriculture in Beaufort (Bordeaux), he succeeded his father and immediately began harvesting by *tri*, cluster thinning, and joining in Didier Coutenceau's experiments. In addition to making spectacular Layons in great years like '89 and '90, he also made fine versions in "off" years like '83 and '87. In '93 both the generic and the Grains Nobles were well-structured, sapid Layons, with fine flavors of honey, oak, and ripe fruit. The Grains Nobles, however, was deeper, with more intense flavors. Two *cuvées* of '92 were knockouts: a densely layered, pure gold, super *tri* with high pineapple accents, and a Cuvée l'Imprévue (unexpected). Harvested in November, fermented and aged in oak, it was a sumptuous concentration of honey, ginger, oak, and fruit. His '88 and '85 Grains Nobles are terrific, too.

Domaine Philippe Delesvaux, Chaudefonds-sur-Layon: A fortyish Parisian (via Savoie), Philippe Delesvaux was studying agriculture in Picardy and came to Anjou for a *stage*, the equivalent of our clinical programs. He worked at a typical farm, raising cereal crops and cattle, and some grapes, too. One thing led to another, as they say, and by 1983 Delesvaux found vineyards in Anjou and began making his own wine in a toolshed. He read and he worked with Didier Coutenceau as well as other local enologists. He put out some glorious Grains Nobles (which won him lots of deserved press coverage), built a new winery, and has extended his vineyard holdings to 14.5 hectares.

His '89 and '90 Grains Nobles were masterpieces. The '90 is 14.5 percent alcohol with 160 grams residual sugar and layer upon layer of honey, apple, quinine, peach, apricot, melon, and currants. It's also aristocratic and long, still unfolding a full minute after you've swallowed. The '94, despite a streak of the year's earthiness, is a thick wave of honey balanced by lively acidity. The '93 was a velvet blend of raisins and honey.

My sole misgiving about rating Delesvaux "Outstanding" is that his generic *cuvées* of Layon, and even some of his Layon-Villages, have been rather simple and bland. But I have confidence in Delesvaux's desire to make great Layon, and I've witnessed progress, notably in two single-vineyard bottlings.

Delesvaux's most recent acquisition is a parcel in Saint-Aubin called Clos du Pavillon. The discreet, balanced '93 is a deep blend of honey, ripe fruit, and minerals. I've also admired the wines from another plot in Saint-Aubin, La Moque: '92 was lovely; '94 was layered and nearly viscous, with bright flavors of minerals, apricots, and honey.

EXCELLENT

Domaine des Baumard (Quarts): The estate's generic Layon is on a lot of wine lists and is sometimes disappointing. Bottles tasted at the winery or at the homes of friends, however, have always been excellent. There are two superior *cuvées*—Clos Sainte-Catherine, whose sandy soils make tender, very pretty, early-drinking Layons; and, in fine vintages like '89 and '90, Paon (peacock), a crystal clear Layon, with layers of tropical fruit and honey and an elegant quinine finish.

Domaine des Forges, Saint-Aubin-de-Luigné: "Coteaux du Layon is my passion," says fiftyish Claude Branchereau. A third-generation winemaker, Branchereau works thirty hectares and makes the gamut of Anjou wines. His Layons are hand harvested, by *tris*. There are several different bottlings, including a delicious Séléction de Grains Nobles from his vines in Saint-Aubin and another beauty from his fifty-plus-year-old vines on Les Onnis (also Aunis) in Chaume. Earthy notes undermined the otherwise gorgeous '94 Saint-Aubin SGN and the Les Onnis but both '93s were lovely—complex Layons with generous flavors. The discreet '90 Les Onnis, well structured, with a graceful honey–bitter lemon balance, was divine. An extremely concentrated, exquisitely balanced '88 Les Onnis expressed powerful aromas of quince, pear, apricot, and all sorts of flowers. It will be gorgeous in 2000.

TO WATCH

Château de la Genaiserie, Saint-Aubin-de-Luigné: It seems that Yves Soulez was born to make *moelleux*. While he was at Château de Chamboureau, making Savennières, his wines were hit-or-miss; the best was often the *moelleux* from his one hectare of Quarts-de-Chaume. In 1990 he moved across the river to Genaiserie, and since then, has been turning out sublime Layons from his forty-two hectares in Chaume and Saint-Aubin-de-Luigné. (It's more than just destiny, however. It's work, too. Soulez, who harvested mostly by machine in Savennières, for example, has now become one of the most ardent *tri*-ers, and is often among the last to pick.)

Soulez offers several *cuvées* of Layon, including three *lieux dits*—Les Petits Houx, Les Simonelles, and La Roche. Thus far I've found the generic Layon rather bland. Things get interesting with the Saint-Aubin and Chaume bottlings: A '91 Saint-Aubin was lacy, fine, and lovely; the '92 Saint-Aubin was concentrated with clear, high floral notes, though the '92 Chaume was meatier, more honeyed, and more nuanced.

The '90 Les Petits Houx was honey syrup; Les Simonelles was richer still, alluring in every respect, and more nuanced than Petits Houx. La Roche was even lusher, if less fine-boned. A burnished gold, it had 150 grams of residual sugar and was a nectar of honey, herbal tea, orange peel, and quinine. Gorgeous.

Soulez won't let anyone taste his Layons till they've passed their first birthday. For now, Les Simonelles is my favorite in the '92 and '93 vintages, particularly the richly honeyed '93, with its intriguing accents of star anise.

Domaine Cady, Saint-Aubin-de-Luigné: Anjou buffs really started noticing Philippe Cady in 1990. In general his Layons come on strong, with broad flavors of honey and pineapple and intriguing notes of amaretto and coconut. The simpler *cuvées*—such as his generic Layon—can be a bit two-dimensional, but the top *cuvées* are super. Favorites include a layered, delicate '90 Les Varennes; a concentrated, honeyed, and mineral '91 from the same parcel; a lush, bitter-orange flavored '90 Chaume; and an aristocratic, hyacinth-scented '91 from that plot.

But when you hear people rave about Cady, it's usually about his Cuvée Anatole Pierre, the nectar he makes from a *tri* in Saint-Aubin. Both '89 and '90 are glorious but the edge goes to the '90: 22.5 percent potential alcohol at harvest with 80 percent noble rot, the wine has lavish flavors of fruit and honey and a long, long finish.

Domaine de l'Echalier, Rablay-sur-Layon: Isabelle Lorent and François Bureau, a husband-and-wife team of enologists, came to Anjou to work for Pascal Laffourcade. In 1990 they found their own land, taking over the thirteen hectares of a retired vigneron. Their first vintage was textbook, including a number of fine-boned, tasty Layons—a Rablay, a Cuvée Jean Cesbrun (aged in oak barrels), and my favorite, a nuanced and velvety Vieilles Vignes which ferments in barrel. The fine work continues with pretty '92s and a string of lovely '93s. Once again, my favorite is the richly honeyed Vieilles Vignes.

Domaine de Juchepie, Faye-d'Anjou: You could call it a midlife career change. Or you could call it the realization of a long-held dream. Eddy and Marie-Madeleine Osterlinck had always wanted to make wine. They happen to live in Belgium, where Eddy is "in hardware." But now they also have four hectares of well-exposed slopes in the heart of Layon (with a possible total of seventeen when all is planted). They have built a small cellar under their house and, for now, produce 3,000 to 4,000 bottles a year.

It's obvious that the Osterlincks love wine, particularly sweet ones, and that they've thought about what makes one wine wonderful and another merely good. And they're in the Layon to make wonderful *liquoreux*. By pruning severely, yields are kept to an average of ten hectoliters per hectare. Viticulture is organic. Harvest waits until the grapes are overripe or attacked by botrytis. Wines ferment in newish oak barrels (without the addition of yeasts) and stay in barrel from six months (for dry whites) to eighteen months for *moelleux*.

The Osterlincks' first vintage was '89. I believe I've tasted every year and, I think, every *cuvée*, from the extraordinary dry white sold as Anjou blanc to the divine *moelleux*. The dry whites made me think of Yquem's dry white, called "Y" (the Osterlincks call their version "J") because the color, the power, the breed, as well as various aromas and flavors, recall *moelleux* but the wines are utterly dry.

There are two *cuvées* of Layon—a Layon-Faye and, since '92, La Quintessence. Each of the '94s was among the triumphs of the vintage. Though each had minuscule traces of earthiness, that aspect was nearly impossible to detect under the plush layers of honey, oak, citrus zests, and ripe fruit. Other sublime bottles include the lavish and brightly focused '92 Quintessence; the fresh, chamomile-tinged '91; the mind-blowing '90 which, in ten years (and for another fifty thereafter) will be a monument; and the beautifully balanced '89, a velvet blanket of honey, oak, and licorice.

Domaine Jo Pithon, Saint-Lambert-du-Lattay: A born-again vigneron, Jo Pithon was an average Angevin, working thirteen hectares of vines, with Anjou's gamut of grape varieties. After the '91 spring frosts, however, he grabbed the opportunity to reinvent himself. Why? "Opting for quality seemed the only way to succeed." Pithon reduced his acreage to 4.12 hectares—almost exclusively Chenin. He makes Anjou blanc, Layon, and a tiny bit of Anjou-Villages.

Pithon's Layon vineyards are in Saint-Lambert and in Saint-Aubin. He tries to make two versions of each, a Grains Nobles and an earlier-drinking variety. All ferment and age in *barriques*, some for as long as eighteen months.

I found the '93 and the '92 Saint-Lamberts attractive, two-dimensional Layons. My decided weakness for Layons from Saint-Aubin was confirmed by Pithon's versions. There were three *cuvées* of '93, one richer than the last, though all quite appetizing. My favorite was Le Clos des Bois, Grains Nobles, the middle *cuvée*, with its ravishing weave of peach, apricot, oak, coffee, and honey.

HIGHLY RECOMMENDED

Château du Breuil, Beaulieu-sur-Layon: The Château du Breuil, a historic thirty-two-hectare Layon estate, was bought by Chantal Morgat's father some fifty years ago. Chantal's husband, Marc, who comes to wine from computers (IBM), studied at Montreuil-Bellay when he assumed wine-making responsibilities. As his son Eric says, he makes very rational wines.

Dry wines are more important commercially but Layon is the star, particularly the barrel-aged Vieilles Vignes *cuvée* (from vines planted in 1894). The '94 Vieilles Vignes had hints of earthiness but was fine, aromatic, and rich. The '93 was very pretty indeed, with its discreet blend of honey, oak, citrus zests, and pear. The '91 was an admirable, multiple-award-winner. The '90 was a ripe, California-style Layon, with broad flavors of toast, coconut, quince, banana, and orange.

Château de Passavant, Passavant-sur-Layon: This popular winery, near the source of the Layon, is a sure bet for easy-drinking *moelleux*. The wines seem to resemble the family: They are nice, reasonable, and reliable.

Château de Plaisance, Rochefort-sur-Loire: This may be one of the last strongholds of the harvest meal. The harvesters come from all over France—there's a parish priest from Brittany, two couples from Alsace, several widows from Auvergne—to spend their yearly vacations picking the Rochais family's grapes. As they all bring regional specialties—sausage, foie gras, cheese—meals are long. There is wine, of course, and song, and one wonders how the harvest gets done. But it does.

Rochais' Layons are somewhat rustic but not without appeal—both for the evident quality of the land and the grape, as well as for the rough edges of workmanship that has not yet reached the level of neighbors like Pierre-Yves Tijou and Claude Papin.

The normal *cuvée*, from less-well-situated parcels, is a good Layon, rarely more. The Vieilles Vignes is lusher, more expressive. A '94 Les Zerzilles (eighty-year-old vines) showed traces of earthiness but was rich enough to cover a multitude of sins. A '90 Les Charmelles was full of honey, quince, and herbal tea flavors, rather coarsely expressed. Those who buy it won't be disappointed ten years from now, despite the missed chance to make a sensational Layon. I loved the barrel-fermented '85 Vieilles Vignes, however, which seemed to have been steeped in honey, ginger, and quince. And I had no problem whatsoever downing the blossomy '88.

Château des Rochettes, Concourson-sur-Layon: You'll find this winery's Layons on many restaurant lists. In top vintages, like '90, the generic Layon is truly delicious and classic. Generally, however, the wines to look for are Séléction de Grains Nobles. They're not mind-blowing, but they can be lovely in lesser vintages (like '87) and excellent in years like '85 and '88.

Domaine de Brizé, Martigné-Briand: The Delhumeaus' eighty hectares of vines are at the foot of Bonnezeaux and just outside the Layon-Villages appellation. And the Layons from this house do tend to be less epic than those from more privileged sites. But skill often compensates for nature's oversights. Luc Delhumeau (University of Bordeaux) makes excellent Layons that tend to get overlooked because he also turns out spectacular sparkling wine, luscious fruit liqueurs (like *crème de cassis* or *framboise*), and lovely reds. The '90 Layon was super. As rich as anything from Rochefort, it exploded with flavors of honey, apple skins, and lemon zest. The '88 was deeply fruity, too, with layers of honey, citrus zests, and pineapple.

Domaine des Closserons, Faye-d'Anjou: Truly lovely Fayes, ample, syrupy, with Muscat, apricot, and licorice notes. Also a good source for Bonnezeaux.

Domaine du Petit Val (Bonnezeaux): Goizil's major *moelleux* statement is Bonnezeaux, but don't overlook his fine Layon: '90 was a knockout; '91 wasn't far behind.

Domaine de la Pierre Blanche, Champ-sur-Layon: Vincent Lecointre is the young winemaker whose family saga I selected to tell the tale of Anjou—and of the Loire—in chapter 1. "My style could be called demi-sec," he says of his Layon. "I hate fraudulent wines. Alcohol should just support the aromas and flavors. The old Layons weren't strong, but they lasted for fifty years. So will mine."

It's true that in average years like '86, Lecointre's Layons do come across as demi-sec; in great vintages like '89 and '90, they seem like normal *moelleux* compared with the Grains Nobles of Rochefort. But Lecointre's top Layon, Château la Tomaze Cuvée des Lys, is usually accurate, well-structured, restrained, and pretty. I detected some earthiness in both the '94 and the '92, but note that the former won a gold medal in a respected competition and that the latter, which was also pure botrytis, has devoted fans among some of Paris's leading restaurateurs. My favorites include the '89 and '90 Cuvée des Lys, with their mix of honey, brown sugar, pineapple, and caramel, and the '88 Layon-Rablay, which was all pears and quince, elegance and finesse, with a long, citrus-scented finish.

Sechet-Carret, Maligné: If every Layon coming out of this winery were in the same ballpark as its versions from Maligné, Sechet-Carret would be among the top producers of Layon. Maligné is an exceptional vineyard that, in the nineteenth century, was considered as *grand* a *cru* as Bonnezeaux. (When the INAO named Anjou's *crus*, no one lobbied for Maligné's inclusion.) Sechet-Carret's versions certainly reveal the extraordinary "personality" of this site. The normal '90 *cuvée* had an "if you've got it, flaunt it" nose of honey and pineapple. It overwhelmed the palate with layers of ripe fruit, honey, and minerals and a stunning finish that explored every medicinal plant in the herb book. The special *cuvée*, partially fermented and aged in new oak, was a blockbuster—sumptuous, velvety, lick-your-lips delicious. I prefer the unoaked special *cuvée* of '89; fine and potent, it perused each possible expression of orange—from blossom to fruit to zest. Spring frosts resulted in a single '91 Layon—a graceful wine with ample pineapple aromas and a long mineral and tisane finish. The '92 Maligné was excellent; full and rich with delicious flavor. You get the picture. What troubles me is the considerable amount of quite uninteresting Layon one can also find here—such as a string of very earthy '94s.

Vignobles Touchais, Doué-la-Fontaine: Don't go to this *domaine* to taste recent vintages. Touchais believes that a wine needs twenty years before it can be called Layon. One of the largest Loire houses, the *domaine* has 145 hectares of vineyards. (A separate *négociant* business shares the winery facilities, offering such *cuvées* as "Cuisses de Bergère" [Thighs of the Shepherdess]). Coteaux du Layon accounts for only 5 to 10 percent of Touchais's production. But the top Layon, Moulin Touchais, as well as the seemingly endless supply of old Layons, have given the *domaine* its distinction.

Moulin Touchais is the proprietary name of a Layon from a good vintage with a minimum of ten years' age. It is usually very good, if rarely stunning. There are currently eight Moulin Touchais being offered; the youngest is '85. (It has attractive flavors of pine, honey, macaroon, and anise but is rather soft for my liking, though some might consider it supple.)

If you visit, you're likely to go way back in time. My tasting spanned the 1960s (a sapid '64 stood out), then hopped to a show-stopping 1892 that washed the palate with orange zest, toffee, chocolate, and dried apricots mingled with honey. Fresh, eternal, extraordinary.

RECOMMENDED

Patrick Baudoin, Chaudefonds-sur-Layon: Several of my favorite Layon producers steered me to Baudoin, a former bookshop employee who reclaimed the family vines in 1990. Baudoin generally makes a Layon, a Saint-Aubin, and a Grains Nobles. The '93s and '94s I tasted displayed good work but they were rather blunt and two-dimensional. The '94 Grains Nobles had strong balsamic, orange, and mint notes but was fairly oxidized. Baudoin is a beginner and it shows. But there's cause for optimism here. To watch.

Michel Blouin, Saint-Aubin-de-Luigné: Among his twenty hectares of vines, Blouin has nice parcels in Saint-Aubin and in Chaume. The wines have been fairly rustic, but they seem to be improving. I favor the Chaume, especially the complex, rich, and rather elegant '90 and the floral and lovely '92.

Château Montbenault, Faye-d'Anjou: Until 1982 Pierre Leduc directed the *domaine* and made fabulous Layons. The jury is still out on son Yves (Montreuil-Bellay) who sometimes makes lovely Layons, but more often, not. The best come from La Herse (ungrafted vines on a south-facing slope with clay-schist soils) and Le Poirier Bourgeaux (another south-facing slope, with more pebbly soils). Both ferment in used Bordeaux barrels and should, by rights, always be special. Indeed, they were both wonderful in '89, '88, and '85. But all the '94s were marred by stem rot; the '90 Poirier Bourgeaux had a hot finish and vegetal flavors.

Older vintages are awesome. The '59 is the type of Layon that brings tears to the eyes. A velvet syrup, it was impossible to isolate all the flavors, so subtly did they melt into one sublime whole. There was butterscotch and honey, white currants, lemon, pine, maple syrup, and chamomile. "When the wine is really good," Leduc noted, "we say, 'The tongue goes out for a stroll.' "

Château de Montgueret, Nueil-sur-Layon: This large *domaine* has twenty-five hectares in Vaudelnay (in the Saumurois) and seventy-five in the Passavant area. It makes a full range of Anjou-Saumur wines. The best is its old-vines Layon Le Petit Saint-Louis. In '88, '89, and '90 this was a luscious crowd-pleaser.

Domaine Banchereau, Saint-Aubin-de-Luigné: Numerous *cuvées* of alcoholic Layon with big, flashy flavors—like the '90 Cuvée Privilège with 16.6 percent alcohol (*sic*) and 200 grams of residual sugar: It didn't have a lot of finesse, but it sure was impressive.

Domaine Grosset, Rochefort-sur-Loire: *Le père* (Raymond) Grosset is a sommelier's trap. Beret worn at a jaunty angle, he negotiates the aisles between his barrels. Stooped and gnarled, yes, but still spry. There are photos of old vintages. There are diplomas and awards. And Raymond, with his toothless grin, is holding forth on how he harvested his first Layons in 1932, how he worked the vines with a horse before getting his first tractor in 1956, how he cranked the press by hand. Folklore, plus a glass of '71—after an extensive tasting—and you're bound to walk out with several cases of mixed vintages. And the prices are, well, rather attractive. So you're not surprised to see Domaine Grosset on many prestigious wine lists.

Far from perfect, the Grosset Layon is Anjou sociology in a glass. The great grape is there. The fine *terroir* is there. And there's a kind of dishonest honesty. All the crafty little tricks used in making wine that aren't really cheating but . . . So I think, with pleasure, of a '90 served by the glass at a café on the banks of the Loire. It radiated charmingly all the old flaws. It was hot, it was sugary, it was rough, there was a trace of rot and an overdose of sulfur. But it was undeniably a Layon—from a certain epoch. And perversely, when you have fallen in love with Layon, this version has its appeal.

Serge Grosset, who learned from his father, makes three Layons, all vinified in barrel. In most years, including '93, I prefer the Layon-Rochefort, although the Chaume always shows more breed and was my favorite among the '94s. I enjoyed both bottlings in '88 and '85. The Rochefort was a mix of honey and chamomile; the Chaume, clear yet syrupy-rich, had flavors of pine and quinine against a backdrop of honey. A favorite older vintage is the '76 Rochefort. My sophisticated tasting notes end with "yummy."

Domaine Touche Noire, Chavagnes-les-Eaux: A serious Montreuil-Bellay grad, who has worked with Didier Dagueneau in Pouilly, Thierry Templai is out to make great wines. He seems to have hit his stride with his '90 Le Brochoire, a classic Layon that rings true from the first fine whiff to the succulent finish.

TASTED AND CONSIDERED

Domaine Gaudart, Chaudefonds-sur-Layon
Domaine Jean-Louis Robin, Chaudefonds-sur-Layon
Domaine Leduc-Frouin, Martigné-Briand
Domaine de la Motte, Rochefort-sur-Loire
Domaine des Maurières, Saint-Lambert-du-Lattay
Domaine du Sauveroy, Saint-Lambert-du-Lattay

IN TRANSITION

Château de la Guimonière, Beaulieu-sur-Layon, and *Domaine de la Roulerie,* Saint-Aubin-de-Luigné: Both recently purchased by Gaston Lenôtre. La Guimonière comprises seventeen hectares of prime Layon-Chaume; La Roulerie, until recently the *domaine* of Dominique Jaudeau, a grand seigneur of Chenin, has eight hectares of Les Aunis, a parcel of Chaume regarded as the peer of Quarts. Many restaurants carry old vintages of La Roulerie on their lists. Don't miss it.

SAVENNIERES

STATUS: *AOC 1952. There are two* crus, *Coulée de Serrant and La Roche aux Moines.*
TYPES OF WINE: *Dry and off-dry whites*
ZONE AND PRODUCTION: *Roughly 80 of a possible 343 hectares within three communes, producing an average of 2,976 hectoliters yearly*
GRAPES: *Chenin Blanc*
SOILS: *Shallow sandy topsoils covering schist with complex striations of volcanic rock (spilite and rhyolite) as well as sandstone and clay*
PRICE: *25 to 150ff*
BEST VINTAGES: (see *Layon*)

The sole Angevin vineyard north of the Loire, Savennières makes the ultimate dry Chenin Blanc. If Layon pushes the grape to its limits in its *moelleux* expression, Savennières takes it to the outer edges of dry.

It is, I think, the most cerebral wine in the world. When fully mature, it is breathtaking. All about majesty, the wine spreads across the palate like cream, revealing glimpses of flavor like an ever-changing landscape, a bale of hay, a whiff of chamomile, a basket of dried flowers, honey blended with quince and apricot or peach, the sting of citrus zests, a sonorous wave of minerals. Simultaneously taut and lyrical, bone-dry yet marrowy, it is a stroll along steep slate hillsides with Chenin. A wine of discovery, of reflection, Savennières is not for the uninitiated.

The style of Savennières has fluctuated, however. When it received its appellation, Savennières was demi-sec. When the *moelleux* market slumped in the '60s, Savennières found its vocation as a producer of extraordinary dry whites (which is the style of Savennières I prefer). Grapes in Savennières are always less ripe than those in the Layon. In great vintages they may reach 15 or 16 percent potential alcohol; across the river they shoot above 25 percent. Demi-sec is still made but accounts for about 10 percent of production. It can be a lovely, mellifluous wine, but the dry version can, and should, be monumental. As one vintner rightly said, "It's a wine you'll never finish discovering."

The archetypal Savennières proprietor is the *grand bourgeois* from Angers or Paris. The seigneurs of Serrant were followed by the Baron Brincard, the Jolys, the Bizards. Vines ornamented their country homes, the wines lubricated their dinners, and in theory, supported the lifestyle of the country squire. Usually, however, the squire found his recherché Savennières as costly and demanding as a *danseuse*. And winemaking, for the most part, was more or less competent.

This could be changing for the better, however, as an increasing number of top Layon producers cross the river to try their hands at Savennières. Since 1992 Jean and Florent Baumard have been joined by other rigorous professionals, among them Claude Papin, Pierre-Yves Tijou, and Claude Branchereau. Gaston Lenôtre now directs the Château du Chamboureau. And Eric Morgat, the son of the Château-du-Breuil Morgats, bought a small vineyard and will harvest his first Savennières in 1995.

⪻ PRODUCER RATINGS ⪼

OUTSTANDING
Domaine des Baumard

TO WATCH
Clos de Coulaine   Clos des Perrières

HIGHLY RECOMMENDED
Château d'Epiré   Domaine du Closel

RECOMMENDED
Clos des Maurières   Domaine de Laroche
Vignobles Laffourcade

OTHER
Clos de la Coulée de Serrant

⪻ ⪼

OUTSTANDING

Domaine des Baumard (Quarts):   The technical mastery and precise expression that distinguish Baumard's Quarts-de-Chaume separate his Savennières from a "family style," often marked by sulfur and quick, hot fermentations. For this he is indicted for making "technological" wines. Hogwash. Until 1992 Baumard was the only vintner consistently honoring the appellation.

I suspect that what sticks in the craw of so many of his naysayers is that Baumard's wines are unfailingly professional. However, some legitimate concerns have been raised. First, that Baumard makes Savennières to drink young. (To the extent that that's true, he's certainly not alone.) Second, that he would like to change the law to have the right to add Sauvignon Blanc or Chardonnay to his Chenin as producers do with Anjou blanc. Indeed, some say he's already done this and presented the wine under the Savennières label, which Baumard denies.

It is true that Jean Baumard makes Savennières that tastes good right away. Scrupulous protection against oxidation, low-temperature fermentation, and in high-acid years, malolactic fermentation, result in a young Savennières marked by vivacious fruit, a backdrop of minerals, and a bit of carbonic gas which Baumard leaves deliberately for its thirst-quenching zestiness. But his fresh, floral Savennières also ages beautifully.

I have sampled every vintage since '68 (his first in the appellation). Among these was a '75 Clos du Papillon so glorious it brought tears to my eyes. It is one of the six most memorable whites I've ever tasted. A fine weave of fleeting aromas and flavors, a whiff of menthol, then ginger, the mellow toast of the best oak (though it never saw a barrel), quinine, cranberries, and chamomile, and a long, sapid, citrus zest and mineral finish. It was fully evolved yet fresh as dew. It was Balanchine, Petipa. Nothing could better express the combination of lyricism and tensile strength, the sensuality underlying sheer intellect, the ethereal floating above a solid base. *Les Sylphides* in a glass. It was like nothing else in the world.

I'm sure Baumard's '88s, '89s, and '90s will be masterpieces in fifteen or twenty years. In both '89 and '90 the Clos de Saint-Yves, the generic bottling, was a beautiful knit of apple, Chenin, lemon zest, and Badoit-like minerals. There was a special *tri*, too, that was even better; everything you could ask for in a white. The Clos du Papillon, a vineyard whose soils make very distinctive wines, was equally magnificent, powerful and long, full of ripe fruit and minerals.

Papillon, often my favorite when Jean was in charge, continues to be, under Florent's stewardship. The lacy '93 should be magnificent, with its subtle blend of apricots and minerals and its fine structure.

TO WATCH

Clos de Coulaine, Savennières: François Roussier, the owner of Coulaine, is one of the great gentlemen of Anjou. His Cabernets were the most elegant in the region. But he wasn't known for his Savennières. When his cellar master retired, Roussier rented his vines to Claude Papin whose

'92s and '93s seem in keeping with Coulaine's light, floral-mineral style. I expect this will change as Papin begins to test the limits of this plot as he has done so brilliantly with his parcels in Layon. (The 1995 vintage may well reveal the direction. Papin has set aside one *cuvée* of Super-ripe Savennières—picked at a potential of 20 percent alcohol—to make a Séléction de Grains Nobles.)

Clos des Perrières (Layon): The excellent winemaker Pierre-Yves Tijou isn't a major Savennières player acreage-wise but his skills should catapult him to the top quality-wise. Very dry, very crisp, the '92 had clear peach and mineral flavors. The perfumed '91 was beautifully knit, floral and fresh. (I was not crazy about another version, which had gone through malolactic fermentation and was aging in barrel.) Both '89 and '90 are demi-sec and need time to show their stuff, but they are redolent of flowers, pears, and minerals. The '88 presented an exciting blend of fruit, fine structure, and elegant balance.

HIGHLY RECOMMENDED

Château d'Epiré, Savennières: This venerable *domaine* has been in the Bizard family for a century. Until 1990 the wines were made by Robert Daguin, who had a good way with old wood, and the nonfiltered *cuvées* that importer Kermit Lynch brought to the U.S. were lovely Savennières. (A mellow '88 was a subtle mix of bitter almonds, lemon, and quince, more complex than the normal bottling.)

Daguin was succeeded by his assistant, and the Bizards replaced a number of barrels with stainless steel tanks. Most of the Savennières ages in barrel, however. And Lynch still gets his nonfiltered *cuvée*. In '93 this was a curious wine, vaguely oxidized, with flavors of pineapple Lifesaver, among other things. I preferred the '94, with its basso profundo notes of anise and herbal tea. The regular bottling of '92 was lovely, a light but structured Savennières with delicate mineral and pear notes. The '91 was relatively concentrated, with fine balance and a long finish. The '90 sec was a personalized wine, rich and firm yet supple, with good grip and intense flavors, ending on a powerful bitter-lemon and licorice note. The '90 demi-sec was floral and creamy. An easier wine to get to know than the sec, it was well-rounded with a lavish mix of fruit.

Domaine du Closel, Savennières: Madame de Jessey is a large woman with a warm, imperious manner and a high, trilling voice that penetrates enormous rooms and vast expanses of vines. She inherited the Domaine du

Closel by way of her great-grandfather, Comte Las Cases, chamberlain of Napoléon Ier and the author of *Mémorial de Sainte-Hélène*. Under her direction Closel is moving away from traditional Savennières dilettantism toward something approaching professionalism. She has increased the acreage to fifteen hectares. She invested in stainless steel and fiberglass tanks. (Some wines, such as her Clos du Papillon, still ferment in barrel, others age in them.) There are usually four *cuvées,* including a Vieilles Vignes, the Papillon (which Mme. de Jessey describes as "*my* wine: When I like the way it tastes, I stop the fermentation") and a Cuvée Spéciale (a *sec-tendre*).

Many of the *domaine's* wines seem like diamonds in the rough. Such was the case with both the '93 Vieilles Vignes and the '94 Papillon. Each had a hint of oxidation and the very slight rasp of old wood, combined with fine aromas of distilled honey and exotic fruit and a strong undertow of chamomile. Papillon, often my favorite, offered delicate floral aromas in '91, with good underlying tension. A rich wine that combined power and freshness, the '90 displayed some old wood along with texture that epitomized Rabelais's *vin de taffeta,* as well as aromas of blossoms, honey, minerals, quince, quinine, and truffles—another diamond in the rough. Papillon was the most structured and complex of the *domaine's* '89s. The '88s are all nuanced and fairly elegant.

RECOMMENDED

***Clos des Maurières* (Coteaux du Layon):**   In 1988 the Rochais family released its first Savennières; it was light, lean, and steely. The '91 Cuvée Prestige was rather short and diffuse but had nice flavors of pear, quince, and minerals; '94 was beset by earthiness.

***Domaine de Laroche (Domaine aux Moines),* Savennières:**   In 1981 Mme. Laroche, a former pharmacist, bought this ten-hectare property, most of it in the *cru* La Roche aux Moines (the similarity of names is coincidental). She is a serious and able woman. One senses she wants to make the best Savennières she can but that she is by nature neither a risk-taker nor a visionary. So far her Savennières are competent but unexciting. They are Savennières for chic bistros.

***Vignobles Laffourcade* (Quarts-de-Chaume):**   "People in Savennières should learn to make wines that drink more easily," Pascal Laffourcade once said to me. Laffourcade rents seven hectares in Savennières and uses a variety of techniques (skin contact, barrel aging, malolactic fermentation) to make user-friendly versions. Since 1990 he has offered an old-vines, barrel-fermented Clos la Royauté. I found the '90 soft, tasting of milk chocolate. In general, these are Savennières for noisy brasseries.

OTHER

***Clos de la Coulée de Serrant,* Savennières:** At times the *terroir* speaks despite the vintner. And that is why you sometimes find a magnificent Coulée de Serrant made since 1976, when Nicolas Joly took over the direction of this phenomenal property.

The Jolys are the sole owners of the Coulée de Serrant, a seven-hectare vineyard so clearly blessed in exposition and soil it can only have been destined to make wine. The steep southwest-facing slope forms an amphitheater perpendicular to the Loire. It has been called the Yquem of Anjou. Curnonsky, Prince of Gastronomes, classed it as one of the five great white wines of France (along with Yquem, Le Montrachet, Château-Grillet, and Château-Châlon). The Jolys also have five hectares of La Roche aux Moines called the Clos de la Bergerie, which, to a Savennières lover, is a bit like having sole ownership of Le Montrachet plus a piece of Bâtard.

The *domaine* was purchased by Nicolas Joly's father, a Paris surgeon, in the 1960s. Mme. Denise Joly, who knew nothing about wine at the time, took the property in hand, turned it into a profit-making operation, and placed the wine in France's top restaurants. I tasted a Coulée de Serrant from her era, a '73, a goodish year. The wine took my breath away. All about breed and elegance, it spread across the palate like cream, with mingled flavors of wax, hay, toast, and oak. It was still fresh and lively, with an extraordinary expression of minerals.

Enter Nicolas: A self-styled firebrand, one senses he's a clever, restless malcontent; a born subversive. After earning an MBA at Columbia University, he worked for Morgan Guaranty on Wall Street and then in London, where he advised on investments in the chemical industry. After returning to the family vineyards he read a book on biodynamics. By 1985 he had converted the entire *domaine* to this system of holistic agriculture as laid out by Rudolf Steiner, the Austrian philosopher.

Biodynamics can sound New Age zany but it embodies a wealth of folk wisdom. Homeopathic vine treatments replace synthetic fertilizers, insecticides, and herbicides. Planting, pruning, and so forth are scheduled according to the positions of the planets. Farmers have always sown grain and vignerons bottled wine by phases of the moon. And while those traditions may have fallen into disuse, some impressive wine people (Lalou Bize-Leroy of Burgundy and the Huets of Vouvray, for example) are reclaiming them in biodynamics.

Joly can be a persuasive speaker on the subject, and despite gossip to the contrary, his vines appear in good shape. But when he inveighs against current winemaking practices he gets into trouble. When I asked him where he learned the craft—didn't he study at the University of Bordeaux with the revered enologist Ribéreau-Gayon?—he dismissed techniques of vinification as so much "tra-la-la."

Well, the proof is in the tasting. My overall impression of his three Savennières—Coulée de Serrant, Clos de la Bergerie (La Roche aux Moines), and Becherelle (a recent addition)—is one of tragic near and not-so-near misses. Always the *terroir* comes through. You sense the power, the distinction, the magnificence of this privileged site. And you sense what might have been. As with the '92s and the '91s, you perceive fabulous raw material in search of a vintner.

I think the problem is this: Nicolas Joly doesn't like wine. Biodynamics is not the problem. And the world has known many nuts and narcissists who've made brilliant wine. Joly is infatuated with biodynamics, but the love affair ends there. Wine, as you and I love it, doesn't interest him. If he ever makes a Coulée de Serrant that lives up to its potential, it will be by accident.

The '89 and '90 vintages of both the Coulée de Serrant and the Clos de la Bergerie were cases in point. Disappointing. It's depressing to taste what *is* and imagine what *might* have been: Coulée should rival Le Montrachet. The '90 Coulée de Serrant greeted me with a bouquet of industrial pollution (happily, it blew off), a rather oxidized color, and a hot statement of alcohol. But the natural power of the wine, the sap, the structure, spoke of its glorious *terroir*. And what fine streaks of minerals, of bitter lemon-lime, of bitter almonds! The '89 was even more oxidized. Also, despite the discreet flavors of almonds, minerals, wax, tilleul, and an appetizing saltiness, the wine seemed soft, diffuse, merely good, its virtues outweighing its flaws. The '89 Roches aux Moines had better grip and offered attractive flavors of apricot, ash, minerals, and menthol. A bit of carbonic gas remained, and there were candied notes in the finish. Not uninteresting. But 150ff?

Both '88s were cloudy when tasted in the fall of '89. The Coulée was a bit soft and short but had attractive, if muted, flavors of apples and almonds and that flintiness born of schist. The Bergerie displayed quince, minerals, nuts, and aggressive tartness against a flinty-steely finish. The '86 Coulée de Serrant seemed to be in an awkward adolescence when tasted in January '91, but one sensed the wine's massive power as well as its breed. There was something dirty in the nose but there were also lovely evolving Chenin notes, hints of pine, grapefruit zest, some old wood. The impression in the bouquet alone was of an opulent wine. On the palate it was almost viscous. The texture was impressively rich; the acid, still painfully high, was melding with flavors of minerals, barrels, wax, butterscotch, and quinine.

But these should be profound, commanding wines to come back to again and again and still feel that you've barely understood them. That's why I would give this land to Guy Bossard.

THE COTEAUX DE L'AUBANCE

STATUS: *AOC 1950*
TYPES OF WINE: *Off-dry or* moelleux *whites*
ZONE AND PRODUCTION: *Average 3,000 hectoliters, made from 88 out of a possible 1,051 hectares within ten communes at the southern tip of Angers*
GRAPES: *Chenin Blanc*
SOILS: *Slate*
PRICE: *40 to 150ff*
BEST VINTAGES: (see *Layon*)

My introduction to Coteaux de l'Aubance was a tasting for an agricultural fair in the village of Saint-Mélaine-sur-Aubance during my first week in Anjou. In wine regions, juried competitions precede such fairs; the winners are announced and prizes awarded in public ceremonies. Along with a local chef and a vintner from Bonnezeaux, I judged 1988 Coteaux de l'Aubance, a dozen or so, ranging from sulfured sugar water, through floral charmers, to a stunning wine that was clearly the best of the lot.

It was pure gold, with endless layers of honey, peach, apricot, and minerals. The chef and the vigneron admired it, too, but refused to place it first because it was "atypical," starting with that deep, burnished gold.

"Must be skin contact," sniffed one disdainfully. "More Sauternes than Aubance," the other concurred. "Typical" Aubance was supposed to be lighter in every respect. When I refused to budge from my gold-medal vote, we called over one of the tasting's organizers, a highly regarded young vigneron, Jean-Yves Lebreton, who said: "I know that wine. The deep color doesn't come from skin contact but from successive *tris*. It's one hundred percent botrytis." The wine had been made by his cousin, Victor Lebreton. It placed second, over my dissent: Atypical only in its extraordinariness, the wine was absolute proof of what Aubance *could* be—with rigor, talent, and a little help from Mother Nature.

The village of Saint-Mélaine-sur-Aubance is one of ten communes comprising the Coteaux de l'Aubance, an appellation whose vines form a pocket around the southern tip of Angers, to the east of the Coteaux du Layon. The appellation takes its name from a virtually unfindable river. Unlike the Coteaux du Layon, which is practically one continuous slope from Passavant to Chalonnes, the Coteaux de l'Aubance consists of many low hills. Its soils, composed of blue schist, have less of the clay that makes Layons so rich; its wines tend to be lighter, less alcoholic, and more "nervy." In great years, however, or when made by someone like Victor Lebreton, Aubance comes across as lush as any Layon.

Among the roughly thirty full-time producers in Aubance are some of the most exciting in Anjou: Victor Lebreton, Didier Richou, Jean-Yves Lebreton, and Christophe Daviau.

⫸ PRODUCER RATINGS ⫷

OUTSTANDING
Domaine de Montgilet   Domaine Richou

EXCELLENT
Domaine des Rochelles

TO WATCH
Domaine de Bablut

HIGHLY RECOMMENDED
Domaine de Haute Perche   Domaine de Rochambeau

BY THE GLASS
Château la Varière   Domaine de Prince

⫸ ⫷

OUTSTANDING

***Domaine de Montgilet*, Juigné-sur-Loire:** Victor Lebreton's Aubance is the new benchmark. A Montreuil-Bellay graduate, he took over the family winery in '84, doubled its acreage to twenty-four hectares, built new cellars (always immaculate), and filled them with stainless steel tanks and used Bordeaux barrels.

When I visited during the '89 harvest Victor led me out to the vineyards where a team of harvesters was picking his least ripe Chenin for Anjou blanc sec. There was an INAO inspector (and admirer) walking through the rows, tasting the shriveled grapes and occasionally testing one with his refractometer, a kind of thermometer that measures grape sugars. The super-concentrated Chenin sent the mercury above the instrument's limit of 21 percent potential alcohol.

Victor, who bears a strong resemblance to *Sesame Street*'s Big Bird, was sniffing the grape clusters for volatile acidity. He is painstaking and goes about his perfectionist way with constant good cheer. I have never seen him not working, and I have never seen him ill-tempered. Meticulous in the vineyards, meticulous in the winery, he pampers his twelve hectares of Coteaux de l'Aubance—removing bunches to leave four to seven clusters per vine, passing through the vineyards as many as five times a harvest, placing the grapes in small cases. For the most part the wines ferment in stainless steel, but Victor has recently begun some newish oak experiments. He makes at least two *cuvées* of Coteaux de l'Aubance. The two best are the Tête de Cave and the Cuvée Prestige, Lebreton's top wine.

The mind-blowing Aubance I tasted at the Saint-Mélaine competition was the Cuvée Prestige of 1988. The Tête de Cave, no slouch either, had rich floral and apricot notes. The '89 was lusher, and '90, 60 percent noble rot, was radiant. Unctuous and syrupy, the wine was balanced by a refreshing quinine bitterness with long flavors of honey, tilleul, lemon zest, and butterscotch.

Lebreton's nearly viscous '93 Cuvée Prestige Le Terteraux had opulent flavors of peach, apricot, and medicinal herbs—wonderful. The tender '92 Cuvée Prestige was a blend of pear, honey, and minerals, with a trace of earthiness. The '91 was lovely. It had 58 percent noble rot and was a crisp but honeyed and supple Aubance, accented with tilleul. And the '89 and '90 were staggering: the former, a profound compote of peach, quince, white currants, and quinine, napped with honey; the latter, 90 percent noble rot, pure velvet, layers of honey and toffee, lemon zest, pineapple—a masterpiece.

Domaine Richou, Mozé-sur-Louet: Archives in the town hall of nearby Denée trace Didier Richou's family as far back as 1550, when an ancestor furnished wine to the king—François Ier, perhaps, or Louis XIII. A gentle rebel in his thirties, Didier Richou (Montreuil-Bellay) succeeded his father on this thirty-seven-hectare estate in the 1980s. He is one of the most respected Young Turks in Anjou. You will never be disappointed by this *domaine*. Didier Richou doesn't know how to make bad wine.

Aubance is harvested in a series of *tris*, then vinified in barrel, 20 percent of which are new. The top wine is an old-vines bottling called Les Trois Demoiselles. The '94, despite a whiff of earthiness, was rich, textured, and honeyed, with light apple-skin flavors. Richou made only one *cuvée* of Aubance in '91. A harmonious, nervy, and delicate wine, it was an object lesson in what can be done in a less-than-monumental vintage. A heavily botrytized '90 Les Trois Demoiselles had potent aromas of apples and honey. The wine was so rich it overwhelmed the flavors of new oak—sheer pleasure, as were both *cuvées* of '88 and '89.

EXCELLENT

Domaine des Rochelles, Saint-Jean-des-Mauvrets: Vivacious and straightforward, often elegant, Aubance. The style is lighter than cousin Victor's, but the versions from Jean-Yves and Hubert Lebreton are beautifully made. As Didier Coutenceau is Hubert's son-in-law, the *domaine's* wines are always on the cutting edge. And the super *tri cuvée* of '90 rivals Victor's Cuvée Prestige of that year, a weave of apricots, ginger, honey, lemon zest, and licorice.

TO WATCH

Domaine de Bablut, Brissac-Quincé: The evolution of this important eighty-five-hectare estate may be one of the most thrilling in Anjou. Christophe Daviau, a University of Bordeaux graduate who studied with Denis Dubourdieu and worked as an enologist in Australia, is ambitious and exacting. He has grafted Chenin onto old Gamay vines (bringing in Mexican workers for the job); he experiments with methods of training and trellising; he thins clusters, passes through his Aubance vines at least three times (for his deluxe *cuvée*, his GN, he waits for botrytis); and he is drastically reducing the amount of sulfur in the finished wines.

Part of the harvest undergoes skin contact. The wines ferment in tank as well as in barrel (the *barriques* are both new and used, Nevers and Allier, with a range of toast levels). The size of the barrels and the slight aeration they afford, not the oak flavor, is what enchants Daviau. The wines ferment slowly and stop by themselves, thus minimizing the need for sulfur; barrel aging further diminishes the threat of refermentation, particularly for his botrytis-affected SGN. "All flavor, no headaches," he says.

A barrel sample of the '94 GN was one of the best *moelleux* I tasted from that vintage. The impressive '93 was a blanket of honey and oak; the more restrained '92 had accents of minerals and herbal tea.

Perhaps anyone could make super *moelleux* in '89 and '90, but versions as exquisite as Bablut's Vin Noble require hard work as well as craft. The '90, in particular, was so packed with lush fruit and honey that the oak influence was reduced to a whisper. Yet the wine showed breed and restraint. It was a *boulevardière*, Dietrich in white-tie and tails, with its satiny shimmer and its voluptuous flavors of white currants, honey, apricot, and peach nectar, and light nuances of toast, *crème brûlée*, and toffee.

HIGHLY RECOMMENDED

Domaine de Haute Perche, Saint-Mélaine-sur-Aubance: Christian Papin, a solid team player, seems to keep up with his teammates. His '90 was by far the best Aubance he's ever made—more focused, more concentrated than his erstwhile style of light, flowery, and peachy *moelleux*.

Domaine de Rochambeau, Soulaine: Maurice Forrest is becoming a very good practitioner, turning out a beguiling, perfumed Vieilles Vignes called Cuvée Mathilde de Rochambeau.

BY THE GLASS

Château la Varière, Vauchrétien: Jacques Beaujeau is known for his reds and his innovative dry Chenins. Aubance seems to get lost in the shuffle here.

Domaine de Prince, Saint-Mélaine-sur-Aubance: No revelations in the *moelleux* from this nineteen-hectare property. Alex Vaillant's Aubances are pleasant, supple with light honey and herbal notes. The Cuvée Vieilles Vignes often has good structure and good stuffing, though in difficult vintages it can seem confected.

ANJOU–COTEAUX DE LA LOIRE

STATUS: *AOC 1946*
TYPES OF WINE: *Off-dry and* moelleux *whites*

ZONE AND PRODUCTION: *Formed by an arc in the Loire, the zone covers 1,396 hectares between Ingrandes and Chalonnes, though only about 47 hectares produce the 1,500 hectoliters of wine made under this appellation.*
GRAPES: *Chenin Blanc*
SOILS: A *variety of schists*
PRICE: *20 to 40ff*
BEST VINTAGES: (see *Layon*)

This is where noble Chenin takes over from Muscadet and Gros Plant. Most of the Anjou repertory is produced here—which is why most of the zone is given over to grapes other than Chenin. Anjou–Coteaux de la Loire tends to be less *moelleux* than Layon and, in my experience, Aubance. And the wines seem less marked; they are gentler, less vivid.

Roughly a dozen vintners live off their wine. The best of them are former classmates who help each other, taste together, and share equipment.

❧ PRODUCER RATINGS ❧

HIGHLY RECOMMENDED
Château de Putille   Domaine du Fresche
Domaine Musset-Rouillier   Domaine de Putille

❧ ❧

Château de Putille, La Pommeraye: The best wine from this *domaine* is its Tri du Clos du Pirouet. The normal *cuvée* is full, fruity, and clean with engaging flavors of pineapple and grapefruit zest. But the Tri du Clos du Pirouet is richer, more elegant, and more complex.

Domaine du Fresche, La Pommeraye: After World War II Fortuné Boré and his brothers bought some thirty hectares of vines they had formerly rented or sharecropped. "We bought our own work. Why leave it to the neighbors?" said this aging dean of Coteaux de la Loire. "We refer to each *clos* by the profession of the person who owned it—the veterinarian, the doctor, the mayor."

Fortuné is a walking history of the region. He has kept a journal of the weather, his vineyard practices, and thoughts thereon, of every vintage of his life. When the next generation took over, however, the wines seemed to lack character and concentration. A stellar '92 and a sapid, tisane-scented '90, however, recall the lip-smacking '59 Fortuné opened for me. A reason for celebration.

Domaine Musset-Rouillier, La Pommeraye: Gilles Musset is the president of the appellation's *syndicat* and among its leading practitioners. In 1994 he joined forces with Serge Rouillier, another good producer, to work a shared twenty-nine hectares.

Their '94 Coteaux de la Loire was fresh, honeyed, and pleasing, despite minor earthiness. In the past, Musset put out some impressive special bottlings. His '90 Cuvée Antoine, for example, was a delicious blend of honey and chamomile. The '93 Tris Séléctionnés was, if anything, even more delectable.

Domaine de Putille, La Pommeraye: Pierre Sécher's Coteaux de la Loire comes from north-facing slopes with clay-rich soils. A thirtysomething graduate of Briacé, Sécher is a conscientious winemaker. He removes bunches, leaving only three clusters per vine. He harvests by *tri* and then lets the grapes undergo twenty-four hours of skin contact before fermenting at low temperatures. The '91 Tri was a bit thin—so was the vintage—but it was a pleasant wine, with scents of pear, apricot, and banana. Sécher's '89 and '90 Coteaux de la Loire were ample, pleasant, straightforward *moelleux*.

ANJOU BLANC ET ROUGE

STATUS: *AOC 1936 (revised 1957); Anjou-Villages, 1987 (revised 1991); Anjou-Gamay, 1957*

TYPES OF WINE: *Dry whites and reds; Villages, red only*

ZONE AND PRODUCTION: *An average of 182,260 hectoliters produced in 168 communes in the Maine-et-Loire, plus northern communes in Deux-Sèvres and Vienne. The average of 63,400 hectoliters of Anjou blanc is made on 1,260 hectares. The average of 98,230 hectoliters of Anjou rouge and Villages is made on 1,780 hectares (though the latter is limited to 56 communes). The average of 20,630 hectoliters of Anjou-Gamay is made on 370 hectares.*

GRAPES: *Whites—Chenin (minimum 80 percent), Chardonnay, Sauvignon (maximum 20 percent); reds—Cabernet Franc and Sauvignon. Pineau d'Aunis may be used in Anjou rouge; Gamay for Anjou-Gamay.*

SOILS: *Varied*

PRICE: *15 to 60ff (for a special* cuvée)

BEST VINTAGES: *(see* Layon)

Though less attention-grabbing than the rebirth of Anjou's great *moelleux,* the evolution of Anjou blanc as a refreshing, even characterful, white and of Anjou rouge and Anjou-Villages as exciting reds, represents some of the most significant and hard-won progress in Angevin viticulture.

Turning a recalcitrant, green Chenin into a charmer was no mean feat. It demanded every experiment in the book as well as the determination of Anjou's vignerons and the hands-on aid of enologists like Didier Coutenceau. Using techniques such as skin contact, barrel aging, extended lees contact, and malolactic fermentation, vintners now make crisp, floral Anjou blancs. Increasingly, they bottle Chenin pure. Some are beginning to turn out ringers for Savennières.

The wines are instantly likeable, with the vivacity that marks Loire wines combined with the fruit, body, and up-front charm that have made Chardonnay and Sauvignon Blanc worldwide best-sellers—all without banalizing their origins. In their professionalism, the wines seem UC–Davis. In their souls, they're Angevin. A number of producers also make lovely Sauvignon Blancs and Chardonnays, sold as Vins de Pays.

Red wine production is very new to Anjou. California has been making red wine in commercial quantities longer than Anjou has. In 1955, production of red wine amounted to only 1 percent of the region's output. When the rosé market began to decline, growers started vinifying reds from the grapes they had used for their sweet rosés—Cabernet d'Anjou and Rosé d'Anjou. During the 1970s and 1980s vintners learned the ABCs of red-winemaking. Now reds account for roughly 25 percent of overall production.

Designed to be drunk within three years of the harvest, Anjou rouge is a perfect wine-bar red, a fruity quaffer loaded with flavors of red berries. As one producer nicely put it, Anjou rouge is a wine to drink with your buddies.

Anjou-Villages is the region's most prestigious red. In theory, and increasingly in practice, it is a serious Cabernet, in the league of Champigny. Often it is made from a producer's oldest vines and vatting tends to last two weeks or more—compared with five or six days for Anjou rouge. By law, Anjou-Villages may not be sold until September following the harvest. Its production is limited to fifty-six communes, basically in the Layon, Savennières, the Coteaux de la Loire, and the Coteaux de l'Aubance. (Vintners in Aubance took an early lead in Anjou-Villages production. They are lobbying for, and are likely to get, a subappellation, Anjou-Villages-Brissac.)

Anjou-Villages does not taste like Champigny, however. The grapes are the same, though Angevins tend to use more Cabernet Sauvignon. Soils account for the fact that Anjou Cabernets seem chunkier, more foursquare and aggressive than their ineffably elegant cousins born of tuffeau. In comparison with a nuanced Champigny, Anjou-Villages often seems a plain-spoken red whose robust pleasures are best savored by its sixth birthday.

But enormous progress has been, and continues to be, made. (Indeed, it has become easier to find a serious, handcrafted Cabernet in Anjou than in the Saumurois or Touraine.) Anjou-Villages now ranges from silky, raspberry-scented charmers to tannic blockbusters with intense spice, blueberry, and black cherry flavors. Most at home as part of a French Sunday lunch or in an upscale bistro, Anjou-Villages is adaptable; it can handsomely accompany a three-star roast duck or hang loose with *steak-frites* in a café.

Anjou-Gamay is the third local appellation for red wines. Some are made like Beaujolais Nouveau, but the best are the regular bottlings, Gamays with surging fruit flavors, fine structure, and an enticing mineral backdrop. Grolleau completes the red wine picture. It is mainly used for rosé, but you occasionally find a red version sold as Vin de Pays. When made by Victor Lebreton—or by Gérard Dépardieu—it can be a tasty, gutsy, chillable light red, the kind you like to discover in a wine bar.

❧ PRODUCER RATINGS ❧

EXCELLENT
Château Pierre-Bise   Domaine de Montgilet   Domaine Ogereau
Domaine Richou   Domaine des Rochelles

TO WATCH
Patrick Baudoin   Château de Tigné
Domaine de Bablut   Domaine de l'Echalier   Domaine Jo Pithon
Domaine de la Sansonnière   Sechet-Carret

HIGHLY RECOMMENDED
Château du Breuil   Château de la Genaiserie
Château de Passavant
Château Soucherie   Château la Varière   Domaine de Brizé
Domaine de Haute Perche
Domaine de l'Homois   Domaine Philippe Delesvaux
Domaine de la Pierre Blanche   Domaine de Sainte-Anne
Domaine de la Victorie

RECOMMENDED
Château d'Epiré   Château de Fesles   Château de Putille
Château de Rochambeau   Château des Rochettes
Domaine des Baumard   Domaine Cady   Domaine du Closel

Domaine des Closserons   Domaine des Forges
Domaine du Fresche   Domaine des Hautes Ouches
Domaine Musset-Rouillier   Domaine du Petit Val
Domaine de Putille   Domaine de Touche Noire   Leduc-Frouin
Vignerons de la Noëlle   Vignobles Laffourcade

BY THE GLASS
Château Montbenault   Domaine Gaudart
Domaine des Maurières   Domaine de Sauveroy
Domaine des Soulaies   Domaine des Trahan

⋘ ⋙

EXCELLENT

Château Pierre-Bise (Layon):   Soil remains Claude Papin's obsession. His Anjou blancs generally come from La Haute de la Garde, a vineyard with soils like those of Savennières. The '92 was clear, fresh with powerful flavors of medicinal herbs. The supple '90 (20 percent barrel aged) was a compact weave of pineapple and oak with an undertow of minerals. Papin's '86 was one of the best Anjou blancs I've tasted. A vigorous thoroughbred, it was finer than many a Savennières.

Papin's tasty Gamay is marked by mineral, cherry, and kirsch. Three-quarters of his Anjou-Villages, predominantly Sauvignon, ages in used Bordeaux barrels. The '90 was fine-grained, with lovely structure and a hint of oak. But everyone's waiting to see what Papin will do with the reds at Clos de Coulaine. Under François Roussier, these were Anjou's benchmark Cabernets, long-stemmed beauties that proved graceful reds could be made in the region. Barrel samples of the '92, Papin's first vintage, were truly promising but too raw to call.

Domaine de Montgilet (Aubance):   Victor Lebreton makes over-the-top Cabernets. He says his model is Haut-Brion, but if anyone makes Latour-style Anjou-Villages, it's Victor. Bigger, bolder, more concentrated Cabernets don't exist in Anjou. My initiation was an '88 Villages, half each of Franc and Sauvignon. A tidal wave of purple fruit obliterated the chewy tannins.

When I visited during the '89 harvest, one lot of rich, tannic Cabernet was finishing its fermentation in used *barriques* from Château Margaux. (Lebreton likes the way wood rounds out the tannins and lets the wine evolve, and that particular *cuvée* remains a favorite of mine.) To keep "Loire fruit," the rest ferments in stainless steel tanks. During the two- to three-week vatting, Lebreton experimented with at least four methods of breaking up the fermenting cap.

I have tasted every vintage (and almost every *cuvée*) since '85. The '93 was a bit too brawny and gamy for me; the '92, too tannic (though it seems to be calming down). In other years the Lebreton tannins are balanced by plush black cherry fruit and spices. Recently, at a restaurant not far from Lebreton's cellars, I drank his non-oaked '89. A well-upholstered red with tons of plush fruit, it was sheer pleasure with grilled rabbit and salty fries.

Lebreton also makes manly Anjou rouge and charming Gamay and Grolleau. His Anjou blancs secs and his Sauvignons are always very good, if not in the same league as his Aubance and Cabernet.

Domaine Ogereau (Layon): Fruit intensity and fine winemaking characterize Ogereau's Anjou blancs and rouges. The creamy '93 Anjou blanc had pleasant oak notes; the potent '90 (15.3 percent alcohol) was truly tasty, its floral aromas supported by tight structure and a bitter-almond finish.

Ogereau's Anjou rouge has a short, four- to seven-day vatting and is mostly Cabernet Franc. Both '92 and '93, each silky and vibrant, charmed with *cassis* and blackberry flavors.

Anjou-Villages vats for ten to fifteen days and, when ripeness permits, Sauvignon accounts for as much as 80 percent of the assemblage. The velvety '93 and the fine-grained '92, each lightly tannic and vividly fruity, would make lovely lunch reds at an upscale bistro. The '90 was a powerful brew of violets, plum, and cherry covering abundant tannins. I could linger for a long while over the nose of his '89 Villages—a mix of black olives, violets, plum, licorice, Morello cherries, and black, ripe fruit.

Domaine Richou (Aubance): In blind tastings Didier Richou's Anjou blancs often beat Savennières. Some tasters hit the nail on the head, and say, "This could only be Richou." He doesn't do anything snazzy, but his Anjou blancs are excellent in bad vintages as well as in good—floral, structured, fruity, with lots of minerals.

In reds, Richou produces tender Gamays bursting with fruit, and exemplary Anjou rouge and Villages. The latter, Richou's most important red, comes from vines more than forty-five years old and is often pure Cabernet Franc. Firm structure and luxuriant black cherry fruit are its hallmarks. I often find my notes on Richou's Anjou-Villages repeating "supple and handsome, discreet but strong"—rather like Didier.

Domaine des Rochelles (Aubance): Hubert Lebreton is to Anjou rouge what Jean Boivin was to Bonnezeaux. He was instrumental in bringing about the Anjou rouge and Villages appellations; he was among the first to produce the wine and one of the first to master its production, from vine-yard to cellar.

"My father was probably the first to discover that this type of Cabernet could come from our schisty soils," Hubert's son Jean-Yves told me. "His first breakthrough was planting Cabernet Sauvignon on land that was very hot. People used to plant Cabernet Sauvignon on lowlands because, as it's a late ripener, it's less subject to frost. But it didn't ripen in those vineyards and was, consequently, very herbaceous, very green."

The *domaine*'s Cabernet Sauvignon vineyards are on slopes of decomposed schist, which Jean-Yves thinks accounts for their "typicity." They are, in his words, both lively and fleshy, with round—not drying—tannins as well as distinctive fruit character. Suppler than cousin Victor's, these are among Anjou's pleasantest "serious" Cabs.

The Lebretons make two types of Cabernet—one dominated by Sauvignon, the other by Franc. They're both heartily recommended but, when I review my notes, I find I systematically prefer the silky, surefooted, Sauvignon-based *cuvées*, with their vivid flavors of black cherry, strawberry, clove, cinnamon, and licorice, as well as a whisper of bell pepper.

TO WATCH

Patrick Baudoin (**Layon**):   For the moment, Baudoin's reds interest me more than his Layons. He harvests his Cabernet by hand, by *tri*. The grapes vat for eighteen days, and the fermenting must is both punched down and pumped over. The '94 Anjou rouge (mostly Cabernet Franc) had good, brambly fruit; the Villages (mostly Sauvignon) had intriguing fruit and fairly serious structure. The '93 Villages offered brambly fruit mixed with ivy and truffle flavors. It was a bit rough, but there was a lot to chew over.

Château de Tigné: "This is *red* wine country," insists the actor Gérard Dépardieu, an irresistible force, charging through *barrique*-lined *caves*, pipette in hand. We are still in the Layon, but Dépardieu wants to point out that his fifty hectares—at the juncture of the Paris Basin and the Massif Armoricain—have chalky, hot, pebbly soils, and Cabernet does better here than Chenin.

Dépardieu bought the Château de Tigné in 1989. He had been looking to buy vineyards in Anjou for some time. And he's got strong, Loire-leaning, vinous preferences: His favorite grapes are Chenin, Cabernet Franc, and the non-Ligerian Syrah. (Right on!) And he wants to make *real* wines. His cellar master, Dominique Polleau (the mayor of Tigné), explains the châtelain's philosophy thus: "It's not traditional vinification but vinification and viticulture to rediscover the grape and the land." In practical terms that means low yields, severe pruning, cluster thinning, hand harvest, partial (or no) destemming, a minimum of three weeks' vatting, followed by a year or two (or more) in *barriques* (of one wine, from Bordeaux or Burgundy). His top *cuvées*, made only in good years, are called Cyrano and Mozart; these come from Dépardieu's oldest vines on his best-exposed parcels. Cyrano is the more "generous" of the two; Mozart, made from pure Cabernet Franc, has more finesse.

Oak is the dominant feature, at least when they are young. But as the oak is good oak, the wines are tasty. Most of the Cabs I've tasted have been from barrel. Thus, a '90 Franc that was kirschy, oaky, a tad oxidized, and due for another year in wood; an opaque Cyrano '90 with potent kirsch flavors; a thick, tannic '90 Mozart that tasted like raspberry coulis.

I appreciate Dépardieu's decision to vinify grapes from his fifty-year-old Grolleau vines as a red. The '90 was a charmer with orange zest and kirsch flavors; just enough acid to make it appetizing and just enough tannins to give it oomph. An honest-to-God wine-bar red, a wine of memory and sentiment. I like his term for the wine, too, *vin de cave* (wine-cellar wine). And that may be where his wines—even Mozart and Cyrano—will always taste best, mixed with the mushroomy, dank cellar smells. The wines, so far, are like the châtelain: in a class by themselves.

Domaine de Bablut (Aubance): Christophe Daviau's experiments with Anjou blanc have wrought some stunning successes. His '90, with its green-apple and *eau-de-vie* notes nicely melded with oak, seemed a perfect example of New World technology building on an Angevin base. Daviau also offers brisk Sauvignons and crisp, fruity Chardonnays.

I had always liked the *domaine*'s reds—more or less. While the evolution hasn't been as dramatic as it has been with the *domaine*'s whites, it is real and satisfying. The latest vintages tasted—'91 and '90—were suave, silky Anjou-Villages, with warm flavors of black cherries and plums.

The Daviaus also make two types of Gamay—a *primeur* and an Anjou-Gamay—and they make the wines of the Château de Brissac.

Domaine de l'Echalier (Layon): Lorent-Bureau's first vintage of Anjou-Villages, '90, was mighty impressive. First, the wine was elegant; it was also inviting, with flavors of plums, black cherries, and black olives. Soft without being flabby, it recalled a good Bordeaux while retaining its Loire fruit. The *domaine*'s Anjou-Villages have fit that profile ever since. (The '93 is particularly tasty.) Not to be overlooked, either, are the *domaine*'s exuberant Anjou-Gamays or its vivacious, well-defined Anjou blancs and Sauvignons.

Domaine Jo Pithon (Layon): Anjou blanc is an afterthought, for the moment, but I think Pithon will eventually do something interesting with his dry whites. The very ripe, barrel-fermented '93 didn't have a lot to say, but I expect that will change.

Domaine de la Sansonnière (Bonnezeaux): One cuvée of Mark Angeli's '92 Anjou blanc reminded me of the Domaine de la Taille aux Loup's terrific Montlouis. Fermented in barrel, it was fine, textured, haunting. A simpler '92, a blend of Chenin and Sauvignon with no wood age, was fruity and uncomplicated. Then there was a fragrant cuvée of '91. A blend of Grolleau Gris and Sauvignon, it was not the legal Anjou blanc mix but it was fresh and lovely, with flavors of apricots, blossoms, and bitter almonds.

Frankly, I did not love any of Angeli's dry wines in '94—too much earthiness in the whites and Gamays and a bit of acetic acid in the Cabernet. But I was very fond of his honest, wonderful '93 Gamay (20 hectoliters per hectare). And several vintages of his unfiltered Anjou-Villages have been extraordinary. Both '91 and '92 are delicious, and the '90 Cuvée Martial is phenomenal, an avalanche of dark red fruit, mingled with oak and tannin—massive, fine, and elegant.

Sechet-Carret (Layon): This domaine made its first Anjou-Villages in 1989. Oh la la! What a nose! The Martha's Vineyard of Anjou. Pure eucalyptus mixed with berries and cassis, a Rhône-like intensity, lush fruit, fine structure, and minerals. The '90 Villages, rawer and more tannic, needs two more years ('98). The '93 was good, though somewhat vegetal and foursquare. Anjou blancs, regrettably, are an afterthought. The wines reveal raw material potentially as fascinating as Savennières. An optimistic nature says "To Watch."

HIGHLY RECOMMENDED

Château du Breuil (Layon): Cool, clean Vins de Pays in four flavors: Pinot Blanc, Sauvignon Blanc, Chardonnay, and Gris Fumé; also, aromatic Gamays. The '94 Anjou blanc was tart and lively; the Anjou rouge, light but nicely focused, with cheerful fruit and bell pepper flavors. The '93 Anjou-Villages was supple and perfumed.

Château de la Genaiserie (Layon): Yves Soulez's barrel-fermented '93 Anjou blanc was a discreet, textured wine with peach and mineral flavors. Lovely. His '93 Anjou rouge, with its dark, jammy fruit, would be a great find in a wine bar.

Château de Passavant (Layon): Adapting techniques like skin contact and malolactic fermentation, the Davids turn out reliably good Anjou blancs. A '91 was floral and sprightly, with good structure and pleasant Chenin-apple-pineapple notes. Reds are equally rational, friendly Cabernet Francs. The '91 Anjou rouge offered soft black cherry and cherry pit flavors and lively acidity. The '93 and the '90 Villages were warmly fruity and generous.

Château Soucherie (Layon): Tijou's '88 Anjou blanc had the punch of a Sauvignon Blanc and the discretion of well-bred Chenin. His '87 was one of the finest Anjou blancs I've tasted. Harvested on November 18, it was explosively fragrant, fresh, regal, and steely with immense tensile strength and sinuous flavors of *eau-de-vie*. I wish he'd make one every year. Tijou also offers a flavory Anjou rouge.

Château la Varière (Aubance): One of the first vintners to collaborate with Didier Coutenceau, Jacques Beaujeau makes dry Chenins that might appeal to Americans hooked on Chardonnay. Using skin contact, barrel fermentation, malolactic fermentation, and so forth, Beaujeau makes supple, creamy Anjou blancs with pleasant fruit, and suggestions of oak.

Beaujeau has also mastered the art of rounding off the hard edges of Anjou Cabernet. Still on the rustic side but usually successful, the reds are characterized by warm, accessible fruit mixed with bell peppers and mint.

Domaine de Brizé (Layon): My introduction to the Delhumeaus' wines was an '88 Gamay. There are stars all over that notebook entry, along with some babble about the wine's surprising grandeur and its succulent fruit (a ringer for Cab Franc, with cherry pit, black cherry, and plum flavors). The '90 was every bit as luscious—really lovely fruit, black cherries, cherry pits, violets, orange zest. These Gamays are the result of low yields and both carbonic maceration and a week of traditional vatting.

Cabernet vats for two weeks. The best, a Villages called Clos Médecin, is made only in good vintages and is not released for two years. I admire these wines more than I love them; they tend to toughen up. A '90 Clos Médecin was extracty, rugged, and tannic, with flavors of tar and violets. But it was suppler than the tarry '89 which was profoundly flavored with blueberries, mint, *cassis*, and brawny tannins. In this sense, Delhumeau should be in the "To Watch" category. Luc Delhumeau is not yet satisfied. He knows he can do more. Someday (and soon, I think) that Clos Médecin will be as glorious as the *domaine*'s Gamays. Then, Domaine de Brizé moves to "Outstanding."

Domaine de Haute Perche (Aubance): Papin's Cabernets seem to be meeting the challenge presented by the Cabs of young winemakers like Victor Lebreton. The '90 Villages (the pure Sauvignon *cuvée*) was the best red I've tasted from this winery. It was warm and ripe, with rich plum, prune, tar, and tobacco. The '91 was no slouch, either, but a bit sharp—the vintage *oblige*. Papin also makes spirited Gamays, and his Anjou blanc is clean, correct, and up-to-the-minute (thanks to Didier Coutenceau).

Domaine de l'Homois, Saint-Jean-de-Mauvrets: Shy, low-key Alain Moget tends to get overlooked—except by wine juries who frequently single out his extremely pretty Cabernets for awards. At the limit of the Massif Armoricain, the *domaine's* clay-chalk soils contribute to the suppleness and elegance characteristic of Moget's reds. Both his '89 and '90 Villages had intense aromas of crushed raspberries, to which the '89 added *crème de framboise* as well as black olives. Moget also makes a winsome floral Gamay.

Domaine Philippe Delesvaux (Layon): At their best (a juicy '91, a generous '90, and a lush '89), Delesvaux's Cabs seem a cross between an elegant Champigny and a macho, Victor Lebreton Villages. A thinking woman's jock. Less ravishing versions, such as a flat '92 and a light '93, are still pleasant drinking. The whites aren't bad either. The '93, which had gone through malolactic fermentation, was supple and mineral-rich.

Domaine de la Pierre Blanche (Layon): One of my favorite Anjou blancs was Lecointre's '88. Picked during his last pass through the vineyards, it had rich perfumes of pear and quince, the tight taffeta texture of Chenin, and a beautifully long finish of fruit and minerals. I wish he'd make it every year, but even when he doesn't, his Anjou blancs are fresh and fruity. (His supple '93 would make a nice house Chenin.) Lecointre also makes crisp Chardonnays and vivacious Sauvignons, hard and dry with a fine thread of minerals.

His structured '88 Gamay was vibrant with suggestions of mint, spices, and tannin. The '91 was less vivid, but it is a cute wine-bar red. The '90 Anjou rouge was a bit short, but an alluring bistro Cab with attractive plum and black cherry flavors. I preferred it to his Villages, Château la Tomaze, a prettyish sort of weak soprano in a full-throated mezzo of a vintage.

Domaine de Sainte-Anne, Brissac-Quincé: The Braults produce generous Cabernets. Two *cuvées* of '90—one a blend of Sauvignon and Franc, the other pure Franc—were "walk right in, sit right down" reds, with warm, ripe fruit. Even in light years, the Braults turn out bighearted Cabernets.

Domaine de la Victorie, Cersay: The Thoreaus are passionate about wine, in general, and about the expression of Chenin on the unique soils of the Thouars area, in particular. They pamper their Vieilles Vignes bottling of Chenin: It's hand harvested, by *tri*, and ferments in new oak barrels. An admirable blend of apple *eau-de-vie* and pears, it seems as noble and tasty as

Chenin from this region can ever be. I prefer the Thoreaus' Anjou rouge and Villages, however. Chiefly Cabernet Franc, the latter vats for three weeks in stainless steel tanks and ages in used Bordeaux barrels. The several *cuvées* of '93 were all impressive; the '90 La Treille (from chalky soils) was plushy, fruity, and bright. Delicious.

RECOMMENDED

Château d'Epiré (Savennières): Clos de la Cerisaie is the *domaine's* appetizing Anjou rouge, a lean, mouth-watering red.

Château de Fesles (Bonnezeaux): Gaston Lenôtre's greatest vinous success to date is his '92 Vielles Vignes Anjou rouge. A supple Cabernet with soft fruit and a hint of bell peppers, it won the Guide Hachette's *coup de coeur* as well as a gold medal at the Salon des Vins de Loire.

Château de Putille (Coteaux de la Loire): Relatively high percentages of Cabernet Sauvignon, vatting of a week for Anjou rouge and nearly two weeks for Villages, and 5 percent press wine (aged in oak) blended back into the final assemblage make for flavory reds with good structure and pleasant mineral undertones (though I often prefer the suppler Anjou rouge to the denser, more tannic Villages). Also, attractive Sauvignon Blancs and very good Anjou blancs (Chenin vinified on the lees of Sauvignon Blanc).

Château de Rochambeau (Aubance): Pleasant reds for satisfying near-term drinking, particularly the '90 Villages, with black cherry, plum, and *cassis*, and soft tannins.

Château des Rochettes (Layon): Anjou blancs for Chenin converts—floral, with flavors of pineapple and quince supported by a framework of steel. The satisfying Anjou rouges are good lunch reds.

Domaine des Baumard (Quarts-de-Chaume): Fruity Chardonnays and light Cabernets to drink up.

Domaine Cady (Layon): The Anjou-Villages, packed with plum, black cherry, and black olive flavors, are a bit "easy come, easy go," but nice, friendly reds, among the few Loire Cabs I'd pair with osso buco or polenta with sausages.

Domaine du Closel (Savennières): Attractive, medium-bodied Villages.

Domaine des Closserons (Layon): Solid, creamy Anjou blancs with big, Broadway flavors.

Domaine des Forges (Layon): Crisp, green-beany Sauvignon Blancs; light, appley Chardonnays; fragrant, steely Anjou blancs. User-friendly

Anjou rouge to drink with friends, and florid Villages packed with *cassis* and blueberry fruit. (The '94 Anjou rouge was particularly amiable.)

Domaine du Fresche (Coteaux de la Loire):   Chewy, satisfying wine-bar reds.

Domaine des Hautes Ouches, Brigné-sur-Layon: The Lhumeaus are red wine specialists, offering punchy, vivid Cabernets characterized by kirsch, black cherry, mint, and bacon flavors. The '93 and '92 both seemed coarse and confected, but the '90 and the intense '89 were very good. An '86 was lovely with bacon-, herb-, and garlic-scented wild rabbit in a local restaurant.

Domaine Musset-Rouillier (Coteaux de la Loire):   Good work behind that bunch-selected '93 Anjou blanc; it was firm, creamy, and textured. The Anjou-Villages Clos de Rinières is a dark, dense Cab.

Domaine du Petit Val (Bonnezeaux):   Appley Chardonnays; supple yet crisp Anjou blanc; increasingly pretty Cabernets and Gamays.

Domaine de Putille (Coteaux de la Loire):   Pierre Sécher makes fragrant, firm Anjou blancs, delicate despite high alcohol; chewy, tannic Anjou rouges with a solid backdrop of berry fruit.

Domaine de Touche Noire (Layon):   Tart, appley Chardonnays; herbaceous, nicely structured Sauvignons; tannic, brawny Anjous from a serious young vigneron whose wines seem to get better every year.

Leduc-Frouin (Layon):   Tart, peachy Anjou blanc secs; pleasant Gamays; rustic, generous Anjou-Villages with vivid plum, blackberry, bell pepper, and mint flavors.

Vignerons de la Noëlle, Ancenis: In a better world the sturdy Anjou rouge and Villages from this co-op would be the carafe red in every café in the region.

Vignobles Laffourcade (Quarts-de-Chaume):   The Château Perray Jouannet, in the Chavagnes-les-Eaux area, is where Laffourcade makes all of his wines. Its vineyards produce the *domaine*'s Anjou rouge and Villages. For the most part, these are beefy, bistro reds; one-dimensional but otherwise agreeable.

BY THE GLASS

Château Montbenault (Layon):   Once again, it's hit-or-miss. The '94s and '92s are discouraging, but there's a firm, graceful '91 Anjou-Villages.

Domaine Gaudart (Layon):   Bland Anjou blanc; competent, easygoing reds.

Domaine des Maurières (Layon): Light, floral, flinty whites, tart Gamays, and tannic Cabernets in search of pâtés and cheeses to soften rough edges.

Domaine de Sauveroy, Saint-Lambert-du-Lattay: Neutral, hard Anjou blancs. The tannic, chewy reds, certain *cuvées* of which win medals, show improvement, particularly the plush '90 Villages that came before me on a jury.

Domaine des Soulaies (Layon): Crisp Sauvignon Blanc.

Domaine des Trahan, Cersay: In the northern reaches of the Deux-Sèvres, this family winery produces fragrant, simple Anjou blancs, Sauvignons (Vin de Pays), and modest *moelleux* with pretty flavors of pineapple and herbal tea.

THE WINES OF SAUMUR

Saumur straddles the Loire forty-five kilometers southeast of Angers. Its stern castle commands a high hill, and rows of houses descend in bands under it, ending at a tree-lined quay. The landscape seems unchanged since it was depicted in *Les Très Riches Heures du Duc de Berry*, a fifteenth-century illuminated manuscript.

Known today for its elite school of cavalry, its mushrooms, and its wine, Saumur was the subject of conflicts between the counts of Blois and those of Anjou in the eleventh century and was a center of Protestantism in the seventeenth century. Saumur has always been as vigorous a wine center as Angers. (It is here that Balzac's miserly Père Grandet, a wine broker, cheated his fellow Saumurois while cutting a deal with Dutch exporters.)

Saumur's vines form a crescent south of the Loire. The grape varieties are the same as in Anjou; the appellations are similar. But the wines are quite different. Near Gennes the sedimentary soils of the Paris Basin take over from the schists of the Massif Armoricain, marking the start of archetypal Loire. It is a sweet landscape of vast clouds and slow streams, of fairytale castles and priories all made of tuffeau, the creamy stone that is as central to our image of the Loire as its soft skies. Tuffeau was quarried for the region's homes as well as for its châteaux. The excavations left caves which were converted into dwellings or into mushroom or wine cellars. They pock the cliffsides between Saumur and Montsoreau as well as between Tours and Vouvray. The plateaus above them are prime vineyard land.

Wines from tuffeau are suave compared with earnest Anjous. Even in very good years Chenin is likely to be demi-sec, not *moelleux*. Reds are lissome, more carefree. And while sparkling wine seems an afterthought in Anjou's wine scheme, it is key to Saumur's.

Until World War II, Chenin was king. Its great *crus* were similar to Vouvray. Tasting old bottles, one can't but regret that Chenin has largely been replaced by red varieties, now 60 percent of Saumur's acreage.

That said, the harvest bins are full of purple fruit in *Les Très Riches Heures*. Menus from the 1950s list vintage Champigny. Within the past fifteen years, Champigny has become the image of Saumur.

SAUMUR-CHAMPIGNY

STATUS: *AOC 1957*

TYPES OF WINE: *Reds*

ZONE AND PRODUCTION: *An average of 70,000 hectoliters made on 1,000 hectares within nine communes that form a rough triangle between Saumur, Montsoreau, and Saint-Cyr-en-Bourg. The other communes are Dampierre-sur-Loire, Turquant, Parnay, Chacé, Varrains, and Souzay in which lies the lieu dit Champigny.*

GRAPES: *Cabernet Franc and Sauvignon; also Pineau d'Aunis*

SOILS: *Tuffeau covered by a shallow topsoil of sand and gravel; soils may be layered with differing percentages of clay and silex.*

PRICE: *25 to 50ff, or more*

BEST VINTAGES: *'95, '93, '90, '89, '88, '86, '85, '76*

Saumur-Champigny burst onto the wine scene in the late 1970s, becoming the darling of the Paris wine bar, the ideal wine to serve with the new cooking. A succulent Cabernet that benefits from light chilling, Champigny is relatively low in alcohol and relatively high in acidity. It is mellow yet vivacious, with incredible fruit intensity as well as personality—Loire wine in a nutshell.

Two people can be credited for Champigny's celebrity. The first is *le père* Cristal (1837–1931), who created an eponymous *clos* in Champigny (a *lieu dit* in the commune of Souzay) and whose Saumur whites and reds were loved by Clemenceau and Edward VII. The second is Paul Filliatreau, who, in 1978, shocked his neighbors by introducing a new style of Champigny. The wine, fermented in stainless steel tanks rather than old barrels, and in an aluminum-siding *chais* rather than in tuffeau caves, was brisk, fresh, and as thirst-quenching as Beaujolais. It swept awards in Paris and sold like proverbial hot-cakes. Filliatreau's neighbors followed suit: Volume has increased tenfold.

Easy-drinking Champigny is still the prevailing style, though, not surprisingly, the pendulum has begun to swing the other way. Winemakers (including Filliatreau) increasingly offer at least two versions, a light "young-vines" and a more serious bottling. In general, beefier Champignys come from vineyards on the cliff facing the Loire, where soils are chalk covered with alluvial silt; silkier ones, from soils of sand, clay, and gravel, come from communes farther from the river (though one finds enough exceptions to swallow this rule). And while there's something of a trend to make Champignys that can age for ten years or more, most should be drunk within five. To date, only the Foucault brothers' Champignys improve after that.

This may change, however. Champigny's success brought abuses of overproduction as well as slipshod vinifications. With rare exception Champignys could be nobler. But the appellation is young, and it's evolving quickly. A flat market has many vintners turning to a revolutionary concept—quality—as a selling point. As I write this, in the summer of 1995, I have just spoken with Pascal Cellier, the director of the INAO in Anjou, who has been carrying out on-the-spot inspections in Champigny's vineyards. When he sees too heavy a charge of grapes on vines, he delivers this ultimatum: Remove clusters (to lower yields) or face declassification of the wines. And even now, despite all the work that needs to be done, the wines are mighty tasty.

⇜ PRODUCER RATINGS ⇝

OUTSTANDING
Clos Rougéard

LEADER
Domaine Filliatreau

TO WATCH
Château de Villeneuve   Domaine des Roches Neuves

HIGHLY RECOMMENDED
Cave des Vignerons de Saumur
Château du Hureau
Château de Targé   Domaine Saint-Vincent   Domaine de Nerleux
Michel et Jean-Claude Dubois
Lavigne Père et Fils   René-Noël Legrand

RECOMMENDED
Daheuiller Père et Fils   Domaine des Bonnevaux
Domaine des Galmoises
Domaine du Val Brun   Domaine du Vieux Bourg
Gérard et Yves Drouineau

TASTED AND CONSIDERED
Château de Chaintres   Clos des Cordeliers   Hospices de Saumur

⊲⊱⊷ ⊲⊱⊷

OUTSTANDING

Clos Rougéard, Chacé: As the credits roll in *Champigny! the Western*, the mustachioed Foucault brothers swagger off into the sunset having whupped the High-Yield Gang and chased the *négociants* out of town.

Rigorously original, Jean-Louis and Bernard Foucault make a virtue of iconoclasm. They make wine the way their great-granddaddy did. They replant with mass selection, not industrial clones; they hand harvest; they don't add yeasts; they foot-stomp the fermenting grapes to break up the cap; they age the wines in *barriques*—either new or used (from top Bordeaux châteaux)—for eighteen months to two years. The wines are not filtered, though they may be fined with egg whites. The results are mostly magnificent, though some are over-oaked and a few have been ever-so-slightly volatile. Whatever: They are must-taste Champignys. Always fine of grain, clear as a bell, complex, and mouth-watering.

From their eight hectares of vines, the Foucaults bottle three versions of Champigny. The first, assembled from diverse parcels, is Clos Rougéard (a proprietary name registered by *grandpère* in 1904). Les Poyeux (a 2.7-hectare plot with chalky soils) and Le Bourg (a hectare of old vines grown on the tuffeau soils of a *clos* behind the cellar) are the two single-vineyard bottlings. Le Bourg ages in new oak barrels; Les Poyeux in used Bordeaux *barriques*.

The Foucaults lost 60 percent of the '94 crop to spring frosts, but what remained was harvested at 10.5 to 12 percent potential alcohol. Some find them over-oaked. I place them among the Loire's triumphs in '94. Les Poyeux was svelte and harmonious, tasting of cranberries and minerals. Le Bourg was tighter, with more stuffing as well as accents of vanilla and black cherry.

Both '93s, again tasted from barrel in the summer of 1995, fit the family image, with Le Bourg, of course, the deeper of the two. Classic, in the best sense of the word, they expressed every beautiful aspect of Loire Breton—

from its sapid fruit, through its sweet spiciness, to its hints of musk and sandalwood.

The '92 Les Poyeux, while not as resplendent as the '93 or '94, was lovely.
And frost wiped out the '91 harvest. But with '89 and '90 I get to "how many
angels on the head of a pin" ruminations. All the wines are phenomenal. But
my two favorites are the '89 Les Poyeux and the '90 Le Bourg. After trotting
out many adjectives to describe the former, I finally noted: "It's the sum-
mum." Of the plush weave of fruit and oak and caramel and coffee and spices
and dried fruit that is the '90 Le Bourg, I just wrote: "WOW!"

Many Loire restaurants carry older vintages of the Foucaults' wines, like
the subtle, gorgeous '88; the sumptuous, nuanced '86, and the smoky, well-
structured '85.

LEADER

Domaine Filliatreau, Chaintres: Like it or lump it, Paul Filliatreau
reinvented Champigny in the style of red he loved, a fresh quaffing wine
with plenty of fruit. He was the first in Champigny to bottle separate *cuvées*
of old and young vines. He built Saumur's first modern *chai*, which he filled
with stainless steel tanks with chilling systems and punching-down devices.
The wines are generally excellent (some are better), and anyone wanting a
quick introduction to Champigny should taste here.

Filliatreau works fifty hectares, including Château Fouquet, a generic
Saumur which is discussed here, and La Vignolle, above the troglodyte
dwellings in Turquant. (He also restored the derelict caves, which now
include a restaurant and a tasting room.) All *domaine* wines are hand
harvested. Filliatreau never adds yeasts. Vatting lasts ten to twelve days at
cool temperatures. The five Champigny bottlings are Jeunes Vignes (ten- to
fifteen-year-old vines); Vieilles Vignes; La Grande Vignolle; a *primeur*; and
Lena Filliatreau, from purchased grapes, which has always been my least
favorite.

Jeunes Vignes is quintessential Filliatreau, generally lively and bursting
with berry, plum, and cherry flavors. Even the '94 was pretty, with attractive
cherry pit notes. The '90 La Grande Vignolle was a mouth-filling wine, with
breed galore as well as lush fruit and a fine mineral undertow. The '94
Vieilles Vignes, from pure tuffeau, was supple and pretty, with vivid cherry
pit flavors, and in spring '95, was showing better than the bigger, harder '93,
which will need several years. The '90 is an elegant Champigny with notes
of *cassis* and eucalyptus.

Filliatreau aged part of his best '89 in barrels from Château Margaux. He prefers the non-oaked *cuvée*. I like the oaked; barrel age seems to have reduced the wine's baby fat. Both, however, are velvet blankets of plum, black cherries, and cherry pits. Fine and elegant, they recall the Chinons of Bernard Baudry.

Château Fouquet, on a superb hillside in Brézé, is generic Saumur but is often as fine as Filliatreau's finest Champigny. (The '90 is a perfect example.) Even the '94 was a lovely red, with pretty cherry pit flavors. The '93 was meatier and more tannic. Both won gold medals in Paris.

TO WATCH

Château de Villeneuve, Souzay-Champigny: Jean-Pierre Chevallier, an enologist and the president of the ITV for the Maine-et-Loire, succeeded his father on the family *domaine* in 1990, though he'd been assisting since 1982. Wines from this property had always been good—particularly the singular, often breathtaking whites—but they are in the process of getting a lot better.

Chevallier, as committed to making great wine as any of Anjou's artist-vignerons, started making three types of Champigny in 1993. Low-yielding old vines from the *lieu dit* Le Grand Clos produce his deluxe red, which ages in newish barrels and is bottled unfiltered. The '93, still in barrel in September '95, was oakier and slightly more concentrated than the '93 Vieilles Vignes. The latter was gorgeous. Surehanded, intelligent, and focused, it was a blanket of black cherry, Morello cherry, and plum. Outstanding.

Previous vintages worth tasting, while not on the level of the '93, include the plummy '91; the black cherry– and black olive–flavored '90 Vieilles Vignes; and an opulent '89 with a strong mineral undertow.

Domaine des Roches Neuves, Varrains: Thierry Germain, a young Bordelais, came to Saumur in 1991 to make great wine. He is already making very good wine, including a supple '94 Jeunes Vignes with pretty cherry pit flavors; a tasty '93 Vieilles Vignes Terre Chaude, a plush red with a firm backbone; and a discreet, fluid '92 Vieilles Vignes. The 1990 Cuvée Marginale, a barrel-aged blockbuster by the *domaine's* former owner, Denis Duveau, is still on many French wine lists. It is worth tasting, if you like oak.

HIGHLY RECOMFMENDED

Cave des Vignerons de Saumur, Saint-Cyr-en-Bourg: "Born of misery and despair," the cooperative was created in the 1950s by several local vignerons. Today, it produces 30 percent of Saumur's wine. Its 260 members must bring 70 percent of their harvest. Champigny accounts for 27 percent of production. There are four *cuvées* and they always represent good value for the dollar. You won't see stars, but you'll get a good picture of good Champigny. Even the '94s were pleasant.

Château du Hureau, Dampierre-sur-Loire: An agronomist by training, Philippe Vatan is a hardworking, unsentimental pro who says, "I want to make the best wine possible but I'm not bitten by the wine bug." He offers a normal and an old-vines *cuvée* and often an experimental one, either pure Cabernet Sauvignon or wine aged in used Bordeaux barrels. His "normal" '94 was among the three or four best Champignys I tasted from that vintage, brambly and full of focused cherry pit flavors. The jammy '93s were pretty and supple; the '92s were minty and fluid; his '90s were pungent with berry and tar flavors; and the '89s were intensely fruity, with *cassis*, black cherry, and cherry pit flavors finishing on an appetizing bitter-almond note.

Château de Targé, Parnay: "People say I'm one of the most Chinonais of Champigny," said Edouard Pisani-Ferry, meaning that his Champignys tend to be powerful, tannic, and long-lived—and that he likes them that way. A Montpellier graduate, the son of the minister of agriculture for both De Gaulle and Pompidou and the owner of Targé's nine hectares, Pisani explains: "My vatting is relatively long [twelve to fifteen days] and I often age the wine in oak. Targé has a hard attack [that] softens within months. This is Targé," he continued, indicating the '89 we were tasting.

It had lovely cherry fruit, elegant structure, and a fine mineral finish, but it needed to shed its abundant tannins. The '90 and '93, too, will want time to integrate the tannins with the fruit and spice flavors. And they are the three vintages of Targé that seem the most likely to evolve well. Other years come off as blunt but honorable.

Domaine Saint-Vincent, Saumur: Young Patrick Vadé (Montreuil-Bellay) wins lots of awards for his Champignys. Vintages as different as '94 and '89 demonstrate Vadé in his award-winning mode: plush plum and cherry fruit and heady floral aromas; charming wines for elegant lunches. Other versions—a '90 Les Adrialys, a '91 Les Trézellières—were too bell-peppery for my taste, and too rough. I suspect Vadé can do better.

Domaine de Nerleux, Saint-Cyr-en-Bourg: Robert Nau founded the co-op. Régis (Lycée Viticole de Beaune) concentrates on the family *domaine,* increasing the acreage, building new cellars, and bottling his own wine. His regular *cuvée* of Champigny is always adequate (a stolid '94; a pleasant '92; a tart, bell-peppery '91) and sometimes more (a plush, fruit-packed '89). Les Châtains, from old vines, is deeper, more intense. An '89, with dark red fruit, black olive, leather, smoke, and game flavors, recalled Bourgueil more than Champigny. The silkier '90 offered plum, black cherry, and bell pepper flavors. The '93, while relatively rich, had the sharp edge characteristic of the vintage.

Michel et Jean-Claude Dubois, Saint-Cyr-en-Bourg. The Dubois don't do anything special, but their Champignys are always lissome and harmonious, notably in difficult vintages like '94 and '87 (their version of which won Anjou's most prestigious award, the Médaille Capus).

Lavigne Père et Fils, Varrains: Sometimes ravishing, sometimes not, but always better-than-average Champignys from Gilbert Lavigne, one of the appellation's most respected producers. The '89 was ravishing; the '88 was leaner but equally seductive. The '90 was gamy and brawny; '94 was pleasant. Two *cuvées* of '93, tasted in '95, displayed the hardness typical of the year.

René-Noël Legrand, Varrains: Soils are the passion of this honest and enthusiastic vigneron. During the course of a long tasting—conducted over the kitchen sink—Legrand spoke simply but movingly of the tuffeau of his plot in Chaintres and of the sand, clay, and gravel of his butte in Saumur.

Legrand doesn't assemble his wines. Rather, as each bottling corresponds to specific parcels, he effectively offers single-vineyard *cuvées*. "I want to keep the personality of each *cuvée*, because I like soils a lot but I'm not a great taster," he explained with his characteristic blend of candor and modesty. "I don't think I'm great at doing assemblages. So I respect the character of the soils."

Legrand's wines aren't perfect—you'll find some rough edges—but they can be wonderful and are always personal. A '93 Vieilles Vignes was an inky, deep Cabernet with a bit of acid. It needs about five years. A structured '89 was pungent, ripe, and jammy. Another *cuvée* was pruney and tannic, more Bourgueil than Champigny. The '85 was a classic, with flavors of musk and truffles.

RECOMMENDED

Daheuiller Père et Fils, Varrains: Claude Daheuiller and son Laurent (Montreuil-Bellay, Amboise), and the wines they make, give as accurate a picture as any of your average well-heeled Champigny *domaine*, circa 1995. They have thirty hectares of vines, a modern *chai* (Bucher press, thermoregulated stainless steel tanks, including two *à pigéage*), and a list of prestigious clients, including some of Paris's top restaurants. Most of the grapes are machine-harvested and ferment for a little more than a week. There are at least two *cuvées* of Champigny—a normal and an old-vines. The wines are generally pretty without being distinguished. By far the best I tasted was a '90 Vieilles Vignes. Classic, in the best sense, it was succulent, fruity, and supple; a pleasure. The Vieilles Vignes bottlings in both '93 and '94 are pleasant bistro reds.

Domaine des Bonnevaux, Varrains: A retired plumber, Camille Bourdoux makes distinctive Champigny. As he says, "It's always blacker and more tannic than the rest." His success seems a mix of beginner's luck and good land. Some *cuvées* were volatile but others were iron-fist-in-velvet-glove Champignys, like the sumptuous '89 with its potent wave of plum, berries, and violets. His '94 was a curious mix of rose petals and stem rot.

Domaine des Galmoises, Chacé: Young Didier Pasquier's raw material seems attractive, but the Champignys are often awkward: The '89, the '90, even the '91, were dense and chewy, enjoyable; the '92 seemed a mix of pretty fruit and a variety of flaws.

Domaine du Val Brun, Parnay: Pleasant Champignys from a pleasant family winery. The best—'89 and '90—are chunky and flavorful, to drink now.

Domaine du Vieux Bourg, Varrains: Amiable, rather coarse Champignys with plush fruit and licorice flavors. They can be awfully pleasant drinking but one senses they could be better—as in the clumsy but pretty '93 Le Clos; the fruity–bell peppery '92 Vieilles Vignes (the generic was better, with very pretty fruit); the green olive– and Cabernet-rich '90; and the thickish '90 Vieilles Vignes with its winsome plum and cherry fruit.

Gérard et Yves Drouineau, Dampierre: Things may change as Yves, a Beaune graduate, takes over; for now the wines are forthright, rustic, and engaging.

TASTED AND CONSIDERED

Château de Chaintres, Dampierre-sur-Loire: This seventeenth-century *domaine*, with a seventeen-hectare vineyard enclosed by tuffeau walls, was once the workshop of an order of monks attached to nearby Fontevraud. Their mission was to teach agriculture, and it was likely they who first planted its vineyards. The château's current owner is Baron Gaël de Tigny. One of the first to recognize the potential of Saumur's reds, he sold to local restaurants (in bottle) and was always out of stock. Today, his bland Champignys seem mostly to be out of the loop.

***Clos des Cordeliers*, Champigny:** The Ratron brothers produce soft, blurry Champignys.

***Hospices de Saumur*, Souzay-Champigny:** The ten-hectare *clos* is considered a historic monument. Created by the *père* Cristal, who bequeathed it to the hospital of Saumur, it is nothing if not original. Between every two rows of vines is a tuffeau wall. Vines are planted to the north and are trained through the wall to face due south. The site is worth a visit.

SAUMUR BLANC ET ROUGE

STATUS: *AOC 1957*
TYPES OF WINE: *Whites and reds*
ZONE AND PRODUCTION: *31,000 hectoliters white; 40,800 hectoliters red; made on 1,200 hectares within thirty-seven communes, principally on the banks of the Dive and the Thouet south of Saumur around Tourtenay, Montreuil-Bellay, Le Puy Nôtre Dame, and Vaudelnay*
GRAPES: *Whites—Chenin (minimum 80 percent), Chardonnay, and Sauvignon; reds—Cabernet Franc and Sauvignon, Pineau d'Aunis*
SOILS: *Sedimentary; chalky subsoils*
PRICE: *20ff*
BEST VINTAGES: (see *Champigny*)

Saumur blanc, like Anjou blanc, is usually a fruity, uncomplicated white. Those from Turquant and Parnay, within the Champigny zone, as well as from Brézé, approach Savennières in breed and distinction. Saumur rouge is Champigny's charming country cousin. And production has doubled since 1983. There has also been a great deal of progress, particularly in the area around Le Puy Notre Dame.

⊰⊱ PRODUCER RATINGS ⊰⊱

TO WATCH
Château de Villeneuve

HIGHLY RECOMMENDED
Cave des Vignerons de Saumur
Château de Beauregard   Château du Hureau
Clos de Boisménard

RECOMMENDED
Château de Montreuil-Bellay
Domaine Armand David   Domaine Langlois-Château
Domaine Lucazeau   Domaine Saint-Vincent   Lavigne Père et Fils
René-Noël Legrand

TASTED AND CONSIDERED
Lycée Viticole de Montreuil-Bellay   Jean-Marie Réclu

❧ ❧

TO WATCH

Château de Villeneuve (Champigny): Virtually every Saumurois will affirm that Villeneuve is one of the region's best *crus* for Chenin. As in Champigny, the wines here already qualify as "Excellent." I think they're headed for "Outstanding," though. Even before the recent improvements, I was stunned by the Saumur blancs of this *domaine*. The unique expression of *terroir*, the explosion of the gorgeous scents of a *moelleux*—of spring blossoms, ginger, honey—all the more startling because the wine (an '89) was as dry and mineraly as Badoit. The '90 was equally great, a voluptuous, glinting Chenin; '92 was a fabulous expression of peach and minerals.

In 1994, Chevallier inaugurated a new *cuvée*, Les Cormiers, which ferments and ages in new oak barrels. It is bottled off its fine lees without filtration at the end of June following the harvest. The '94 had just been bottled when I tasted it. I'm not surprised, therefore, that flavors of oak, licorice, and ripe fruit obscured the stark originality of the *terroir*. I think that will emerge as the wine ages. For now, Les Cormiers is a marrowy, beautifully textured, delicious wine. I'd love to watch it evolve. In a way, it expresses a new approach to Chenin; as valid as any, and fascinating.

HIGHLY RECOMMENDED

Cave des Vignerons de Saumur (Champigny): The co-op makes 60 percent of all Saumur blanc and 33 percent of all Saumur rouge. The whites are accurate, light, and fruity; the reds, while not as succulent as Champigny, are tasty and are good values. The '93, which won Anjou's top awards, was a generous glass of red.

Château de Beauregard, Le Puy Notre Dame: Philippe Gourdon makes pleasant Saumur rouge and very pretty Saumur blanc. His floral, nicely textured '94 was a lovely quaffing Chenin.

Château du Hureau (Champigny): Philippe Vatan used to sell his Chenin to houses like Gratien et Meyer, but in 1989 he started making Saumur blanc himself. Over the years, the wine has seemed very much a work in progress. The most interesting so far was the '94, which, though marred by a hint of stem rot, had lovely flavors of pear and mineral. To watch.

Clos de Boisménard, Tourtenay: The Clos de Boisménard is the sole producer of AOC Saumur in the Deux-Sèvres. It's worth a detour, if only to visit the huge subterranean dovecote, carved into the tuffeau, where you'll sample light, fragrant Chenins and delicate Cabernets, with bright flavors of cherry, strawberry, and mint.

RECOMMENDED

Château de Montreuil-Bellay: The Cabernets made at this enchanting château are usually expressive, with good stuffing. While the '93 was a bit acid and hard, other vintages—such as '90, '89, '88, and '87—are gutsy, the kind of user-friendly reds I like with meat loaf and mashed potatoes. The château also makes pleasant Saumur blanc, which often has some residual sugar.

Domaine Armand David, Vaudelnay: Barrel-aged Saumur blancs; upfront, slightly rustic Cabernets, for lunch in a wine bar.

Domaine Langlois-Château, Saint-Hilaire-Saint-Florent: From the *domaine*'s own vineyards come crisp, clean, New Age Chenins (with 20 percent Chardonnay), which can be delightful in good years and fragrant, if a bit watery, in less propitious vintages like '94 and '93. At their best, the Saumur reds are supple, berry-packed Cabernets with notes of mint, rosemary, and thyme ('89), bell peppers ('88), and cherry and raspberry jam (an oak-aged '87 Vieilles Vignes). Both '93 and '94 were fair representatives of their respective vintages.

Domaine Lucazeau, Vaudelnay: Restaurant reds and whites that, to their credit, keep a Saumurois personality. Whites made from old vines display rich texture and depth of fruit with long mineral finishes. In ripe vintages, like '89 and '90, the reds tend to be chewy and jammy, with flavors of berries and bell peppers; in lighter years, like '91 and '92, they are soft and spicy, with green-olive accents.

Domaine Saint-Vincent (Champigny): Given the fine mineral expression of his '90, Patrick Vadé clearly has land meant for Chenin. The wine itself was very pleasant, with lively grapefruit flavors, but it should have been nobler.

Lavigne Père et Fils (Champigny): Brawny and mineral-rich, these Saumur blancs are slightly rustic, sometimes slightly oxidized. Good, old-fashioned country whites—for initiates.

René-Noël Legrand (Champigny): Count on Legrand to make a handcrafted, highly personal Saumur blanc, vibrant with flavors of tropical fruit, ginger, and Granny Smith apples.

TASTED AND CONSIDERED

Lycée Viticole de Montreuil-Bellay: The enology students get a C for the Saumur blanc, fragrant but too light and tart and a bit bubble-gummy (in a variety of vintages), as well as for leathery, thick Saumur rouge—either too pruney, too tannic, or too bell-peppery.

Jean-Marie Réclu, Montreuil-Bellay: Clean, aromatic reds to be drunk before the next harvest.

COTEAUX DE SAUMUR

STATUS: *AOC 1962*
TYPES OF WINE: *Off-dry white*
ZONE AND PRODUCTION: *Thirteen communes, including most of the Champigny zone as well as Brézé, Epieds, Fontevraud, Saint-Hilaire-Saint-Florent, and Saix (in the Vienne) make an average of 380 hectoliters yearly.*
GRAPES: *Chenin Blanc*
SOILS: *Essentially the chalky soils of cliffs cut by narrow valleys, running along the Loire, the Thouet, and the Dive*
PRICE: *20 to 60ff*
BEST VINTAGES: (see *Layon*)

For centuries sweet Chenins from this region have been referred to as Coteaux de Saumur. *Monseigneur le Vin*, the old Nicolas guide, classified its best *lieux dits* in Montsoreau, Brézé, Parnay, Saint-Cyr-en-Bourg, Turquant, and Dampierre. Less alcoholic than the Chenins of Anjou, Coteaux de Saumur gives us a foretaste of the Chenins we'll find in Vouvray and Montlouis—more often "tender" than *moelleux*, but nervy and aristocratic, with fine fruit.

Coteaux de Saumur is one of the Loire's rarest wines. Most producers make it only in great years. In '94, a little more than one hundred hecto-liters were made; in '87, only twenty-three.

⋖ PRODUCERS RATED ⋗

OUTSTANDING
Clos Rougéard

HIGHLY RECOMMENDED
Château du Hureau   Domaine Saint-Vincent
Domaine du Val Brun
Lavigne Père et Fils   René-Noël Legrand

RECOMMENDED
Cave des Vignerons de Saumur   Domaine de Nerleux

⋖ ⋗

OUTSTANDING

Clos Rougéard (Champigny): This half-hectare of hundred-year-old Chenin, yielding twenty hectoliters per hectare, makes extraordinary Coteaux de Saumur. It blends classic flavors of honey, herbal tea, and oak but in a way that is unique. *Sui generis*. (It is not for sale, but is usually available for tasting if you visit.)

HIGHLY RECOMMENDED

Château du Hureau (Champigny): Philippe Vatan put a lot of work into his '94 Coteaux de Saumur, harvested at an impressive 17 percent potential alcohol. The wine is impressive, too, with tart flavors of sour lemon candies, honey, and minerals. Earlier efforts include Vatan's first, a floral, soft, pretty '89; and a firmer, finer '90.

Domaine Saint-Vincent (Champigny): Vadé usually sells his Chenin to Bouvet Ladubay. As a top supplier, he won a *barrique* in which Bouvet's deluxe Trésor had aged. He used this, in '89, to ferment his Coteaux de Saumur, a lush honey-ginger and lemon zest *moelleux*.

Domaine du Val Brun (Champigny): Eighteen hectoliters of awesome '89 Coteaux de Saumur. Pure noble rot, it fermented in barrel until January when it stopped on its own, leaving an opulent Chenin with layers of honey and ginger. An '85, while lighter, was pure botrytis, too. A delightful aperitif Chenin.

Lavigne Père et Fils (Champigny):   The '89 was a late-harvest beauty, structured, floral, lemony, absolutely lovely.

René-Noël Legrand (Champigny):   The '89 was a lush Chenin syrup with flavors of bananas and pineapples, ginger, pear, and quince.

RECOMMENDED

Cave des Vignerons de Saumur (Champigny):   Correct wines that give a glimpse of the appellation without making converts.

Domaine de Nerleux (Champigny):   Competent, supple Coteaux de Saumur with aromas of tropical fruit.

VIN DU THOUARSAIS

STATUS: *VDQS 1966*
TYPES OF WINE: *Red, white, and rosé*
ZONE AND PRODUCTION: *680 hectoliters produced on 17.43 hectares within a zone spanning fifteen communes in the Deux-Sèvres, mostly around Oiron.*
GRAPES: *Whites—Chenin, Chardonnay (maximum 20 percent); reds and rosés—Cabernet Franc and Sauvignon and Gamay*
SOILS: *Groies (a shallow layer of pebbly clay-chalk soils on limestone)*
PRICE: *14ff*
BEST VINTAGES: *'95, '93*

Michel Gigon, Oiron: Gigon, the only local producer with a commercial presence, makes light, appley Chenins which his clients buy for *kirs*; light, fruity Cabs and Gamays, good for barbecues. My favorite is his rosé, dry, with firm strawberry and hazelnut flavors.

THE ROSES OF ANJOU AND SAUMUR

STATUS: *Rosé d'Anjou, 1957; Cabernet d'Anjou and de Saumur, 1964; Rosé de Loire, 1974*
TYPES OF WINE: *The first three are off-dry or sweet rosés; the last is a dry rosé.*

ZONE AND PRODUCTION: *Throughout Anjou and Saumur for the first two;
throughout the Saumurois for Rosé de Saumur; Anjou and Touraine for Rosé
de Loire. The sweet rosés account for roughly 250,000 hectoliters a year;
Rosé de Loire, an average of 39,600 hectoliters on 670 hectares; Cabernet de
Saumur, an average of 3,100 hectoliters on 56 hectares; Cabernet d'Anjou,
an average of 116,860 hectoliters on 2,000 hectares; Rosé d'Anjou, an average of 135,800 hectoliters on 2,000 hectares.*

GRAPES: *Grolleau, Cabernet, Gamay, Cot, Pineau d'Aunis for Rosé d'Anjou;
the two Cabernets for Cabernet d'Anjou and de Saumur; Cabernet (minimum 30 percent), Pinot Noir, Gamay, Grolleau, and Pineau d'Aunis for
Rosé de Loire*

SOILS: *Varied*

PRICE: *10 to 20ff*

BEST VINTAGES: *'95*

It all started in 1905 when M. Taveau, a Saumurois, vinified his Cabernet as a rosé. By the 1950s rosés had conquered Anjou. Some speculate that
the wines were vinified sweet to offset the naturally high acidity. But it's also
true that Angevins were accustomed to making *moelleux*. Perhaps they simply continued. In any event, "sweet" was what consumers wanted. The
workers' cafés, where much of Anjou's rosés were sold, emptied fifteen barrels of sweet rosé for every barrel of dry. They were preferred over the oxidized rosés of southern France and they competed successfully with
confected aperitifs like Ricard.

That Anjou rosé was liberally quaffed during the weekly broadcasts of
the popular soap opera *La Famille Duraton* over Radio-Luxembourg further
stoked the craze for the stuff, which accounted for 58 percent of Anjou wine
production. By the early 1970s, Pierre Bréjoux would note that the fashionable wines of the Paris bar were Muscadet, Beaujolais, and the Anjou rosés.
And the vogue spawned such dubious contributions to French viticulture as
Nectarosé and Saumurosé.

Success proved a double-edged sword, however. The region's reputation as
a producer of breathtaking Chenins was obliterated as Anjou became synonymous with sweet plonk. Winemakers abandoned their hillsides, planted on
flatlands, and replaced much of their Chenin with Grolleau. Their rosés sold
for as much as Bonnezeaux. Author Pierre-Marie Doutrelant, in his *Les Bons
Vins et les Autres*, reflected the chagrin of many when, in comparing the celestial aged Layons of his memory with the cheapo sweet Cabernets d'Anjou current in the mid-'70s, he lamented: "Where are the Anjous of yesteryear?"

The postwar decline in the *moelleux* market hit sweet rosés, too. To counter the downward spiral, the appellation Rosé de Loire, which covers dry rosés from Anjou, Saumur, and Touraine, was created in 1974.

All four rosés are made by a direct press of the harvest, a brief maceration or a bleeding of the vats destined for red wine. Rosé de Loire is usually firm yet delicate. Floral, crisp, and vibrantly fruity, it is a refreshing summer wine and as delicious with Indian or Chinese food as with local *rillettes* and *rillauds*.

Rosé d'Anjou, Cabernet d'Anjou, and Cabernet de Saumur must have a minimum of 10 grams residual sugar, though the last is generally somewhat drier. To me, the sweet Cabernets taste like green bell peppers mixed with sugary strawberry juice—not a winning combination. Rosé d'Anjou is blander. "Vinous" would be a big compliment.

The sweet rosés *do* have their fans, however. In Anjou they are often paired with local charcuterie or melon—and they're not bad in that context. They also show some affinity with corn on the cob. And a herbaceous Cabernet d'Anjou maybe the ideal partner for one of the most wine-difficult foods, asparagus, particularly the white ones from the Loire.

⋙ PRODUCER RATINGS ⋘

HIGHLY RECOMMENDED
Cave des Vignerons de Saumur   Château de Beauregard
Château de Passavant   Domaine de Bablut   René-Noël Legrand

⋙ ⋘

Cave des Vignerons de Saumur **(Champigny):**   Among the best Cabernets de Saumur I've tasted, they seem almost as dry as Rosé de Loire.

Château de Beauregard **(Saumur):**   When making their Cabernet de Saumur, Philippe and Alain Gourdon let their Cabernet Franc macerate for two days before pressing; they ferment at low temperatures, and leave the wine on its lees until bottling in June. Their '94 was my kind of rosé—firm, dry (relatively), with appetizing mineral flavors.

Château de Passavant **(Layon):**   The Davids make only Rosé de Loire and it's a lovely one, lacy and floral with a savory bitter nut finish.

Domaine de Bablut **(Aubance):**   When old rosés are uncorked, they invariably come from Bablut's cellars. (Two memorable examples are the '59 and the '61, deliciously honeyed, with flavors of licorice, hay, coffee, and grapefruit.) Though recent vintages don't promise that kind of ageability, the wines are very good. A crisp, rather dry '93 Cabernet d'Anjou was quite refreshing. The deeply colored '90 Rosé de Loire was big, taut, and dry, with rich strawberry flavors subtly accented with green peppers and orange peel.

René-Noël Legrand (Champigny):   Legrand's '89 Cabernet de Saumur (13 percent alcohol, with 22 grams residual sugar) fermented in used Bordeaux barrels. Supple, with intense strawberry and peach flavors, it justified the appellation.

EXTREMELY GOOD *DOMAINES* WITH VERY GOOD ROSES

Château Pierre-Bise (Layon)
Domaine des Closserons (Layon)
Domaine de Brizé (Layon)
Domaine de Montgilet (Aubance)
Domaine Ogereau (Layon)

ALSO RECOMMENDED

Château Montbenault (Layon)
Domaine Gaudart (Layon)
Domaine des Hautes Ouches (Anjou)
Domaine de la Pierre Blanche (Layon)
Leduc-Frouin (Layon)
Jean-Marie Réclu (Saumur)

SPARKLING WINES

STATUS: *AOC. Anjou* mousseux *(1957); Saumur* mousseux *(1976); Crémant de Loire (1975; 1994)*

TYPES OF WINE: *Sparkling whites and rosés*

ZONE AND PRODUCTION: *Anjou* mousseux: *Roughly 4,600 hectoliters are made throughout the entire Anjou zone. Saumur* mousseux: *More extensive than the zone for still wines, the Saumur* mousseux *zone extends into the Layon in places like Martigné-Briand and Passavant and the Aubance around Coutures, and produces 104,000 hectoliters. Crémant de Loire: Covering Anjou, Saumur, Cheverny, and Touraine, the zone produces 30,300 hectoliters.*

GRAPES: Anjou: *Whites—Chenin, Cabernet, Cot, Gamay, Grolleau, Pineau d'Aunis (maximum of 60 percent red grapes); rosés—Cabernet, Cot, Gamay, Grolleau, Pineau d'Aunis.*

Saumur: *Whites—Chenin, Chardonnay, Sauvignon (the last two, maximum of 20 percent), Cabernet, Cot, Grolleau, Pineau d'Aunis, Pinot Noir (maximum of 60 percent red grapes for whites); rosés—Cabernet, Cot, Grolleau, Gamay, Pineau d'Aunis, Pinot Noir*

Crémant de Loire: *Chenin Blanc, Cabernet, Pineau d'Aunis, Pinot Noir, Chardonnay, Arbois, with the possible addition of up to 30 percent Grolleau*

SOILS: *Varied*

PRICE: *30 to 150ff*

BEST VINTAGES: *Most mousseux are not vintage dated. Those that are generally represent special or reserve bottlings.*

Saumur produces more sparkling wine than any region in France aside from Champagne. It is a distant second, however: Champagne makes about 250 million bottles a year; Saumur, 14 to 15 million, to which Anjou adds another 600,000. But Saumur shares with Champagne chalky soils as well as miles of underground tunnels carved into rock—caves whose constant, cool temperatures are perfect for the stocking of wine as well as for secondary fermentation. And like the wines of Reims, the *crus* of Saumur have a tendency to sparkle naturally, a phenomenon remarked upon as early as the fifteenth century. (The similarities between the two regions were not lost on Jean Ackerman, a Belgian who studied banking in Champagne. When he married a Saumurois girl, née Laurance, he founded Saumur's first sparkling wine firm, Ackerman-Laurance, in 1811.)

Saumur and Anjou produce a number of different styles of sparkling wine, all made by the *méthode champenoise*. Most are Saumur non-vintage *mousseux* and most are white. The wines are usually brut, occasionally off-dry, and tend to be pungent, fruity, and full.

Many of the region's best sparkling wines are Crémant de Loire. The laws governing its production are more restrictive than those for *mousseux*. Grapes must be harvested by hand in non-watertight cases. (The letter of the INAO's law fixes lower yields for Crémant than it does for Anjou and Saumur *mousseux*—fifty hectoliters per hectare, as compared with sixty—but in practice, Crémant's yields have been *higher*, at least as reported by the INAO for the '94 harvest!) Restrictions are set on the types of presses that may be used, the amount of pressure that may be applied when pressing the grapes, the use of press wine, and so forth. While *mousseux* is required to age for nine months, Crémant must age for twelve months, with nine months on its lees. Additionally, Crémant is, by nature, less aggressively bubbly than *mousseux* or most Champagnes; the law sets a limit of 3.5 atmospheres of pressure as compared with 6 for Champagne, which makes for a gentler, creamier fizz. In general, the wines are finer than *mousseux* in every respect; the bead elegant, the structure firm, the flavors subtle, the finish long and toasty.

Saumur also produces an off-dry red *mousseux* based on Cabernet. Its sweet, bell-peppery flavors are surprisingly tasty when paired with local strawberries macerated in Champigny.

Most of the region's sparkling wine is made and sold by *négociant* houses located on the outskirts of Saumur in Saint-Hilaire-Saint-Florent. The top four are Ackerman-Laurance (Jean Ackerman's *domaine*, Saumur's largest, is now part of the Rémy Pannier portfolio); Veuve Amiot, number two, owned by Martini and Rossi; Bouvet-Ladubay (founded in 1851 and now owned by Taittinger); and Gratien et Meyer (founded in 1864 by Alfred Gratien). Each markets well over a million bottles of wine a year. The Cave des Vignerons de Saumur and Langlois-Château (founded in 1885, now owned by Bollinger) are important players, too, though neither matches the big four in volume.

Few houses rely on their own vines for their sparkling wine. Most buy must or finished wine. And many of Anjou's small *domaines* offer sparkling wines but are insufficiently equipped to handle on their own operations such as disgorging. They send the base wine to the Coopérative or to Langlois-Château for champenization.

❧ PRODUCER RATINGS ❧

LEADERS
Bouvet-Ladubay   Langlois-Château

EXCELLENT
Domaine des Baumard   Domaine de Brizé

TO WATCH
Domaine de la Gloriette

HIGHLY RECOMMENDED
Château de Passavant

RECOMMENDED
Gratien et Meyer

BY THE GLASS
Cave des Vignerons de Saumur
Domaine de Nerleux   Domaine du Val Brun

❧ ❧

LEADERS

Bouvet-Ladubay, **Saint-Hilaire-Saint-Florent:** Founded in 1851 by Etienne Bouvet, this house was purchased by the Monmousseau family in the 1930s, then by Champagne Taittinger in 1974. Patrice Monmousseau stayed on as director. A graduate of the Institut de Beaune, the dynamic Monmousseau invented the *gyropalette* (a rotating case, holding up to 500 bottles, which facilitates the laborious riddling process), conceived the delectable barrel-fermented Cuvée Trésor, and is forever dreaming up new wines as well as publicity links between Saumur brut and other passions—antique cars, car racing, modern art. It is no wonder that Bouvet-Ladubay seems the most vigorous of all of Saumur's—indeed, the Loire's—sparkling wine producers.

Bouvet-Ladubay has no vines but it does have eight kilometers of cellars snaking through tuffeau caves. It buys must from growers in the Saumur area and sends its enologists to supervise pressing at harvest.

Both Bouvet brut and the vintage brut are pure Chenin. The first is assertively bubbly and fruity. Saphir, the vintage brut, is made every year from selected juices. It is delicious and a real step up—fuller, richer, subtler, with finer balance. Bouvet's basic rosé is made from Cabernet Franc and Grolleau. It tends to be aggressive, too, but it is a pleasant blend of tart fruit with ripe strawberry notes. Rubis, the off-dry Cabernet-Gamay blend, is one of the more restrained and balanced versions of this unusual wine.

Bouvet's deluxe wine is Trésor, which is made using the same exigent standards as a Crémant and which costs as much as Champagne. The blend is Chenin with 20 percent Chardonnay. The grapes are hand harvested by *tri*. The base wine, a selection of free-run and juice of the first gentle pressing, ferments in Tronçais oak barrels (with a four-year rotation) and stainless steel tanks. After racking, the wines go back into barrel where they will age until the September following the harvest, when they are bottled for the *prise de mousse*. Trésor ages for two to three years before release.

This is a wonderful wine, beautifully balanced and layered with savory nut and toast flavors. It has spawned two offspring: a Saumur demi-sec,

Grand Vin de Dessert, made from Chenin with a bit of Chardonnay; and Trésor rosé, based on Cabernet Franc. Each ferments partially or entirely in barrel.

The demi-sec recalls a big Vouvray *pétillant*. It is meaty and flavory, with excellent sugar-to-acid balance. The rosé is lacy and urbane. There are lots of flavors, many nuances, none of them loud, just whispers—of fig, strawberry, truffle, a wee suggestion of oak. An English wine writer I know described (appropriately) the original Trésor as "desperately sexy." I think he'd find Trésor rosé "desperately elegant."

Langlois-Château, Saint-Hilaire-Saint-Florent: Owned by Bollinger and managed by Jean Leroux, a grandson of the founders, who still holds 45 percent of the stock, Langlois-Château is a big firm that works like a boutique winery. It makes a number of still wines from its own vines in Loire appellations from Muscadet to Sancerre. Its specialty, however, is Crémant de Loire.

For its Crémant, Langlois-Château buys grapes from around thirty growers. A premium is paid for choice grapes and the house feels, rightly, that it knows which growers work best, as it champenizes the base wines of many of the region's vignerons.

The wines age a minimum of three years. Crémant brut accounts for 70 percent. Primarily Chenin, it includes Chardonnay, Cabernet Franc, and Grolleau. The bouquet can be blowsy, as pungent as a raspberry *kir*, but the wine is more restrained on the palate, with dry, nutty flavors.

Langlois's best wine, a vintage Crémant de Loire, could serve as a role model for Saumur sparkling wines. Not everyone can invest in new oak barrels, but with exigence, one can produce discreet, layered Crémants like Langlois's '90 (currently on the market), its '89, and its '85. I'm also extremely fond of Langlois's refined Crémant rosé (Cabernet Franc with 30 percent Grolleau). I recall, with pleasure, a sunny summer lunch on a patio under Saumur's château. The Crémant rosé was as pretty as the setting and a fine match for my smoked salmon as well as a *salade de gésiers* (gizzard salad).

EXCELLENT

Domaine des Baumard (Quarts-de-Chaume): Baumard's bubblies are always crisp and clean, with a kind of patrician formality. There are three types: Crémant, Anjou brut, and Carte Corail brut (a rosé of Cabernet). Crémant, usually pure Chardonnay, is the best. Firm but delicate, with fine, persistent bubbles, it is lacy, ephemeral, and regal. A splendid aperitif.

***Domaine de Brizé* (Layon):** After two years in Champagne, Luc Del-humeau returned to Anjou to make some of its best sparkling wine. The *cuvée* to look for is Crémant. Red grapes make up half the blend; the bal-ance, Chenin and Chardonnay. The wines usually age two years. They are wonderful: fine, fresh, and layered with subtle flavors of toast and fruit. (The Delhumeaus also make *crèmes* of various fruits, like *framboise* and *cassis*. For family celebrations they bottle a Crémant with just a whisper of *crème de framboise*—the best *kir royale* I ever tasted. Alas, it's not for sale. But you can buy the components.)

TO WATCH

***Domaine de la Gloriette*, Le Puy Notre Dame:** When young Sébastien Crépaux decided to go into the family business—wine—father Jean-François decided they needed more than four hectares in Champagne. So, in 1990, they bought another ten in the Saumurois. Most of their 60,000-bottle production is sparkling wine, headed by Saumur brut and Crémant. These aren't perfect, but they're mighty impressive. The latest Saumur brut, pure Chardonnay, was well structured, with lovely fruit and some depth. A crisp Saumur rosé, based chiefly on Cabernet Franc, had brawny, almost raspberry liqueur–like fruit. A bracing aperitif.

HIGHLY RECOMMENDED

***Château de Passavant* (Layon):** Lovely Crémants. The regular *cuvée*, Chenin with Chardonnay, ages for two years. It is a zesty palate freshener, lightly toasty with lemon and quince flavors. The rosé (half each of Caber-net and Grolleau) is crisp, fruity, and dry, a very pretty summer sparkler.

RECOMMENDED

***Gratien et Meyer*, Saumur:** Founded in 1864 by Alfred Gratien, who at the same time founded a house in Epernay, Gratien et Meyer is still owned by the family. Alain Seydoux, the director, is the great-grandson of Gratien's partner, Jean Meyer.

The firm purchases grapes and makes a gamut of sparkling wines, posi-tioned as "supermarket bubbly." The Saumur brut, Chenin with Cabernet Franc, tends to be fat, fruity, and aggressive. The Cabernet-based Blanc de Noirs ranges from crisp and strawberry-scented to heavy and herbaceous.

The off-dry Cabernet-based Crémant rouge, simultaneously tart and sweet, is competent. The most expensive wines are Crémant de Loire and Cuvée Flamme. Each makes a pleasant aperitif.

BY THE GLASS

Cave des Vignerons de Saumur (Champigny): Respectable versions of the full-range of Saumur sparkling wines at reasonable prices.

Domaine de Nerleux (Champigny): The Crémants lack oomph but they are tasty, even a bit elegant.

Domaine du Val Brun (Parnay): Competent, if aggressive, *mousseux*.

THE ANJOU TABLE

France's Prince of Gastronomes, Maurice Edmond Sailland, better known as Curnonsky, came from Angers and placed Anjou above all other gastronomic regions. In his *Les Trésors Gastronomiques de la France* (1933), he wrote: "This land without excess has created a cuisine which reflects its purity and finesse. . . . Angevin cooking, in which the delicious butter of the land predominates, is bourgeois and simple. It doesn't aim to impress; it sums up what French people of taste eat in their homes. . . . One doesn't find stuffings or *coulis* or spices or sophisticated, complicated sauces; essentially reasonable and sincere, Angevin cooking reflects the *douceur* of its skies, the limpidity of its air, the calm of its horizons."

Anjou has changed, of course, since Curnonsky's time. Yet a modern chef can still describe a richness of produce that would have seemed normal to Curnonsky, telling me: "We're spoiled. The *douceur Angevine* isn't false. We don't use many spices because produce here has so much flavor. Our vegetables and fruits are exceptional. So are the river fish. I get my frogs from the Vendée, my meat from Cholet, my poultry is all local. I get my wild mushrooms from a producer in Jumelles who also does asparagus; another guy does my salads, tomatoes, white radishes, herbs, and the gray shallots indispensable for good *beurre blanc*. Anjou has the best strawberries, raspberries, *fraises des bois*, white peaches; many varieties of apples; apricots (the ones from Roussillon are grainy and insipid). I buy potatoes only from one guy who supplies me with the *la ratte du Touquet*." Here the chef pauses to kiss his fingers, then adds that he makes sorbets from physalis, an exotic fruit in the tomatillo family, and he garnishes dishes with sautéed sea kale, an endangered plant that once grew wild on the Breton coast. Each is now grown locally, in Anjou's experimental gardens.

That shopping list gives a pretty good picture of the local larder. With Curnonsky's description, it also summarizes Loire cooking, particularly the cooking of the western Loire. Where Anjou meets the Nantais, recipes still feature butter, cream, and white wine. Progressing east, toward Champigny and Chinon, red wine takes over, for use in sauces, stews, and soups.

The Loire's fields of white asparagus, as well as its mushroom caves, begin between Angers and Saumur. Two Saumur-area companies—Royal Champignon and Champi-Jandou—market more than 80 percent of France's cultivated mushrooms, of which more than 40 percent comes from the Saumurois. And Anjou introduces us to a style of charcuterie born in the west-central Loire, *rillauds*, *rillettes*, and *rillons*.

While Angevins rightly take pride in their preparation of each, *rillettes* and *rillons* are just as rightly the purview of Tours, where they originated. Anjou, however, contributes *rillauds* and *gogue*. *Rillauds*, allegedly invented by the monks of Saint-Georges-sur-Loire, consist of cubes of pork cooked slowly until fork-tender. *Gogue* is a dense, blood-thickened sausage, filled with onions, which in flavor recalls the Vendéen *fressure*.

Other Angevin dishes include pigs trotters à l'Aubance, served in cabbage leaves; pike stuffed into cabbage and sauced with *beurre blanc*; *cul de veau Angevine* (a three-hour braise, the meat basted with dry Anjou wine and aromatized with carrots and onions); chicken in tarragon cream sauce and *poulet Angevine*, sautéed with local wine, local cream, and local mushrooms.

La Sarthe and Loué, a bit north of the wine route, are known for their flavorful poultry. In Maine-et-Loire as well as in Deux-Sèvres, entrepreneurs raise *pigeonneaux* and ducks, the latter mostly for foie gras. (Local foie gras usually accompanies old vintages of *moelleux* at special Angevin dinners.)

Crémet, fresh cheese molded with cream and egg whites, eaten with cream and sugar or with a fruit coulis, is Anjou's sole cheese tradition. But cheese—artisanal and industrial—is made all around it. Chèvre country starts in Touraine to the east and in Deux-Sèvres to the south, where the appellation goat cheese, Chabichou du Poitou, overlaps with the outer limits of the Anjou wine zone. A small, drum-shaped chèvre, aged for ten to twenty days, it is made around Thouars, in Poitou and Charente.

France's leading producer of eating apples and of *cassis*, Anjou employs its many fruits in desserts ranging from strawberries in red wine (often served with the sweet sparkling red wine of Saumur) to all varieties of fruit tart, the most famous being *pâté de prunes*, a buttery two-crusted pie filled with *reine-claude* plums. (I have only seen the pie when *reines-claude* are in season, from mid-July to mid-September.) Pears, usually the *belle Angevine*, are often stewed in wine or they are sautéed and stuffed into crêpes and laced with Cointreau, a treatment also given to apple jam. This is purely regional: Cointreau was invented in the nineteenth century in a small confectioner's shop in Angers.

Anjou's Charcuterie

Serge Chauvin, a three-time gold-medal winner for the best *rillauds* in Brissac's annual Rillaudée, makes the finest version I have ever tasted. I visited him one afternoon in the back of his shop to see how he made his *rillauds*. Brownish pink cubes of meat simmered in a big kettle and the kitchen smelled of meat and salt. Before putting them up to boil, Chauvin had salted the *rillauds* for twenty-four hours. During the cooking, he, like most, added a tablespoon of commercial onion extract to the cooking liquid to deepen the color to a dark brown. After the *rillauds* had cooked for an hour and a quarter, Chauvin pulled them off the stove, saying, "They're done."

He sliced each *rillaud* and, using his knife as a pointer, demonstrated how they should be eaten: "From top to bottom, a vertical slice. You must take some skin with each bite. The skin is important. It adds a jellied texture and strengthens the flavor. I like them warm," he continued, opening a bottle of Brissac red to accompany our tasting. "Others like them cold. But they should be supple. You should be able to eat everything on a *rillaud*. The flavor should be very slightly salty and natural."

Serge Chauvin, Les-Rosiers-sur-Loire: Chauvin's *rillauds* have a warm spiciness reminiscent of pastrami and corned beef that comes from the meat alone. I've also sliced them very thin and served them cold, or reheated, with aperitifs.

Robert Gasté, Rochefort-sur-Loire: This excellent charcutier adds pepper and bay leaf to his boiling *rillauds*. He often places second, just behind Chauvin, in the Brissac Rillaudée. And he regularly wins first prize for his *gogues*, which include Chinese cabbage, lettuce, leeks, and spring onions.

Eaux-de-Vie and Liqueurs

Angers's tradition of liqueur production dates from the Middle Ages when such brews were used as digestives or medicines. *Guignolet,* a liqueur made from the sour cherry of the same name, was invented by Loire Valley nuns in either the fifteenth or seventeenth centuries (sources differ). By the nineteenth century, *guignolet* had become a *liqueur de salon.* Among those who produced it were Adolphe Cointreau, then a confectioner on the rue Saint-Laud in Angers, and by Emile Giffard, a pharmacist. Cointreau later invented an eponymous orange-flavored liqueur; Giffard created a peppermint liqueur called Menthe-Pastille. Today the two are joined in the Angers area by newer distilleries who use Anjou's excellent fruit to produce intense *eaux-de-vie* as well as liqueurs, *crème de cassis, crème de framboise,* and so forth—for *kirs* or for flavoring the confections of Angers's chocolatiers.

Cointreau, Angers: Cointreau, which merged with Rémy-Martin, is one of the most powerful spirits concerns in France. Now located on the outskirts of Angers, the company produces more than nine million liters of Cointreau annually. The liqueur's distinctive flavor comes from macerating orange skins (sweet ones from Spain and dark, bitter ones from Haiti) in grain neutral alcohol prior to distillation, and later adding sugar, gentian, and quinine. Among Cointreau's other products is Royal Guignolet.

Giffard, Angers: This family company specializes in liqueurs made by macerating regional fruit and herbs in alcohol. The most famous of Giffard's more than forty varieties are the peppermint-based Menthe-Pastille, its best-seller, and Guignolet d'Angers.

Hardouin Distillery, Mazé: A family distillery between Angers and Saumur producing *eau-de-vie* of Poire William, Prune Sainte-Catherine, and Prune de Quetsche, all from Loire Valley fruit. Potent and concentrated, the Hardouin *eaux-de-vie* are served in the Loire's top restaurants.

Caves de la Loire: The Poire William, though not as fine as Hardouin's, is quite good, pungent and strong.

Combier, Saumur: Intense *crèmes de fruit*—*cassis,* blackberry, peach, and raspberry—as well as fruit brandies and cherries macerated in *eau-de-vie*.

Domaine de Brizé, Martigné-Briand: In addition to wonderful wine, the Delhumeaus make the region's best *crèmes de fruit*—raspberry, blackberry, and *cassis*—from their own crop.

Langlois-Château: A leading producer of Crémant de Loire, Langlois-Château also makes a light, oaky Eau de Vie de Vin Originaire des Coteaux de la Loire.

Vegetables: Back to the Future

Throughout its history, Angers has been a center of horticultural research. Streets are named after celebrated nurserymen such as André Leroy, who also authored an important pomology dictionary. Fruits and vegetables developed here are duly commemorated as well: A plaque in the park of Angers's Beaux-Arts building reads, "In this garden was raised in 1849–50 the celebrated pear *doyenné du Comice* by the gardener Dhommé and by Millet de la Turtaudière, President of the Comice Agricole."

Horticultural research continues at ENITH (Ecole Nationale d'Ingénieurs des Techniques Horticoles), where professor Jean-Yves Peron, the son of a Breton farmer, acclimatizes exotic vegetables like Peruvian physalis (Cape gooseberry) to French growing conditions, while saving forgotten plants like *crosne* (Chinese artichoke) and *crambé maritime* (sea kale) from extinction.

Working in the greenhouses and labs of Angers's Belle Beille campus and with market gardeners in Les-Ponts-de-Cé, Peron hopes to further expand the choice of vegetables on the market to include *cerfeuil tubereux* (root chervil), a very tasty tuber that can replace chestnuts in purées, and *metulon*, a cucurbit appreciated for its decorative value as well as for its taste.

Most of Peron's vegetables had been introduced at the end of the nineteenth century by horticultural researchers at the Société d'Acclimatation, near Paris. Initially successful, each subsequently disappeared after World War II, when French industry began overproducing easily cultivated vegetables like potatoes, peas, beans, and tomatoes at the expense of both quality and diversity.

To date, only *crosne* and physalis seem to have established a market presence. But it's worth remembering that French consumers only recently got to know kiwis, avocados, and bean sprouts. And that, once upon a time, the *doyenné du Comice* was a "new" pear and tomatoes and potatoes were "new" vegetables.

Anjou's leading chefs work with Peron's vegetables (as do innovative chefs in other regions). The three you are most likely to taste are:

Physalis, the Coqueret du Pérou, is part of a family that includes the Mexican tomatillo (*P. ixocarpa*) and the orange Chinese lantern plant (*P. alkekengi*). Technically a fruit, physalis grows on low-trellised vines. Its round orange "berry," roughly the size of a cherry tomato, is encased in a papery husk. Its flavor is more tart than sweet, highly acidulated, with hints of pineapple and coconut.

Physalis disappeared from the market until 1982–83 when Peron resuscitated its cultivation, locating plants in Egypt. Now, he reports, "It's going too well. It's easily reproduced. And it's been developing chaotically all over France—with all levels of quality—some terrible, some fine. We'd like to create an association of producers of physalis which will be open to anyone who will adhere to a certain level of quality."

Often served as finger food to accompany Saumur's sparkling wine, physalis is also used much as it was between the two World Wars, when Parisian confectioners baked the berries in tarts and petit fours or used them as the base for bonbons, napped in fondant or caramel.

Crambé maritime, sea kale, once grew wild on the coasts of Brittany and England, where it likely originated. It looks like designer celery, with tapered, milky white branches and lavender tips. Author Jane Grigson called it "our one English contribution to the basic treasury of the best vegetables." In her *Vegetable Book*, Grigson recounts this charming history of the plant she considers "an aristocrat of the northern coasts":

> Sea kale was being grown in English gardens by the early decades of the 18th century, transferred from its natural habitat, which Gerard in his *Herball* had evocatively described as the "bayches and brimmes of the sea, where is no earth to be seen, but sande and rolling pebble stones." . . . On the beaches along the drift lines where sea kale grew, from seeds which floated around with the tide, country people bleached it by heaping sand round the shoots, which they cut and carried to market. . . . The French took to it cautiously. . . . But the great Carème appreciated it, calling it "Sickell" . . . mentioning it in a breath with celery and asparagus and describing several ways of serving it.

Now an endangered species, sea kale had all but disappeared until Peron found a plant in *le potager du roy* in Versailles. He developed a method of propagating sea kale as well as procedures for blanching it, like endive, in dark rooms.

Best eaten raw, sea kale needs no peeling, no cooking—though you can sauté it briefly and serve it like asparagus, with a hollandaise. The flavor is nutty and subtly cabbagy. It has none of the fibrous or slick qualities of celery; it's crisp and crunchy and thirst-quenching. It's full of vitamins and fiber and has no calories!

The French, however, are once again taking to sea kale rather cautiously. I think Americans would love it immediately: We snack on raw celery; the French don't.

Crosne (Chinese artichoke):   Also known as Japanese artichoke, this tiny, knobby tuber takes its French name from Crosne, the Paris-area experimental garden in which it was cultivated at the turn of the century. Among the Chinese names for *Crosne* is the poetic *kan lu,* which translates as "sweet morning dew." Chinese singers reportedly ate *crosne* to maintain their voices. In France, *crosne* became a theatrical footnote as well: At the end of the nineteenth century an important Parisian restaurateur used *crosne* in his fashionable *salade Japonaise,* the recipe for which was recited in Alexandre Dumas's play *Francillon.*

Because *crosne* doesn't lend itself to mass production, it began to disappear after World War II. When Peron started to work with it in 1975, there was barely a half hectare left in France. He found his plants with traditional Angevin market gardeners—Anjou's sandy soils had made it one of the major producers of *crosne*—and set about raising *crosne*'s yields and ridding the plant of viruses. There are now over two hundred hectares in cultivation.

VI

Touraine

There are two Touraines. The first is a crossroads, a land of passage, of perfect French, and of 650 classified châteaux such as Chenonceau and Azay-le-Rideau. The other Touraine is a land of vines, goats, orchards, and fields, of villages where, after centuries of intermarriage, everyone has the same name, Renault or Sourdais or Raffault, and speaks a ribald patois in which the Vallée de Grottes is transformed into a Rabelaisian Vallée de Crottes (dung), the Cabernet Franc grape is called Breton but pronounced *bairrrton*, the goat, *chieuve*, and there are as many names for snacks as there are hours in which to eat them: *casse-croûte, mangement, gueuleton, dinette, souper,* and so forth.

Named after its principal city, Tours, the ancient province is largely encompassed by the Indre-et-Loire department. Locals often sum up the region's attributes—its skies, its climate, its landscape, its calm way of life—with the word *douceur*, sweetness or tenderness. While this *douceur* extends throughout the Loire Valley, its expression is purest here: Touraine is archetypal Loire.

The wines of Touraine have been called a "vinous" mirror of the landscape, as *doux* as its languid rivers and its splendid châteaux. Unlike its châteaux, however, the wines are perennial secrets. Vouvray, as thrilling a wine as exists and one of the most complex whites in the world, heads a ros-

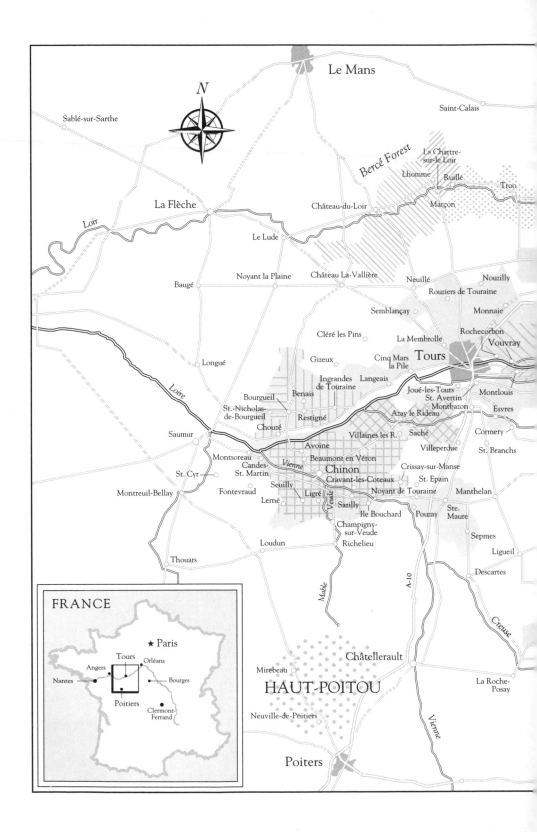

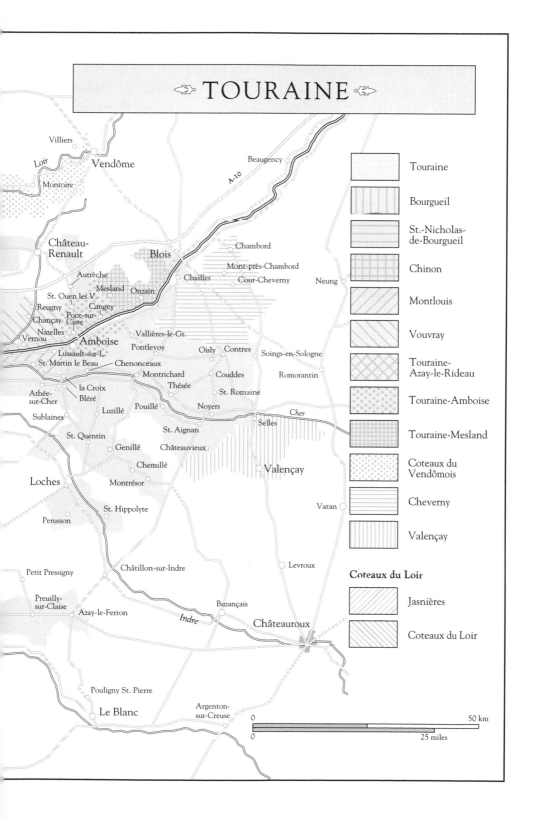

TOURAINE

Villiers

Loir

Vendôme

Montoire

Beaugency

A-10

Château-Renault

Blois

Chambord

Mont-près-Chambord

Autrèche

Chailles

Cour-Cheverny

Neung

Mesland

Onzain

St. Ouen les V.

Reugny

Cangey

Poce-sur-Cisse

Chançay

Nazelles

Vernou

Amboise

Vallières-le-Gr.

Pontlevoy

Oisly

Contres

Soings-en-Sologne

Lussault-sur-L.

St. Martin le Beau

Chenonceaux

Montrichard

Couddes

Romorantin

la Croix

Thésée

St. Romaine

Athée-sur-Cher

Bléré

Pouillé

Noyers

Cher

Sublaines

Luzillé

Selles

St. Quentin

St. Aignan

Châteauvieux

Genillé

Chemillé

Valençay

Loches

Montrésor

Vatan

St. Hippolyte

Perusson

Châtillon-sur-Indre

Levroux

Petit Pressigny

Preuilly-sur-Claise

Buzançais

Azay-le-Ferron

Indre

Châteauroux

Pouligny St. Pierre

Le Blanc

Argenton-sur-Creuse

Touraine

Bourgueil

St.-Nicholas-de-Bourgueil

Chinon

Montlouis

Vouvray

Touraine-Azay-le-Rideau

Touraine-Amboise

Touraine-Mesland

Coteaux du Vendômois

Cheverny

Valençay

Coteaux du Loir

Jasnières

Coteaux du Loir

0   50 km

0   25 miles

ter of sixteen unsung appellations, including most of the Loire's best reds—Chinon, Bourgueil, and Saint-Nicolas-de-Bourgueil.

Touraine's 15,000 hectares of AOC vines start where Saumur-Champigny leaves off and extend almost to Sancerre, seventy kilometers to the east. They continue north to Jasnières and the Vendômois and south to Poitou. It is a large region, sprawling over five departments, with incremental changes in weather, variations in the types of soils covering the tuffeau base, and a multiplicity of grapes.

At the temperate western limits of the appellation, the Chinonais, the major grape is Cabernet Franc; Chenin Blanc takes over at the outskirts of Tours, in and around Vouvray. Approaching the hills of Sancerre the climate becomes more continental and the major grapes are the earlier-ripening Sauvignon Blanc and Gamay.

Two soil types account for the best *crus* in western Touraine, slopes whose hot, permeable soils have been given the local names *aubuis* and *perruches*. *Aubuis* (limestone) is said to produce the finest whites—the *première côte* of Vouvray, for example—but is also found in many of Chinon's best parcels. *Perruches* (flinty, silex-streaked clay) produces excellent reds and whites, contributing strong mineral and flint flavors. The Varennes soils of the riverbanks—light, fertile soils often mixed with gravel—produce up-front, charming Chinons and Bourgueils.

Our Touraine wine route opens with the noblest whites, Vouvray and Montlouis. Next, we'll explore Chinon and Bourgueil, then the pack of delicious Touraines, including Touraine-Amboise, Touraine-Azay-le-Rideau, Touraine-Mesland, and Noble Joué (not yet an appellation but likely to become one). Azay can make gorgeous Chenin. Were it not for the confusion that might come from splitting it off from the other Touraines, I'd include it with Vouvray and Montlouis. Ditto for Jasnières. The interests of clarity dictate that this wine, an hour north of Vouvray, be discussed with its sister appellation, Coteaux du Loir. The Touraine wine tour concludes with Cheverny-Cour-Cheverny (recently promoted to AOC) and three VDQS: Valençay, Haut-Poitou, and Coteaux du Vendômois.

With the exception of producers in the Chinonais, most Touraine vignerons offer at least one sparkling wine. These are discussed under the specific appellation, Vouvray (or Montlouis), for example, as well as Touraine *mousseux*. Those wines will be included in the producer's main write-up, as will be Vin de Pays du Jardin de la France. And if a Montlouis producer makes Touraine rosé, for example, it will be in Montlouis. In one or two cases I have included the producer of Vin de Pays in the Touraine section.

VOUVRAY

STATUS: *AOC 1936*

TYPES OF WINE: *Still white—dry, off-dry,* moelleux. *Sparkling white*—méthode traditionnelle *and* pétillant; *brut or demi-sec*

ZONE AND PRODUCTION: *A rough average of 94,000 hectoliters, made from 2,000 hectares in eight communes, beginning six kilometers east of Tours and stretching along the Loire's right bank for some sixteen kilometers*

GRAPES: *Chenin Blanc*

SOILS: *A base of tuffeau overlaid with limestone (aubuis) or with* argile à silex (perruches)

PRICE: *20 to 150ff*

BEST VINTAGES: '95, '90, '89, '88, '85, '76, '71, '69, '59, '49, '47

It is a hot June day in Vouvray. The air doesn't budge. In Gaston Huet's cellars, however, it is a chilly 11 degrees Celsius. My breath vaporizes as I follow Huet through his labyrinthine cellars carved into rock, parts of which date from the fifteenth century. Huet, mayor of Vouvray for more than forty years, sets up glasses on a trestle table. He uncorks a grimy, wet bottle, pours, and waits. The wine is superb. A gleaming topaz, it has beautiful structure, layers of flavor integrating lemon, honey, wax, herbal tea, and sautéed mushrooms. The finish is succulent and long. It makes you smack your lips.

The vintage is '47; the wine, a *moelleux* from one of Huet's best vineyards. He says, without ceremony, "It is the best wine I ever made." It is a truly glorious wine, one that makes tasters giddy. It is the wine that made me fall in love with Vouvray, with Chenin Blanc, and with the Loire.

Unlike the Chenins of Anjou, which are always sweet, good vintage or bad, Vouvrays are more likely to be dry (sec); off-dry (*sec-tendre*), with between 4 and 15 grams residual sugar; or half-dry (demi-sec), with 15 to 30 grams residual sugar. *Moelleux* (sweet wines), with residual sugars ranging from 30 grams in an average good year to 60 or 70 grams (or more) in a great vintage, are relatively rare: Huet, for example, made no *moelleux* between '76 and '85. And there is a movement afoot to position the appellation as a producer of *sec-tendre* in most years, as well as a source of *moelleux* in fine vintages. (It is worth repeating here that the EEC defines the sweetness levels differently. Its regulations mandate that wines labeled sec contain no more than 4 grams residual sugar; demi-sec, no more than

12 grams; *moelleux*, no more than 45. Sweeter wines are *doux* or *liquoreux*. The EEC does not recognize *sec-tendre* as a category.)

Sec-tendre Vouvray is not a compromise. Alexander Monmousseau, who specializes in the style, turns out glorious Vouvrays no matter the vintage. Didier Champalou makes every style permitted by nature. His '92s, all *sec-tendres*, were concentrated, firmly focused, fresh, and lacy.

Within Vouvray, distinctions are drawn between wines from the *aubuis* soils of vineyards closest to the Loire, in Rochecorbon, Vouvray, Noizay, and Vernou. Called *la première côte*, these parcels make what are considered the finest and longest-lived Vouvrays. The soils of Reugny, Parçay-Meslay, and Chançay tend toward *perruches*, as do those of the backlands of the riverside communes. Nervy, trenchant, and rectilinear, these Vouvrays have a strong undertow of chamomile, tilleul, and quinine that I find exciting.

Vouvray's sparkling wine is the tail that wags the dog. You rarely meet a producer who's wild about it, yet most say that client demand, not to mention climate, require that it account for half their wine. While it is true that the noblest expression of Vouvray is still wine, the effervescent can be wonderful.

Vouvray has a tendency to *pétiller*—to sparkle naturally. In the old days, it started to bubble once the weather warmed up. But this natural *pétillant* was neither regular nor controllable, so a vintner named Marc Brédif set out to systematize production. This was in the 1920s. *Mousseux* were already being made in the region by the Champagne method. Brédif used the same techniques to produce less fizzy sparkling wine, a *pétillant* whose light thread of bubbles tends to disperse in the glass.

Méthode champenoise, also called *méthode traditionnelle*, is the more popular of the two with consumers accustomed to the bubbles of Champagne; most vintners prefer *pétillant*. It is more "wine," more "Vouvray." As one producer said, "Clients who come for *pétillant* come for wine; those who buy *méthode traditionnelle* buy the celebration."

Both must spend nine months *sur lie*. If I could change policy I would mandate longer aging. Chenin is Chenin. With age it's extraordinary. I recall a gorgeous '62 *pétillant* from Huet, with flavors of toast and honey and caramel. A '49 from Daniel Allias was a crisp, exciting wine with layers of honey, lemon, and toffee. Even his fresh '82 was elegant, bready and full.

Of Vouvray's 350 growers, roughly 200 live off the wine they make. The past decade has seen great qualitative improvement in the wines due to the change in spirit of its vignerons. In the recent past, most sold their wine to *négociants* or to one of Vouvray's two cooperatives. You could count the artisanal producers on one hand. As of the '89 vintage, at least 95 percent kept part of their production to sell on their own.

Several vintages presented tasting problems. The first was the highly regarded '85, which everyone agreed was blocked in its development. Most were utterly closed from '89 through '95. In many '94s and '88s (and some '93s) I detected stem rot—in some cases, barely perceptible; in others, a clear flaw. In the '93 vintage, there is a big difference between the Vouvrays harvested before the rain and those harvested after. Among the latter are a number of classic Vouvrays that will age beautifully.

⤏ PRODUCER RATINGS ⤎

OUTSTANDING
Didier et Catherine Champalou   Domaine des Aubuisières
Domaine du Clos Naudin   Le Haut Lieu (Huet-Pinguet)

EXCELLENT
Daniel Allias   Château Gaudrelle

TO WATCH
Alain et Christophe Le Capitaine   Domaine d'Orfeuilles
François Pinon

HIGHLY RECOMMENDED
Marc Brédif   Clos Baudoin   Domaine de la Robinière
Domaine de la Saboterie   Domaine Vigneau-Chevreau
Domaine du Viking   Benoit Gautier   Alain Rohart

OTHER PROMISING YOUNG VOUVRILLONS
(AND SOME WINES THAT DEMONSTRATE THEIR POTENTIAL)
Georges Brunet   Thierry Cosmes   Domaine de la Galinière
Domaine de la Mabillière   Régis Fortineau

RECOMMENDED
Cave des Producteurs la Vallée Coquette   Cave de Vaudenuits
Gilles Champion   Régis Cruchet   Darragon Père et Fils
Domaine de la Fontainerie   Domaine du Margalleau
Jean-Pierre Freslier   Jean-Pierre Laisement

BY THE GLASS
Domaine Bourillon-Dorléans   Philippe Brisebarre
Domaine de la Limacière   Domaine de Vaugondy
Le Peu de Moriette

⤏ ⤎

OUTSTANDING

Didier et Catherine Champalou, **Vouvray:**   Graduates of Montreuil-Bellay and offspring of vignerons, this young couple set up their own *domaine* in 1984. By applying rigorous standards, they have created one of the most exciting wineries in Vouvray.

Champalou chaptalized only in 1984—not even in '92, when, with *tris*, he arrived at ripenesses of between 13.5 and 15.5 percent potential alcohol. The grapes are pressed slowly, for five hours, and fermentation is slow, cool, and long. Dry wines, which are always *sec-tendre*, ferment in tank; sweet ones in barrel.

I have tasted every vintage (and almost every *cuvée*) from '86 to '93 and each is strongly recommended. Among the '93s, my preference is for the lyrical Cuvée des Fondraux, a floral, elegant wine with layers of honey-mineral flavor and fine focus. Actually, des Fondraux always stands out. It was one of my favorites among Champalou's '92s as well as among the incredible '90s, with its superb flavors of minerals and citrus zests.

Champalou's '90 Cuvée CC is an extraordinary *moelleux*, the result of a *tri* with 90 percent noble rot, 10.5 percent alcohol, and 180 grams residual sugar. Champalou deliberately kept the alcohol level low, leaving the balance in residual sugar because, he says, that is how the legendary Vouvrays of '21 and '47 were made. Honeyed, intense, with full-blown flavors of menthol, apricot, pineapple, currants, and peach, it is gorgeous.

Champalou's '89s—which include three different *moelleux*—were equally spectacular; the most magnificent being, again, the Cuvée CC, with its fine structure and its ravishing, complex flavors of honey, citrus zests, and white currants.

Domaine des Aubuisières, **Vouvray:**   Bernard Fouquet (Montreuil-Bellay) shares the seriousness of purpose of the best of the young Vouvrillons and has an edge: His father is also a nurseryman, and the two developed their own selection of Chenin grafted from their own vines and adapted to their soils. This Chenin is prone to noble rot and is usually a degree riper than industrial clones. Perhaps that explains why his '93s were the best I tasted. Fabulous. The Le Bouchet demi-sec had the heady fruitiness of Champagne, plus pear, mineral, and truffle flavors held together by a taut thread of honey and quinine. Bravo! And the '93 Le Marigny, a *moelleux*, was nothing less than extraordinary: a fine, lacy weave of honey, fruit, and chamomile, with a lemon-lime finish. Again, Bravo!

Fouquet's luxuriant '90 Grains Nobles Vieilles Vignes was a ringer for a Layon, flashy, opulent, bordering on decadent. I loved his racy '89 sec, an explosion of fruit—banana, pineapple, quince—accented with ginger and unified by a strong mineral core. The *moelleux* Vieilles Vignes was a knockout. Nearly pure botrytis, it was a taffeta blanket of honey, pineapple, licorice, and a million other things. With time and a bottomless bottle I could write tomes on Fouquet's '86 sec, a fascinating Vouvray with a stunning unity of the appellation's characteristic flavors. An "Ah Vouvray!" kind of wine.

Fouquet's *méthode traditionnelle* resembles a *pétillant*—toasty, fruity, and clean, with a touch of pineapple and minerals.

Domaine du Clos Naudin, Vouvray: The Foreaus turn out benchmarks, vintage after vintage. Everything is recommended. Yields are low, averaging 33 hectoliters per hectare. (Here, too, grafts are developed from the *domaine*'s vines.) Foreau has not chaptalized since 1984 and never adds yeast. Wines ferment in 300-liter oak barrels (stainless steel for secs) for a month and a half. Later they go into tanks; the secs age in wood.

Foreau can wax inspirational on the subject of Chenin, which he believes has an aromatic palette second to none. An avid cook, Foreau also dreams up dishes to marry with various vintages of Vouvray. I'd love to taste what he ultimately pairs with his '93 demi-sec, a taut, lyrical Vouvray, with firm pear, honey, and quinine notes and an appetizing undertow of citrus zests and herbal tea. The result of a rigorous *tri*, Foreau's '92 sec was a tender wine (4 grams residual sugar), with a framework of steel and finely etched honey and lemon-lime flavors. Both promise to be extremely food-friendly, and each is a lovely evocation of its vintage.

Foreau made numerous *cuvées* of *moelleux* in both '89 and '90. The '90 Goutte d'Or, with more than 27 percent potential alcohol, should be sipped all by itself. A wine of meditation, it was one of the most talked-about '90s in the Loire; a masterpiece. Secs and demi-secs were gorgeous, too, structured, with firm mineral cores, and long, luscious flavors ranging from apricots and ginger to Poire William and licorice. The heavily botrytized first *tri* of '89 tasted like nectar, an exceptional wine with exquisite fruit and structure. (Another *cuvée*, partially fermented in new oak barrels, was a toothsome *moelleux* with apricot, honey, litchi, and ginger flavors and a whisper of oak.)

Foreau's sparkling wine ages for two years, though Foreau is aiming for four; a swell idea, as his *mousseux* is particularly savory when it has aged a bit longer. An '83, tasted in '95, was fresh, nuanced, discreet, and succulent.

Le Haut Lieu (Huet-Pinguet), Vouvray: Now in his eighties, Gaston Huet has become a legend in his own time. Although the *domaine* and the man are one in most minds, Huet turned over day-to-day operation of his *domaine* to his son-in-law, Noël Pinguet, more than a decade ago. A former math major, Pinguet has taken the winery even further in search of quality. He led the *domaine* into biodynamics, a shift he undertook sensibly and gradually, starting with a single plot in 1986. By 1991 the entire thirty-five hectares had been converted.

The *domaine*'s best wines are single-vineyard bottlings from three parcels: Le Haut Lieu, Le Clos du Bourg (the first to be converted to biodynamics), and Le Mont. Pinguet turned out some rather miraculous '94 secs, notably Le Mont and Clos du Bourg, each with tart Granny Smith flavors, seasoned with honey. The impressive '93s began with a fragrant, gingery Haut Lieu sec—which seemed simultaneously big-boned and delicate—and culminated with a delectable, vibrant *moelleux*. Pinguet had the best lineup of '92s I tasted. Le Mont, an extremely pretty *sec-tendre*, had lovely flavors of apple skin and quinine. The Clos du Bourg was an intense, mineral demi-sec with nuances of orange peel and ginger; Le Haut Lieu, an elegant blend of apples, apricots, and quinine.

The '90s are all magnificent. Honors go to the first *tri* of the Clos du Bourg, an exquisite syrup that spread its flavors of honey, apricots, lemon, and licorice across the palate. None of Pinguet's '89s is less than stupendous. The biodynamic Clos du Bourg was my favorite: Glinting with green and orange reflections, it was profound and delicate, with crystalline flavors of apricot, orange, quinine, herbal tea, and butterscotch as well as the purest expression of honey I've ever tasted.

Not to be overlooked is Huet's fine sparkling wine. Much of the 5,000 square meters of wine cellar is given over to its production. When young, the *pétillants* tend to be a bit pungent—too Cheniny—but with age they are sublime. Toasty, layered, fresh, and exciting.

EXCELLENT

Daniel Allias, Vouvray: When he's on target—and he often is—Daniel Allias makes perfect Vouvrays. The family style is floral and fruity with underpinnings of steel. The overall impression is one of well-knit, finely tuned wines. They are bottled under two labels: Domaine Allias and Clos du Petit Mont, a single vineyard with thin, extremely chalky soils.

I did not much admire the '92s but Allias made some lovely '90s, from a toothsome *sec-tendre* to an astonishing Réserve *moelleux*, lushly honeyed, with flavors of cinnamon, apples, and quinine. A must-taste. All three levels of '89 were excellent. The ample sec could convert blockbuster-Chardonnay fans. But it was fine, too, and tightly knit, with savory bitter-almond and quinine flavors. The demi-sec was a rich blend of pear, ginger, quince, and blossoms, with an undertow of quinine and minerals that seemed to deepen and accentuate the other flavors. The '89 Petit Mont *moelleux* was fine-boned yet sumptuous. And you already know about his extraordinary *pétillants*.

Château Gaudrelle, Vouvray: My afterimage of Château Gaudrelle always places the *domaine* in "Outstanding"—and that's where it should be—but some wines fall slightly short of the mark. Brash, intense Alexander Monmousseau physically resembles his father, Armand (formerly head of the sparkling wine firm Monmousseau, in Montrichard); temperamentally, he recalls his uncle Patrice (the brash, intense director of Bouvet-Ladubay). A Beaune graduate, Monmousseau works a fourteen-hectare vineyard and leads Vouvray's *sec-tendre* movement. All his wines are off-dry—excepting his over-the-top *cuvées* of syrupy *doux*.

I like to think that Monmousseau's '88 *sec-tendre* represents the kind of wine Vouvray could be making most years. It was fresh, with pungent apple skin aromas, supported by ripe fruit, herbal tea, lemon zest, honey, licorice, and quinine. Gaudrelle at its most classic, it was aerodynamic, and clear and fresh as a waterfall.

Monmousseau's '93, while not quite as invigorating, was a suave, textbook Vouvray with delicate, well-integrated flavors. Less traditional was his '92 Réserve *sec-tendre*, which was still fermenting in February '93. A fascinating wine, pure botrytis, it came on like a *moelleux* but was dryish, honeyed, concentrated, and firm. The '90 Clos le Vigneau was a fine *sec-tendre* with mouth-filling marrowy texture from aging on its fine lees. His dense Réserve Passerillé, 10 percent alcohol and 235 grams residual sugar, was sheer nectar. It brought to mind his '89 Vendange Tardive made from botrytized and shriveled grapes with between 25 and 30 percent potential alcohol. It was dazzling—like biting into a honeycomb.

TO WATCH

Alain et Christophe Le Capitaine, Rochecorbon: These recent graduates of Amboise have made impressive Vouvrays on their seventeen hectares with admirable consistency—in weak years (a well-knit, pear-scented '94 sec), in fair ones ('93 sec and demi-sec, each with vivid flavors of minerals and Granny Smith apples), and strong ones ('89 and '90 *moelleux*, layered with flavors of honey, fruit, and minerals).

Domaine d'Orfeuilles, Reugny: Bernard Herivault's wines get better all the time. His '93 sec and demi-sec each presented an accurate portrait of Herivault's Vouvrays—floral-scented, crystal clear wines, supported by a stony, mineral undertow characteristic of Reugny's soils. Ditto the '92 sec. I love Herivault's '90s and '89s, particularly the '89 *moelleux*, a flinty, long Vouvray with lots of breed as well as flavors of ginger, honey, and ripe fruit.

François Pinon, Vernou: "When I took over the *domaine* it wasn't to make just anything," said Pinon, a child psychologist who succeeded his father in 1987. "I had an interesting life as an analyst. As a winemaker I want to keep the typicity of both the appellation and the vintage. I've always lived in the Vallée de Cousse. You're either sensitive to that or not. I am."

A love of living things informs Pinon's winemaking. Vineyards are plowed, not chemically treated; vines are replaced by mass selection, not clones; grapes are harvested by *tri*, in small cases, and pressed gently. He adds no yeast and vinifies by parcel.

Of the minuscule amount of Vouvray he made in '94, Pinon offered a bracing sec with a strong personality. His impressive lineup of '92s and '93s includes lacy but taut and mineral-rich demi-secs in each vintage and a characterful late-harvest *moelleux* in '93.

Tasting Pinon's separate *cuvées* of normal '90 *moelleux* graphically demonstrated the impact of *terroir*. The first, from clayey soils, offered peach, minerals, and honey. But the second, from *perruches*, showed more breed and was more complex. Then there was a *tri*, Réserve Botrytisé, a lush and complex weave of many types of fruit, honey, minerals, and bitter lemon; and finally, a Goutte d'Or, which was all of the above, five shades deeper. Less elegant than the *tri* but celestial. Other beauties include Pinon's hauntingly nuanced '89 sec; his luscious '89 Réserve Passerillé, an old-vines *moelleux*; and his '88 demi-sec, a *tri* of old vines, which explodes with minerals and quinine.

Pinon's flavory, characterful *méthode traditionnelle* and *pétillant* age for three to four years. His ample Touraine *mousseux*, a rosé of Gamay, Cot, and Grolleau, goes well with both curries and plum tarts.

HIGHLY RECOMMENDED

Marc Brédif, Rochecorbon: Created in 1882 by Ernest Brédif, then directed by nephew Marc, the house was purchased in 1980 by Patrick de

Ladoucette. Most of Brédif's twenty hectares are on the *première côte* of Vouvray. The firm also buys must and wine, mostly for sparkling wines, which account for half of production.

Brédif turns out tasty, textbook Vouvrays, of which '93, a well-made *sec-tendre*, is a good example. *Moelleux* are cellared for three or four years prior to release. The '89 *moelleux*, drier and more alcoholic than many, was flowery, fine, and nicely structured. An '86 sec was a creamy, two-dimensional Vouvray, well structured and savory. The elegant *moelleux* balanced honey and quinine.

Brédif's sparkling wines age for a minimum of two years (five, if vintage-dated). The *Méthode traditionnelle* Brut is fresh, airy, layered, and elegant; the *Pétillant* brut, toasty and fruity, with savory mineral and licorice notes.

Clos Baudoin, Vouvray: Prince Philippe Poniatowski makes two sparkling wines: a rosé (Touraine *mousseux*) and a Vouvray called Aigle d'Or Brut. In still wines his line includes AC Touraine, Aigle Blanc (a Vouvray), and three single-vineyard Vouvrays: Clos des Patys, Clos de l'Avenir, and the signature wine, Clos Baudoin.

Yes, the title's for real. Poniatowski's great-great-uncle was the last king of Poland, Stanislaus Auguste. The logo on the label of Aigle Blanc comes from the old Polish flag. The family came to France in 1855. Poniatowski's grandfather used to eat at a Paris restaurant called La Petite Riche. Sometime after the first World War he was told that he could no longer order his favorite wine, as the vineyard was being sold. So he bought it himself. It was the Clos Baudoin. Philippe Poniatowski later bought twenty-four additional hectares.

Poniatowski says his wines are on the dry side, except in exceptional vintages. And he keeps them dry, often under 5 grams residual sugar. I have often been disappointed in Aigle Blanc; the single-vineyards are more interesting. Restaurateur Jean Bardet (Tours) has an exclusive on the Clos des Patys, which in good years is a vigorous Vouvray softened by underlying sweetness. Of the versions of Clos de l'Avenir I've tasted, the best was the '89 *moelleux*, with its intriguing layers of honey, minerals, pineapple, and herbal tea.

The Clos Baudoins are usually nervy, discreet Vouvrays with fine sugar-to-acid balance. An '89, 50 percent botrytis, embodied this elegance. A velvety wine with layers of honey, quince, and quinine, it was focused, every inch a Vouvray. A nicely built '93 had pleasant peach and floral notes.

Poniatowski's Vouvray brut is usually characterful and full-bodied, with flavors of toast and mushrooms.

Domaine de la Robinière, **Chançay:** Vincent Raimbault, a young Clark Kent look-alike, graduated from Amboise and took over his father's fifteen hectares of vines on the hillsides between the Loire and the Brenne. His Vouvrays give an honorable, if not always inspired, image of the appellation, often missing the higher mark by a hair. My favorites include his sapid '89 *doux* and the even more impressive *liquoreux*, a *tri* of old vines, with 100 grams residual sugar. His lovely '90 Réserve *moelleux* was hydromel for the gods. And his nicely textured '93 demi-sec had intriguing mineral flavors.

Domaine de la Saboterie, **Rochecorbon:** Christian Chaussard, a former technician for public works projects, began making Vouvray in 1987 (after studying at La Tour Blanche in Bordeaux). For a latecomer to wine, he plays the role of folkloric vigneron to the hilt—forever beret-clad, discoursing on organic viticulture, and introducing his latest novelties. One such was a '93 with 17 grams residual sugar. As he had barely filtered it, the wine had started going through a second fermentation: Voilà! a natural *pétillant*—just the way they used to make them. Well, it was a nice wine. Not all that bubbly, but appetizing, with intriguing fruit flavors and a pleasantly oxidized note.

Chaussard made five different '90s and six different '89s, including a number of *moelleux*. All should be quite lovely, but when tasted in '95, they seemed closed. I recall with particular pleasure an earlier encounter with Chaussard's top *cuvée* of '89. It offered mellow flavors of oak, honey, apple, and rum, linked by a strong citrus thread.

Domaine Vigneau-Chevreau, **Vernou:** This family *domaine* consists of twenty hectares on the *perruches* of Vernou and the *aubuis* of Chançay and Noizay. Lots ferment separately and, when the vintage warrants, are bottled separately. In '89, for example, the *domaine* offered six *moelleux*, a demi-sec, and numerous secs.

"Our clients come to find an original product and discover a *terroir* and a *cépage*, and I have fun," explains Jean-Michel Vigneau. His wines are always a discovery. In his lineup of beautiful '90s I adored a limpid sec and a crystalline, honeyed *moelleux*, a *tri* of very old vines. I tasted three of the '89 secs, each one more luscious than the last. My favorite was the astonishing Vernou, tight and rich, with apricots, minerals, and amazing personality.

From a gingery young-vines bottling to an overwhelming old-vines (a jam of apricot and quince), Vigneau's six '89 *moelleux* were divine. I also love the way he talks about off-years. As we tasted a tart, lemon-mineral '92 sec, he shrugged and said, "This, too, is Vouvray." Vigneau's five different sparkling Vouvrays are as personal as his still wines.

***Domaine du Viking,* Reugny:** Lionel Gauthier, a strapping blond whose Nordic roots inspired the *domaine*'s name, specializes in *pétillant* because, he explains, his *terroir* produces wines that are particularly vivacious. Indeed, his bracing '84, tasted in a local restaurant, inspired my visit. And Gauthier's '83 *Méthode traditionnelle* was layered, rich, and fruity, with a flinty finish. His still wines are recommended, albeit less categorically. The '90 demi-sec resembled the vigneron, vigorous and briskly citric.

***Benoît Gautier,* Rochecorbon:** An Amboise grad with ten hectares, Gauthier sometimes makes excellent Vouvray but not every time—yet. I liked his ultra-dry '93 sec and his curious, rather cidery, barrel-fermented '93 Clos la Lanterne. The '92 Lanterne accidentally went through a second fermentation and was too flabby for my taste. Most of Gauthier's '89s and '90s were lovely, particularly the '89 Cuvée Arnaud Grains Nobles, a syrup of honey and pineapple.

***Alain Rohart,* Vouvray:** Laid off from his job as an industrial designer, Rohart decided to realize a long-held dream of studying wine. He enrolled at Amboise and later found six hectares on Vouvray's *première côte*. His '92s and '93s were honest and ambitious. (The '93 demi-sec Cuvée Michel Lelarge was a fine blend of pear and minerals.) All the '89s and '90s are recommended. My three favorites, all '89s, were a refined demi-sec Cuvée du Clos du Pin; the Cuvée de la Chataigneraie, a *moelleux* from old vines, complex and noble; the Cuvée des Loges, all pears and orange zest drenched in honey.

For his *méthode traditionnelle*, Rohart follows the more stringent rules governing Crémant. His sparkling Vouvray is among the best.

OTHER PROMISING YOUNG *VOUVRILLONS*
(AND SOME WINES THAT DEMONSTRATE
THEIR POTENTIAL)

***Georges Brunet,* Vouvray:** '90 *doux*, '85 demi-sec.
***Thierry Cosmes,* Noizay:** '93 demi-sec, '89 demi-sec; '88 and '85 sec.
***Domaine de la Galinière,* Vernou:** '89 sec and *moelleux*.
***Domaine de la Mabillière,* Vernou:** '90 Cuvée Louis Philippe, a Grains Nobles, and the normal '89 *moelleux*.
***Régis Fortineau,* Vouvray:** '90 *sec-tendre* and normal *moelleux* and *doux*; '89 sec and late-harvest *moelleux* and the extremely tart '93 sec, with its intense Granny Smith flavors.

RECOMMENDED

Cave des Producteurs la Vallée Coquette, **Vouvray:** This co-op's best wines are its sound commercial sparklers, particularly the Cuvée Extra Réserve.

Cave de Vaudenuits, **Vouvray:** Ditto, for full-bodied, fruity *mousseux.*

Gilles Champion, **Vernou:** A practical vigneron who makes early-drinking Vouvrays. *Doux* from '90 and '89 are recommended.

Régis Cruchet, **Noizay:** Pleasant, honest Vouvrays from a pleasant, honest vigneron.

Darragon Père et Fils, **Vouvray:** A respected family *domaine* making virile Vouvrays.

Domaine de la Fontainerie, **Vallée Coquette:** In '90, Catherine Dhoye-Deruet took over her family's six hectares on the chalky soils of well-exposed slopes. The '90 *moelleux* Coteaux les Brulées is truly lovely, complex and fine, with light, roasted notes said to be characteristic of this parcel.

Domaine du Margalleau, **Chançay:** Jean-Michel Pieaux describes his Vouvrays as tending toward the demi-sec. The '89 *moelleux* was, indeed, less powerful than many but was a lovely Vouvray with a beautiful interweaving of honey, fruit, and quinine, which gave it sublime balance. The sec was beautiful, too (ironically, the '89 demi-sec disappointed). His '90 *doux* was fetching.

Jean-Pierre Freslier, **Vouvray:** Characterful '89s and delicious '90 *moelleux.* The '93 sec would be fine to sip in a wine bar. The full-bodied *mousseux* are "*bien* [very] Vouvray."

Jean-Pierre Laisement, **Vouvray:** Hit-or-miss, but I admired the '90 *doux* and the '88 sec.

BY THE GLASS

Domaine Bourillon-Dorléans, **Rochecorbon:** The '89 *tri moelleux* and the '90 Goutte d'Or are recommended. The '93s and '94s seemed like bad faux Burgundies, a blend of barrel fermentation and malolactic.

Philippe Brisebarre, **Vouvray:** Brisebarre's wines seem to be slipping. His '89 demi-sec was rich and vivacious. The '90 *moelleux* Réserve was fair, but the '92s and '93s were bland.

Domaine de la Limacière, **Vouvray:** Bernard Courson's Vouvrays often win awards. Not from me.

Domaine de Vaugondy, **Vouvray:**   The '93 demi-sec is pretty in a sweet-sour way. The '90 *moelleux,* Cuvée Sélecte, would be nice to taste in a wine bar or as a *vin d'honneur.*

Le Peu de Moriette, **Vouvray:**   A family enterprise with a strong commercial presence and lackluster Vouvrays.

MONTLOUIS

STATUS: *AOC 1938*

TYPES OF WINE: (See *Vouvray*)

ZONE AND PRODUCTION: *Between 12,000 and 16,000 hectoliters of wine yearly, of which two-thirds is still, the rest sparkling, from 400 hectares in three communes, beginning just beyond Tours, on a triangle formed by the confluence of the Loire and Cher*

GRAPES: *Chenin Blanc*

SOILS: *Clay-silica on tuffeau. Parcels near the Loire tend to be covered with large pebbles; those approaching the Cher are sandier (and make the lightest wines); and those approaching the Amboise Forest contain the silex-streaked pebbles you find in cement.*

PRICE: (see *Vouvray*)

BEST VINTAGES: (see *Vouvray*)

Montlouis faces Vouvray across the Loire. Only an intrepid taster would claim to distinguish them blind. Said one vigneron, "We're easily tricked, but our soils are sandier and have less clay so the wines are leaner, demi-sec rather than *moelleux.* They express themselves more quickly and may be somewhat less long-lived." The wines do seem leaner, which makes the mineral aspect stand out in bolder relief. They age beautifully, however.

Nearly half Montlouis's vineyards are used to make Touraines. And many *domaines* offer Sauvignon, Cabernet Franc, Gamay, and Rosé.

Montlouis was severely hit by frost in 1994. Most vintners made only a quarter of their normal volume, much of that sparkling.

❧ PRODUCER RATINGS ❧

LEADER
G&G Deletang

EXCELLENT
Yves et François Chidaine   Dominique Moyer

TO WATCH
Domaine de la Taille aux Loups

HIGHLY RECOMMENDED
Domaine de la Bigarrière   Domaine des Liards
Alain Lelarge

BY THE GLASS
Château de Pintray   Domaine des Chardonnets
Domaine de Saint-Jérôme   Georges Fradin   Alain Joulin
Claude Levasseur   Jean-Claude Thiellin

❧ ❧

LEADER

G&G Deletang, **Saint-Martin-le-Beau:** Olivier Deletang turns out textbook Montlouis year after year. He offers six versions in a normal "good" vintage, two each of sec, demi-sec, and *moelleux.* The first bottling is Saint-Martin-le-Beau; the second, Les Batisses, the *lieu dit* which makes Deletang's fullest, most nuanced wines.

Focus, fine structure, a blend of minerals, pineapple, and flint are the family traits. Since '91, Deletang has made only sec. The '93 Saint-Martin bottling was a lacy, floral wine with a backbone of steel—guns and roses. In '89 and '90 Deletang presented a super *tri* of Les Batisses that went over the top—fat, deep, syrupy, and voluptuous. In the secs and demi-secs of those years, I give the edge to the floral Les Batisses with their fine mineral-nut finishes. Deletang also makes crisp Touraine Sauvignons, pleasant Cabernets, and several *pétillants,* including a perfumed Montlouis brut.

EXCELLENT

Yves et François Chidaine, **Husseau:** Father and son turn out well-knit Montlouis, both floral and razor sharp. François's '92 sec Les Choisilles was among the best Montlouis I tasted of that difficult vintage; a late-harvest wine made from very old vines, it was textured and creamy, with intriguing flavors of balsam. The '90 secs were clean and hard, with flavors of minerals, apples, and pears. Yves's '90 Taille du Loup demi-sec was an exciting mix of minerals, honey, quince, and citrus zests. François's '90 *tri moelleux*, with 60 to 70 percent noble rot, was one of the richest Montlouis I've ever tasted. Yves's *moelleux* was equally regal, a lush and concentrated Montlouis.

The '89s are recommended across the board, particularly François's Cuvée Le Lys, a ravishing *moelleux*. By *tri*-ing severely, the Chidaines turned out lovely, nuanced '88 secs and demi-secs.

Yves also makes supple, fruity rosé and very pleasant Gamays. Sparkling wines, mostly *méthode traditionnelle,* from both Chidaines are characterful, full, broad, and bready, with flavors of fruit and mirabelle.

Dominique Moyer, Husseau: Moyer's wines are very much like the man: gentle, intelligent, honest. They are good company. The vines producing the wine Moyer bottles must be at least twenty years old; wine from younger vines, or vintages like '91, is sold to *négociants*. Harvest is by *tri*. *Moelleux* is made only in great years. Both the floral '93 sec and layered demi-sec are good ambassadors. The '92 sec was nervy and lean, with excellent grip and flavor. Of his four *cuvées* of '90 I preferred the gorgeous normal *moelleux*, a finely etched, honeyed Montlouis. Both the sec and demi-sec seemed a bit coarse and hot. All of Moyer's '89s were excellent. My favorite, the *moelleux* Vielles Vignes, was crystal clear and floral, with ripe pear and mineral flavors, a lyrical Montlouis. His '88s were among the best I tasted.

TO WATCH

Domaine de la Taille aux Loups, Husseau: This one's a cliff-hanger. Act I: 1988. Christian Prudhomme, a hotshot from Bordeaux, saunters into Montlouis, puts together a *domaine* consisting of seven hectares of prime vineyard land—in many parcels, all with old vines, nary a clone among them—and sets the appellation on its ear with his theories about winemaking. His principle: "We're making haute cuisine here."

Prudhomme has the experience to back up his swagger. He has been a roving player for Baron de Rothschild, working in the *chais*, the vineyards, on Baronnie and Opus One in Napa. In Montlouis, he reduces yields to twenty-five hectoliters per hectare by cluster thinning in June; he sends teams of harvesters to pass through the vineyards with their little plastic cases five times, telling them the grapes must taste like jam, then *tris* the harvest again in the cellar. He crushes without destemming and, adding no yeasts, puts the juice in barrels, including *barriques* from Yquem. The wines ferment at their leisure. Ten months. No sulfur, no sugar, no filtration. Those with less than 4 grams residual sugar are blended for the sec; up to 12, demi-sec; 13 to 45, *moelleux*; and above, *liquoreux*.

Yes, the wines are magnificent. "Complex" is an understatement. The wines have the same throbbing sensuality as Jacques Lalanne's Quarts-de-Chaume. And they're intellectual, restrained, refreshing. I retaste them every chance I get. The '90s are resplendent. A pure botrytis *liquoreux* is ravishing in its intensity and purity of flavor. The '89 sec is a joy. The '89 demi-sec exudes every aspect of peach, as well as quince, tisane, oak, and minerals. The first *moelleux* is statuesque; the more botrytized Cuvée Spéciale is pure honey, licorice, toast, and apple skins; sapid, long, fine, and powerful.

Act II: 1991. Prudhomme goes belly-up. Enter Jacky Blot, a local wine broker who says he was Prudhomme's major shareholder. And who says he's determined to make wines the way Prudhomme did, even keeping the cellar master.

So far, the results have been encouraging. Both the sec and demi-secs of '93 were layered, mineral-rich wines. There's also a tiny amount of elegant *moelleux*. Fragrant and dignified when tasted in 1993, the '92 demi-sec seemed closed and coarse in the fall of 1995. A barrel-fermented *pétillant*, from the '93 vintage, was a mouth-filling, extraordinarily appetizing wine, however, with nuances of cider and dried flowers. Another must-taste.

HIGHLY RECOMMENDED

***Domaine de la Bigarrière*, Saint-Martin-le-Beau:** Claude Boureau created his *domaine* "from A to Z" in 1975. He greeted me in khaki shorts, a T-shirt that read FISHING PARTY, and running shoes, and said, with feeling, that what interests him is making "honest wine—of one grape, of one *terroir*. Made by the vigneron, aged in barrel. I'm the one who made it; I'm the one who sells it."

Frost killed off most of his '94 and '91 crops. His somewhat oxidized '93 Les Maisonettes recalled a high-quality dry sherry. The '90s and '89s are all recommended, particularly the vibrant, flinty '89 sec, with intense pear flavors, and the demi-sec Les Chemaudières, from very old vines. Brisk and mineraly, the wine explored the theme of apples—Granny Smiths, apple skins, appie blossoms—with accents of honey and pear. Boureau's '88 sec was as bracing as a mountain stream.

Boureau also produces chewy, *cassis*-flavored Touraine rouge. In his range of sparkling wines, I prefer the Montlouis brut.

***Domaine des Liards*, Saint-Martin-le-Beau:** The Berger brothers run a bifurcated estate: One half champenizes the base wines of Touraine vignerons; the other makes competent, clean, fruity wine (still and sparkling) from its twenty-one hectares. Berger's '93 demi-sec Vieilles Vignes was a supple, accurate Montlouis. The very good '90 Grains Nobles de Pineau offered masses of honey; a two-dimensional *moelleux*. In other vintages, I have liked a floral '89 demi-sec; a silky '89 *moelleux*, with pungent fruit and honey flavors; and a tart, toasty '81 demi-sec.

***Alain Lelarge*, Saint-Martin-le-Beau:** A University of Bordeaux–trained enologist, Lelarge makes classic, clear-cut Montlouis. His floral '92 demi-sec was a supple, pretty wine for the vintage. His '90 *moelleux* Cuvée de Clos de la Touche was a lovely blend of menthol, honey, and quinine. And his '89 *moelleux* Taille du Loup was a refined expression of honey, minerals, quinine, and licorice.

BY THE GLASS

***Château de Pintray*, Lussault:** Marius Rault, who recently took over this historic château, makes rough-hewn, often characterful, and always quirky Montlouis.

***Domaine des Chardonnets*, Saint-Martin-le-Beau:** Quirky Montlouis worth sampling in a wine bar, particularly the pretty '89 demi-sec and the pungent and lively '88 sec and flowery demi-sec.

***Domaine de Saint-Jérôme*, Montlouis:** Jacky Supligeau and Michel Hardy get around. The name is known. Their range of '89s did not kindle interest, but I've come across some tasty '90s.

***Georges Fradin*, Husseau:** Pleasant Montlouis for those already in the camp.

***Alain Joulin*, Saint-Martin-le-Beau:** His '93 Cuvée Cristal *moelleux* (harvested at the end of November) is an engaging blend of honey and truffles, with a strong citric core. Joulin at his best.

***Claude Levasseur*, Husseau:** A man about Montlouis, Levasseur produces very commercial wines which often win medals. They get distinctly mixed reviews from this taster.

***Jean-Claude Thiellin*, Husseau:** Rustic but often appealing Montlouis, with flavors of pear and old wood.

CHINON

STATUS: *AOC 1937*

TYPES OF WINE: *Red, rosé, and white*

ZONE AND PRODUCTION: *80,000 to 95,000 hectoliters on 1,990 hectares in nineteen communes, mostly on the right bank of the Vienne. Cravant is the most viticulturally oriented.*

GRAPES: *Red and rosé—Cabernet Franc and Sauvignon (maximum 10 percent); white—Chenin Blanc*

SOILS: *Gravelly, alluvial soils on the banks of the Vienne; argilo-calcaire or argilo-siliceux hillsides and plateaus*

PRICE: *20ff for a young-vines to 65ff or more for an old-vines*

BEST VINTAGES: *'95, '93, '90, '89, '88, '86, '85, '76, '71, '69, '64, '59, '55, '49, '47*

Wine-lovers, be forewarned! You will not be able to resist the deep-seated sociability of the Chinonais. Bon vivants like these you have never met. Feeling rebuffed by the frosty formality of Bordeaux? Can't get a rendezvous with Henri Jayer? You cannot help but fall in love with Chinon.

In a folkloric cellar carved in rock, in a beautiful, historic town, a garrulous vigneron has *cuvée* after tasty *cuvée* and vintage after riveting vintage awaiting your delectation. The tractor salesman shows up. Great! A reason to uncork more bottles. Then another vigneron accompanied by his mason. More vintages. A bowl of *rillettes*. A '55. Finally, a dulcet old Vouvray from Old-Man-Whatzizface and a searing marc from the farmer next door.

If François Rabelais had not been born, the Chinonais would have had to invent him. The native son's statue sits on the quay above the Vienne, smack in the middle of town, directing traffic, as it were, to Chinon's main square. He gave its townsfolk a motto (which they have adopted quite literally): "*Beuvez toujours, vous ne mourrez jamais.*" ("Drink constantly, never die" is my translation.) His Caves Painctes, the temple of Bacchus in which Panurge seeks the truth, is now the home of Chinon's wine society, the Entonneurs Rabelaisiens, a group which has turned organized merrymaking into a local industry.

Chinon sits near the tip of a triangle formed by the confluence of the Loire and the Vienne. The ruins of a medieval castle look down on a tree-lined quay. And it is from its battlements that most visitors get their first glimpse of Chinon's vineyards.

Chinon is the key to the Loire's great Cabernet Francs. Simultaneously silky and potent, it is capable of expressing the easy elegance one associates with Saumur-Champigny and the power of the manliest of Bourgueils. (I *am* generalizing here!) It is made in essentially two styles: The lightest come from alluvial soils on the banks of the Vienne; the most age-worthy and distinguished from hillsides of clay and chalk. An intermediary style, of moderate ageability, is produced on siliceous slopes and plateaus.

When Rabelais wrote "I know where Chinon lies and I know the Caves Painctes for I have drunk many a glass of fresh wine there," he might well have been describing the friendly little Chinons of Paris wine bars, the Chinon that most people know. Rightly considered a *vin de soif* (thirst-quenching wine), this version ferments in tank, vatting for less than a week, and is bottled by Easter. A buoyant wine, it seems a cross between a juicy Beaujolais and a young claret. Sometimes herbaceous but more often downright jammy, it tastes best lightly chilled. It is often labeled Jeunes Vignes.

Most producers also offer a Vieilles Vignes Chinon. (As there is no legal definition of what constitutes "Old Vines," you have to trust the vigneron.) Vatting for these lasts from between fourteen to forty days or longer. Producers generally punch down to extract maximum flavor, color, and aroma (and to keep the fermentation going). Wines usually age in barrel—either before or after they have gone through malolactic fermentation—for four months to more than four years. Oak and chestnut *demi-muids*, traditional in the region, are still the most widespread. But many are eliminating chestnut (which leaves a bitter taste) and some are experimenting with used Bordeaux *barriques*.

These Chinons benefit from cellaring for five years to several decades. They pass from an exuberant fruitiness through a musky, visceral stage, evolving toward a finespun fabric of sandalwood, spice, dried fruit, licorice, and faded flowers.

Chinon rosés, made from bleeding the vats for the reds, can be real charmers. Firm, vinous, with pungent strawberry and mineral flavors, they are robust and perfumed. There is also a minuscule—though increasing—amount of Chinon blanc. Nervy and austere, it is capable, in great years, of aging like a fine Montlouis. I recall Olga Raffault's extraordinary '59 Champs-Chenin (the name of the *lieu dit* alone confirms Chenin's history in Chinon). Drunk in '92, the wine was sublime, a fresh, complex weave of honey, herbal tea, citrus, and spices. Today the trend is to make Chinon blanc to drink right away. With techniques like skin contact, producers such as Couly-Dutheil and Domaine de la Noblaie succeed in making immediately amiable Chenins.

Chinon has roughly three hundred producers. Most sell at least part of their production to *négociants* and to cubi customers. About half belong to the recently formed SICA (Société d'Intérêt Collectif Agricole) des Vins de Rabelais which claims at least 20 percent of their harvest, from which it makes a range of cheap, rather dull Chinons, to sell to supermarkets. An increasing number, however, save a percentage of their production to bottle under their own labels.

Now here's the rub: With rare exception, every single Chinon could—and should—be better. And the obstacle is that seductive sociability. The Chinonais' "eat, drink, and be merry" lifestyle is a double-edged sword. More than anything, the Chinonais vigneron makes wine for his buddies, for endless afternoons that melt into late nights in the bowels of cellars. The outside world—of other wines and other markets, of progress, of comparison, of the sheer desire to excel—doesn't exist. Life's so damned easy here. Why change? This doesn't mean the Chinons aren't delicious. They are. But they could be better, almost across the board.

Note: When green bell pepper flavors are just a nuance in a red wine, that's fine; more than that is a turnoff. The Loire Cabernets of two very good vintages—'78 and '85—were marked by strong flavors of green bell peppers. This explains why I'm not more enthusiastic about the highly considered '85s.

⋘ PRODUCER RATINGS ⋙

OUTSTANDING
Charles Joguet

LEADER
Couly-Dutheil

EXCELLENT
Philippe Alliet   Château de la Grille
Domaine Bernard Baudry

HIGHLY RECOMMENDED
Clos du Parc   Domaine Olga Raffault
Guy Lenoir

RECOMMENDED
Centre Viti-Vinicole de Chinon   Domaine Francis Haerty
Domaine de la Noblaie   Domaine de Pallus

Domaine de la Perrière   Domaine de la Roche Honneur
Moulin à Tan   Jean-Maurice Raffault   Wilfred Rousse
Gérard Sourdais

BY THE GLASS
Château de Ligré   Clos de la Croix Marie
Clos du Saut au Loup   Guy Coton   Domaine de Beauséjour
Domaine du Colombier   Domaine des Rouet
Domaine du Raifault
Domaine de la Tour (Guy Jamet)   Philippe et Charles Pain
Gérard Spelty

⤜⤛

OUTSTANDING

Charles Joguet, Sazilly: Joguet's wines have a cult following (which includes me). A graduate of the Ecole des Beaux-Arts in Paris, he returned to Chinon after his father died in order to help his mother tend the vines. He was one of the first small proprietors in the region to bottle his own wine rather than sell in bulk. The first Chinonais to bottle young- and old-vines separately as well as to systematically bottle his wines by vineyard, he was the first to employ once-used Bordeaux barrels for aging and he helped "invent" the *cuve à pigéage,* a tank equipped with a device for punching down the cap of the fermenting must.

Joguet's Chinons are fine-grained reds with silky texture, great concentration, and plush flavors. When young, they surge with raspberries, plums, and violets; with age, spices, musk, prunes, fennel, dried fruit, smoke, and minerals. His three lightest bottlings are Jeunes Vignes, Clos de la Cure, and Varennes du Grand Clos. His finest, and most expensive, are Clos de la Dioterie, made from eighty-year-old vines on the clay-and-chalk soils of a north-facing hillside, and Clos du Chêne Vert, a two-hectare plot on a southwest-facing hillside overlooking Chinon. (The eponymous nine-hundred-year-old oak demarcates the point at which the soils change from a mix of silica, clay, and chalk that produces powerful wines to a more friable soil that produces perfumed ones.)

Joguet treats all of his grapes similarly—up to a point—and then makes distinctions based on age of vines and the characteristics of each parcel. In broad strokes, his yields are generally low. He hand harvests, using plastic Champagne cases. Nearly all of the harvest is destemmed, placed under a blanket of carbon dioxide, and fermented in stainless steel. Beyond that, however, he treats each *cuvée* differently, with Jeunes Vignes and Dioterie at either extreme. With the first, he aims to "to snatch the fruit, the vivacity of the young vine." Fermentation is cool but short—25 degrees Celsius for eight to twenty days. The wine is vibrant and appetizing, with flavors of raspberry, cherry, *cassis*, and plum.

To extract as much perfume and elegance as possible from Dioterie's old vines, Joguet adapted techniques used for the perfumed Chenins of Vouvray, keeping temperatures at 20 to 22 degrees Celsius for the first month, then raising them to 35 degrees to extract color and tannins. Chêne Vert is vinified similarly. Both age in used Bordeaux *barriques*, and neither is fined or filtered.

Chêne Vert is a generous Chinon, a manly version, with strong fruit and warm, meaty solidity. In its youth it is flashier than Dioterie, more Broadway; it's Gene Kelly to Dioterie's Fred Astaire. Dioterie, which takes longer to open, is regal and complex. It can age indefinitely.

I love the Varennes du Grand Clos, too. It is Dioterie on a smaller scale. Finely tuned, silky fruit, effortless elegance, but it's less complex, its finish is slightly shorter, and you can drink it sooner. It's fascinating to taste this *cuvée* next to Joguet's Plant Direct. In 1983, with the permission of the INAO, he planted a hectare of ungrafted Cabernet Franc vines in the Varennes vineyard. Its yields are naturally half those of the grafted vines, and though Joguet does not chaptalize this wine, it seems to have more extract than the normal Varennes, which is usually 1 percent higher in alcohol. The '89 was spectacular, giving even Dioterie and Chêne Vert a run for the money.

In 1985 Joguet formed a society with an accountant in Chinon who has vines in Beaumont-en-Véron. This permitted him to hire employees and to delegate responsibility to Alain Delaunay and Michel Pinard, who have taken over most day-to-day functions. The experimentation that informed earlier years seems to have halted. Nevertheless, vintage after vintage and bottle for bottle, Joguet continues to make the best Chinon.

In '94, Joguet produced a string of pretty kirsch- and cherry pit–scented Chinons, beginning with a juicy press wine, bottled as Cuvée de Printemps, and culminating with the fine-grained Chêne Vert. (What little Dioterie remained after spring frosts went into Varennes.) Joguet's '93s should age as beautifully as his '86s, particularly the berry-rich Varennes, the clove-accented Chêne Vert, and Dioterie, whose rich plum, *cassis*, raspberry, and musk flavors obscured the wine's characteristically hard mineral core.

The '89 and '90 Varennes are drinking splendidly now: The baby fat's been replaced by a svelter, finer line; spicy nuances, as well as the wine's firm mineral underpinnings, are beginning to flash through the plush fruit. The '89 and '90 Chêne Vert and Dioterie are, of course, sublime now—but will continue to develop. It's time to taste the very classic, very beautiful '88s, and the harder '86s (one of my favorite vintages chez Joguet). I'd put the peppery '85 Chêne Vert with a garlicky roast leg of lamb and I'd open an '87 Dioterie just for its firm, elegant, inimitable expression of *terroir*.

LEADER

Couly-Dutheil, Chinon: Considered "the motor of the region," this grower-*négociant* house is run by Pierre and Jacques Couly and by Pierre's son Bertrand, an agronomist. The firm, which also sells purchased wine from other Loire regions, works seventy-five hectares in Chinon and has contracts covering another one hundred.

In 1989 Couly completed computerized cellars, investing in a pneumatic press and thermoregulated stainless steel fermentation tanks. Its richest reds age in fifty-hectoliter barrels made of local oak—from the forests of Chinon and Blois, for example. (The Coulys feel that the closer the wood was to the appellation, the better its effect on the wine.)

The Coulys are evidently commited to wine, in general, and to Chinon, in particular. But since the death of founder René Couly, the *domaine* seems to lack a distinctive voice. There's a sense of too many cooks spoiling the broth; or of too much time spent trying to second-guess what consumers want. For a while, the supposition was that people wanted lighter, more supple Chinons. And even the *domaine*'s top wines have seemed less concentrated, designed to drink young. Lately, in what seems a positive move, the Coulys say they have abandoned all machine-harvesting and are picking only by hand, by *tri*. A Chinon lover hopes this means Couly's back on track. It's an important house and has wonderful vineyards.

Les Chanteaux, Chinon blanc, is a recent but worthwhile addition to the Couly portfolio. The vibrant, floral house-style holds in rich years, like '89 and '90, as well as in terrible ones, like '94, when the Coulys succeeded handily with a crisp, perfumed white that ended on a fine mineral note.

Les Gravières, Couly's lightest red Chinon, is made from purchased wine and is generally intensely fruity with raspberry and bell pepper notes. The Domaine René Couly, a red for near-term drinking, is usually an attractive, if somewhat two-dimensional, Chinon: even '94 is pleasing.

Along with a handful of stars of French culture and gastronomy (e.g., Alain Senderens and the omnipresent enologist Jacques Puisais), the

Coulys purchased a six-and-a-half-hectare vineyard, La Diligence, a gentle south-facing slope outside of Chinon. Judging from the respectable '94 and the fruitier, more focused '93, it seems to make a gentle Chinon, bridging the René Couly bottling and the winery's three prestige *cuvées*: Clos de l'Echo, from a seventeen-hectare vineyard facing Chinon's château; Clos de l'Olive, a two-and-a-half-hectare vineyard; and Baronnie Madeleine, a blend of the best *crus*, usually of purchased wine.

I've tasted both the '90 and the '89 Clos de l'Echo many times. At the winery each has been expressive, layered, tannic, plummy, with spice and mineral flavors. Elsewhere they have seemed ripe but neutral and soft. The '88 has had penetrating flavors of raspberry and violet mixed with spice, tobacco, and bell pepper. My preference in more recent vintages is for the '93, with its attractive blend of bell pepper, musk, black cherry, *cassis*, and clove.

That the Coulys are capable of making extraordinary wine is evidenced by older vintages. The most fascinating, and the most demonstrative of a *grand cru*, was the '55 Echo, a lacy knit of dried red fruit, hay, and cinnamon. Not powerful, simply haunting, it embodied my old-handkerchief image of Breton.

EXCELLENT

***Philippe Alliet,* Cravant-les-Coteaux:** A Bordeaux fanatic, Alliet (Montreuil-Bellay) makes fine-grained, oak-aged Chinons from eight hectares of vines, either on clay and gravel or on the gravelly, sandy soils of the banks of the Vienne. Vatting lasts four to five weeks at moderately high temperatures. The wines age in used Bordeaux barrels. The finished wines are fined with egg whites but not filtered.

Detractors say that Alliet's soils don't produce Chinons that can support long barrel age, and as a result, his wines are too drying, too tannic. I disagree, though I see the point. For me, Alliet's Chinons are always full of extract and plush fruit. They are focused and fine and, good vintage ('90, '89, '88) or bad ('92), always among the best in the appellation. The very small amount of '94 Alliet made was a light, savory red; a bit too hot, however. But his '93 was all you could want in a near-term drinking Chinon—elegant, fruity, and appetizing. Delicious. His '90 Cuvée Prestige Vieilles Vignes exuded aromas of violets, prunes, black cherries, cherry pits, and *eau-de-vie*. Intense and tannic, it should evolve beautifully. The '89s are silky, fine, and beautifully fruity.

Château de la Grille, Chinon: In 1950 Alfred Gosset of the Champagne Gossets bought this venerable vineyard—and held on to it after the sale of the Champagne property. His son Laurent recently bought his siblings' shares and is now at La Grille full-time. The Gossets make every effort to produce as deluxe a version of Chinon as they did of Champagne. They have built ultramodern cellars with stainless steel tanks (some *à pigéage*) and used Bordeaux *barriques* in which the wines age for twelve to eighteen months. Grapes are hand harvested, by *tri*, in small Champagne cases; yields are kept low by cluster thinning. Vatting lasts a month or longer. The wines are kept for more than two years before release.

La Grille has detractors who criticize the wine's price (63ff) and its oakiness. But the Chinonais don't exactly welcome new kids to the block. I admire the wines and I like the image of style, care, and quality the *domaine* gives to Chinon. La Grille may not make a typical Chinon but it certainly makes a very good one.

Jean-Max Manceau, the winemaker, started in 1982, and there isn't one of his vintages I wouldn't be happy drinking. The family-style is rich and concentrated. The younger Chinons are chewy and tannic with dark fruit, violets, occasional green bell pepper notes, and oak. With age, sweet spices such as cinnamon and clove develop, along with musk and dried fruit, and the abundant oak melts into the whole. A trial blend of the '93 (to be bottled in autumn 1995) offered the classic weave of sandalwood, dried fruit, and spice. Lovely. The '92, however, was well-nigh spectacular. A luscious mix of *cassis* and subdued bell peppers, it was suave, concentrated, and rich—the proof of what rigorously low yields can do! It would be difficult to find a better '92 Loire Cabernet. Both '90 and '89 are dense, with profound purple fruit, spices, jam, and oak. By 1996 both the '88 and the '86 should be luscious, nuanced Chinons.

La Grille also makes a tiny amount of big, barrel-fermented rosé, with pretty fruit and a solid bitter-almond finish. The '94 was truly lovely—strong, flavory, and endlessly appetizing.

Domaine Bernard Baudry, Cravant-les-Coteaux: Chinon has no more conscientious winemaker than Baudry, a graduate of the Lycée de Beaune, who worked at the Tours enology lab before creating his own twenty-five-hectare *domaine*. His wines are intelligent, discreet, and well-conceived. They reveal Chinon's surging fruit, sweet spice, and fruit pit flavors but express that succulence clearly and cleanly. When they go over the top, they do so rationally.

Most of Baudry's vines grow on the alluvial soils of the banks of the Vienne. (When the river overflows, Baudry prunes these vines from a rowboat.) Filtration is not systematic, particularly for his more age-worthy *cuvées*.

Les Granges, Baudry's simplest wine, is quintessential young-vines Chinon, sappy, plush, delicious. The '94 was one of the most honest tasted, a supple, light red, accurate for the vintage. The winsome '93 had focused *cassis* and berry flavors and soft tannins. The '94 Domaine Bernard Baudry, from old vines (tasted from tank), was really quite pretty (a surprise from this vintage), with a strong sour cherry finish; the '93 was silkier and finer, with plum and *eau-de-vie de prune* notes, though it displayed the hardness characteristic of the year; the '90 had everything you could want in a Chinon, finesse, structure, and concentrated flavors of black cherry, cherry pit, and birch bark. The sapid '89, at once lush and austere, mixed cinnamon, musk, cherry pits, and licorice, ending on a pleasantly bitter note.

Baudry's Les Grézaux, old vines from a gravelly *lieu dit,* is aged in barrels either from Burgundy or Bordeaux. I've tasted most of the vintages from '76 to '93 (Baudry made none in '94) at least twice. The family resemblance is one of breed, great freshness, youthful aromas of raspberries and linden blossoms, blended with the more evolved aromas of leather, musk, and tobacco. The structure is steely; the texture, *moelleux.* The '90, ample and suave, is the one to drink now.

HIGHLY RECOMMENDED

Clos du Parc, Chinon: The Chinons from this *domaine,* served at Tabac Henri IV in Paris, always got me through the worst hours of jet lag and made me want to get to know the appellation. The style is "enlightened rustic," chewy and tannic, with good fruit, bell pepper, spice, and oak flavors, and in good years, good ageability. Older vintages—'76, '69, '64, '59— offer true portraits of Chinon, with clear flavors of dried fruit, spices, black olives, oak, and bark. In younger wines, the soft, ripe '90, the ample, smoky '89, and the plummy '88 should be drinking well by 1996.

Domaine Olga Raffault, Savigny-en-Véron: "I'm completely opposed to making our wine taste like a Bordeaux," says Olga Raffault, the eightyish doyenne of Chinon and one of its most accomplished flirts. "Our style is fruity and friendly."

Raffault's wines perk up many Tourangeaux lists. Her twenty hectares include several *lieux dits:* La Poplinière (a sandy riverbank); Barnabé (gravelly); and Les Picasses, whose chalky soils produce the *domaine's* longest-lived Chinon. Raffault also produces a rosé and a white Chinon. The latter seems lean and unexpressive when young, but those from great years (like '89 and '90) should evolve to the wondrous complexity of that '59.

The reds are "fruity and friendly"—and often, a lot more: They can offer gorgeous fruit, fine structure, and infinite nuances, all with a slightly rustic edge. The wines ferment in stainless steel tanks or in barrel, vatting for roughly a month. With the exception of Jeunes Vignes, most age in barrel. (Some stay in barrel over four years, at which point they're too dried out, and less tasty than earlier-bottled versions.)

Les Picasses, the most "serious" of Raffault's Chinons, is also the bottling you're most likely to find in restaurants—often in several vintages. It's a good opportunity to taste how a well-made Chinon from a great *terroir* evolves. (The '90, curiously, is disappointing. A pleasant Chinon, but no more than that. Older vintages are more rewarding.) Orange zest lifts the dense *cassis* and cherry flavors of the '89; the deeply fruity '88 offers a fine thread of minerals; '86 is smooth and silky, its musk flavors accented with eucalyptus; '85 displays dried fruit, musk, and spice. The '76, as memory-scented as an attic, is as delicate as an infusion made of dried fruit and sweet spice, with undertones of leather.

Guy Lenoir, Beaumont-en-Véron: Lenoir is a wine-buff trap—in the most amiable sense. A born raconteur, lean and wily, with the feisty appeal of Ross Perot, he holds court in a cellar lined with small barrels, the ground pocked with sand piles encasing demijohns of wine. Between the mono-logue about clones and the aria against filtration, Lenoir suctions some '89 Chenin (from pre-phylloxera vines) from barrel. It is off-dry, a compact blend of quince and pineapple. Then comes an '89 Chinon. It's beautiful and personal, with blueberries, vanilla, and caramel.

In the clear light of day, the wines don't always live up to expectation. Barrel aging, for one, is often too long (more than five years). Despite lovely fruit and spice flavors and nuanced bouquets, most of the reds seem to be drying out by the time they're bottled. But they are always true, original Lenoir and Chinon. He's unique. Crafty and enterprising, he's also a hair-dresser and owns a hotel that caters to traveling salesmen. And his '64 was a fascinating weave of hay, leather, dried fruit, musk, sandalwood, and bacon.

RECOMMENDED

Centre Viti-Vinicole de Chinon: This experimental facility, with twenty-three hectares of vines, is part of the Lycée Agricole de Tours. Its

Chinons are good, sometimes very good—friends get tasty cubitainer Chinons here—to be drunk within six years of the harvest.

Domaine Francis Haerty, Savigny-en-Véron: Usually charming, these are good, middle-of-the-road, early-drinking Chinons. Haerty has vines in the Saumurois from which he makes pleasant Champignys and Chenin-based *mousseux*. He also grows asparagus.

Domaine de la Noblaie (Manzagol-Billard), Ligré: That some of Chinon's vineyards are ideally suited for Chenin is proven year after year by the perfumed, tightly knit Chinon blancs from this *domaine*, which are, by far, the best wines it makes.

Domaine de Pallus, Cravant-les-Coteaux: Daniel Chauveau makes silky, charming, cherry-, raspberry-, and blueberry-scented Chinons to drink in the near term. There is a non-wood-aged Easter bottling, an intermediary bottling with some wood aging, and a September bottling with additional barrel age. The '93, with its focused raspberry fruit, is recommended.

Domaine de la Perrière, Cravant-les-Coteaux: Jean and Christophe Baudry make supple Chinons to drink within five years of the harvest. At their best—as in the '89 La Perrière and Vieilles Vignes—they are quasi-serious Chinons with lively fruit. The Baudrys also make the wines of Gaston Angelliaume.

Domaine de la Roche Honneur, Beaumont-en-Véron: Stéphane Mureau makes potent, muscular Chinon, particularly his Cuvée Diamant Prestige.

Moulin à Tan, Cravant-les-Coteaux: Pierre Sourdais's Chinons have lots of fans. Try his old-vines bottling, Réserve Stanislas, of which the cherry-scented '93 would be a tasty choice in a wine bar.

Jean-Maurice Raffault, Savigny-en-Véron: Raffault has forty hectares of vines, including parcels on some of Chinon's best *lieux dits*, Les Picasses and Isoré. His wines can be very good but they can also disappoint. In general, one senses the quality of the fruit and the excellence of the *terroir*, but too often the wines seem thick and sloppy. Raffault is also one of the founders of the SICA and, with two partners, owns the Caves de Monplaisir, a tasting cellar that sells their wines. He also makes Chinon blanc, a marc of Chinon aged in oak, and a lovely, potent *eau-de-vie de poire*.

Wilfred Rousse, Savigny-en-Véron: Warm, supple Chinons from a conscientious young vigneron who pieced together six hectares on Savigny's sandy soils, invested in temperature-controlled tanks and used Bordeaux barrels, and began turning out some very creditable, generously fruity Chinons in three styles: Easter (no oak); a blend of old and young vines (eight months in barrel); and a Vieilles Vignes which spends a year in barrel.

Gérard Sourdais, **Cravant-les-Coteaux:** Very pretty, juicy Chinons from the producer who formerly supplied Couly with its Bouqueries bottling. I often buy in "cubi" from this *domaine*.

BY THE GLASS

Château de Ligré, **Ligré:** Gatien Ferrand and son Pierre are pure Rabelais. Big eaters, big drinkers, epic partyers, they're ambassadors of the Chinon spirit and fun to be around. But their wines, which are on many lists, are dull, dull, dull.

Clos de la Croix Marie, **Rivière:** André Barc has something of a cult following for his dark, tannic Chinons. I find them unbalanced, hot, graceless, and coarse, occasionally portish, becoming leathery and bouillony with age. If you like that black, hit-'em-over-the-head style, try the '89.

Clos du Saut au Loup, **Ligré:** Passable Chinons. Look for the special *cuvées*.

Guy Coton, **Crouzilles:** Terrific *eau-de-vie de poire*, average Chinon.

Domaine de Beauséjour, **Panzoult:** Light Chinons from a producer who wants to make serious wine. To watch.

Domaine du Colombier, **Beaumont-en-Véron:** Yves Loiseau makes correct, pleasant Chinons.

Domaine des Rouet, **Cravant-les-Coteaux:** Rouet, a young, ex–car salesman, took over the family's fifteen hectares of vines (which he works "homeopathically") and turns out interesting, if not always perfect, Chinons. Try the homeopathic bottling.

Domaine du Raifault, **Savigny-en-Véron:** Though I find many of Raymond Raffault's wines lack concentration, I have admired special *cuvées* like Le Villy and Les Allets.

Domaine de la Tour (Guy Jamet), **Beaumont-en-Véron:** Pleasant, grapey Jeunes Vignes; his Les Picasses and Vieilles Vignes seem to have excellent raw material in search of an author.

Philippe et Charles Pain, **Panzoult:** The brothers Pain supply the house red for Jeanne d'Arc, a bar with a good 58ff lunch menu in Chinon. It's the perfect setting for the wine they make.

Gérard Spelty, **Cravant-les-Coteaux:** Of the many types of wines and special bottlings Spelty makes, the Clos de Neuilly, from fifty-year-old vines, is the most interesting.

Note: A number of wineries in other appellations put out Chinons. Excellent versions come from *Pierre-Jacques Druet* (*see* Bourgueil), particularly his Clos du Danzay.

BOURGUEIL AND
SAINT-NICOLAS-DE-BOURGUEIL

STATUS: *AOC 1937*
TYPES OF WINE: *Red and rosé*
ZONE AND PRODUCTION: *94,000 to 100,000 hectoliters split 60-40 between Bourgueil and Saint-Nicolas. Bourgueil's 2,000 hectares span eight communes. Saint-Nicolas, the farthest west, is included in the Bourgueil appellation though it has its own, too, making it the only Loire red appellation consisting of a sole commune.*
GRAPES: *Cabernet Franc and Sauvignon (maximum 10 percent)*
SOILS: *Sandy, silty soils (Varennes); sand and gravel; and chalky clay*
PRICE: (see *Chinon*)
BEST VINTAGES: (see *Chinon*)

When the red-wine producers of Touraine want promotional photos of their most picturesque sites, they focus on Bourgueil. Here they find an unbroken panorama of vines covering plateaus and hillsides, bordered on the south by the Loire and on the north by forests that provide shelter from winds.

At the western rim of Touraine, the Bourgueil region was part of Anjou until 1790, when it was included within the Indre-et-Loire. Its microclimate is particularly mild. One finds banana plants and palm trees, but more typically, its sandy riverbanks are given over to strawberries and asparagus. Local produce is usually on display in Bourgueil's lively Tuesday-morning market, which spills from under the timbered ceilings of its ancient market hall onto surrounding side streets up to its historic abbey. (Founded in the tenth century by the Benedictines, the abbey's prominence in local viticulture was secured by the abbot Baudry, who first planted Cabernet Franc in the Chinonais in 1089.)

Most of Bourgueil's vines stretch along a plateau of light, hot soils which produce fine, fruity reds. The richest, most complex and age-worthy reds come from gentle, south-facing slopes where the mix of soils changes from sand and gravel to clay and chalk. (Saint-Nicolas is usually considered lighter than Bourgueil because most of its vines grow on gravelly terraces.

But Bourgueil's riverbanks have similar soils. There is no practical reason to distinguish the two.)

Wines are made as they are in Chinon. Many now harvest at least part of their crop by machine. (I often detect a chlorophyll flavor that I associate with machine-harvesting.) Most offer at least two *cuvées*, a spring bottling (with shorter vatting times and no wood age) and a more full-bodied version which usually passes several months in old wood barrels.

Ask someone the difference between Chinon and Bourgueil and you'll get either "Chinon smells of raspberries, Bourgueil of violets"; or "Bourgueil is the more rustic of the two and needs bottle age to reveal its charms." Nothing I've tasted leads me to credit the first theory. The second, however, seems truer, but I'm not sure if that rusticity comes from the *terroir* or from the winemaking. Bourgueil, too, needs shaking up.

❧ PRODUCER RATINGS ❧

OUTSTANDING
Pierre-Jacques Druet

EXCELLENT
Domaine de la Lande

TO WATCH
Pierre Breton   Nau Frères

HIGHLY RECOMMENDED
Domaine de la Chevalerie   Domaine de la Coudraye
Domaine des Forges   Lamé-Delille-Boucard

RECOMMENDED
Christophe Chasles   Clos de l'Abbaye
Jean-Paul et Michel Delanoue   Domaine de la Chanteleuserie
Domaine des Galluches   Domaine de la Gaucherie
Domaine des Mailloches   Domaine des Ouches
Domaine des Raguenières   Maison Audebert et Fils

❧ ❧

SAINT-NICOLAS-DE-BOURGUEIL
❧ PRODUCER RATINGS ❧

LEADER
Domaine Joël Taluau

HIGHLY RECOMMENDED
Cognard-Taluau   Vignoble de la Jarnoterie

BY THE GLASS
Clos des Quarterons   Domaine du Bourg
Domaine Jacques Mabileau   Pascal Lorieux

❧ ❧

Bourgueil

OUTSTANDING

Pierre-Jacques Druet, Benais: When you are talking Pierre-Jacques Druet you are talking extremes. Matinee-idol handsome, he comes on like a snake oil salesman, but passion and knowledge underlie the boulevardier charm. And his wines are fine-grained, focused, and opulent.

The son of a *négociant* in Montrichard, Druet graduated from the Lycée de Beaune and received diplomas from Montpellier and the University of Bordeaux. He sold pneumatic presses, made wine in Switzerland and the Var, and managed an export firm in Bordeaux. He pieced together his twenty hectares in time for the '80 vintage, swept all the awards, and became an "overnight" star.

Druet makes wine like Leonard Bernstein conducted. He chews the scenery. He has studied the ripening dates of each of his parcels over the decades and he harvests, by hand, "by the expression of the land and the soils." Sometimes he's the first, sometimes the last. Yields are among the lowest in the red wine producing Loire. Vatting and temperatures are adapted to a given vintage. Punching down is systematic, even in bad vintages—a practice that provoked an argument with the great enologist Emile Peynaud. (According to Druet, Peynaud later wrote him from California, telling him to continue what he was doing.) He ages some of his wine in new Tronçais barrels—experimenting with different methods of drying the staves—and filters only his rosé.

Druet's rosés (old-vines, fermented in barrel) are terrific: floral, firm, and layered, with rich strawberry, apricot, and almond flavors. He also has vines in Chinon, including a parcel of old vines in the Clos du Danzay. I found the '91 honest but thin—a '91 Bourgueil was only slightly better—but both the '93 and '89 Clos de Danzay were excellent Chinons; limpid, serious, with intense flavors of fruit and spice.

Druet makes four different Bourgueils; the progression from one to the next is always precise. Les Cent Boissellées, a juicy quaffer with clearly etched fruit, is the simplest; next is the Beauvais. Its mellow fruit-spice-oak flavors make it seem simultaneously fine-grained and rustic—a hugely satisfying Bourgueil to drink while waiting for Grand Mont to mature.

Made from old vines on chalky soils, Grand Mont is a long-lived, intensely concentrated Bourgueil. The '89 and '90 were profound. Velvety, rich, and tannic, each was packed with plums and blueberries. The '93, its lush black-cherry fruit accented with licorice, should age as regally as the '88 and '86. If you don't like this, you basically don't like Bourgueil.

But if I must pick one *cuvée* chez Druet, it's Vaumoreau, the black wine of Bourgueil. Made from fifty- to one-hundred-year-old vines, it's majestic. A barrel sample of '93, tasted in '95, revealed dark, cinnamon-scented fruit, sandalwood, and spices. A very evocative wine, deeply complex, it should be a monument, as is the mind-blowing '89. So concentrated it seems a distillate—of berries, violets, oak, and minerals—the '89 Vaumoreau is the essence of Bourgueil.

EXCELLENT

Domaine de la Lande, **Bourgueil:** Vintage after vintage, Marc Delaunay's wines are ambassadors for Bourgueil. No magic recipes—quality is simply due to a respect for basic principles. Delaunay, who works nine hectares with his son, François, hand harvests, by *tri* (with the exception of a small parcel of Chinon, which is seven kilometers away); he doesn't push his vines to overproduce; and he vinifies carefully, at low temperatures, in either stainless steel tanks or barrels.

The family traits of Delaunay's Bourgueils are silkiness, fine balance, and radiant cherry and cherry pit fruit. (That silky, fine-grained texture hardly fits the traditional image of Bourgueil. I think Delaunay achieves this, in part, because he almost never blends in his press wine—though even *that* is good.)

His '94s were among the best I tasted, light and fine-grained, with bright, focused cherry and cherry pit flavors. He bottled only two *cuvées* of '94. Usually there are four (as well as the Chinon and a Saint-Nicolas-de-Bourgueil): a succulent Jeunes Vignes Domaine de la Lande; Cuvée des Pins, for near-term drinking; the richer, longer Les Graviers, from pebbly clay soils; and Cuvée Prestige, an old-vines bottling. Delaunay made each version in '93, one prettier than the last. The Cuvée Prestige was the richest, amplest, and most complex of all, with soft fruit tannins supporting its elegant blend of cherry pit and spice. His '92s were also among the best I tasted, particularly the Cuvée Prestige, which was light in alcohol, long on finesse.

His lightest '90 offered a perfect portrait of Loire Breton. But the '90 Cuvée des Pins was a notch above, with its intense, floral aromas, its silky texture, and its insistent "listen up!" Bourgueil fruit. The Cuvée Prestige was beautiful, too, with gorgeous fruit and a smoky finish. The '89 Cuvée Prestige was a marrowy blanket of cherry pits, *cassis*, and minerals.

TO WATCH

***Pierre Breton,* Restigné:** Breton (Montreuil-Bellay) seems every bit a yuppie—nice Gap-style clothes, nicely renovated house, nicely outfitted new cellars (stainless steel tanks and used Bordeaux *barriques*). Breton's ideas about wine, however, go well beyond the homogenized image. Above all, he wants to respect the character of his *terroir* and to this end he prac-tices organic viticulture. He has all but eliminated filtration. He's beginning to make sleek, stylish Bourgueils with pretty fruit, which he's also smart about marketing. And I sense that he is just starting to hit his stride as a winemaker.

Breton made some lovely '89s and '90s: grapey Jeunes Vignes; limpid, smoky, serious Les Galichets; silky, inviting Clos du Sénéchal; a Schwarzeneg-ger-ish '90 Cuvée Grand Mont; and complex, layered La Perrière Vieilles Vignes, with flavors of cherries and cooked fruit, black olives, and spices. His '93 Les Galichets was a bit too brawny and gamy (in summer '95), but La Perrière Vieilles Vignes was one of the best '93 Loire reds I've tasted. It has terrific concentration, lovely balance, flavors that go on forever—focused fruit (blackberry, blueberry, plum, black cherry, and more), minerals, and now and then the wonderful funky taste of the crust of a good Saint-Nectaire. It's major league.

***Nau Frères,* Ingrandes:** The honest Bourgueils of Jean Nau were long admired. In 1990 he passed the torch to the next generation and the early signs are encouraging. If anything, the wines seem somewhat sleeker, finer of grain. A barrel-aged '93 Vieilles Vignes, from a south-facing slope, was nicely structured, with ample fruit, mixed with bell pepper and balsamic notes. The graceful '91 was full of cherry pit flavors. The '90 had good up-front fruit, spices, and musk. The Vieilles Vignes was an absolutely lovely Breton, with a whiff of bell peppers to season the blend of wood, raspberry, and cherries. Like so many of Nau's Bourgueils, it was both elegant and rustic.

HIGHLY RECOMMENDED

***Domaine de la Chevalerie,* Restigné:** The afterimage of a visit here is of a handsome, sprawling stone farmhouse built around a hot plant-and-dog-filled court; of cool, endless underground cellars with different vintages and different *cuvées* in every last niche; and of course, of the boyish, enthusiastic vigneron, Pierre Caslot, and the fascinating wines he uncorked.

Caslot's lightest wine, Cuvée du Peu Muleau, is good but never my favorite. La Bretesche, Caslot's newest *cuvée,* comes from old vines on chalky-clay soils. Caslot believes the '93 is one of the best wines he's made. Perhaps, but the '92 was no slouch, either, with its fine mineral and plum flavors, soft tannins, and graceful structure.

The Cuvée Galichets is both sturdy and silky—and heartily recommended, as is the Vieilles Vignes bottling, which is always richer, more structured, and more concentrated. Des Buzardières, from fifty-year-old vines, is the *cuvée* Caslot keeps for himself. Every vintage from '81 to '93 is recommended. (There was none in '91, however, as Caslot lost most of his crop to spring frosts.) Favorites include the compact '93, the seductive '92, the characterful '90, and the lissome '89, with endless flavors of dried cherry, sweet spices, and sandalwood.

***Domaine de la Coudraye,* Bourgueil:** Yannick Amirault, a thoughtful, youngish vigneron, doesn't make headlines but has won the respect of his confreres with the high quality of his work, his seriousness of purpose, and his basic human decency. He experiments, he mixes old techniques with new, he questions, he tastes, and he reflects on what he's tasted. The results—in great years like '89 and '90 as well as diffuse ones like '92 and quixotic ones like '93—are dependably honest, well made, serious, rather feminine (and pretty) Bourgueils and Saint-Nicolas-de-Bourgueils. Amirault makes several versions of each. My favorites are the silky Saint-Nicolas, particularly the old-vines, nonfiltered Malgagnes and Les Graviers, with their concentrated flavors of plum and black cherry, and a nonfiltered, old-vines Bourgueil, Les Quartiers.

***Domaine des Forges,* Restigné:** Jean-Yves Billet makes several *cuvées* of Bourgueil, including a spring bottling, Les Bézards (a *lieu dit* in Ingrandes), and a Vieilles Vignes. Whether a rich vintage like '90 and '89, a lean one like '93, or a light one like '92 and '87, Billet's Bourgueils are invariably well made, feminine. At their best, as in a generic '92 and an '89 Les Bézards, they beguile with their silky texture and mouth-watering cherry pit, blueberry, plum, and orange zest flavors.

Lamé-Delille-Boucard, Ingrandes: Despite machine-harvesting, Lamé-Delille is old-guard Bourgueil. Their best wines are masculine Bretons. Let them age and they won't let you down. They evolve to a soft, pleasant rusticity, with warm flavors of spice, musk, and bacon. I drank the '86 Vieilles Vignes at a small restaurant in the middle of the woods north of Bourgueil one cool, gray Saturday. The smoky, supple red, with its plummy fruit, game, and old-wood notes, was just what was wanted on a winter day with a winy stag stew.

Grapes ferment in old wood vats. All wines, except the spring bottling, age in oak barrels for one to four years. Cabernet Sauvignon may account for as much as 40 percent of the blend. I'd pass on the flat, herbaceous '93 and the dull '91, but both '89 and '90 were classic Lamé-Delille—strong, with lots of stuffing, and spiced with clove. Multiply that by five for the Vieilles Vignes and the Cuvée Prestige (also old-vines, usually in Benais). In 1995 the '88 Prestige should have evolved from the rawly visceral stages to spices and sandalwood. And the fine-boned '86 should still be going strong.

RECOMMENDED

Christophe Chasles, Saint-Patrice: This thirty-seven-year-old vigneron, who studied at the Lycée de Beaune and Amboise, has seven and a half hectares located at the eastern rim of the appellation. His best wines come from a parcel called Rochecot, and they can be riveting Bourgueils.

Clos de l'Abbaye, Bourgueil: This seven-hectare vineyard within the stone walls of Bourgueil's thousand-year-old abbey is considered the "cradle of Breton." The monks of Bourgueil are thought to have planted the grape here in the eleventh century. The vines were cultivated by religious orders until recently, when the abbey's current occupants, the sisters of Saint-Martin, found the job too much for them and rented the plot to two honest young vignerons, Jean-Baptiste Thouet and Michel Lorieux, who make pleasant, if leathery, Bourgueils. Thouet also produces amiable Bourgueils from his own vines, under the label Domaine Thouet-Bosseau.

Jean-Paul et Michel Delanoue, Benais: Tasty, charcuterie-friendly light reds.

Domaine de la Chanteleuserie, Benais: Moise and Thierry Boucard make pretty bistro Bretons to drink within six years of harvest. Of particular interest are the Cuvée Beauvais and the Vieilles Vignes bottlings, as well as the Saint-Nicolas.

Domaine des Galluches, Bourgueil: Jean Gambier, one of Bourgueil's most helpful vignerons, makes wines that are as generous as he is. Issued from gravelly soils, they are immediately appealing, with a rustic charm that makes them ideal with *rillettes*. The normal *cuvée* appears under the Les Galluches label. In exceptional years Gambier bottles a Cuvée Ronsard.

Domaine de la Gaucherie, Ingrandes: Régis Mureau makes good wines from Bourgueil's two soil types. The gravelly soils of his vineyards near Restigné produce a thirst-quenching, juicy version. The tuffeau soils of a hillside in Ingrandes make his barrel-aged Cuvée de la Gaucherie, a supple Bourgueil with lush fruit and minerals.

Domaine des Mailloches, Restigné: Jean-François Demont makes some lovely Bourgueils, notably the Cuvée Vieilles Vignes, from seventy- to one-hundred-year-old vines in Benais and Restigné, and the lighter Cuvée Sophie, from old vines on gravelly soils, for drinking within five years. The normal *domaine* bottling is a good, easy-drinking Bourgueil. The '91 was an honest job for a difficult year, and not a bad wine.

Domaine des Ouches, Ingrandes: Paul Gambier makes friendly, medium-bodied Bourgueils to drink within five years.

Domaine des Raguenières, Benais: The Bourgueils of Maître et Viemont get around. They're on lots of local lists as well as in many Paris wine bars. (My introduction to the house was an herbaceous, pleasant '86 at Tabac Henri IV.) Despite the chlorophyll taste suggestive of machine-harvesting, these are old-guard Bourgueils, visceral, musky, and tannic.

Maison Audebert et Fils, Bourgueil: A *négociant* with the soul of a vigneron, Audebert puts his heart into his own wine from Grand Clos and La Marquise, two of Bourgueil's finest *crus*.

Saint-Nicolas-de-Bourgueil

LEADER

Domaine Joël Taluau: The inevitable reference for the appellation as well as for non-barrel-aged Breton, Joël Taluau is a conscientious producer who makes irreproachable Saint-Nicolas. Although I rarely find them inspiring, I always enjoy drinking Taluau's wines—for their well-defined fruit as well as for the solid work they represent—and wholeheartedly recommend them to tasters who want a quick fix on Saint-Nicolas.

Taluau ferments his wines in stainless steel tanks in climate-controlled cellars. There are three *cuvées:* Jeunes Vignes, *domaine,* and a hand-harvested Vieilles Vignes. The '94 Jeunes Vignes was lean but forthright, with bell pepper and crushed-ivy flavors. The Vieilles Vignes bottling stood up honorably to the rigors of '94, offering sturdy cherry fruit accented with bell peppers. The '93 was a lean blend of fruit and bell peppers; '91 was concentrated and seductive. I was disappointed by the '90s, however; they were good, very good, but a bit hot. In '89, the *domaine* bottling was almost as good as the Vieilles Vignes *cuvée;* they were both plush wines with flavors of *cassis,* violets, and raspberries.

HIGHLY RECOMMENDED

Cognard-Taluau: It's a pity that Max Cognard is not a bit more obsessed with wine. He makes lovely Saint-Nicolas, but an ounce of passion would make a pound of improvement here. As it is, Cognard makes a bright, lively rosé and two *cuvées* of red, regular and Les Malgagnes (which I always prefer). The '93, '90, '89, '88, and '86 Malgagnes are all heartily recommended. The '93, for example, is an extremely pretty Breton with delicious fruit and excellent balance. The '86 is a weave of berries, musk, and spices. Cognard also makes a bit of brawny, gamy Bourgueil (from one hectare of what he calls "very interesting soils"). I always prefer his Saint-Nicolas, Les Malgagnes.

Vignoble de la Jarnoterie: Jean-Claude Mabileau's light, feminine wines are tempting to drink right away. But the older ones hold up—and hold on to that pretty expression, picking up additional flavors of dried cherries, hay, orange zest, mint, and sandalwood.

BY THE GLASS

Clos des Quarterons: Claude and Thierry Amirault bottle several varieties of Saint-Nicolas; the best is Clos des Quarterons Vieilles Vignes, an elegant, drink-me-up Breton.

Domaine du Bourg: Jean-Paul Mabileau makes easygoing reds to drink with roast chicken and *frites* in a bistro; look for the prestige *cuvée,* Clos Lorioux.

Domaine Jacques Mabileau: Planted on a well-exposed hillside, the *domaine*'s thirteen hectares of vines produce full-bodied Saint-Nicolas. The

Vieilles Vignes usually has good fruit with an appetizing thread of minerals. It benefits from cellaring for a year or two.

Pascal Lorieux: Young Lorieux studied at Briacé and in Bordeaux before setting up his own *domaine* in 1985 in a converted garage. Lorieux's eight and a half hectares of vines are on sand and gravel. Grapes are machine-harvested and ferment in stainless steel tanks. All are assembled to make one *cuvée*. They are often good and often win awards. I have never found them delicious. But Lorieux's very ambitious, so I'm hopeful.

THE TOURAINES

STATUS: *AOC 1939*
WINES: *Red, white (dry, demi-sec, and* moelleux*), rosé; still and sparkling*
ZONE AND PRODUCTION: *Touraine AOC: Roughly 333,600 hectoliters made on 6,100 hectares on 104 communes in the Indre-et-Loire, 42 communes in the Loir-et-Cher, and one commune in the Indre department.*
GRAPES: *Whites—Chenin Blanc, Arbois, Sauvignon, Chardonnay (maximum 20 percent); reds and rosés—Cabernet Franc and Sauvignon, Cot, Pinot Noir, Pinot Meunier, Pinot Gris, Gamay, Pineau d'Aunis, Grolleau (rosés only)*
SOILS: *Largely sand and clay, more or less siliceous or chalky*
PRICE: *12 to 60ff*
BEST VINTAGES: *'95, '93 (some), '90, '89, '88, '86 (reds), '85*

The Touraine appellation spans the entire Indre-et-Loire and a good portion of the Loir-et-Cher as well. Its vineyards chart a three-star itinerary of France's most beloved châteaux, including Azay-le-Rideau, Chenonceau, and Amboise. Valençay marks the southern limit; Chambord, the eastern boundary.

Three of its subregions are super-Touraines—Touraine-Amboise, Touraine-Azay-le-Rideau, and Touraine-Mesland—and Noble Joué is trying to join the list. Aside from its best zones, however, the Touraine countryside is not blanketed with vines. Vineyards seem to be designated parcel by parcel, where expositions are favorable and soils lend themselves to the cultivation of vines rather than the more prevalent fruits, vegetables, and grains.

Chenin's dominion begins in Azay-le-Rideau and runs as far east as Amboise. It is also the base of Touraine brut, made by the *méthode champenoise*. With the exception of Azay-le-Rideau, the Chenins can be lovely but are clearly second-string, with none of the distinction of Touraine's top *crus*. Much more interesting are the Sauvignon Blancs, which are perfect bistro whites. The finest come from the Oisly and Soings regions.

Cabernet Franc spreads across Touraine. Its best ambassadors are made on the fringes of Chinon. Reds from eastern Touraine are, increasingly, blends. (Indeed, the INAO recently revised laws governing the production of Touraine-Mesland to require a mix of grapes rather than varietal wines.) Generally dominated by forward, fruity Gamay, these blends typically include Cot, which adds deeper fruit as well as structure, and Cabernet Franc, for body, framework, and tannin. The blends usually have a regional "proprietary" name: Touraine Tradition, for example; or, in Amboise, François Ier. Many producers also offer a Gamay *primeur* as well as one—or several—sparkling wines, most of which are Touraine Brut, Touraine *Méthode traditionnelle*, or Crémant de Loire. Producers generally send the base wine to specialists for champenization.

PRODUCER RATINGS

OUTSTANDING
Clos Neuf des Archambaults   Domaine de la Charmoise

LEADER
Confrérie des Vignerons de Oisly et Thésée

EXCELLENT
Château du Petit Thouars   Domaine des Acacias
Domaine de Bergerie (Jacky Marteau)   Domaine des Corbillières

HIGHLY RECOMMENDED
Paul Buisse   Caves de Pré Auguste   Château de Chenonceau
Jean-Michel Desroches   Domaine Octavie   Domaine de la Presle
Domaine des Perrets   Roche Blanche (Clos)

RECOMMENDED
Château de Maulevrier   Le Chai de Varennes
Domaine de la Bourdelière   Domaine de la Méchinière
Domaine de Peumen   Domaine du Pré Baron
Domaine de la Rénaudie   Domaine des Sablons
Domaine de Saint-Gennefort   Domaine Sauvète   Pascal Ricotier
Les Vignerons des Coteaux Romanais

OUTSTANDING

This was unintentional, but the two *domaines* rated "Outstanding" reveal the extremes within the appellation Touraine: The first is a minuscule property at the southern rim, a distant satellite of Chinon; the second is a large commercial property at the eastern limits of Touraine, where we enter the world of Sauvignon. The differences in the way each vigneron works could also not be more radical, save their commitment to quality.

Clos Neuf des Archambaults, Sainte-Maure-de-Touraine: Talk about confidential. Jean-François Dehelly has 1.43 hectares of vines, all Breton, in the southern reaches of Touraine. My kind of fanatic, he keeps yields low by rigorous pruning and cluster thinning. He uses no insecticides or fertilizers. Grapes are hand harvested and destemmed, and they ferment in open stainless steel tanks. Vatting lasts a month and punching down is done by foot. The wines age in used Bordeaux barrels and are rarely filtered.

Dehelly's rosé is always a delight; in '92 it was closer to a miracle. Unchaptalized, it was fragrant, firm, and scented with fruit and bell peppers. The '94 was crisp, ample, and citric.

I've tasted reds back to a sandalwood-scented '75. "Pretty, pretty, pretty!" were the first three words I noted upon tasting a barrel sample of Dehelly's '94 (10.4 percent alcohol with no chaptalization). It was an explosion of raspberry jam, oak, spices, light tannins, and light citrus notes. So true; so authentic, too. And better than just about every '94 Chinon I'd tasted, as was Dehelly's '89 Vieilles Vignes, a supple, structured red, with fabulous flavors of crushed raspberries and musk. The '93s, '92s, '90s, and so forth, are all of this quality.

Domaine de la Charmoise, Soings-en-Sologne: Henry Marionnet is a wine adventurer with a genius for innovation in the vineyards, in the cellars, and in marketing. (He's currently consulting for Terra Noble in Chile.) On my first visit to Soings, he immediately swept me into his office and planted me before a topographical map to prove that Charmoise was an island of flinty clay; soils hospitable to the vine, unlike those of the rest of Soings, where sandy soils dictated the cultivation of strawberries and asparagus. Topographical maps not withstanding, Soings is not Sancerre. Marionnet is like the kibbutzniks who made lush Edens of former Israeli deserts. It's impossible to imagine extracting more from Soings than Marionnet has.

With fifty hectares, he is one of the largest proprietors in the Loir-et-Cher. And he was the first in the region to make Gamay by carbonic maceration (which he calls *fermentation intracellulaire*). The tastiness of the wine, combined with the publicity it reaped (thanks to Marionnet's assiduous and creative courting of press and sommeliers), was a wake-up call to Loir-et-Cher vignerons. His Sauvignon proved equally influential, as have recent releases: M de Marionnet, a potent, pricey, late-harvest Sauvignon Blanc which won Gault Millau's worldwide Sauvignon sweepstakes, and his Première Vendange (First Harvest), a Gamay which he promotes as the modern world's first all-natural wine.

Sauvignon is planted on his lightest soils; Gamay on soils rich in both clay and gravel. Wines ferment in hundred-hectoliter stainless steel tanks. Yeast is never added. Sauvignon harvested by machine is pressed immediately; half the hand-harvested Sauvignon undergoes *fermentation intracellulaire*, as does the Gamay.

Cluster thinning and rigorous harvest selection resulted in delicious '92s, both in Sauvignon and Gamay. His '94 Sauvignon, one of the best I tasted, was sprightly, clean, and herbaceous.

There's a school of thought that says Sauvignon must be nervy, green beany, and tart. Such people prefer Marionnet's generic Sauvignon. Everyone else likes his M de Marionnet. Made in vintages with good Indian summers—1995 will be his first since 1990—its grapes come from old vines harvested three weeks to a month after the rest of Marionnet's Sauvignon. The '89 (14.8 percent alcohol) was richly textured and tightly woven, with peach and apricot aromas. The '90, a ringer for a Tokay from Alsace in a great vintage, was velvety and full, with delicious mineral undertones.

Marionnet likes to say his Gamay de-intoxicates, quenches thirst, and cures hangovers. Whatever—it is all too easy to drink a lot of. The common threads are freshness, bright structure, vibrant flavors of red berries, and a backdrop of minerals. (Only '94 fell short, through no fault of Marionnet's.) Then there's Première Vendange, the *première année* of which was '90. This is a hand-harvested Gamay fermented without added sulfur, sugar, or yeast. It's a delight, with rich strawberry-raspberry flavors and undertones of *cassis*, cherry pits, and orange zest. It's cute and fascinating, the ultimate seductive wine-bar Gamay, without a scintilla of banalized Gamay flavors. And though it's less potent than the regular bottling, it's deeper; less beefy but finer—even in '94.

LEADER

Confrérie des Vignerons de Oisly et Thésée, Oisly: A reliable address for very good to excellent Touraines, this association is admirable in every way. It was founded in 1962 by six winemakers to lift the region out of its bulk-wine doldrums. Today it has fifty-eight members. Payment is based on the quality of the harvest. (A bonus is paid for harvesting by hand, for example, and standards concerning quality factors such as yields seem to get stricter every year.)

Most of its 30,000 hectoliters yearly is Touraine (chiefly Sauvignon and Gamay), though there are also Crémants and Vins de Pays. Many smart local restaurants serve its base Sauvignon and Gamay as house wines.

The Confrérie offers a range of proprietary blends, such as Baronnie d'Aîgnan and Prestige de la Vallée des Rois, as well as a number of characterful *domaine* bottlings, such as the plump, aggressive Sauvignons from the Domaine du Bouc, the subtler ones from the Château de Vallagon, and the raspberry-rich Cabernets from Domaine de la Châtoire.

Of the Confrérie's '94s (all tank samples) the Sauvignons were respectable, citric and herbacous. The Prestige de la Vallée des Rois bottling was a bit more than that; ampler, with finer fruit. The Gamays and Pinot Noirs were equally respectable, though the evident good work behind them was undermined by traces of stem rot. The most unusual of their '94s was a late-harvest Sauvignon. Ample, with strong grapefruit and mineral flavors, it managed to carry its 13.5 percent alcohol gracefully.

In '93 the Confrérie inaugurated a new prestige bottling, a hand-harvested, low-yielding, old-vines *cuvée* called Excellence, in both Sauvignon and Gamay. A fine debut, particularly for the '93 Sauvignon, which was creamy and richly fruity, with ample exotic fruit flavors and a citric finish.

Baronnie d'Aîgnan is the proprietary name for a top *cuvée* of white and red, each an assemblage. The white, a blend of Chenin, Sauvignon, and Chardonnay, is open and grassy, with an attractive mineral expression. The red, a blend of Cabernet Franc, Gamay, and Cot, is a food-friendly, berry- and mint-flavored wine. I imagined the '93, with its soft fruit and light tannins, alongside a young goat cheese. (I put a kirschy, mellow '93 Cot with *petit salé* and lentils.)

EXCELLENT

Château du Petit Thouars, Saint-Germain-sur-Vienne: *Noblesse*, not to mention the cost of supporting a château, *oblige*. Marguerite, a wine writer, and Yves, Comte du Petit Thouars, have twelve hectares of vines on this historic property which Cardinal Richelieu gave to Aubert du Petit Thouars in 1636.

A cellar master makes the wines, but Marguerite knows what she admires and practices what she preaches. Yields are kept to sixty hectoliters per hectare. Grapes are hand harvested in Champagne cases. They travel by gravity to a destemmer and ferment in stainless steel tanks, vatting for roughly three weeks. The wines age in chestnut barrels for up to four months. The result is a tasty, often elegant, and always user-friendly Touraine Cabernet. The '92 and '93 were fine-grained, fruity country reds, only a tad herbaceous. The '89 was so deep, the fruit seemed sweet.

Domaine des Acacias, Chémery: From his twenty-three hectares of vines, Charles Guerbois makes pretty terrific wines. His Sauvignons in '91, '90, and '89 were vibrant, with aromas of peaches and flowers. He didn't bottle his small amount of '94; '92 was just so-so; but in '93 Guerbois came out with Vinovorax, a stunning special *cuvée*. One half of the harvest was picked at the normal time, at 11 percent potential alcohol; the rest, a month later, at nearly 13 percent. The two finished fermenting together and spent a year on their lees before bottling. The wine is admirable in every respect. It's ample yet discreet, with marrowy texture and fine mineral and fruit flavors—flashes of Muscat, Pinot Gris, grapefruit. Like Marionnet's "M," it's difficult to imagine better wine coming from the Loir-et-Cher.

Guerbois's '92 Gamay was fruity and firm. His '91 had the freshness of carbonic maceration as well as more serious flavors of plum and black olive. Delicious. But the most remarkable is his Delirium Caroli Bellum Silva, from thirty-year-old vines. Yields are kept at twenty-five hectoliters per hectare. He harvests these grapes three weeks after the rest of the Gamay is in, looking for overripeness. He starts fermentation by tossing a bucket of Sauvignon into the tank, something he learned from a pal in Morgon. Vatting lasts three weeks. The '90, the last Guerbois made, was incredibly potent (13.7 percent alcohol), with plum, black olive, licorice, and cherry pit flavors and a long finish. (Presented blind on a French TV show about sommeliers, the wine stumped every single one of the country's top tasters.)

Domaine de Bergerie (Jacky Marteau), Pouillé-sur-Cher: No one presents a more positive image of the average Loir-et-Cher vigneron than Jacky Marteau. Marteau, in his mid-forties, has eighteen hectares of vines on the plateaus above the Cher. He does nothing really remarkable—he machine-harvests, fermenting his white wines in enameled steel tanks, his reds in cement; vatting his Gamay for about a week, his Cabernet for twelve days; with ordinary methods of temperature control and pumping over. He has, however, invested in a pneumatic press and makes an even greater investment in his harvest, keeping yields low, particularly for his signature wine, Gamay—which is simply too delicious. His '89 through '93 were structured, vibrant, and meaty, tasting of cherries and cherry pits. Perfect bistro Gamays. Marteau's next-best wine is his sprightly, slightly herbaceous Sauvignon Blanc. I also like his vinous and appetizing rosés from Pineau d'Aunis and his fleshy, well-focused Cabernets.

Domaine des Corbillières, **Oisly:** In 1910 Grandfather Fabel noticed that a Sauvignon vine growing along his garden wall did rather well. He grafted a cutting onto his post-phylloxera hybrids. The only drinkable wine in the region, it sold like hotcakes in nearby Blois. Fabel, later awarded the Legion of Honor for his contributions to French viticulture, was also jovial and folkloric. Stamps featuring him in his habitual cap and wood sabots were printed to promote Loir-et-Cher wines.

Today 75 percent of the *domaine*'s production is Sauvignon, made by Fabel's grandson, Maurice Barbou, and *his* son, Dominique. In tastings, Barbou, who looks like Jimmy Carter and speaks with the same fixed smile, presents his Sauvignons last because they are the most perfumed of his wines. He begins with a solid, peppery Cabernet; then pours a potent blend of Gamay, Cabernet, and Cot, rich with flavors of kirsch and spices; then culminates with several fragrant, mouth-filling, and rather complex Sauvignons from '90, '89, and '88.

A pungent '94 could hold its own against many a Pouilly. A crisp, sharp '93 was appetizing but left me thinking that the *domaine*'s best grapes had gone into a special *cuvée*. This may have been the case. In '93 the Barbous made an extraordinary Sauvignon, a *tri* of low-yielding old vines, that could have been a ringer for a Sancerre. Subtle, rich, almost viscous, it was a wave of minerals accented with ginger and lime. Super. The name of this *cuvée* is Fabel Barbou.

HIGHLY RECOMMENDED

Paul Buisse, **Montrichard:** One of the most quality-conscious *négociants* in the Loire, Paul Buisse offers a complete range of Touraine appellations. His Cristal Buisse, a floral, fruity Sauvignon, is his best wine.

Caves du Pré Auguste, **Civray-de-Touraine:** The Godeaus produce the complete range of Touraine wines, of which my favorites are the bright Gamays, loaded with cherries, and the spice- and kirsch-flavored Cots.

Château de Chenonceau: Off to the side of the château are sixteenth- to eighteenth-century cellars, newly outfitted with high-tech equipment and new oak barrels for reds. The château makes nice *mousseux*, but I prefer its ambitious Chenins and its stylish Cabernets.

Jean-Michel Desroches, Saint-Georges-sur-Cher: Alluring, studied, silky Touraine wines—to wit, delicate, floral rosés; vibrant, fluid Gamays; classic bistro Cabernets.

Domaine Octavie, Oisly: Jean-Claude Barbeillon is a very good producer whose best wines are his pretty Gamays, his fleshy Sauvignons, and his Touraine Tradition, a rather refined country red with flavors of kirsch, cherries, and spice.

Domaine de la Presle, Oisly: Jean-Marie Penet is a reliable source for extremely tasty Touraine wines—for Sauvignons long on grapefruit and minerals; kirsch- and cherry pit–flavored Gamays; firm, vinous *vin gris* from Pineau d'Aunis; and delectable, stew-friendly Cabernets.

Domaine des Perrets, Saint-Georges-sur-Cher: Young Bruno Bouges shows real promise with his lovely, flavorful Gamays, his honest Touraine Tradition, and his ambitious off-dry Chenins.

Roche Blanche (Clos), Mareuil-sur-Cher: Appetizing Sauvignons with licorice and basil notes; firm, peppery rosé of Aunis; toothsome Tradition, mingling rich red fruits and orange zest; Cot, from hundred-year-old vines, juicy as cherry jam.

RECOMMENDED

Château de Maulevrier, Lerné: A clos of pre-phylloxera vines makes concentrated, singular Touraine Cabs, rustic but charming.

Le Chai de Varennes, Thésée: Potent Sauvignons, pretty Gamays, jammy Cabs, and chewy Cots.

Domaine de la Bourdelière, Pouillé-sur-Cher: René Angier sells 95 percent of his production to Oisly et Thésée, where his son is the marketing director. If you come across his structured, smoky Pinot Gris, try it.

Domaine de la Méchinière, Mareuil-sur-Cher: Vivacious Sauvignons and supple Touraine Traditions.

Domaine de Peumen, Pouillé-sur-Cher: Ripe, mango-y Sauvignons; herb- and raspberry-scented Gamays.

Domaine du Pré Baron, Oisly: Prototypical wine-bar Sauvignons, Gamays, and Cabs—rough-and-ready and tasty—and a silky, chewy Tradition.

Domaine de la Rénaudie, Mareuil-sur-Cher: Cherry- and cherry pit–flavored Traditions.

Domaine des Sablons, Pouillé-sur-Cher: Quality varies, but you can find Cabernets that are fruity, supple, and satisfying country reds. Not at all anonymous or generic, they speak of a region, a man.

Domaine de Saint-Gennefort, Seigy: Most of the wines are light and bland, but Max Meunier can turn out feisty little Sauvignons.

Domaine Sauvète, Monthou-sur-Cher: The rosé of Pineau d'Aunis is fragrant, hard, and dry; the Gamay, sapid and fruity; the Cabernet, a lovely country red, supple and engaging, with just the right amount of bell peppers; and the Tradition is a lissome charmer.

Pascal Ricotier, Crissay-sur-Manse: Vin de Pays du Jardin de la France is the appellation for Ricotier's rustic, tasty Cabernets.

Les Vignerons des Coteaux Romanais, Saint-Romain-sur-Cher: This sixty-member co-op makes crisp, herbaceous Sauvignons; cute little Gamays; and gutsy Cabernets.

Touraine-Amboise

STATUS: *AOC 1955*
TYPES OF WINE: *Red, white, and rosé*
ZONE AND PRODUCTION: *10,000 to 12,000 hectoliters yearly, made on 180 hectares spanning nine communes on both banks of the Loire*
GRAPES: *Whites—Chenin Blanc; reds and rosés—Cabernet Franc and Sauvignon, Cot, and Gamay*
SOILS: *Chalky clay, occasionally thin and sandy*
PRICE: *12 to 40ff*
BEST VINTAGES: (see *Touraine*)

Amboise lies on the south bank of the Loire, twenty-five kilometers east of Tours. The remains of its splendid castle look down on stone bridges, twisty streets, lush walled parks, and exuberant markets.

Known for its white wines, Amboise once furnished the royal table. Today red grapes represent two-thirds of the acreage, and reds are its most interesting and delicious wines. They are the best kind of country wine, both comfortable and personal. Increasingly they are blends of Gamay, Cot, and Cabernet Franc called François Ier.

There is an exciting sense in Amboise that the appellation is beginning to hit its stride. There is still a long way to go, but one sees progress at every turn and in every winery.

◁ᴲ· PRODUCER RATINGS ·ᴲ▷

LEADER
Domaine Dutertre

TO WATCH
Xavier Frissant   Catherine Moreau

HIGHLY RECOMMENDED
Jacques Bonnigal et Fils
Domaine du Breuil   Domaine de la Gabillière   Guy Durand

BY THE GLASS
Daniel et Philippe Catroux   Joël Cosmes
Jacques Gandon

◁ᴲ· ·ᴲ▷

LEADER

Domaine Dutertre, **Limeray:** With thirty-five hectares of vines, Jacques Dutertre and son Gilles (Lycée de Beaune) have one of the largest estates in Touraine and increasingly turn out fine, and ever improving, versions of its wines—fragrant rosés; delicious, supple, and fruity François Ier; and some impressive Chenins.

The firm, juicy '94 rosé—a blend of Gamay, Cabernet, and Cot—was like biting into garden strawberries just before they're totally ripe. The '93 François Ier was not the best I've tasted from this winery (though it's a pleasant wine-bar red), but the '93 Clos du Pavillon—old-vines Chenin— was such an ample yet discreet blend of pear, minerals, and citrus zests, it lent credence to the locally advanced proposition that Amboise is indeed a viticultural extension of Montlouis.

TO WATCH

Xavier Frissant, **Mosnes:** Young Frissant has plenty of good, strong opinions, and he puts his money where his mouth is. He hand harvests, vinifies by parcel, and, in ripe years like '89 and '90, turns out supple Sauvignons with solid mineral cores, as well as heroic reds: His François Ier and his Cabernet were chewy and tannic, with intense flavors of cherries and cooked fruit.

In difficult vintages, Frissant more than holds his own. His piquant '94 Sauvignon was quite honorable; a '93 was meaty and attractive. His '93 Cuvée Angélique (with no added yeasts or sugar) was crisper and less ample, but fresher and more discreet.

The lightly rustic '94 François Ier wanted only a goat cheese to round off its rough edges, as did the jammy, acidulated '93. Supple and kirsch-scented, the '92s (both a François Ier and a blend of Cabernet and Cot) were spicy, berried, and warm; to be drunk on cold autumn nights.

Catherine Moreau, Cangey: Unhappy working as a secretary in Paris, Moreau returned to the family *domaine* in 1983, took courses at Amboise, rebuilt and climatized the cellars, and installed stainless steel tanks and a couple of newish barrels. By '90 she was making delicious wine. Her '90 François Ier was the best I tasted. A blend of Gamay (50 percent), Cab Franc (25 percent), and Cot (25 percent), the wine spent several months in barrel. The result was supple, generous, and fruity; everything you want in an easy, near-term drinking red. Ditto for the '93. Only a party pooper wouldn't warm to its comforting, berried fruit.

HIGHLY RECOMMENDED

Jacques Bonnigal et Fils, Limeray: With sons Serge and Pascal, Jacques Bonnigal works thirty-five hectares of vines—next door to the country home of Mick Jagger. The herbaceous, mineraly Sauvignons are tart wake-up calls; the off-dry Chenins are suave; the reds (even Gamays) are tannic, though appetizing and fruity.

Domaine du Breuil, Amboise: One of the founders of the Lycée Viticole d'Amboise, as well as the self-appointed protector of the grape variety Cot, Hubert Denay is a must-visit for his barrel-fermented Chenins in several levels of sweetness and his vintage Cots.

An '89 *moelleux*, a *tri* picked at over 14 percent potential alcohol, was pear-scented, sweet, soft, and syrupy. A '59, with lovely wax and honey flavors, though not epic, was a fine-aged Chenin, a delight to discover and to drink. The Cots age in barrel for nine to eighteen months. They are fined but not filtered. Denay says that the clients who like his Cot are *chevronné*; to wit, they must be connoisseurs who have earned their spurs. His best—like an '85 which offered rich flavors of plum, kirsch, cherries, spice, leather, and minerals—need a couple of years of cellaring before drinking with hearty meals.

Domaine de la Gabillière, Amboise: Founded in 1975, the Lycée Viticole d'Amboise trains the current generation of Touraine winemakers, whose clinical studies take place on the school's fifteen hectares of vines (on the twenty-five-hectare Domaine de la Gabillière) and in its modern cellars.

The Lycée focuses on Chenin Blanc, usually a nicely made middle-of-the-road *sec-tendre* with light flavors of corn, pear, and pineapple. In exceptional years, like '89 and '90, there is *moelleux* with huge creamed-corn flavors. The Lycée also makes a bit of rosé; clean, ripe, herbaceous Sauvignon; a full-flavored François Ier; and competent Crémant.

Guy Durand, Mosnes: Durand and his son Philippe make delicious, grassy, minerally Sauvignon; textbook Gamay; warm, minty François Ier; amiable Cabernets; kirsch- and cherry-flavored Cot; and in great years, delightful Chenins.

BY THE GLASS

Daniel et Philippe Catroux, Limeray: Chenins and rosés, both off-dry.
Joël Cosmes, Montreuil: Thick, potent, old-vines Gamays.
Jacques Gandon, Nazelles-Négron: Off-dry Chenins (in great vintages) and curious, though not unpleasant, *méthode traditionnelle.*

Touraine-Azay-le-Rideau

STATUS: *AOC 1953 (white); 1977 (rosé)*
TYPES OF WINE: *Dry or off-dry white and rosé*
ZONE AND PRODUCTION: *2,000 hectoliters from 44 hectares within eight communes*
GRAPES: *Whites—Chenin Blanc; rosés—Grolleau (minimum 60 percent), Cot, Gamay, Cabernet Franc, and Sauvignon (maximum 10 percent)*
SOILS: *Varied, including* perruches *(clay with silex) and chalky clay*
PRICE: *12 to 50ff*
BEST VINTAGES: *'95, '90, '89, '88*

This appellation is blessed with two magical villages, Azay-le-Rideau and Saché. You enter the first by crossing a serene river edged with tall trees. Follow its narrow streets lined with medieval houses to a leafy park in which sits a gem of a Renaissance château, perfectly symmetrical, perfectly situated. Lush green valleys and ivy-covered farmhouses lead you to Saché, where Balzac wrote *Le Lys dans la Vallée* and where Alexander Calder lived and worked. (A mobile commands the village square.)

It is also blessed with a white wine that offers yet another expression of Chenin. It comes across as extremely dry, even when sweet. Often difficult to appreciate young, it begins to unfold after its tenth birthday, revealing a splendid specificity, a fine core of minerals and lively scents of apples and pears, as if the grapes transmitted the flavors of the orchards whose neat rows of espaliered fruit trees dominate the landscape.

Rosé Azay-le-Rideau, made by a direct press of the grapes, is firm, aromatic, and fruity. It even ages well, its aromas evolving toward wax, quinine, and herbal tea.

Most of Azay's fifty growers earn the major part of their income from other crops, principally fruit. Many make one or more Touraine reds, and some, an *eau-de-vie de poire* from their own orchards. Ask to taste this; it is usually not for sale.

PRODUCER RATINGS

OUTSTANDING
Robert Denis

TO WATCH
Thierry Bésard   Château de la Roche

RECOMMENDED
Château de l'Aulée   James Paget   Pibaleau Père et Fils

BY THE GLASS
Marc Badiller   Michel et Frédéric Hardy
Daniel Jahan   Jean-Pierre Perdriau
Pierre Rivry   Franck Verroneau

OUTSTANDING

Robert Denis, La Chapelle-Saint-Blaise, Cheillé: Denis is the heart and soul of Azay-le-Rideau. President of its *syndicat* for twenty years he was, for much of that time, the only producer in the appellation making wines worthy of being called Azay-le-Rideau—pure, straight, rigorous Chenins and characterful rosés.

Denis hand harvests and vinifies his wines in oak *demi-muids*, letting the wine ferment until Christmas. He bottles in April and cellars the wines for two to four years—or until he deems them ready for release. His rosés are sapid and firm, often with sour-apple or cherry notes, a bit of oak, and a savory bitter-nut-and-mineral finish. They can age beautifully (an intriguing '76 evolved like a minor Chenin). But Chenin's where the action is.

Due to spring frost, Denis did not bother harvesting in 1994. His '93 sec was a strong, tight expression of pear and minerals. By cluster thinning two-thirds of his potential crop, Denis made stupendous '92s. The dry Chenin was elegant and concentrated, with flavors of minerals and pears. The focused demi-sec was a marvel, with delicious fruit and a clear statement of *terroir*.

Denis feels his '90 sec is the best he's ever made. Indeed, a delicate weave of honey, tea, minerals, apple, and licorice, it could rival a good Montlouis. All of Denis's 1980s are recommended. (It's a good idea to de-cant them an hour in advance; Denis often adds too much sulfur, but it blows off with aeration.) The '89 demi-sec—supple, with flavors of quinine and pineapple *eau-de-vie*—will be gorgeous by 2000.

TO WATCH

Thierry Bésard, Lignières-de-Touraine: A Montreuil-Bellay gradu-ate, Bésard took over the family's vines in 1988 and has been modernizing the cellar, buying new equipment, and making better and better wine. What first drew my attention was a '90 *moelleux*. Bésard harvested the grapes for this *cuvée* by *tri*, selecting only those affected by noble rot. Richly honeyed, with clear, appetizing flavors of citrus zests and minerals, it was super. His '93 sec was one of those waterfall-y Chenins, with firm pear and mineral flavors. Lovely. And his '93 Touraine Cabernet was one of the best I've tasted from the Azay area. Smooth, slightly tart and bell-peppery, it was brilliant paired with a three-week-old chèvre.

Château de la Roche, Cheillé: A tweedy ex-Parisian who made his debut with the '90 vintage, Bernard Gentil has four hectares of vines and eighteen of fruit trees. He laid in a good supply of used Bordeaux *barriques* and hired Bourgueil's Pierre-Jacques Druet as his consulting enologist. The results are fragrant, stylish Azays. The tart '94 white showed honest work; the '93 and '92 whites were perfumed Chenins, blending flavors of oak, lemon, and minerals. Rosés—Grolleau, often with a bit of Cot—are particu-larly successful. A '93 was a bit oaky, but a '91 was sprightly, with pretty fruit, and a deeply colored '90 was lovely and mellow. Part of the Grolleau harvest makes a creamy rosé brut. And Gentil puts out a great *eau-de-vie de poire* from his own orchards.

RECOMMENDED

Château de l'Aulée, Azay-le-Rideau: Owned by Mme. Lallier-Deutz (of the Champagne Deutz family), this thirty-eight-hectare *domaine* (the largest in the appellation) makes sleek Azay whites and stylish Touraine *mousseux*.

James Paget, Rivarennes: The Pagets, a hardworking young couple, have ten hectares of vines in Azay-le-Rideau as well as several hectares of Chinon. Their impeccable cellars stretch along a sun-dappled country lane on the boundary of Cheillé and Rivarennes. James, a fourth-generation vintner, makes pleasant, barrel-fermented rosés with a trace of residual sugar; agreeable, one-dimensional Chenins; and congenial reds for *soirées dansantes*.

Pibaleau Père et Fils, Azay-le-Rideau: Gaston Pibaleau and his son Pascal (Amboise and a *stage* in Champagne) represent state-of-the-art Azay: six hectares (augmented by a small orchard); machine-harvesting; more or less competent fermentations in tank as well as in barrel; overuse of sulfur; effective experimentation with aromatic yeasts. What results are good enough rosés, Chenins, Crémants, and Touraine Cabs, all of which could be better.

BY THE GLASS

Marc Badiller, Cheillé: Appealingly rough-hewn Azays, often on the tart side.

Michel et Frédéric Hardy, Vallères: As Frédéric (Amboise) succeeds his father the wines may improve. His clean, fruity '90 Touraine Tradition showed promise.

Daniel Jahan, Saché: The owner of Le Balzac, a café on Saché's main square, Jahan pours his bitingly tart Chenin, tasting of Granny Smith apples, as the house white. If you're having lunch, order Jahan's tart rosé to accompany the *rillettes*; with the roast chicken, insist on the best *cuvée* of the latest good vintage of Breton.

Jean-Pierre Perdriau, Cheillé: A lumberjack of a man, Perdriau is tall, dark, and ruggedly handsome. His best wines resemble him, notably a vigorous '90 rosé and thick, dark Cabernets.

Pierre Rivry, Lignières-de-Touraine: Rustic, barrel-fermented Azays.

Franck Verroneau, Cheillé: As this young vigneron, who studied in Bordeaux, learns the ropes, the wines here should improve. Promising signs: a '90 Chenin, a *sec-tendre*, with attractive grapefruit and mineral flavors.

Touraine-Mesland

STATUS: *AOC 1955*

TYPES OF WINE: *Red, white, and rosé*

ZONE AND PRODUCTION: *9,000 hectoliters, of which 80 percent is red, produced on 200 hectares within six communes on the north bank of the Loire, between Limeray and Blois*

GRAPES: *Whites—Chenin Blanc (minimum 60 percent), Sauvignon (maximum 30 percent), Chardonnay (maximum 15 percent); rosés—Gamay (minimum 80 percent), Cot, Cabernet Franc; reds—Gamay (minimum 60 percent), Cot, Cabernet Franc (between 10 and 30 percent)*

SOILS: *Mostly on thin soils dominated by sand, clay, and gravel, with outcroppings of silex, quartz, and chalk*

PRICE: *15 to 50ff*

BEST VINTAGES: (see *Touraine*)

One of Touraine's oldest viticultural regions, Mesland specializes in red wines. You can also find attractive dry rosés (as well as the occasional demi-sec, or even *moelleux*) and pleasant Chenins, but the best wines are the warm, easy-drinking reds. As of 1994, these must be blends of Gamay, Cot, and Cabernet Franc. Beefy and well-structured, with savory fruit flavors, they often taste of cherries, cherry pits, kirsch, and sweet spices. They are perfect bistro reds, made to be drunk within five years of the harvest.

❧ PRODUCER RATINGS ❧

EXCELLENT
Château Gaillard   Clos de la Briderie

BY THE GLASS
Château de Monteaux   Serge Cordier   Jean-Louis Darde
Domaine d'Artois   Domaine de la Besnerie
Domaine du Chemin de Rabelais
Domaine Closerie du Val de Laleu   Domaine du Prieuré

❧ ❧

EXCELLENT

Château Gaillard, Mesland: When young Vincent Girault (Lycée Viticole de Beaune and Bordeaux) set up his own *domaine*, he called in experts to determine where specific grapes should be planted (early-ripening Gamay went on clayey-sandy soils; later grapes like Cabernet on clay-flint and chalky soils). And like his father, François Girault, he practices biodynamic viticulture.

Having worked at Champagne Roederer, Girault produces discreet, Chenin-dominated Crémants. But his finest wines are his fleshy, fruity reds. The best is his Vieilles Vignes *cuvée,* generally 60 percent Gamay, 25 percent Cot, and 15 percent Cabernet. At first blush, the '93 was just a tasty country red. But as it opened, it revealed flavors of Morello cherries mixed with minerals and orange zest. There was a real "There" there. The '92 was a smooth, soft blanket of flavor; '89 and '90 were generous blends of plum, cinnamon, and kirsch.

Clos de la Briderie, Monteaux: I find my notes on François Girault's wines peppered with "delicious" and "an ambassador" and "if only all Touraines were this good . . ."

The wines are that good because Girault keeps yields low, hand harvests—he also practices biodynamic viticulture—and is exigent in his vinification. Girault makes a meaty *vin gris* from a direct press of Gamay. His whites are particularly impressive. Whether the deeply intelligent, serious, and concentrated '93 sec (Bravo!) or the beguiling late-harvest wines of '89 and '90, Girault's Chenins present the most persuasive argument for that grape's cultivation in eastern Touraine.

Though I found the '93 a bit too kirsch-flavored for me, Girault's red blend (usually a third each of Gamay, Cot, and Cabernet Franc) has been delicious in difficult years like '94 and '91. In vintages like '90, '89, and '88, the wine was a lip-smacking knit of ripe, warm fruit, with flavors of kirsch, plum, and macerated cherries.

BY THE GLASS

Château de Monteaux, Monteaux: The rustic, slightly oxidized whites are not without charm.

Serge Cordier, Mesland: Satisfying Mesland reds, particularly the Tradition, a friendly, tasty, country wine.

Jean-Louis Darde, Onzain: Solid, tasty bistro Chenins and silky red blends with splendid fruit.

Domaine d'Artois, Mesland: Formerly owned by François Girault, now part of the Guy Saget portfolio.

Domaine de la Besnerie, Monteaux: Gamay only.

Domaine du Chemin de Rabelais, Onzain: Pleasant light whites, fragrant rosés, and slightly rustic Gamays and Cabernets.

Domaine Closerie du Val de Laleu, Chouzy-sur-Cisse: Much is dull and overworked, but the Gamays can charm.

Domaine du Prieuré, Mesland: Chewy reds and herby Sauvignons, with intense aromas of mint and basil, which seemed destined to pair with pesto.

Touraine-Noble Joué

On the outskirts of Tours—a bleak stretch of gas stations, discount centers, and high-rises—a wine with the lyrical name of Noble Joué is resurfacing. A *vin gris* made from Pinot Meunier, Pinot Gris, and Pinot Noir, it is produced in five communes immediately south of Tours, and it is as pretty as its name. Its robe is coppery, *oeil de perdrix*; its flavor, vinous and fruity; its structure firm; its finish dry and nutty.

The wine is said to have existed before the fifteenth century. Historians place it on the table of Louis XI in his château in Plessis-les-Tours. It was drunk in Tourangeaux inns in the eighteenth century and won numerous awards in the Paris exposition of 1900. Climatic problems and the expansion of the city of Tours led to the disappearance of its vineyards, perhaps nowhere more radically than in Joué-les-Tours, the wine's commune of origin.

In 1976 the Chambre d'Agriculture, the INAO, and enologist Jacques Puisais counseled replanting the vines that made the traditional blend. Pinot Gris, which usually represents 60 percent of the blend, is always the most alcoholic of the three and provides the wine's structure, power, and body. Meunier, usually 30 percent, adds fruit and finesse; Pinot Noir, 10 percent, length as well as historical accuracy. The harvest is pressed immediately, and the wine is fermented like a white. Noble Joué is best in its first year.

For now Noble Joué is merely a name—it has no legal protection. But its half-dozen producers are demanding recognition from the INAO and are likely to get it. There are only twenty hectares in production and one *domaine* makes more than half of its wine. It is:

Rousseau Frères, Esvres-sur-Indre: Allowing for vintage differences, the Noble Joués are fruity, vinous, and firm, with strawberry notes and appetizing bitter-almond finishes. Even the '94 was fragrant and floral with appealing peach notes. The Rousseaus also make pleasant sparkling Noble Joué and soft Touraine reds.

ALSO RECOMMENDED

Lucien Leroux, Saint-Avertin: Hand harvested and fermented and aged in oak and chestnut *demi-muids*, these Noble Joués are heavier than the rest and richer, with some wood character and mallowy nuances.

Jean-Jacques Sard, Esvres-sur-Indre: Marginally leaner and drier Noble Joués, often with light tangerine flavors.

JASNIERES AND
COTEAUX DU LOIR

Jasnières

STATUS: *AOC 1937*
TYPES OF WINE: *Dry and off-dry white*
ZONE AND PRODUCTION: *600 to 1,000 hectoliters, made on 37 hectares on a thin, four-kilometer-long, crescent-shaped band midway up a hillside in the communes of Lhomme and Ruillé above the Loir*
GRAPES: *Chenin Blanc*
SOILS: *Tufa with outcroppings of silex, often covered with pebbles and rocks*
PRICE: *25 to 98ff*
BEST VINTAGES: (see *Vouvray*)

Coteaux du Loir

STATUS: *AOC 1948*
TYPES OF WINE: *Red, white, and rosé*
ZONE AND PRODUCTION: *1,200 to 1,500 hectoliters, from about 48 hectares within twenty-three communes; seventeen in the Sarthe, six in the Indre-et-Loire*
GRAPES: *Whites—Chenin Blanc; reds and rosés—Pineau d'Aunis, Gamay, Cot, and Cabernet. Up to 25 percent Grolleau may be used in rosés.*
SOILS: *Marl with silica on tuffeau*
PRICE: *20 to 50ff*
BEST VINTAGES: (see *Vouvray*)

Thirty-five kilometers north of Tours, where cider- and wine-country meet, are the two northernmost AOCs of the Loire, each of which adds an intriguing shade to the Loire palette. Jasnières, which takes its name from a one-and-a-half-hectare *clos*, is a variation on Savennières's theme of austere, mineral-rich Chenins. Drier and more delicate, it is Mosel to Savennières's Rheingau. The Pineau d'Aunis–based Coteaux du Loir are peppery, spicy country reds.

By rights it should be too cold here to grow grapes. But the region has a microclimate resembling that of Touraine, thanks to the Loir, a 350-kilometer-long river running from the Ile-de-France to Anjou. This *is* the northern limit, however. Harvest is late, usually from the end of October to mid-November, and the wines are always less alcoholic than Vouvray.

In great years like '89 and '90, Jasnières can be *moelleux*—and, when harvested by *tri*, can be heavily botrytized. Most, however, range from chalk dry to off-dry. (Many winemakers leave about 3 grams residual sugar to offset acidity.)

Anyone who wants a quick definition of *terroir* might start in Jasnières. The wines have a persuasive mineral undertow, a distinct flintiness due to the rich streaks of silex in the soil. They are also floral and seem to dance every variation on the theme of Apple: green apples, apple skins, *eau-de-vie de pomme*, Calvados. From the bouquet you often think Jasnières will be sweet, but it astonishes you with a dryness that nevertheless reprises impressions of flowers, apples, quince, acacia, and honey. Jasnières pulls you up short. It makes you think about wine.

The Coteaux du Loirs to look for are the peppery, characterful Pineau d'Aunis, followed by impressive, mineral Gamays. Some bottle Aunis pure—as they do their Gamays—but the local wine *syndicat* recommends blending, counseling 65 to 75 percent Aunis, 15 to 25 percent Gamay (for roundness and pretty aromas); 5 to 10 percent Cabernet Franc (for body and power); and 5 to 10 percent Cot (for color). Pure or blended, these are reds to drink chilled—at 13 to 14 degrees Celsius—and despite their youthful charm, they can age. A succulent '76 Aunis that some pegged for Chinon and others for Burgundy was fresh, honest, and delicious, a well-knit blanket of dried raspberries, hay, leather, tobacco, truffles, roasted green peppers, and caramel.

Few of the region's producers live solely off wine. Cereal crops, poultry, and cattle are their principal sources of income. This is changing, however, as young winemakers take over vineyards and renovate cellars. In addition to their appellation wines, many producers make sparkling wines; these are *vins de table*. All but one producer I met machine-harvest at least part of their production; old vines and those on the steepest slopes are done by hand. *Tris* are recent and not, as yet, widespread.

⋘ PRODUCER RATINGS ⋙

LEADER
Domaine de la Charrière

TO WATCH
Aubert de Rycke

HIGHLY RECOMMENDED
Domaine de Cézin

RECOMMENDED
Gaston Cartereau   Jable d'Or   Tuffeau Mont Veillon

⋘ ⋙

LEADER

Domaine de la Charrière, **La Chartre-sur-le-Loir:** Joël Gigou took Jasnières out of the Middle Ages and into top restaurants. He lost 80 percent of his '94 crop to frost. His '93 Clos Saint-Jacques (his best vineyard) was an intriguing, steely blend of green apple and minerals; it should age beautifully. In '92 Gigou rose to the challenge of a difficult vintage with elegant, mineral-rich Jasnières, particularly his Sélection de Raisins Nobles, a dry wine from heavily botrytized grapes. Curiously, I was underwhelmed by the '90s, but all three versions of both '88 and '89 are elegant and gorgeous, their many attributes perhaps best summarized by the lacy, beautifully focused '89 Clos Saint-Jacques. An explosion of floral aromas as well as apples and Calvados, it added on the palate nuances of ginger, minerals, sandalwood, and flashes of smoke and flint, mallow and herbal tea.

Gigou's sparkling wines are impressive, too. And his Coteaux du Loir blanc and rosé are always among the best. I'm crazy about his Aunis and barrel-aged Cuvée Cénomane. Pure Gamay, the latter is a compact, peppery, light red that can develop aromas as penetrating as incense—cinnamon, carnation, orange zest, tea, and sandalwood.

TO WATCH

***Aubert de Rycke*, Marçon:**   Jean-Michel Aubert and Bénédictine de Rycke both graduated from Macon's enology program. Aubert was formerly the director of the Cheverny cooperative, Mont Près Chambord, a post he left when the couple expanded its vineyard holdings from seven to fifteen hectares. The two make ambitious Coteaux du Loir blanc (from a parcel once included in Jasnières); hard, dry, cinnamon-scented rosé made from Pineau d'Aunis; engaging barrel-aged Aunis rouge and delicate Jasnières.

The '94 Jasnières Cuvée Prestige was remarkable. Not only was it by far the best wine they made in that vintage, it could stand up well to a lot of '94 Vouvrays. Nicely focused and quite suave, it had 55 grams residual sugar, making it seem almost as lush as the complex, honeyed Jasnières the couple made in '89 and '90.

HIGHLY RECOMMENDED

***Domaine de Cézin*, Marçon:**   André Fresnau and son François are the pillars of Coteaux du Loir and are among its best producers. They have a little over a hectare in Jasnières from which they made a firm, mineral-rich '92; a flinty, ginger-scented '89; and a mind-blowing '90, a lush weave of honey, licorice, and herbal tea that brought to mind Curnonsky's dictum, "Three times a century, Jasnières is the best white wine in the world."

The Fresnaus make attractive Coteaux du Loir blanc, but I have a crush on their reds, especially the pure Aunis. The '92 drank like a wonderfully firm, dry, dark rosé, with pepper and cinnamon flavors. The '90 was love at first taste—and the wine grew on me with each additional sip. It wasn't complex or powerful; it was just wonderful and cozy and interesting and satisfying.

RECOMMENDED

***Gaston Cartereau*, Lhomme:**   I first tasted Cartereau's rustic, quirkily honest Jasnières at Tabac Henri IV, a wine bar in Paris. Alone among the producers I met, Cartereau harvests entirely by hand. He's got an ancient press, he ferments everything in wood, and he neither fines nor filters. The Jasnières is hard and tart, with a thread of carbon dioxide and flavors of apple skins and the mushroomy-moldy smell of a good Saint-Nectaire. The fragrant Aunis is a sinewy country red with guts and allure.

Jable d'Or, Château-du-Loir: A proprietary name given to the clean, pleasant, commercial Jasnières and Coteaux du Loir made by assembling wines from a group of local growers.

Tuffeau Mont Veillon: In 1991 Thierry Honnons, a non-vigneron wine nut, took control of ten hectares of vines. He signed up for some adult classes in Tours, invested in temperature-controlled stainless steel tanks, and, with brother-in-law Philippe Sévault (a professional vintner), began turning out some promising wines, even in the difficult '91 and '92 vintages. His '92 Jasnières, the best, was appley, austere, and mineral, downright classy.

CHEVERNY AND COUR-CHEVERNY

Cheverny

STATUS: *AOC 1993*

TYPES OF WINE: *Red, white, and rosé*

ZONE AND PRODUCTION: *7,000 to 16,000 hectoliters, on 335 hectares within twenty-three communes south of the Loire, between Blois and Contres*

GRAPES: *Whites—Sauvignon (minimum 40 percent, 60 percent after 1997); Chardonnay, Chenin, Arbois; reds—Gamay (40 to 65 percent); Pinot Noir, Cabernet Franc, Cabernet Sauvignon (until 2000 only), Cot; rosés— Gamay (more than 50 percent), Pinot Noir, Cabernet, Cot, Pineau d'Aunis*

SOILS: *Clay or sand mixed with silica as well as isolated clay-chalk parcels*

PRICE: *15 to 20ff*

BEST VINTAGES: (see *Touraine*)

Cour-Cheverny

STATUS: *AOC 1993*

TYPES OF WINE: *White*

ZONE AND PRODUCTION: *41 hectares within eleven communes at the heart of the Cheverny appellation*

GRAPES: *Romorantin*

PRICE: *15 to 20ff*

BEST VINTAGES: (see *Touraine*)

Cheverny's pleasant whites, reds, and rosés resemble those of Touraine. One wine, however, is unique. Cour-Cheverny, a dry white which received its own appellation in 1993, is made from Romorantin, a grape introduced to the region by François Ier in 1519. Romorantin's origins are unknown. High in acid, lightly viscous, it has a suggestion of oxidization that seems integral to the wine. Relatively neutral in its youth, it can age for five years or more, developing Chenin-like flavors of wax, hay, herbal tea, and butterscotch as well as wild fennel and petrol. I always imagine drinking young Romorantins with Italian antipasti.

Certainly not your everyday white, Romorantin is a wine for those of us who revel in footnotes. Two producers make particularly good versions as well as delicious Chevernys. They are:

Domaine des Huards, Cour-Cheverny: The Gendriers make admirable Sauvignons, rosés, and red blends, but they excel with Romorantin. You'll never find a better version. I've tasted every vintage since the early '80s and have invariably found the wines fascinating as well as tasty. The '93 had delightful flavors of balsam, nuts, and green olives. The engaging '92 Cuvée François Ier (an old-vines Romorantin) was meaty and focused. Simultaneously rustic and sleek, it was Romorantin in its Sunday-go-to-meetin' attire. It will age, but it is drinking beautifully now, as is the impressive '89.

Domaine de la Desoucherie, Cour-Cheverny: Christian Tessier makes solid Romorantin, too, as well as pungent Sauvignons and pretty reds. His Gamay blended with 20 percent Pinot Noir is the kind of supple, personal, light red I love to find in a wine bar.

VALENÇAY

STATUS: *VDQS 1970*

TYPES OF WINE: *Red, white, and rosé*

ZONE AND PRODUCTION: *6,350 hectoliters on 152 hectares within fourteen communes stretching along the banks of the Cher immediately upstream of the Touraine appellation*

GRAPES: *Whites—Sauvignon Blanc, Chardonnay, Arbois, with possible additions of up to 40 percent of Chenin or Romorantin; reds and rosés—Cabernet, Cot, Gamay, Pinot Noir, which may be blended with up to 25 percent of Gascon, Pineau d'Aunis, Gamay de Chaudenay, and no more than 10 percent of Grolleau.*

SOILS: *Flinty clay*
PRICE: *15 to 20ff*
BEST VINTAGES: (see *Touraine*)

Valençay takes its name from a sixteenth-century château whose lavishly furnished rooms are considerably more sumptuous than the region's wines. The latter, particularly the whites, are most notable for a distinctive flintiness which comes from the silex-rich soils of its vineyards. Indeed, several of Valençay's towns were known for their gunflint, having for three centuries furnished French armies with that commodity. (Wine labels picture rifles sparking gunfire.)

⋘ PRODUCER RATINGS ⋙

HIGHLY RECOMMENDED
Jacky et Philippe Augis

RECOMMENDED
Jacky Preys   Hubert Sinson

⋘ ⋙

HIGHLY RECOMMENDED

Jacky et Philippe Augis, Meusnes: Look for characterful Touraines and Valençays, particularly the juicy Cot whose rich fruit recalls the tart Montmorency cherry.

RECOMMENDED

Jacky Preys, Meusnes: With fifty-three hectares split between Valençay and Touraine, Jacky Preys runs the largest family *domaine* in the Loir-et-Cher. He furnishes two hundred Paris bistros with soft, grassy Sauvignons, passable Gamay blends, and the pleasant Cuvée Royale. His most unusual wine is a lean and grassy Fié Gris, made from an ancient mutation of Sauvignon.

Hubert Sinson, Meusnes: The '89 Touraine Sauvignon, the wine that "conquered" Japan, is one of the best wines I've tasted from Sinson—firm and herbaceous, with flavors of grapefruit and melon and lots of flint. While many of his wines are bland, some are agreeable, such as the beefy '92

Valençay rouge, a Gamay-dominated blend; and a pungent, barrel-aged '89 Pinot Noir.

HAUT-POITOU

STATUS: *VDQS 1970*
TYPES OF WINE: *Red, white, and rosé*
ZONE AND PRODUCTION: *45,000 hectoliters made on over 800 hectares within forty-seven communes north and west of Poitiers*
GRAPES: *Whites—Sauvignon, Chardonnay, Chenin; reds and rosés—Gamay, Cabernet Franc and Sauvignon, Pinot Noir, some Merlot*
SOILS: *Thin clay-chalk and clay-silica, on a base of hard chalk*
PRICE: *15 to 20ff*
BEST VINTAGES: *'95, '93*

A flat land of cattle, wheat, and sunflowers, Poitou is rainier than either Anjou or Touraine. Its vines occupy slopes and small blocks of land on the warmest plateaus north and west of Poitiers. The most successful grapes are the early-maturing Sauvignon Blanc and Gamay.

There are more than six hundred growers in the Vienne, half of them in the VDQS zone. The Cave du Haut-Poitou, formerly the cooperative, vinifies more than 70 percent of the Vienne's wines.

Cave du Haut-Poitou, Neuville-de Poitou: Several days before the first grapes of 1995 were harvested, Georges Duboeuf (a.k.a. Mr. Beaujolais) purchased 40 percent of the shares of the Cave du Haut-Poitou. In one fell swoop Duboeuf ended the *Cave's* days as a cooperative, covered its debts (some grower-members hadn't been paid for three years), and secured for himself a source of inexpensive and easygoing varietal wines in both VDQS and Vin de Pays appellations.

I was a grudging admirer of the *Cave* in its co-op incarnation. It did everything I hate—high yields, juice pumped through pipes under the highway to 1500-hectoliter fermentation tanks, heavy centrifuging, near-sterile filtration—but the wines were solid, tasty, and commercial, nearly always offering good value.

The Sauvignons were sprightly, clean, and herbaceous. Those from the Domaine de Brizay were the richest and creamiest. The Cabernet-based rosés were firm and robust. The Gamays were jammy and vibrant. Heritage, a barrel-aged blend of Cabernet Franc and Sauvignon, was a warm red with pleasant fruit and spice flavors. The silky Château la Fuye, pure Franc, had engaging flavors of musk, cinnamon, and clove.

For now, staff and methods of vinification remain the same, and the '95s tasted are well within the family style, including a pretty Gamay Primeur whose evolution was followed by an enologist brought in from Beaujolais.

COTEAUX DU VENDOMOIS

STATUS: *VDQS 1968*
TYPES OF WINE: *Red, white, and rosé*
ZONE AND PRODUCTION: *6,600 hectoliters made on 220 hectares within thirty-five communes on both banks of the Loir*
GRAPES: *Whites—Chenin, Chardonnay (maximum 20 percent); reds and rosés—Pineau d'Aunis, Gamay (maximum 30 percent for rosés), Cabernet, Pinot Noir*
SOILS: *Clay with chalk or silica under rocky topsoils*
PRICE: *15 to 18ff*
BEST VINTAGES: *'95, '93, '90*

Where are the vineyards? I wondered, driving along endless fields of sunflowers or of parched stubble with bales of hay set about like Christo installations. The vines? They're on the hillsides, growers told me. Indeed, here and there vines extended in narrow strips at the crest of slopes or occupied small parcels of well-exposed plateaus.

Pineau d'Aunis, which represents half the region's acreage, makes the most interesting of its wines. Either it is pressed directly to make a *vin gris* (pure or blended with Gamay) or it produces a red, increasingly a blend called Tradition, with varying percentages of Gamay, Pinot Noir, Cot, or Cabernet.

Coppery *vin gris*, the Vendômois's most representative wine, is firm, vinous, and peppery. Locals drink it with dessert, particularly with fruit tarts. I like to bring along a couple of bottles when invited for dinner with friends from the Antilles. Its peppery flavors and firm structure nicely complement the spicy dumplings and stews of jackfruit.

Only a handful of the region's growers live off their wine. Most sell their grapes to the cooperative. Things are changing quickly, though, as young winemakers get serious about their craft. The Vendômois also realize they can make more money off wine than cereal crops and hope to reclaim some of the zone's best hillsides. But realtors, too, have their eyes on those slopes: Vendôme is a forty-two-minute TGV ride from Paris.

Note: Many of the '92s and '94s were marred by traces of rot.

◄ PRODUCER RATINGS ►

TO WATCH
Domaine du Four à Chaux

RECOMMENDED
Cave du Vendômois
Patrice Colin
Robert et Claude Minier

BY THE GLASS
Domaine du Carroir   Jean Martellière

◄ ►

TO WATCH

***Domaine du Four à Chaux,* Thoré-la-Rochette:** Dominique Norguet studied at the Lycée de Beaune, worked for Henry Marionnet, and, wine for wine, is the best producer of Coteaux du Vendômois. And he's really just beginning to hit his stride. A tasting is a madcap chase. A rendezvous at the hotel in Thoré segues to a bumpy ride over the river and through the woods and up a hillside where the family has several caves, to taste some whites; then to a brief tour of his best vines, on a well-exposed plateau in Thoré. From there to the family farm to taste '89s and older *vin gris* in Grandma's furniture wax–scented house. Then a sprint to Lavardin where we interrupt a wedding feast in the Relais d'Antan to taste the last bottle of '88 Cabernet. Whew!

My favorites here start with his admirable '94 and '92 Chenins as well as his '92 *vin gris*. Not easy vintages. The '92s, in particular, were utter charmers, fruity and firm, with long, mineral finishes. Norguet's Gamay-Aunis blend is a good bistro red. His more "serious" blend—Pinot Noir and Aunis—is a step up. The '89 was an attractive lunch red, supple and fruity, with appealing flavors of strawberries, ripe hay, and orange zest. The '93 was a congenial, kirsch-flavored, country red.

RECOMMENDED

***Cave du Vendômois,* Villiers-sur-Loir:** The cooperative produces 70 percent of local wines. Its two hundred members deliver the entirety of their crop, which is vinified in the co-op's cellars. Less than 10 percent is sold in bottle; most funnels into cubitainers, at prices rivaling bottled water. But the co-op's bottled wines can be good and are getting better. A fine example is the crisp and fruity '92 Chenin, Tête de Cuvée. A truly admirable job.

***Patrice Colin,* Thoré-la-Rochette:** Colin (Montreuil-Bellay) is serious about wine and was perhaps the first to believe in the potential of the appellation. His wines are good—some are very good—but one senses they could be better if yields were lower, harvest more rigorous, and the wine less manipulated. I often like his pure Chenin, with flavors of green apples and hazelnuts, and his peach- and ginger-flavored *vin gris* of pure Aunis. His general red blend, Aunis-Gamay, can be a pretty quaffer. His Cuvée Emile Colin, Cabernet and 30 percent Aunis with a bit of oak age, is an ample country red with agreeable flavors of kirsch and black cherry.

***Robert et Claude Minier,* Lunay:** The house of Minier is calculated folklore. The family has six hectares of vines and some fifty of corn, barley, and sunflowers. Claude's sister Giselle makes goat cheese and maintains a *table d'hôte* and several rooms for tourists. The three receive cubi customers at a folding table in front of their *caves* dug into the hillside. Robert is shambling and gregarious, with mussed, thinning gray hair that occasionally has a leaf or two stuck in it. He holds forth on "honest wines" with Parisians disenchanted with Bordeaux. Claude is taciturn and sardonic. He shrugs if you compliment a wine, shrugs if you criticize, but finally shows you his wall of awards. Giselle is bossy, chatty, and makes terrific cheese. If only the boys made wine as good!

The wines aren't half bad, considering. Many have a warts-and-all charm. Some even win awards. An '89 Cabernet-Aunis blend was full of engaging flaws—carbon dioxide, flavors of bouillon. But it was also sprightly and fruity and, somehow, fetching. It won a bronze medal in Macon.

BY THE GLASS

***Domaine du Carroir,* Thoré-la-Rochette:** Influenced by young vintners like Dominique Norguet, Jean Brazilier is evolving in the best sense of the word. His wines are still rustic, but the nicest of them, like the fragrant '92 Chenin and the peppery-kirschy Tradition, are pungent, likeable country wines.

Jean Martellière, **Montoire-sur-le-Loir:** The non-filtered Cuvée Jean-Vivien is a characterful local red for pairing with local goat cheese.

THE TOURAINE TABLE

My first typical Tourangeau feast took place on a hot June day in a cold, dark cave outside of Bourgueil. We sat around a trestle table before a huge hearth and dug into platters of thickly sliced potatoes and tomatoes dressed with walnut oil vinaigrette and bowls of indecently delicious *rillettes* from the village charcuterie. Next there was ham marinated in white wine and cooked over the fire, and potatoes that had cooked over the fire, too, followed by salad, local goat cheese in several shapes and stages of maturity, and a homemade walnut tart flavored with local *eau-de-vie de prune*.

I ate like a farmhand, which is to say like a true Tourangelle. Touraine is the land of big eaters. Theme feasts are structured around "Monsieur" (the Pig) or game, around a *tête de veau*, or one of France's innumerable holidays. Whenever or wherever you are in Touraine you can find a major meal in progress—more often than not in one of the thousands of caves carved into the soft rock. (Many of the caves now used for entertaining served as chapels during the Revolution.)

What is eaten, however, and with whatever abandon, seems familiar. Not only do many of the dishes span the Loire, they seem to belong to no particular region at all: They are simply French. The heart of the Loire Valley, and perhaps its spiritual center, Touraine offers cooking as temperate and reassuring as its landscape. There is good sense in the lightness of its pike *quenelles*, moderation in the saucing of its coq au vin, simplicity in its pork roasts, and precision in its fruit tarts. As chef Charles Barrier once said to me, "There is nothing gratuitous in Touraine cooking."

The owner of an eponymous two-Michelin-star restaurant in Tours, Barrier was born in a cave in 1915 and can trace the evolution of many of Touraine's classic dishes—widely appreciated ones like *rillettes,* salmon in *beurre blanc,* shad in sorrel sauce, and chicken stews—as well as more localized favorites like medallions of pork in a prune-and-wine sauce. "In Avoine there were lots of plum trees until the nuclear power plant killed them all," he explains. "So you made *noisettes de porc aux pruneaux,* a dish from the Middle Ages. It's always made with a red wine, not with Vouvray [though many cookbooks specify Vouvray]. It should be a coarse sauce, like a civet."

Prunes still figure in many local recipes. They may be stuffed with apple compote or apricot flambéed with rum. And a Tourangeau matelote of eel or lamprey is garnished with prunes as well as with hard-boiled eggs and croutons fried in walnut oil. This variation, to me, reveals a ruder, less Cartesian side to local cooking, as do *beuchelles*, veal sweetbreads, kidneys, and cockscombs in a vegetable cream sauce.

Poitou, at Touraine's southern border, brings an earthy influence to local fare. Poorer and less polished than Touraine, its cooking has much in common with that of Berry (the two share *pâté de Pâques*, for example) and contributes to the menu several venerable dishes, such as *farci Poitevin*, an elaborate version of stuffed cabbage, and *lièvre à la royale*, the ultimate hare stew, as well as some popular local desserts.

Farci Poitevin was traditional holiday fare for the poor. Everyone has a vegetable garden and much of its contents—cabbage, lettuce, chives, parsley, sorrel, garlic, onion—are chopped and mixed with bacon, eggs, and stale bread and packed into blanched cabbage leaves. The whole is tied into a ball and simmers for three hours, sometimes with the pot-au-feu. (I have also seen the dish prepared in a baking pan, without the wrapping.)

While some authorities claim the recipe for *lièvre à la royale* dates from the fifteenth century, most attribute it to M. Couteaux, a food-loving senator/agronomist/writer from the Vienne, who supposedly concocted in 1898 this dish still featured in restaurants and at festive meals. Place chunks of hare on a bed of lard and goose fat. Add a lot of the following: red wine, red wine vinegar, shallots, garlic, and a bouquet garni. Cook for four hours in a casserole sealed with dough. Remove the hare. Make a hash from its heart, lungs, liver, and lard, and mix with the cooking juices. Put the hare back in the casserole with more red wine and the hash and cook for another hour. Before serving, thicken the sauce with blood.

Broyé Poitevin is a hard, sweet *galette* made from eggs, butter, sugar, and flour. It may be flavored with *eau-de-vie* or lemon zest and topped with hazelnuts. The *torteau fromagé* of Poitou-Charentes, once artisanal, was traditionally made from goat's milk. Poitou-Charentes is France's leading producer of industrial goat cheese. Though the *torteau fromagé* has become industrialized as well, these days it is almost always made from pure cow's milk or a mix of the two. Shaped like a brioche, it has a blackened cap and tastes like a cross between a pound cake and a cheesecake.

In addition to fruit compotes and fruit tarts, plain cakes and confections dominate the dessert course. Many villages bill the macaroon as a specialty.

The Abbey of Cormery, south of Tours, claims its monks invented maca-roons in the eighth century. Formed like sealing-wax stamps (they suppos-edly resemble a monk's bellybutton), the cookies are dry and hard and flavored with bitter almonds and orange zest. Niort's macaroons are sea-soned with local angelica; in Montmorillon they are shaped like crowns.

Fouace, the ancient bread which seems to be reemerging in many French regions, inspires much Tourangeau boosterism, as it was often described by Rabelais. In *Gargantua* the *fouace*-bakers of Lerné (in Rabelais's tale, a kingdom; in reality, a farming village at the southwest limits of Touraine) are transporting their goods to market one fine day when the shepherds of neighboring Seuilly stop them and ask to buy bread. The bak-ers refuse to sell and, in short, war breaks out.

Rabelais's recipe for a deluxe *fouace* includes "fine butter, fine egg yolks, fine saffron, fine spices." (Perhaps it is not accidental that Poitou, which starts at Lerné's border, has cultivated saffron since the Middle Ages.)

I happen to live in Lerné. A neighbor, a retired baker, recalls the post-war days when it was still a bustling little village with lots of small shops and enough commerce to support two bakers. My neighbor made what he con-sidered the classic *fouace*—a puff pastry *galette*, baked, like all his breads, in a wood-fired oven. His competitor's *fouace* was a rustic brioche. The latter has more historical support and is the *fouace* one generally finds now in the local bakeries that have been reviving them. These *fouaces* are likely to be spiced with cinnamon or bergamot, saffron, and orange-blossom water and are studded with walnuts.

My neighbor's version had a particular Rabelaisian appeal, however. It was made with lots of butter and cooked only long enough to melt the inte-rior. When you ate this *fouace,* the buttery juices were supposed to run down your chin. That is precisely what occurs when eating another western Loire bread—the pita-like *fouée*—when it is stuffed with buttered *mogettes,* but-tery *rillettes,* butter and goat cheese, or just plain butter.

Goat cheese eaten, say, as a late-afternoon snack is generally accompanied by farmhouse *vin d'épine* or *vin de pêche.* Powerful, sweet blends of wine and alcohol in which the new shoots of wild sloe (*épine*) or leaves of peach trees (*pêche*) have macerated, these are also popular aperitifs in chèvre and cereal country. Meals generally end with *eau-de-vie.* Once, every village had a dis-tiller—not surprising, given the quantity and quality of local fruit. Because licenses are increasingly hard to come by and increasingly regulated (and alcohol is taxed with an increasingly heavy hand), there is less and less local *eau-de-vie.* But you can still find wonderful *poire,* prune, *quetsche,* and kirsch throughout Touraine and Poitou—whence two additions to the local food-and-drink lexicon: *rincette* is Poitevin for *digestif*; *rincinette* is "one last sip."

La Chieuve

In La Bodinière, a farming hamlet outside the provincial town of Le Blanc, my cheese fantasy of France came to life in the form of Mme. Georgette Blondeau, a sixtyish woman who makes the Eiffel Tower–shaped goat cheese called Pouligny-Saint-Pierre. She appeared from behind a group of outbuildings—preceded by a dog, a farmer with a cane, and a herd of fifty goats who nibbled the ivy and roses climbing up the stone walls. Stocky, buxom, with neatly coiffed gray hair and a purse under her arm (she'd been to the dentist), Mme. Blondeau exuded competence. Her *fromagerie*, a small, free-standing outbuilding, was immaculate but not sterile. It smelled milky, motherly, kitcheny, and clean. The walls were whitewashed and tiled. There were stainless steel draining tables, draining baskets, trays of new cheese, trophies, and ledgers. In a pantry, shelves of aging cheese lined each wall, a kitchen towel draped over each tray—her secret, she said, for developing the blue mold.

At two weeks the Poulignys of Mme. Blondeau embody everything French cheese should be: almost unbearably delicious, specific, the realization of generations of know-how. The cut of a Mme. Blondeau Pouligny is porcelain; the flavor, clean and milky, with hints of citrus and hazelnuts and, at times, a woodsy, mushroom scent on the crust.

Pouligny-Saint-Pierre is one of Touraine's *appellation contrôlée* cheeses. Sainte-Maure-de-Touraine got its appellation in 1990; Selles-sur-Cher, like Pouligny, in 1975–76. Valençay has a *Label Régional* (a guaranty of authenticity, though not as strictly defined or regulated as AOC). The specifics of each appellation follow, along with a list of recommended producers. (Most of these producers sell at regional markets as well as at the farm.)

POULIGNY-SAINT-PIERRE

Made in twenty-two communes in the western part of the Indre department, around the town of Le Blanc, this cheese takes its name from the village of Pouligny. The cheese, in the form of a truncated pyramid, like a fat Eiffel Tower, weighs about eight ounces. There are also miniature versions. Aging generally lasts for two to five weeks.

OUTSTANDING

Mme. Blondeau, Pouligny-Saint-Pierre: You must make the pilgrimage to Georgette to get her cheese. During my first visit four customers arrived, each obsequious, wanting to be sure of getting her cheese. They bought every stage, including fresh—for eating with garlic or onion or with sugar and berries. And though I prefer aged chèvre, the fresh version was truly delicious. The aged ones are sublime.

After Mme. Blondeau, the deluge. There's her Pouligny, and then there are the others. Most comes from Couturier, a big dairy in Pouligny that produces all forms of chèvre. You'll find its cheeses in most shops and restaurants. Sometimes they pass muster, but they'll never make you dream.

RECOMMENDED

Courthial, Pouligny-Saint-Pierre: M. Courthial was the best *affineur* of Touraine-area chèvre, but it is as yet unclear whether his sons have the same talent.

Mme. Geffrault, Mauvières: A likeable woman with good fresh cheeses, which she sells to top boutiques for ripening.

La Ferme des Ages, Le Blanc: A government-owned goat farm making honorable, if not brilliant, Poulignys.

Le Blanc's Saturday market: Farmers, retirees, and widows with a couple of chickens, eggs, favas, and cherries also make a bit of cheese. The cheeses are not within the Pouligny appellation, though they may meet the criteria better and more honestly than industrial versions. I bought such a cheese from a grandmother with cropped white hair and a bright blue sweater. She had nineteen goats and had been making goat cheese since she was twelve. She continues to "keep busy in her old age." Her cheese was the real thing, nicely textured, with the flavor of fresh, grassy milk.

SAINTE-MAURE

The largest appellation, Sainte-Maure is made throughout the Indre-et-Loire as well as in neighboring cantons of the Indre and the Loir-et-Cher, where it overlaps with Pouligny-Saint-Pierre, Valençay, and Selles-sur-Cher.

A six- to eight-inch-long log with a tapered end, Sainte-Maure must be made of fresh goat milk; frozen curds are not permitted. The cheese is usually covered with a mixture of salt and ash, and it ages for a minimum of eight days. Archetypal Sainte-Maure is about three weeks old, its crust covered with a blue-gray or white mold. Many, though not all, Sainte-Maures have a straw running through the center of the cheese. This does not affect quality; Sainte-Maure is a long cheese and the practice of adding a straw came about to prevent crumbling when the log was cut. The custom continues largely because it is unique to Sainte-Maure.

Unlike other cheese regions, the producers of Sainte-Maure have understood the benefits of ripening and marketing their own cheeses rather than selling the milk or the fresh cheese to dairies and *affineurs*.

EXCELLENT

Lydie et Louis Bulté, **Saint-Epain:** Characterful, high-quality Sainte-Maures.

Jacques et Catherine Descré, **Marcilly-sur-Maulne:** A reliably terrific producer.

Jean-Luc Douet, **Bossée:** When well aged, the Sainte-Maures are as complex, layered, and flavorful as fine wine.

Jérôme et Sylvie Huan, **Anché:** Like the dynamic young winemakers of the Layon, the Huans, who are organic farmers, are constantly improving and experimenting. Sylvie also raises free-range chickens and *gélines de Touraine*.

Jean Lepage, **Seuilly:** Sainte-Maures of fresh, pure flavor and texture.

M. et Mme. Ondet, **Crissay-sur-Manse:** Since this young couple began making their own cheese rather than selling goat milk, they've been winning top awards at the yearly Sainte-Maure fair.

Mme. Richard, **Tendu:** (*see* Valençay)

HIGHLY RECOMMENDED

Bacquart, **Braslou:** The president of Sainte-Maure's *syndicat's* chèvres range from fair to sublime.

Castelli, **Saint-Michel-sur-Loire:** Consistently well-made chèvres.

Cuvier, **Vouvray:** Mild, pleasant chèvres.

Fontaine, **Draché:** A dependably fine producer.

Guériteau, **Sainte-Catherine-de-Fierbois:** Very tasty chèvres with good distribution in local shops.

Héribert, **Pussigny:**   Aggressive, pungent chèvres, sometimes with red-orange rinds.

Rabusseau, **Panzoult:**   At times hauntingly delicate chèvres; at times, a bit acid.

SUPERMARKET SAINTE-MAURE

Lamorinière, **Neuillé-Pont-Pierre:**   An intelligent producer who supplies the aptly named mega-market Mammouth feels that goat cheese has become standardized. "The old women could make cheese which 'spoke to God' but they were equally capable of making disasters." He feels his cheese is a very good, very reliable commercial chèvre. He's right.

Marie-Claire Meneau, **Avon-les-Roches:**   Good chèvres from a serious young couple. M. Meneau is an ex-technician for the Chambre d'Agriculture.

Jean-Pierre et Martine Moreau, **Pontlevoy:**   A relatively big farm, making Sainte-Maure, Selles, and numerous non-appellation chèvres of average to good quality.

Vazereau, **La Roche-Clermault:**   Three families, a large herd, chèvres from standard to good.

SELLES-SUR-CHER

Made south of the Loire in Sologne, Touraine, and Berry, it takes its name from the town of Selles at the center of the appellation. The cheese is a disk with a beveled ridge. Covered with charcoal cinders, it weighs roughly five ounces and is aged for ten days to three weeks.

EXCELLENT

Bouland, **Mareuil-sur-Cher:**   This serious young couple, with a goat and sheep farm and an auberge in the heart of Touraine wine country, makes some of the best cheese in the appellation. All the animals pasture, unusual for this region. Cheeses range from a fresh *brebis* (sheep), creamy and lactic, to a *moelleux* herb-coated chèvre in the form of a Pouligny, to a medium-dry, nicely pungent small round (the Boulands' most popular shape), to dry, flavorful six-month-old chèvres.

RECOMMENDED

Christian Egreteau, **Fougères-sur-Bièvre:**   This former technician for the region's goat cheese makers was recommended to me by the Boulands. I found his cheeses bland but correct.

Gaillard, Contres: A reputable *affineur* who also offers a Pavé Blesois.

Jean-Pierre et Martine Moreau (*see* Sainte-Maure)

Jean-Claude Rousseau, Châtillon-sur-Cher: Good, traditional chèvre with fresh, light flavor.

VALENÇAY (OR LEVROUX)

Made in Valençay, Levroux, and the Le Blanc area, this chèvre in the form of a truncated pyramid is shorter and squatter than Pouligny. The cheese is coated with powdered charcoal and must age for a minimum of eight days. A green label signifies a farmhouse Valençay; red, a dairy version, or one from an *affineur* who has used frozen curd, which is permitted.

EXCELLENT

Jean-Michel Chambonneau, Mazères: Grandma makes the cheese, Jean-Michel tends the eighty goats. The results are fabulous.

Yves Jouhanneau, La Châtre: A very good producer.

Mme. Richard, Tendu: Excellent, personalized chèvres—Valençays, Sainte-Maures, and other forms. Mme. Richard's stand at the Châteauroux market always has a long line in front of it.

Mme. Coetemerer, Selles-sur-Nohant;

Ferme du Petit Bellevue, Pruniers.

CHEESE FROM THE VENDOMOIS

La Chèvrerie d'Authon, Authon: A broad range of admirable local goat cheeses in many forms—cylinders, *briques*, disks.

Laiterie Taillard, Villiers-sur-Loir: Several types of local cheese, including Le Petit Troo, which looks like Camembert (originally made from goat milk, now almost always cow's-milk), and Le Petit Vendôme, a creamy, disk-shaped cow's-milk cheese which, to me, recalls a Boursault.

Giselle Minier, Lunay: In the summer Minier's twenty goats pasture in the woods; their milk is scented with the flavor of pine needles. Minier's small, round, hard cheeses are characterized by a hint of hazelnuts.

OTHER CHEESES

At *crémeries* and in local markets you'll also find local cow's-milk cheese. Usually round, they are made like chèvre and eaten rather fresh. They have no appellation.

La Brosse Perusson, **Loches:** Dominique and Geneviève Cornuet make *brebis* (sheep's-milk cheese) in the form of Crottin, Selles, and Tomme (a cake). The cheeses, usually very good, are worth tasting and are carried by many shops and restaurants.

Affineurs and dairies specializing in Loire chèvres include *Couturier* and *Courthial* in Pouligny; *Michel Hardy*, Meusnes; *Fromagerie Jacquin*, Valençay; and *Triballat*, Rians. A number of dairies and milk cooperatives produce the classic Loire chèvres but have specialty cheeses as well. The cooperative *Poitouraine*, Tournon-Saint-Martin, makes Couloummiers de Ligueil and Bleu de Ligueil; the *Coopérative Laiterie Région Lochoise*, Verneuil, turns out good butter as well as Le Sabotier, a round, relatively fresh cow's-milk cheese.

The best shops for local cheese are *Au Parfum de Beurre* and *La Ferme des Vignes* in Tours.

Touraine's Charcuterie

"*Rillettes* are as old as the pig itself," maintains Jacques Hardouin, Touraine's leading producer, adding, "In Tours everything goes into a cauldron or a *marmite* and cooks for five hours without a cover."

Rillettes are made by cooking cubed pork (usually shoulder and breast meat) in its own fat with 20 grams of salt per kilo. Stirred constantly so they don't stick, the *rillettes* cook over a high flame for the first hour—which gives them their golden color—and over a low flame for another four hours. Hardouin also adds a bottle of Vouvray and marc to each batch. Then the *rillettes* are degreased; the large morsels are crushed, cartilage and bones are removed; and the mass is returned to the cauldron, brought to a boil, skimmed of excess fat, and then mixed to incorporate the fat and the threadlike strands of meat.

Rillettes may be made of rabbit, goose, and duck (and in nouvelle hands, salmon) and they may be added to quiches. *Rillons*, or *grillons*, another Touraine specialty, are cubes of pork, salted and then cooked like *rillettes* for two hours until gold. They keep their form and are eaten cold.

Perhaps the best way to find tasty *rillettes*, *rillons*, *andouilles*, *andouillettes*, and *boudins* is to visit charcuteries in wine villages. One theory says that *rillettes de Tours* actually originated in Vouvray. So it's appropriate that the most famous purveyor—*Hardouin*—is located at Vouvray's main intersection, now called the Virage Gastronomique.

Vernou has two excellent producers, *André Mamoux* (*rillettes* as close to homemade as I've found in a charcuterie) and *Jean-Jacques Bergère*. On Restigné's tiny village square, *Michel Fuseau* offers rustic, tasty *rillettes*. In Ile Bouchard, *Didier Arnoult's rillettes* are unusually spicy but very good and creamy; goose *rillettes* are made once a week. In Montrichard, *Perriot* makes classic, if rather bland, *rillettes*. *Pierre le Gal* in Ville-aux-Dames tops the list of many of Touraine's *becs fins*. My favorite Chinon producer is *André Berrier;* in Tours, I like *Jacky Blateau* in the Halles.

VII

The Sancerrois

"In the past we were considered Burgundy; now we're in the Loire."

—Edmond Vatan, vigneron in Chavignol,
part of the Sancerre appellation

T he nine appellations forming an arc from Orléans to George Sand country at the foothills of the Massif Central are known as the Vignobles du Centre. They lie halfway between the vineyards of Touraine and those of Burgundy. You must cross the flatlands of Sologne, lands inhospitable to the vine—past the game forest of the Château of Chambord and stretches of marshes and ponds—before reaching the heart of the zone, the near-perpendicular hills of Sancerre.

This is the kingdom of Sauvignon, the sole grape permitted in Pouilly-Fumé, in white Sancerre, Menetou-Salon, Reuilly, and Quincy and the principal white varietal of VDQS Coteaux du Giennois. The style of Sauvignon made within this constellation of appellations—a full, fresh, instantly recognizable white—has been imitated from Napa to New Zealand to Chile. Often raw and nervy, the aromas and flavors that made the Sancerrois Sauvignon so easily identifiable include grass, grapefruit, green bean, asparagus, and, to this taster, cat's pee. (French tasters use the somehow more polite and less revolting sounding *pipi de chat.*)

Within the past decade, however, the style of Sancerrois Sauvignon has changed. Growers wait to harvest, pick riper grapes, and often use aromatic yeasts—not to mention new oak barrels. Many leave a trace of carbon dioxide in the finished wine. The new Sauvignon is less aggressive, ampler (occasionally blowsy), with aromas and flavors recalling fig, nectarine, peach, and melon, as well as floral and Muscat notes reminiscent of Pinot Gris from Alsace. This development has not been universally well received: Many are the sentimental wine-lovers who, recalling their first love affair with a feisty and green Sauvignon, lament: "Where are the Sancerres of yesteryear?"

Pinot Noir, the region's second most important grape, was first planted in Sancerre in the fifteenth century, and it remained Sancerre's sole grape from the seventeenth century until the end of the nineteenth, when phylloxera struck. (Sauvignon came to dominate the region's vineyards only within the last seventy years.) Pinot Noir now accounts for about a quarter of that appellation's wine. It is also the sole red grape in Menetou-Salon and Reuilly and is used in the reds of the Giennois, Orléans, and Châteaumeillant. Ancillary grapes are Gamay, Pinot Gris, Chardonnay, Pinot Meunier, Cabernet, and Chasselas. (The anecdotal plantings in La Charité-sur-Loire are the Burgundian classics, Chardonnay and Pinot Noir.)

Two soil types predominate in the Sancerrois: *terres blanches* and *caillotes*. *Terres blanches*, chalk on Kimmeridgian marl, have traditionally been considered the finest, making complete, rich, complex Sauvignons that need several months to two years to express themselves. The soil of many of the best vineyards of Sancerre and Pouilly (as well as those of Chablis), *terres blanches* appear in parts of Menetou-Salon, the Giennois, and Reuilly. *Caillotes*, compact chalk found, for example, at the base of hillsides in Sancerre (as well as on some of its most famous slopes), produce fine, highly perfumed wines—quick to express themselves, they are the first to be bottled. (Generally, however, wines from the two soils are blended.)

Vines growing on the sandy or gravelly terraces of ancient alluvial deposits on the banks of the Loire or the Cher make floral, spicy, early-drinking wines. Those growing on silex-streaked soils in Ménétréol or Saint-Andelain make decisive wines with vivid, flinty aromas, wines which can rival those from *terres blanches* in breed and complexity.

The Sauvignons of Sancerre and Pouilly combine the exuberant fruit and nerviness characteristic of Loire wines with a breadth and texture that recall Burgundy. A seemingly unquenchable thirst for this sort of fresh, biggish, dry white has enriched the vignerons of Sancerre and Pouilly to an extent not yet dreamed of by their confreres in the western Loire. They drive fancy sports cars and trendy Jeeps. Their cellars are as spanking new as any in Napa. (Elevators whisk you from a floor of gleaming stainless steel tanks to another lined with new Tronçais barrels.) And they all have major American distributors.

Five years ago I felt that—exceptional wines from producers like Didier Dagueneau, the Cotats, and Lucien Crochet aside—neither appellation was making wine that realized its potential. (One can argue about specifics, but it boils down to overproduction.) Sure, many of the wines were wonderful. And maybe it should be enough that your Sancerre or your Pouilly is delicious, textured, fresh, and marrowy, and that it goes beautifully with your grilled langoustines with a tarragon *beurre blanc*. But when you stand atop the vertiginous slopes of Monts Damnés or look across the sea of vines in Les Loges, you sense that with a bit more commitment on the part of the vigneron, these wines could be mind-blowing. Happily, I've witnessed qualitative progress in Sancerre, particularly with a number of its biggest houses. I hope it continues—and trickles down.

Note: This is not a criticism, just an observation: I don't believe the region's whites age in a way that favors cellaring them. Aside from some anecdotal wonders from the Cotats in Chavignol, even the very best Sancerres and Pouillys taste best if drunk within five years of the harvest.

There's a mini-trend of making late-harvest Sancerre or Pouilly, which, depending on the residual sugar, may or may not get an appellation. Off-dry and sometimes downright sweet Sauvignons are not entirely new. They *are* novelties, but I don't find them all that impressive. Interesting footnotes is about as excited as I can get about most of them.

SANCERRE

STATUS: AOC, *1936 for whites, 1959 for reds and rosés*
TYPES OF WINE: *Dry white, reds, and rosés*
ZONE AND PRODUCTION: *Roughly 148,000 hectoliters, made on 2,298 hectares within fourteen communes in the Cher. Roughly 80 percent is white.*
GRAPES: *Whites—Sauvignon Blanc; reds and rosés—Pinot Noir*
SOILS: *Compact chalk (caillotes), Kimmeridgian marl (terres blanches), and outcroppings of silex*
PRICE: *25 to 90ff*
BEST VINTAGES: *'95, '90, '89, '88; '93 is fair; some very good '94s*

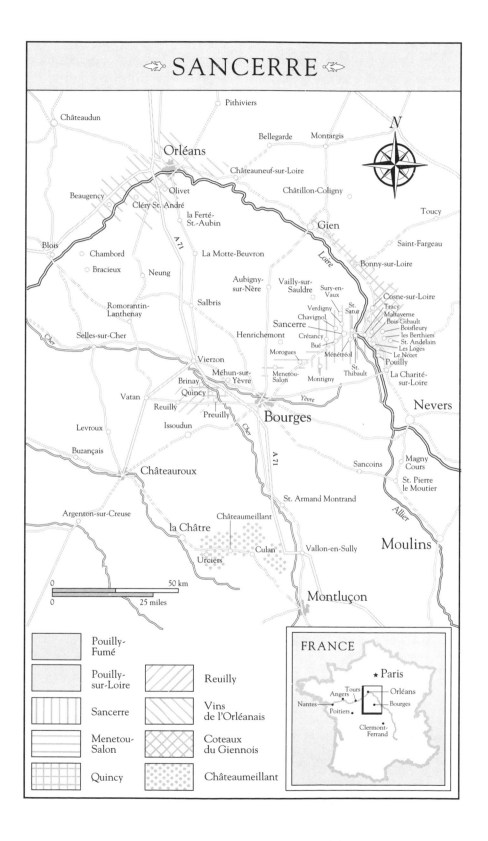

SANCERRE

Châteaudun

Pithiviers

Orléans

Bellegarde   Montargis

Châteauneuf-sur-Loire

Beaugency   Olivet

Cléry St. André

Châtillon-Coligny

la Ferté-
St.-Aubin

Gien

Toucy

Blois

Chambord   La Motte-Beuvron

Saint-Fargeau

Bracieux   Neung

Bonny-sur-Loire

Aubigny-
sur-Nère

Vailly-sur-
Sauldre

Sury-en-
Vaux

Cosne-sur-Loire

Romorantin-
Lanthenay

Salbris

Verdigny   St.
Satur

Tracy
Maltaverne
Bois-Gibault
Boisfleury
les Berthiers
St. Andelain
Les Loges
Le Nozet

Chavignol

Sancerre

Selles-sur-Cher

Henrichemont   Crézancy

Bué

Morogues

Ménétréol

Pouilly

Vierzon

Méhun-sur-
Yèvre

Menetou-
Salon

St.
Thibault

La Charité-
sur-Loire

Brinay

Vatan   Quincy

Montigny

Reuilly

Preuilly

Bourges

Yèvre

Nevers

Levroux

Issoudun

Buzançais

Châteauroux

Sancoins

Magny
Cours

St. Pierre
le Moutier

Argenton-sur-Creuse

St. Armand Montrand

Châteaumeillant

la Châtre

Culan

Vallon-en-Sully

Moulins

Urciers

0   50 km

0   25 miles

Montluçon

Legend

Pouilly-
Fumé

Pouilly-
sur-Loire

Reuilly

Sancerre

Vins
de l'Orléanais

Menetou-
Salon

Coteaux
du Giennois

Quincy

Châteaumeillant

FRANCE

★ Paris

Tours   Orléans

Angers

Nantes   Bourges

Poitiers

Clermont-
Ferrand

The first view of Sancerre is stunning. A steep hill appears out of nowhere, a shock after the flat fields of Sologne. When you drive down from its summit, you feel as if you're in an airplane doing a nosedive. Vine-covered slopes spin around you. In the distance, along the left bank of the Loire, are the hills and valleys of Chavignol, Bué, Saint-Satur, and other hamlets and communes composing the Sancerre appellation. You sense you're in an important wine region.

Sancerre's name is a deformation of the Roman Castrum Sancti Satyri, "fort of the holy satyrs," which as Gerald Asher once observed is an "appropriately Dionysiac reference in a region noted for its vines and its goats." There are no goats left on its hillsides, however. Though the slopes are within the Crottin appellation, they are much too highly valued as vineyards to be turned over to grazing ruminants. The white wines they produce are the Loire's most expensive and sought-after bottles. That they exist at all may be due to that nasty twist of fate, phylloxera.

"Phylloxera had a silver lining," claims Roger Neveu, a vigneron, pointing out that Sancerre was the only region in France to replant white grapes in a vineyard previously planted to red, and that half its young people moved to Paris "where they became police or bureaucrats—and the major ambassadors for our wines."

In 1946 Edmond Alphonse Mellot opened a wine bar called Le Sancerre on the Avenue Rapp. Artists, writers, and gastronomes—from Jean Cocteau to Jean Marais to Curnonsky—regarded Sancerre as the little white they drank with shellfish platters. Then Chablis prices skyrocketed after a killer frost in 1956. And autoroutes took Parisians past Sancerre on their way to the ocean. Its success has not yet peaked.

Most vignerons make more than one style of Sancerre. They have small parcels scattered over various hillsides, giving each a mix of the appellation's soil types. More often than not, the vigneron blends wines from the various soils to make more balanced wines, offering a light *cuvée* and, perhaps, something along the lines of a Vieilles Vignes. Some, however, bottle by parcel to keep the character of the vineyard. Many of the latter wines used to go by the name of the vineyard, or *lieu dit*.

Sancerre's *lieux dits* are many, well known, and much coveted. Pierre Bréjoux organized some of the best-known according to soil type. Those on Kimmeridgian marl, or *terres blanches*, include part of La Poussie in Bué, the Côte de Champtin and Le Clos du Roy in Champtin, Les Monts Damnés, and Le Cul de Beaujeu in Chavignol. *Lieux dits* with *caillotes* soils include Chêne Marchand, Chemarin, and the other half of La Poussie in Bué, Les Bouffants in Chavignol, Le Paradis in Sancerre, and La Perrière in Verdigny.

But using Les Monts Damnés, for example, on a label has become complicated. For one, the legislation is vague. Second, people cheated—using the name of a parcel like Les Monts Damnés for a bottling when only a fraction of the wine came from that plot. Third, the *lieux dits* were restructured to subsume smaller ones into larger blocks, all under the same name. In other words, there's Les Monts Damnés *classico* and the expanded Les Monts Damnés. Many producers now use a proprietary name rather than the name of a vineyard. Jean-Marie Bourgeois, for example, has vines on Monts Damnés, both the heart of the parcel and its extension. He sometimes offers two bottlings, Les Monts Damnés and Le MD de Bourgeois.

Sancerre rouge and rosé became AOCs more than twenty years after Sancerre blanc. In the '70s, Parisian sommeliers began proposing the red with fish. The '82 vintage (good quality and large quantity) put the wine on the map; Sancerre rouge replaced Bouzy rouge (from Champagne) as the chic light red of nouvelle cuisine.

Much of the best comes from chalky clay hillsides in two communes—Crézancy (particularly the Côte de Champtin and the Clos du Roy) and Verdigny. Silex-rich soils are also appreciated, making some of the region's most deeply colored, powerful reds.

Rosés may be made by direct press or by bleeding the vats of the red grapes. They are then vinified like whites. Few vignerons take them seriously, but when they do, the results are extremely pretty tea rose–colored wines, floral, vinous, and mouth-filling.

Producers often make two styles of red, an early-drinking *cuvée* and a more serious version. Depending on the style, the reds ferment for from six days to three weeks. The first *cuvée* may not age in barrel but the rest do, either in new (or newish) *barriques* or old *demi-muids*, for several months or longer.

For the most part these are seductive, light- to medium-bodied Pinots. The simpler version is a succulent red with vibrant flavors of cherries, plums, and strawberries. The more serious *cuvée* is weightier, more structured, with hints of sweet spices and orange zest. They definitely *pinot*. And though most don't plumb the depths of that grape's possibilities, they can be supremely satisfying, absolute charmers. With several notable exceptions, most should be drunk by their fifth birthday.

About 25 percent of Sancerre wine is distributed by local grower-*négociants*; 60 percent is sold by the vigneron.

❧ PRODUCER RATINGS ❧

LEADERS
Domaine Henri Bourgeois   Domaine Lucien Crochet
Domaine Alphonse Mellot

EXCELLENT
Cotat Frères   Domaine Vincent Pinard

TO WATCH
Pascal Jolivet

HIGHLY RECOMMENDED
Les Celliers Saint-Romble   Château de Maimbray
Domaine Vincent Delaporte   Domaine de Montigny
Domaine Paul Millerioux
Domaine Roger Neveu   Domaine de Saint-Pierre
Domaine Vacheron   Bernard Reverdy

RECOMMENDED
Gitton Père et Fils   André et Frédéric Neveu
Jean-Max Roger

BY THE GLASS
Bailly-Reverdy et Fils   Clos la Néore
Domaine du Colombier
Domaine du P'tit Roy   Fernand Girard

TASTED AND CONSIDERED
Balland-Chapuis   Château de Sancerre
Clos la Perrière   Etienne Daulny
Hippolyte Reverdy et Fils   Reverdy-Ducroux
Roger Vimon

❧ ❧

LEADERS

Domaine Henri Bourgeois, **Chavignol:** A substantial family firm and one of the most important high-quality grower-*négociant* houses in Sancerre. Headed by Jean-Marie Bourgeois, the *domaine* has sixty hectares throughout Sancerre and four in Pouilly. Purchased grapes and must represent 40 percent of business.

Bourgeois's cellars—a warren of gleaming, high-tech equipment—sprawl under the steep hills of Chavignol. Sixty percent of harvesting is done by machine. In general, malolactic fermentation is blocked for whites, which stay in tank until March, with a regular stirring up of the lees. The base Sancerre, La Vigne Blanche, from purchased grapes and must, is clean, light, and accurate. The Grande Réserve Sancerre, half *domaine*, half purchased, is squeaky clean. The real action is in the special bottlings. In whites, these are Le MD de Bourgeois, from the slopes abutting the heart of the famous *lieu dit* Les Monts Damnés (Bourgeois also bottles Les Monts Damnés, but not every year); La Bourgeoise, from fifty-year-old vines on the southwest-facing slopes of Saint-Satur; Etienne Henri, the same raw material as La Bourgeoise white, vinified in new oak barrels; and Sancerre d'Antan, the latest of the special bottlings, which had its debut at Vinexpo 1995.

Sancerre d'Antan, which translates as "yesteryear's Sancerre," is an old-vines bottling from silex-rich soils. It is neither fined nor filtered. The first release, a '93, was rich, elegant, and floral, with delicious grapefruit, lime, and peach flavors, a marrowy *sur lie* texture, and appetizing accents of herbal tea and minerals. The '91 MD de Bourgeois was a flavory knit of minerals and grapefruit; ditto for the richer '90. The '89, while very much in the style of the ginger-scented Les Monts Damnés of the same year, was lighter, fruitier, and less site-specific. La Bourgeoise, in both '89 and '90, was lush, generous, and textured, as supple as it was vivacious. Etienne Henri, as engaging as the La Bourgeoise, added notes of oak and ginger.

Bourgeois also sells the Sancerres of Domaine Laporte. The '92 La Cresle de Laporte was a good representative of the different style of the Laporte line—lean, mineral-rich Sancerres, more austere than Bourgeois's own wines, but well structured, characterful, and extremely appealing.

In red Sancerre, Bourgeois's normal bottling is a practiced charmer. The '90 beguiled with mellow flavors of cherries, plums, and *eau-de-vie de mirabelle*. The '93 La Bourgeoise rouge was a delicious blend of very ripe strawberries and sweet spices. The '90, a serious beauty, bordered on Burgundian. A generous light Pinot with lots of nice oak flavors mixing with pretty fruit, it could lure Pinot-hounds to Sancerre.

Bourgeois's late-harvest Sancerres have their fans, but I find them banana-y and sweet.

Domaine Lucien Crochet, **Bué:**   The concentrated, elegant Sancerres from this house have nothing to do with the knock-back Sancerre of the corner bistro. Serious and fine-tuned, these are Sancerres for haute cuisine, and they can be unsettling for first-time tasters with images of the wine as a feisty, raw little white.

Lucien Crochet and son Gilles, an articulate, thoughtful Dijon-trained enologist, have thirty-three hectares of vines, mostly in Bué, including pieces of some of its most famous *lieux dits*. Their spanking new offices with vast meeting rooms and modern underground cellars seem to cover half the village of Bué.

Purchased grapes represent 20 percent of their business but these are not assembled with wines from the *domaine*. They are, however, very good second-string Sancerres. The wines to look for are the *domaine* bottlings, starting with the La Croix du Roy. The white version is a full, austere, bone-dry Sancerre with a strong mineral expression. The Lucien Crochet bottling may or may not be a *négociant* wine—confusing, but just keep in mind that labels with the design of an oak tree signify the *domaine* versions. An elegant Sancerre in so-so years like '94, as well as in great ones like '89, it is mellow, mineral, and satisfying, finishing on fine notes of citrus zests.

Crochet's best Sancerre is the Cuvée Prestige (white and red), an assemblage of old vines (forty-five to sixty-five years) made only in very good years. It is bottled later than other *cuvées*, spends more time on its lees, and is often released several years after the harvest.

The superb '89 white, elegant and full of breed, had discreet Sauvignon aromas. On the palate it was lush, with nuances of minerals, grass, oak, lemon, grapefruit, and melon. The '90, available in the summer of 1995, was a luxuriant mix of melon, fig, creamed corn, and Pinot Gris flavors. Graceful, despite its 14 percent alcohol, it seemed a tad lighter on its feet than Crochet's impressive '90 Vendange du 25 Octobre.

The latter, essentially a late-harvest wine—shriveled and botrytized grapes picked twenty days after the rest—weighed in at 14.5 percent alcohol, with no residual sugar. Bounteous, gargantuan, though not at all awkward, it recalled the old Château Saint-Jean Fumé Blancs from the La Petite Etoile vineyard. I'd happily pair either with turbot, lobster, sweetbreads— nothing less.

Crochet also makes a very pretty rosé. (I drank the '94 with melon and prosciutto.) And his Sancerre reds, which account for about a quarter of production, can be so delectable, you understand why Sancerre was once planted to Pinot Noir.

The '93 La Croix du Roy offered persistent Pinot fruit and spice flavors, with notes of anise, flat cola (which I often find in Burgundies), and orange zest. A perfect lunch red for an upscale bistro, roast chicken and *frites* or *oeufs en meurette*. The '89 and '90 Cuvée Prestige were completely seductive and rather Burgundian, with juicy kirsch and black-cherry flavors, firm structure, and light, bacony finishes. An '88, released in '92, was a deep, fruit-packed wine. Truly delicious and true ambassadors.

Domaine Alphonse Mellot, Sancerre: One of the most venerable houses of the region, Alphonse Mellot is also one of the most visible. From the main square of Sancerre you see its restaurant, tasting room, and boutique; take a side street and you arrive at its modern cellars.

The *domaine,* now run by the eighteenth Alphonse Mellot, was built by the two previous generations. They got the wines into Paris restaurants and began the firm's *négociant* arm—at first to supply their own auberge in Sancerre, later to satisfy the demands of Paris bistros, including their own wine bar, Le Sancerre (no longer in the family). They began building up the *domaine*'s vineyard holdings, which are now at fifty hectares, mostly on La Moussière. The *négociant* arm, extended by Alphonse number eighteen (who now would like to eliminate it to concentrate on *domaine* wines), represents 800,000 bottles yearly. Essentially Sancerre (which is not assembled with *domaine* wine), it also encompasses other Loire appellations.

The *domaine* Sancerres are La Moussière (red and white) and Cuvée Edmond (white only). Reds are not an important part of the Mellot profile. But you can take the squeaky clean, crowd-pleasing La Moussière white anywhere. I brought the '90 to dinner with friends who went nuts over the soft, ripe fruit typical of that vintage. The '92 and '93 were true to form: clean and lightly herbaceous, with pleasant mineral and fruit flavors.

Mellot's pride is his Cuvée Edmond, from forty- to sixty-year-old vines. The grapes are pressed lightly, the must is severely decanted, and half is vinified in oak. The lees are stirred up once or twice a week until the end of the year, and the wine stays on its lees until spring bottling. *Très recher-ché*, it's the kind of stylish, well-made, pedigreed white you'd order with your first course at Lutèce. The fine-grained '94, '91, and '88 embody this *cuvée* for me. Each is Sancerre at its most elegant: discreetly herbaceous, a beautiful weave of citrus, oak, and minerals. The '93 seemed a bit oxidized—though not at all unattractive. And both '89 and '90 were resplendent courtesans, creamy, languid, and cool, with exotic perfumes of Pinot Gris, orange zest, tropical fruit, fancy bath soaps, and whiffs of expensive oak.

EXCELLENT

Cotat Frères (Francis, Paul, and François), Chavignol: *"On n'a pas le droit mais on le prend"* (We don't have the right but we take it) is the unofficial motto of this *domaine* which makes very special, cult Sancerres: big, magnificent, Rhône-like Sancerres; Sancerres bought by Pompidou; Sancerres that M. Bally of shoe fame comes to collect in a truck.

Don't have the right to what, precisely? Well, first, Sancerre sometimes gets distinctly smaller billing than Chavignol on the label because, INAO be damned, the Cotats (brothers Francis and Paul and the latter's son François) believe that, as Chavignol was once more famous than Sancerre, they were cheated out of their rightful appellation.

Then, is it dry or is it sweet? Mostly it's dry, albeit with a bit of residual sugar. But you never know. The Cotat family has been making *moelleux* Sancerre for more than fifty years—long before the trendy *cuvées* of '89. (And the Cotats have always made Sancerre to age. Restaurants lucky enough to carry their wines, often list a half-dozen or more vintages.)

And who, exactly, is the winemaker here? Time was when Francis and Paul worked together. Now they each have their own labels, as does François. But they all operate out of one tiny cellar filled with old *demi-muids* and a press circa 1880. Wines are made as they have always been made. Hand harvested, of course—given the pitch of the Cotats' steep vineyards, they can't even use a tractor. Organic fertilizers. No destemming. The merest decanting to keep most of the "nourishing yeasts." Barrel fermentation. No temperature control. No fining. No filtering. The wines are racked once at the end of January—the week before the new moon—and again two months later, when the phase of the moon favorably affects atmospheric pressure and tides.

So one wonders if the label distinction isn't merely a fiction for the French tax authorities—though the Cotats do seem to divvy up their *lieux dits*, at least on the wine labels. They have four hectares of hillside vines, all on Kimmeridgian marl. The three share part of Les Monts Damnés; Paul and his son have Le Cul de Beaujeu; and Francis and Paul split La Grande Côte.

What a wine, what a sense of winemaking, of tradition and *terroir*, I noted in awe after tasting an '89 Le Cul de Beaujeu. Majestic, with fragrances of the *crus* of the Rhône, Alsace, and Anjou. Discreet and fine, the nose was a blend of chamomile, honey, flowers, and orange zest. On the palate it was the proverbial peacock's tail, a lush, tight tidal wave of licorice, minerals, nuts, and fruit. The '89 La Grande Côte was another completely original expression. Leaner than the Beaujeu, it was still rich and textured, an opulent flow of licorice, peach, apricot, blossoms, and almonds. The '89 La Grande Côte *moelleux*, really more of a demi-sec, reprised the flavors of the sec, adding hints of oak, pineapple, and orange zest. An '88 Monts Damnés was another stunner, simultaneously incisive and luxuriant.

Both the '93 La Grande Côte and the lightly off-dry '94 Les Monts Damnés recalled Champagne (without the bubbles) as well as Chenin. Each was creamy, lime-tinged, and mineral, with mellow fruit flavors and a hint of old wood. A bit rustic for some tastes, but I adore them. They were unique and thought-provoking, like all the Cotat wines. Whenever I review my notes I want to open another bottle.

Domaine Vincent Pinard, Bué: *Pinard*, in French, is one of the many words for *plonk*—precisely what this serious winemaker does *not* make. The hand harvested, handcrafted Sancerres from his twelve hectares include nicely structured rosés; toothsome light reds (the '93 was a delectable cameo of a Pinot); and several bottlings of beautiful whites.

Florès is Pinard's name for a bottling whose grapes come mostly from Chêne Marchand. The inviting '94 was a discreet blend of citrus zests and minerals. Lovely. In richer vintages, like '89 and '90, it is a perfumed, well-knit wine, with succulent flavors of grapefruit, lemon, hay, and minerals.

Old-vines from Chêne Marchand go into two other *cuvées*: Harmonie (100 percent barrel-fermented) and Nuance (one-third barrel- and two-thirds tank-fermented). The delicious '94 Nuance, suave and fine-grained, was a gorgeous weave of mellow pineapple and citrus zests, vanilla, and toast. The somewhat meatier '93 Nuance, a gracious blend of oak and ripe Sauvignon Blanc, was only marginally less captivating. All are perfect for fine dining. No wonder they're on the lists of Lucas-Carton and Guy Savoy.

TO WATCH

Pascal Jolivet, Sancerre: The son of a wine broker (for Savour Club) and the grandson and great-grandson of the cellar master of the Château de Tracy, preppyish Pascal Jolivet is rapidly becoming a high-profile *négociant-grower* of Sancerre and Pouilly. He created his firm in 1985, built Napa-style cellars on the outskirts of Sancerre in 1990, and has been buying up vineyards for a current total of sixteen, split evenly between Sancerre and Pouilly. And Jolivet, who also distributes Silverado in France and a brace of leading French estates within the Sancerre region, has also succeeded in placing his own wines in some of the world's best restaurants—from France to Taiwan.

The focus on *domaine* bottlings is recent. Jolivet still buys grapes and wine and still has exclusive contracts with a number of growers, including Pascal Moreux (Pouilly), who is Jolivet's cellar master, as well as Roger Champault's Domaine du Colombier in Crézancy-en-Sancerre. But what he wants to talk about—and to have you taste—are his *domaine* bottlings, of which there are several in each appellation.

Both today and under his old regime, the Sancerres fare best. Among the latter, I liked two '89 Sancerre blancs, the floral Les Caillotes, an assemblage of wines from Bué, with a steel and mineral core, and a creamy Château du Nozay, with ripe peach, apricot, and Muscat flavors. In more recent bottlings, I admired the '94 Sancerre Le Chêne Marchand, for its appetizing lime, herbal tea, grapefruit, and exotic fruit flavors.

Jolivet's La Grande Cuvée is an old-vines bottling, offered only in "good" years, in both Sancerre and Pouilly. It is made from the juices of the first gentle pressing. After going through malolactic fermentation, the wines stay on their fine lees for a year before bottling. In the summer of 1995, Jolivet was marketing his '92 Sancerre La Grande Cuvée. Crisp, tight, slightly viscous, with rich flavors of minerals and an appealing herbaceousness, it had more focus and flavor than the Pouilly. And it was a very good Sancerre.

Jolivet clearly wants these *cuvées* to be considered the equals of Mellot's Cuvée Edmond, Bourgeois's La Bourgeoise, Crochet's Cuvée Prestige, and Pinard's Nuance. He's not there yet, but he seems headed in the right direction.

HIGHLY RECOMMENDED

Les Celliers Saint-Romble, **Verdigny:** André Dezat, the mayor of Verdigny, is a walking history of Sancerre viticulture—and one of its most charming vignerons. His *domaine* consists of twenty-one hectares in Sancerre and another twelve in Pouilly, from which he and his two sons produce amiable representatives of each appellation. In great vintages like '89, the wines can be quite special. The lip-smackingly delicious '89 red, for example, seemed a cross between a light Burgundy and Pinot from Oregon, with lots of up-front, pretty, wild plum and orange peel fruit. (It went surprisingly well with a mildly spiced jambalaya.) The white was firm and crisp, with fine mineral depth. In lighter years like '94, '93, and '92, the reds are gentle and winsome; the whites have pungent grapefruit and mineral flavors and tart finishes. Tasty and fresh as a breeze, they're perfect for upscale bistros.

Château de Maimbray, **Sury-en-Vaux:** Another wonderful family winery. There's no sizzle here. The Roblins' wines are honest, straightforward, somewhat rustic. Good stuff. Grassy, grapefruity whites with fine mineral undercurrents; full and mellow reds, packed with cherry and oak flavors when young, picking up nuances of coffee, caramel, and mushroom with age.

Domaine Vincent Delaporte, **Chavignol:** Delaporte and son Jean-Yves (Beaune) make firm and pungent Sancerres, perfect for sleek brasseries. Wines from their various soil types are assembled and fermented at low temperatures to achieve the cool, highly aromatic style Delaporte likes. The well-focused '94, with its vivid green bean, grapefruit, and mineral flavors, was a true representative of the Delaporte style.

Reds, which spend eight months in oak, are round, nicely structured, and tasty, developing flavors of dried fruit, cinnamon, leather, sandalwood, and bacon as they age.

Domaine de Montigny, **Montigny:** At the southwest tip of Sancerre, Montigny abuts the Menetou-Salon AOC. Henri and Cécile Natter are new to both the region and to wine. They studied at Beaune and did *stages* at Domaine Ott in Provence before piecing together their twenty hectares of vines. Rather prim and didactic, they make austere Sancerres. This is not a style everyone likes, though it appeals to me, particularly the mineral-rich old-vines bottling. The Natters also make well-structured rosés and light, pleasant reds.

Domaine Paul Millerioux, **Crézancy-en-Sancerre:** Most vignerons of a certain age seem only too eager to retire. Not Millerioux. With sixteen hectares and no successors, he has built spiffy new cellars in which he makes good, solid, personalized Sancerres. His best wine is Clos du Roy. The white is creamy, round, and mineraly, its fruit more discreet than explosive, perhaps a result of Millerioux's preference for long (ninety-day) fermentations at moderate temperatures and the fact that Millerioux chaptalizes a bit to keep the action going, resulting in full, elegant knits of grapefruit, lemon, and minerals.

Grapes for his rosés macerate for several hours for a light coppery color. The wines are floral and fruity, both delicate and firm, with savory mineral–bitter almond finishes. Reds are mellow blends of cinnamon, clove, cherry, and cherry pits, mixed with oak.

Domaine Roger Neveu, Verdigny: Neveu and his sons make lovely Sancerre in all three colors. The whites are full and textured, with generous flavors of grass and grapefruit, and a whiff of minerals, fig, and melon. Reds are seductive light Pinots, compotes of kirsch, cherries, cherry pits, peach and apricot pits, and orange, laced with oak.

Domaine de Saint-Pierre, Verdigny: Brothers Didier and Philippe Prieur produce honest, reliable Sancerres. They want Sauvignons that taste like biting into a grape. And they usually succeed—whether in so-so years like '94 or good ones like '85. The well-knit '89 was more complex—like biting into a salad of grapefruit and peaches seasoned with herbs, but the '92 Cuvée Maréchal Prieur, partially fermented and aged in new barrels, though admirable, was too oaky for me. Rosés are lively and vinous, both tender and bracingly dry, with a firm backbone. The reds, a tasty concentration of cherry, kirsch, and oak, are juicy little bistro Pinots.

Domaine Vacheron, Sancerre: One of the few wineries left in Sancerre, the Vacherons' *caves* are about a ten-minute stroll from the center of town, on a street so twisty and narrow you can't imagine the harvest truck passing through the stone entry.

The Vacherons are known, and rightly so, for their concentrated reds, which are usually best two to three years from the harvest. The '92 and the richer, deeper '93 were absolute charmers, with delightful cherry-oak flavors. The '90, however, reveals the staying power of a great vintage. Satisfyingly delicious at the end of 1995, it showed no signs of losing its tight structure or its succulence. The rosés are flowery and vinous, delightful summer-lunch wines.

Vacheron whites are also heartily recommended, among them the lightly herbaceous '94; the grapefruit- and mineral-flavored '93; the fresh, pleasant '91; and the '89 Le Paradis, a particular favorite. Clear as a bell, with keen grapefruit flavors and hints of Muscat, it finished on a long mineral note.

Bernard Reverdy, Verdigny: The reds and whites are pleasant, but the rosés, for which Bernard and son Noël are known, are exceptional. Made from a direct press of Pinot Noir, vinified like a white, the wines look like tea rose–colored watered silk. Extremely pretty and floral, they are mouthfilling, vinous, and appetizingly dry, with long finishes.

RECOMMENDED

Gitton Père et Fils, Ménétréol-sous-Sancerre: If only Pascal Gitton weren't overextended! An enthusiastic world-traveler, a linguist, Gitton talks really good wine (with EST-like emotionalism) but seems overwhelmed by the six-ring circus he runs: thirty-three hectares in Sancerre, Pouilly, and the Giennois, and another twelve outside of Bergerac in southwest France.

Gitton vinifies and bottles by parcel, offering more than fifteen different *cuvées*. Sancerre bottlings include Les Belles Dames, La Vigne de Larrey, Les Herses, Le Galinot, Les Montachins, Les Cris, Les Romains, La Rey, and Les Frédins; in Pouilly, Jeanne d'Orion, Les Péchignolles. Despite evidence of distinctive raw material, there's a sameness in most of the wines, as well as a lack of concentration and structure and a rough quality. I have, however, appreciated various vintages of Le Galinot, Les Belles Dames, and Les Herses. And I loved a '70 Les Montachins, made by Gitton's father, Marcel, which was a structured, elegant wine, a weave of wax and herbs.

André et Frédéric Neveu, Chavignol: The Neveus have ten hectares of prime vineyard land and an exciting policy of bottling their whites by *cru*. Overall, however, I found their wines lacked concentration. They were too bland for what they should have been, given the pedigree. That said, there are rewarding discoveries in various vintages of Le Grand Fricambault and Le Manoir, as well as a completely anecdotal *cuvée* of Sancerre rouge. Normally the Neveus make goodish versions. Frédéric's special *cuvée* of '85, however, was a remarkable wine which was the result of several coincidences. Winter and spring frosts killed off 90 percent of the crop, leaving just two clusters per vine. That made one barrel of wine at 13.2 percent alcohol. A knockout, it had everything—fruit, body, structure—to spare. Gorgeous.

Jean-Max Roger, Bué: A reliable grower-*négociant* making uniformly good commercial wines in both Sancerre and Menetou-Salon. Purchased wine represents a third of volume and is assembled with wine from the *domaine* in all but the Sancerre Vieilles Vignes. The whites are appetizing, discreetly herbaceous, with a good mineral-citrus presence. Of particular merit is the Vieilles Vignes bottling. Roger's richest, most concentrated wine, it is usually bracing, with fine grapefruit, mint, petrol, and mineral flavors. The reds are light evocations of Pinot, with firm cherry and oak flavors, often ending on a pleasant bitter note.

BY THE GLASS

Bailly-Reverdy et Fils, Bué: A reliable family winery making a pleasant red and four *cuvées* of white, of which I prefer the lemon-tartness of wines from the *terres blanches* of Chavignol.

Clos la Néore, Chavignol: The spiritual father of today's vignerons, Edmond Vatan, colorful and unreconstructed, makes rough, quirky, petrol-, green apple-, and Muscat-scented Sancerres—which you can order at Taillevent.

Domaine du Colombier, Crézancy-en-Sancerre: Roger Champault sells half his output to Pascal Jolivet. The wine he keeps for himself is usually light and pleasant. The whites are agreeable, grapefruity wine-bar Sancerres; the reds, a bit hot and short, but appetizing.

Domaine du P'tit Roy, Sury-en-Vaux: These soft, fragrant white Sancerres and light, pleasant red ones, have been "Séléction Troisgros" for thirty years.

Fernand Girard, Verdigny: A young vigneron who makes attractive, accurate, light Sancerres. The reds have particular charm.

TASTED AND CONSIDERED

Balland-Chapuis, Bué: I find Joseph Balland's Coteaux du Giennois more interesting than his Sancerre. The *domaine*'s eighteen hectares are separated into many different bottlings—ranging from famous *lieux dits* like Chêne Marchand to Vieilles Vignes (red and white) to sweet late-harvest Sauvignons. Quality ranges from diffuse to pleasant.

Château de Sancerre, Sancerre: Marnier-Lapostelle, better known for Grand Marnier, makes bland Sancerres (whites only); a few have orange peel accents reminiscent of the liqueur.

Clos la Perrière, Verdigny: A large grower-*négociant* who makes acceptable restaurant Sancerres from a prime vineyard.

Etienne Daulny, **Verdigny:** At best standard, Daulny's Sancerres frequently win awards.

Hippolyte Reverdy et Fils, **Verdigny:** Fairly bland Sancerres, though some *cuvées* are better than others.

Reverdy-Ducroux, **Verdigny:** Brand-new cellars with high-priced barrels, presses, and tanks, turning out fair, unobjectionable Sancerres.

Roger Vimon, **Ménétréol-sous-Sancerre:** Rustic Sancerres, in all three flavors.

RECOMMENDED PRODUCERS FROM OTHER APPELLATIONS

Château de Fontaine-Audon, **Saint-Gemme:** Saumur's Langlois-Château purchased this vineyard and makes very good, textbook Sancerres.

Henri Pellé **(Menetou-Salon).**

Ladoucette **(Pouilly-sur-Loire):** Under the Comte Lafon label.

POUILLY-FUME AND POUILLY-SUR-LOIRE

STATUS: *AOCs Pouilly-Fumé, Pouilly-sur-Loire 1937*

TYPES OF WINE: *Dry white*

ZONE AND PRODUCTION: *67,000 hectoliters (of which 95 percent is Pouilly-Fumé), made on 1,034 hectares within seven communes in the Nièvre department*

GRAPES: *Pouilly-Fumé—Sauvignon; Pouilly-sur-Loire—Chasselas*

SOILS: *Chalk and marl* (terres blanches); *compact chalk* (caillotes); *and clay with silex*

PRICE: *Pouilly-Fumé, 35 to 190ff; Pouilly-sur-Loire, 25 to 40ff*

BEST VINTAGES: *'95, '90, some '93s, '89, '88*

Pouilly-Fumé

Pouilly faces Sancerre across the Loire. Its name is derived from the Roman Paulica Villa or Villa Paulus, though its vineyards predate the Roman era and have been continuously cultivated since that time. Vines covered nearly 2,000 hectares by 1832 when Jullien issued his *Topographie de Tous les Vignobles Connus*, in which he wrote, "Pouilly-sur-Loire produces white wines which have body and spirit, a light scent of gunflint, and an extremely agreeable flavor. They don't turn yellow and they keep their *douceur* for a long time."

The wine Jullien describes was a blend of Sauvignon and Chasselas, the two grapes which, bottled pure, make today's Pouilly-Fumé and Pouilly-sur-Loire, respectively. Pouilly-Fumé is by far the more important—and the better—wine. But Sauvignon, or Blanc Fumé, as it is often called, was rarely bottled on its own until the 1930s and did not overtake Chasselas in the region's vineyards until the last twenty-five years. It now represents more than 95 percent of planting. And the wine it makes here bears a strong resemblance to Jullien's Pouilly—full, spirited, flinty, tasty, and tender.

What is the difference between Sancerre and Pouilly-Fumé? "Hard to say" was the answer I habitually received from growers, followed by "Sancerre's soils are more varied; there's a greater difference between a Sancerre from Bué and one from Crézancy than there is between Sancerre and Pouilly."

Nevertheless, slight differences in soils, climate, and expositions *do* make for differences in the wines—though I don't pretend to be able to distinguish them blind. The threat of frost, which is more of a problem in Pouilly than in Sancerre, has concentrated production within three communes: Pouilly, Saint-Andelain, and Tracy, a sheltered microclimate with the best soils that runs north of Pouilly for about seven kilometers on either side of RN7.

Pouilly's soils have more clay than those of Sancerre. Thus, its wines take longer to express themselves but are richer, weightier, broader in flavor, and more alcoholic.

An afterimage says Pouilly is more Burgundian than Sancerre. The best of the "regular" *cuvées* have a weight and texture that recall Pouilly-Fuissé. The best of the best, Didier Dagueneau's Silex, for example, or Ladoucette's Baron de L, are ample, deep, structured, creamy whites, with none of Sauvignon's characteristic edginess and little of its green bean–cat's pee aromas. In weight and style they recall Chablis and the Côte d'Or. (That said, Lucien Crochet's Sancerres can seem every bit as Burgundian.)

Pouilly-sur-Loire

With the arrival of the Bourbonnais railroad in 1858, Paris fruiterers came to the Pouilly region in search of Chasselas to sell as table grapes—for which they were willing to pay higher prices than they paid for wine. Sales boomed. In 1865 the railway station of Pouilly, one of three in the area, sent 3,000 metric tons of Chasselas to Paris. By 1890, however, Parisian produce merchants had abandoned the Chasselas of Pouilly for grapes from the Midi which the creation of new rail lines linking Paris with the south of France had made more accessible. The Chasselas crop was turned into wine, but as growers realized that Sauvignon did a better job in that department, they began replacing their Chasselas with Blanc Fumé.

Wine made from Chasselas in the Pouilly-Fumé zone is entitled to the appellation Pouilly-sur-Loire. But it is an endangered species. Generally planted on heavy, clay-siliceous soils, its acreage diminishes with each vintage. A bland, creamy white, it nevertheless has its fans. "Chasselas is a country wine; a bar wine; a thirst-quenching wine," claims producer Michel Redde. "Shellfish lovers seek out Chasselas because it doesn't mask flavors. It's also good with white meats. *Coq au Pouilly* is traditionally made with Chasselas." Redde, for one, is replanting, to "conserve" the wine—which he manages to place on the lists of Lucas-Carton and the Crillon.

Roughly one hundred vignerons make a living from their wines alone. Many are grouped in two hamlets—Les Loges in Pouilly, and Les Berthiers in Saint-Andelain. Les Loges is reputed for its full-bodied, fine wines as well as for its magnificent panorama of vines, river, and the hills of Sancerre beyond. Les Berthiers groups a number of my favorite vignerons.

◁ PRODUCER RATINGS ▷

OUTSTANDING
Didier Dagueneau

LEADERS
De Ladoucette   La Moynerie

EXCELLENT
Alain Cailbourdin   Jean-Claude Chatelain

HIGHLY RECOMMENDED
Château de Favray   Domaine Serge Dagueneau   Masson-Blondelet

RECOMMENDED
Francis Blanchet   Caves de Pouilly-sur-Loire (Les Moulins à Vent)
Château de Tracy   *Friends of the Contrers*
Edmond et André Figéat

BY THE GLASS
Bouchié-Chatellier
Domaine Guy Saget
Tinel-Blondelet

⋘ ⋘

OUTSTANDING

Didier Dagueneau, **Saint-Andelain:** My last visit to Didier Dagueneau's winery, on assignment for the *Wine Spectator,* was on a bright December morning. Didier was about to set off for Slovakia to compete in dogsled
races. As his crew swept cages, he broke off to taste through his '94 Pouilly-
Fumés, ending in a dimly lit cellar lined with barrels. Taut, bone-dry, with
bracing acidity, the wines were the best reflection imaginable of one of the
worst vintages in recent memory. "This year my neighbors made cocktails of
'94, '93, and sugar," he declared.

Fighting words? You bet. Dagueneau, the fortyish enfant terrible of
Pouilly, means them to be. Central casting's dream of a rebel, with his tan-
gled mane of flame red hair, his ice blue stare, his grunge garb (logger shirt,
baggy jeans, trucker's cap), Dagueneau crusades for his idea of authentic
Pouilly-Fumé, denouncing its infidels anywhere he finds an audience.

On French national TV Dagueneau inveighed against overproduction.
At home he has led visitors on tours of Pouilly's vineyards like a prosecu-
tor marshaling evidence, showing not just his own impeccable plots but a
sampling of neighbors' high-yielding, weed-infested parcels as well. He
also sent journalists his declarations of harvest, covering yields, chaptalization, and his bill for harvesters. Like a politician revealing his tax
returns, he was providing proof of purity. And like a politician, he was
throwing down the gauntlet to his confreres. (Like a politician, he sometimes exaggerates: While his claim about "cocktails" may be true in some
cases, it does not apply across the board—at least according to my taste
buds.)

In any event, Dagueneau's best gauntlet is his wine, which has become
the region's new benchmark. Many concur with Denis Dubourdieu, the
Bordeaux enologist credited with revolutionizing white wine production in
that region, who says, "Dagueneau is one of the great winemakers of our
generation; an artist in the truest sense of the word. He makes wine accord-

ing to an ideal in his head. His wines reveal the finesse of Sauvignon Blanc."

Dagueneau cultivates eleven and a half hectares spread over Saint-Andelain. When he made his debut in 1982, he had had no training in wine. He spent his youth as a motocross racer and credits its spirit of competition—which he recaptures today in dogsled racing—for his rigor as a winemaker. "I want to be the best," he says. "If you want to be the best you need the methods and techniques to get you there: Your vines must bear the best grapes; your vinification must be the most meticulous."

In the vineyards Dagueneau goes well beyond the mandates of the INAO. Vine density ranges from the legal minimum of 6,000 to 14,000 plants per hectare. He prunes severely, de-buds, de-leafs, cluster thins, and keeps yields under (often well under) 45 hectoliters per hectare. He judges ripeness not merely by levels of grape sugars but by "aromatic maturity," which will produce flavors like apricot, fig, grapefruit, passion fruit, and *cassis* rather than vegetal ones like green beans or cat's pee. Grapes are then hand harvested by successive passes through the vineyard.

Dagueneau's costly investments include his winery. Built in 1989, it looks like a cathedral—or at least like a church in an affluent suburb. It operates on the gravity principle and is so clean you could eat off the floor. After the devastating spring of '91, he installed Chablis-style antifrost equipment in his vineyards. And he positioned weather posts in key parcels to monitor temperatures, rainfall, humidity, and so forth and thereby to fine-tune his treatment of vine maladies.

Dagueneau claims his winemaking is not systematic. Broadly, grapes may or may not undergo skin contact. If the harvest is ripe and healthy, grapes are not destemmed. Several varieties of yeast are added. Fermentation occurs in small, thermoregulated stainless steel tanks or in oak barrels (some designed to his specifications). After an initial racking the wines stay on their fine lees until bottling. (He is opposed to malolactic fermentation for Sauvignon Blanc no matter how acid the vintage.)

As might be expected, Dagueneau produces some novelties: Pouilly from ungrafted vines, Riesling, and an off-dry Sauvignon which he calls Maudit (Cursed) because it was denied the Pouilly appellation as it was not "typical."

Tasters accustomed to feisty Sauvignons may find *none* of Dagueneau's wines typical. In his Pouilly-Fumés, a creamy texture replaces raw acidity; mineral flavors combined with exotic fruit often recall the wines of Alsace.

He currently bottles four versions: En Chailloux represents half of production. It's a big, friendly wine; as I often find it soft, I tend to prefer years like '94 when it's bracing and steely as well as aromatic. Next is the single-vineyard Buisson Menard, a flinty, mineral-rich Pouilly. The '94, '93, and '92 should develop great complexity. The barrel-fermented Pur Sang (Thoroughbred) tends to be the bridge between En Chailloux and Cuvée Silex. I loved the mellow, pear, and mineral '94 and the suave, almost viscous '93.

Silex, also barrel-fermented and aged, is made from thirty-five- to sixty-year-old vines on the silex-rich soils which Dagueneau believes make the most structured, "intellectual" Pouillys. The '94 was tart, mineraly, with flavors of red currant and grapefruit when tasted from barrel. Promising. The multilayered '93 was a great wine—WINE in capital letters—as were the opulent '90 and '89, and the rectilinear yet sumptuous and complex '88. All confirm Dagueneau's view that Sauvignon is one of the most complex and subtle grapes and that its wines are as noble as great white Burgundies. (Silex is also priced like one, at roughly 191ff. But, cognizant of the work that goes into the wines, customers—collectors and restaurateurs alike—never balk.)

"I'm lucky," Dagueneau reflects. "I make wine without regard to cost. I don't want to know how I'm doing financially—otherwise that will dictate how I make my wine."

Banks underwrote Dagueneau's dazzling ensemble of vineyards, cellars, and seven full-time employees. After his winery was built, Dagueneau conceded that its expense was "disproportionate," adding, "But I didn't want to wait and do it bit by bit. You've got to move quickly. Life is short. I hope in five years I'll still want to be a winemaker, but maybe I'll want something else."

Five years have passed since that statement and Dagueneau is still making wine. And he recently replanted a historic vineyard and bought and trained a mare to maneuver its tight rows.

LEADERS

De Ladoucette, Pouilly-sur-Loire: The home of the world's most famous Pouilly-Fumé is, appropriately, a showplace. A Disney-esque château (you really do expect to see Tinkerbell soar above its pointy towers) is surrounded by vines so neat they look like garden shrubs. These, in turn, are bordered with hedges cut at exactly the same height. Versailles viticulture. New cellars were completed for the '90 harvest.

Baron Patrick de Ladoucette, the great-great-grandson of Comte Lafon, the château's original owner, oversees the *domaine*, which consists of about sixty-five hectares in Pouilly. He buys another sixty-five hectares' worth of wine (including must and grapes) for both his Pouilly and his Sancerre, the latter sold under the Comte Lafon label. Add Marc Brédif in Vouvray and other Touraine appellations sold under the Baron Briare label and de Ladoucette emerges as one of the most important family firms—if not the most important—in the Loire. De Ladoucette also owns the venerable Chablis house Albert Pic; is copartner with Gonzalez-Byass of a small cognac company; directs his Bristol Distribution House (selling Latour, Antinori, and other brands within France); and owns vines in California.

His choice of Montpellier-trained Joël André as cellar master demonstrates a gift for delegating. André, who heads a team of twenty-three full-time employees, speaks like a vintner in his own cellars, describing the whys and wherefores of the decision to use indigenous yeasts, for example, or the particularities of Pouilly's different soil types, all five of which are assembled to make de Ladoucette's normal Pouilly.

For this *cuvée*, de Ladoucette is looking for a house-style. Half the grapes come from the *domaine*'s vines (all in Saint-Andelain). These are vinified by parcel and by press lot. The first press ferments at low temperatures for a month, with a stirring up of the lees; second press and press wine ferment for two weeks. The wines may undergo partial or complete malolactic fermentation. The *domaine*'s wines are assembled in June and blended with the rest according to taste.

Though I prefer a more personalized, idiosyncratic statement, de Ladoucette's Pouilly is generally well made and generous. The '93, the vintage available in the summer of 1995, was rather classic though a bit short.

In 1973 de Ladoucette began producing Baron de L, a deluxe Pouilly made from the first juices of grapes of his oldest vines. The style he is seeking is unabashedly Burgundian—without the oak. "Sauvignon Blanc has more fruit than Chardonnay. Chardonnay has more body and makes up for its lack of fruit with wood," he explains. "In Baron de L, I want the body of Chardonnay and the fruit of Sauvignon without excessive perfumes."

The wine, which stays on its fine lees for eighteen months before bottling, is Pouilly and Sauvignon at their most Côte d'Or–esque. Rich, broad, and creamy, it has the marrowy feel of a wine which has spent a long time on its lees. The bouquet is discreet and rather evolved, though the wine seems youthful, often with Pinot Gris notes in the aroma. Baron de L is usually released three years after the harvest, and that is the best time to drink it. In the summer of 1995, however, de Ladoucette was still selling the '90 Baron de L, a pungent, very ripe, almost viscous Pouilly. Though I was a bit troubled by the hot finish, I found it a lovely white for fine dining. The '89 was Burgundy in the Loire: Ligerian in its liveliness; Burgundian in its breadth. Ditto for the subtle, inviting '88, a pellucid wine, defined not so much by fruit—its definable flavors were flashes of ripe hay, lemon, and minerals—as by texture and finesse.

La Moynerie, Pouilly-sur-Loire: Michel Redde was one of the first producers to systematically bottle his Pouillys. And when he puts his mind to it, he can make one helluva Pouilly. But only part of his production is stellar, due chiefly, I think, to high yields and machine-harvesting.

Fermentation occurs in stainless steel tanks at moderately low temperatures. As Redde dislikes the "technological wine" aromas produced by low temperatures, selected yeasts, and barrel aging, none of these methods is pursued. Malolactic fermentation is not systematic. The wines stay on their fine lees after an initial racking, until bottling, generally within the year.

Redde's normal Pouillys tend to be accurate but not very exciting—though '89 was considerably more than that and both '93 and '94 were rather less. When Redde decides to make great Pouilly it's with his Cuvée Majorum. First released in '73, Majorum consists of selected musts of well-exposed old vines in his best parcels. It is made only in good vintages. The '90, tasted in 1995, disappointed; it had some intriguing, ripe flavors but was hot and undistinguished. The '89, however, was elegant, textured, fresh, and marrowy. Discreetly herbaceous, with grapefruit and Alsace notes and strong flint and mineral character, it had a long bitter-almond and tisane finish.

Redde also makes a bit of vinous, agreeable Pouilly-sur-Loire.

EXCELLENT

Alain Cailbourdin, Maltaverne: As a teenager, Cailbourdin came down from Paris to work harvests. He studied in Beaune and at Cosne, worked for some large Pouilly firms, and in 1980 bought two hectares, rented seven more, and began building his cellars. He is a serious young vintner who makes measured, reasoned investments. There are none of Didier Dagueneau's manic extremes: No new oak barrels. No pneumatic press. No polemics. Just steady, sober progress following the mainstream of viticulture and vinification. Cailbourdin's wines are very much in that image. He makes four different Pouilly-Fumés, bottling by soil type.

The Cuvée de Boisfleury is the appropriately springlike name of the vineyard that makes Cailbourdin's early-drinking Pouilly. Generally supple and pleasant, it has vigorous cat's pee–green bean and mineral flavors in years like '94, '93, and '92. In riper years like '89 it is briskly grapefruity with a mineral–bitter almond finish.

The Les Cris bottling comes from the chalky slopes of Boisgilbaut. With this wine, Cailbourdin can, in years like '90, compete with the top players in the appellation. That excellent '90 was a delicious, fine Pouilly, firm, creamy, with refined varietal notes and a persuasive undertow of minerals. It belongs up with the "L"s and the Silexes. Les Cris is an urbane wine even in off years. Restrained and citric when tasted from tank, the '94 should be very good, given its track record. The '93, well focused, marrowy, and mineral-rich, was fine indeed, as was the '92. More expressive of *terroir* than grape variety, it was firm and concentrated, its lemon and mineral notes merely seasoned with Sauvignon's typical herbaceousness.

Cailbourdin's two other Pouilly-Fumé bottlings are Les Cornets, a *lieu dit* on the Route des Loges, and a Vieilles Vignes from fifty-year-old vines on several parcels with chalky clay soils. Each is admirable, but I give the edge to Les Cornets. Cailbourdin also makes a thoroughly respectable Pouilly-sur-Loire, a clean, light house white.

Jean-Claude Chatelain, Saint-Andelain: No folklore here. No romance, either. But Chatelain, an entrepreneurial winemaker who affects paisley ascots and L.L. Bean–style lumberjack shirts, makes very good, and consistently good, Pouilly. Chatelain has twenty hectares in Pouilly and roughly doubles his production by buying must and new wine.

Most grapes are machine-harvested. Those from similar soils are assembled for vinification at low temperatures in stainless steel tanks. Malolactic fermentation is not systematic. Chatelain's *domaine* bottling is usually good, commercial, and tasty. The '93 had the broad mineral-Sauvignon aromas and flavors that make me think "Pouilly." But I always prefer his special bottlings. These are fine Pouillys for upscale bistros, delicious and satisfying, if not personalized.

Chatelain's Les Charmes bottling comes from a *lieu dit* with both chalky and silex-rich soils. Ten percent ferments in new oak. The '93 offered subtle oak flavors mixed with ripe fig and minerals. Chatelain has a near monopoly in Saint-Laurent-l'Abbaye. That bottling ranges from very good to spectacular: The '90 was Napa-sur-Loire, clear, ripe, luscious fruit with citrus and pineapple accents *and* the breed that comes from a distinguished site.

Chatelain's Cuvée Prestige usually comes from his oldest vines. The grapes are hand harvested and the wine stays on its fine lees until May. The '93, tasted from tank in 1995, seemed rather light, but promising, with flavors of petrol and peach. The '90 was a bit unbalanced by alcohol (13.8 percent), but the '89 was rich and elegant, a fine blend of ripe fruit, almond, and mineral flavors.

Chatelain is also a shareholder in and the technical director of a vineyard in the La Charité-sur-Loire area, south of Pouilly. Fifteen hectares have been planted with Chardonnay, the first vintage of which was '93, and with Pinot Noir, the first vintage of which will be '95. The wines are Vin de Pays des Coteaux Charitois. The '93 Chardonnay, with vague varietal flavors, was just another Chardonnay.

HIGHLY RECOMMENDED

Château de Favray, **Saint-Martin-sur-Nohain:** At the border of Cosne, Quentin David cultivates 12 hectares of vines (he'll ultimately have 25) and another 230 of cereal crops. "Yes, we're at the northern limit of the appellation," he agrees, "but our soils are as interesting as those in the heart of Pouilly. Our vines are on a well-exposed slope where there's very little topsoil and the subsoils are quite chalky. The style of the wines from here is expressive and floral, earlier drinking than those on silex."

His Pouillys *do* seem less intense and complex than those from Pouilly *classico*, a soft fade of the appellation's power. But they also express the seriousness of the vigneron. In '94, by hand harvesting and hand-sorting, David turned out an ample, respectable Pouilly with lemon and petrol notes. It was firmly in the family of the wines he has made since 1986, lively, citrusy, and rather elegant Pouillys, tending toward pungent flavors of grapefruit and green bean, with good mineral notes.

Domaine Serge Dagueneau, **Les Berthiers:** Big, bluff, gruff Serge Dagueneau (Didier's uncle) comes off like a dyed-in-the-wool good ol' boy. But he's the only Loire vigneron I know with "& Filles" (and daughters) blazoned across the winery. Daughters Valérie (Macon) and Florence (Beaune) both worked at Peter Michael winery in Calistoga and now handle day-to-day operations—pressing, pumping, racking, and so forth—alongside Dad.

From his fifteen hectares, the brawny Dagueneau makes full-bodied, creamy Pouillys. They could be finer, more focused, but they *are* characterful. There's definitely a "There" there. His normal bottling of '93 fit that burly image—an ample mix of creamed asparagus and mineral flavors, with accents of ripe peach and apricot.

In good vintages Dagueneau also bottles a special *cuvée* made from late-harvested—and hand-harvested—very ripe grapes from old vines grown on the pure *terres blanches* of his Clos des Chaudoux. There is generally about twelve hours of skin contact, and the wines usually undergo malolactic fermentation. They are bottled the September following the harvest. Dagueneau was offering the '92 in 1995. Broad and rich, with large flavors of asparagus, green bean, melon, and fig and a fine mineral undercurrent, it was not subtle but it *was* satisfying. The '89 resembled Didier's Pouillys in richness and Muscat-Alsace flavors. It was more rustic, however, less fine of grain, but a truly rewarding glass of Pouilly. Ditto for the '90.

Dagueneau also makes incredible Pouilly-sur-Loire—from ninety-year-old Chasselas vines. You'll never taste better.

Masson-Blondelet, Pouilly-sur-Loire: Competent, pleasant wines from a competent, pleasant couple. The Masson-Blondelets bottle five or six different Pouilly-Fumés. Recent favorites have included the '93 Les Pierres Blanches, with attractive apricot and sour lemon flavors, and the nicely focused '93 Villa Paulus, a lively and bracing Pouilly, with appealing peach and mineral flavors. (The '94, tasted from tank, was a thinner version but honorable for the vintage.)

In older vintages ('86 through '90), I have admired the creamy, floral Pouillys from Les Bascoins, a *lieu dit* near de Ladoucette's Nozet; the pungent, flint-and-mineral Les Angelots; and the toasty, mellow Tradition Cullus, an old-vines *cuvée* partially fermented and aged in newish oak barrels.

Masson-Blondelet offers a creamy, lightly nutty Pouilly-sur-Loire. It is a bit pricey but one of the more elegant versions. Their light, perfumed Sancerre blanc is recommended, as are the pleasant, oaky reds and the vinous, nutty rosés.

RECOMMENDED

Francis Blanchet, **Pouilly:** A Lycée de Beaune grad, Blanchet cham-penizes the wines of his neighbors and makes good, slightly rustic Pouillys. In general, Blanchet likes his Pouilly sprightly and herbaceous. Textbook, for him, was a special *cuvée* of '88: A very good Pouilly, it was a supple wine, blending green bean, grapefruit, menthol, and mineral flavors. His '93 may have been a bit too sprightly for his tastes; textured and grapefruity, its hot finish seemed a tad confected, though I found the wine rather charming. And though Blanchet feels vintages like '89 were too ripe, his version of that great year was delicious, with engaging pineapple-Muscat notes.

Caves de Pouilly-sur-Loire (Les Moulins à Vent), **Pouilly:** Creditable versions of both appellations, including the vinous, floral normal bottlings, which would make good house wines for smart bistros, and the full-bodied Pouilly-Fumé Vieilles Vignes Tinelum, with pungent mineral, grapefruit, and, sometimes, petrol flavors.

Château de Tracy: An exquisite, rambling castle in the hollow of a beautiful park, the Château de Tracy has deep roots in Pouilly viticulture; documents from the fourteenth century record the sale of grapes from its vine-yards. Today the *domaine* consists of twenty-five hectares of vines, another eight coming into production—on silex-rich soils around the château and on the Kimmeridgian marl of plateaus stretching east—as well as a newish stock-room and an oldish wine cellar. Henri d'Estutt d'Assay, the well-mannered and otherworldly scion, plans to renovate those ancient cellars and dreams about organic viticulture. His Pouillys could be more focused, more concen-trated; they could have more *éclat.* But they are cool, long versions, grassy and grapefruity, with nice structure and pleasant mineral finishes.

Edmond et André Figéat, **Pouilly:** Edmond (*père*) and André (*fils,* Lycée de Beaune) incarnate Pouilly's recent viticultural history. Their "estate" has evolved from polyculture with a couple of rows of vines to a respected *domaine* with twelve hectares, mostly on prime hillsides between Pouilly and Les Loges. Their cellars, just beyond downtown Pouilly in what looks like a suburban house, are filled with all manner of tank and, at any time of day, all manner of relatives and local schmoozers, tasting different lots and different vintages from small glasses.

Generally flinty, with mineral and strong petrol flavors, the Figéat Pouillys are simultaneously austere and rich. In very ripe years, like '89 and '90, there are accents of Muscat. In less opulent vintages, like '93, the wines can be rather aggressive. The '93 Vieilles Vignes bottling, for example, had powerful petrol and pine flavors as well as that foxy grapeyness characteristic of Concord. The wine would certainly not be to everyone's taste, but I liked its rough-hewn originality.

The Figéats also make a pungent, petroly Pouilly-sur-Loire.

BY THE GLASS

Bouchié-Chatellier, Saint-Andelain: Satisfying, upscale Pouillys from the director of Pouilly's cooperative cellars—from his own vines, on his own time.

Domaine Guy Saget, Pouilly: Crisp, clean, neutral Pouilly-sur-Loire and Fumé from this house which sells four million bottles of Loire wine yearly.

Tinel-Blondelet, Pouilly-sur-Loire: Dependable Pouillys from a hardworking couple.

POUILLYS FROM PRODUCERS IN OTHER APPELLATIONS

Sancerrois:

Henri Bourgeois: With four hectares, Bourgeois makes inviting, elegant Pouilly-Fumés with firm mineral notes.

The Dezats of Celliers Saint-Romble have twelve hectares of Pouilly, labeled Domaine Thibault. The '94 and '93 were very attractive, lively, and grapefruity, though they seemed more like Sancerre than Pouilly.

Pascal Jolivet is definitely worth watching: By 1995 all his Pouilly will come from his own eight hectares, producing a generic Pouilly and two special bottlings, Les Griottes, from a two-hectare vineyard with chalky soils, and La Grande Cuvée, which corresponds to a similar *cuvée* in Sancerre. For now Jolivet seems to be doing a better job with his Sancerres, but he's ambitious and has good ideas.

Balland-Chapuis and **Gitton** Père et fils

Giennois:

Hubert Veneau (see Coteaux du Giennois)

MENETOU-SALON

STATUS: *AOC 1959*
TYPES OF WINE: *White, red, and rosé*

ZONE AND PRODUCTION: *20,500 hectoliters, on 333 hectares within ten communes*

GRAPES: *Whites—Sauvignon; reds and rosés—Pinot Noir*

SOILS: *Similar to those of Sancerre*

PRICE: *30 to 40ff*

BEST VINTAGES: *'95, '90*

Menetou-Salon is a southwest extension of the vineyards of Sancerre, spreading along a band of hillsides 200 to 300 meters high from Morogues to the outskirts of Bourges. It takes its name from its most viticulturally oriented commune, a provincial village with a large tree-lined square girded with cafés (including a favorite, Cheu l'Zib) and a church. A bit farther on is Menetou's sumptuous château, which once belonged to Jacques Coeur, finance minister under Charles XII.

Menetou Sauvignons, generally vinified at low temperatures in all types of tanks, are sprightly and herbaceous, often floral, with firm flavors of grapefruit and minerals. Locals claim that Sancerre is nervier than Menetou and, when produced on the pebbly soils of Bué, more perfumed; Menetou, on the other hand, is rounder, less edgy.

Most of the reds vat for a week to ten days. They may or may not age in barrel before bottling. They are delightful, juicy, wine-bar Pinot Noirs.

Menetou, of course, is riding on Sancerre's coattails. Both volume and acreage are rapidly increasing. Menetou's success is evidenced not only in its expanding acreage but in recent investments. Its two leading producers have built new cellars, equipped with thermoregulated stainless steel tanks and, alas, machine harvesters.

There are about fifteen full-time vintners in Menetou-Salon. Many Sancerrois are buying vineyards—or grapes—here. And young vignerons from other regions are setting up wineries. (For now they sell their grapes.) The ensemble of the appellation is taking steps to improve quality—in vines, in cellars, and in hospitality. An enologist is on retainer, and investments are being made in newer equipment.

I've written up only two producers in this appellation, each of whom rates "Excellent." They are the only ones who consistently make quality wines. Other vintners listed at the end of the section make nice wines from time to time, but it's hit-or-miss. Menetou-Salon has everything going for it and it deserves to be much more well known. Given the current popularity of both Sauvignon Blanc and Pinot Noir, it surely will be.

Note: Morogues, which abuts Montigny, the last of Sancerre's communes, is the only one of Menetou's communes that can put its name on the wine label.

❧ PRODUCER RATINGS ❧

EXCELLENT
Domaine de Châtenoy   Henri Pellé

BY THE GLASS
Georges Chavet et Fils   Jean-Paul Gilbert

❧ ❧

EXCELLENT

Domaine de Châtenoy, **Menetou:**   Bernard Clément and son Pierre, a University of Dijon–trained enologist, make super Menetou-Salon. I often find the Sauvignons ringers for good Sancerres. A portion of the harvest undergoes skin contact. Only indigenous yeasts are used. Fermentation occurs in stainless steel tanks at low temperatures. The wines are left on their fine lees until January bottling. The punchy '93 had lively grapefruity flavors, as did the tart, crisp '92. An experimental *cuvée,* from a hand-harvested *tri,* undergoes a preformentation—the uncrushed grapes are left under a blanket of carbon dioxide for seventy-two hours before pressing, to start a kind of carbonic maceration—before fermenting and aging in new oak barrels. In some vintages the wines go through malolactic fermentation. An '89 seemed a lighter version of Didier Dagueneau's Pouillys, a lush blend of ripe banana, ginger, oak, and Muscat fruit. The lightly oaky '90, full and delicious in 1995, would probably have been even more delectable in 1993.

Clément's reds are lovely, light Pinot Noirs. Supple and silky with bright cherry flavors when young, they evolve nicely for four years, developing nuances of dried cherries, sandalwood, and spices. There is a special barrel-aged *cuvée* here, too, although the oak often seems to overwhelm the pretty fruit.

Henri Pellé, **Morogues:**   The son of a farmworker who wanted him to be a teacher, Henri Pellé recalls thinking, "Thirty kids every day for the rest of my life? Not me!" So, "to the great despair" of his parents, he returned to the land.

Pellé produces about a quarter of the appellation's wine. His are always well made and commercial without sacrificing their sense of place. Pellé seems to do a better job with whites than with his rough-and-ready reds. The normal *cuvée* of white Menetou is textbook—crisp, grapefruity, with an undercurrent of minerals. Les Blanchais is Pellé's special *cuvée* made from thirty- to forty-year-old vines on a slope with Kimmeridgian soils. It is always subtler, as well as deeper, richer, and longer, than the normal bottling. Both are sure bets, year in, year out.

BY THE GLASS

Georges Chavet et Fils, **Menetou-Salon:**   Pungent, if somewhat coarse, reds and whites.

Jean-Paul Gilbert, **Menetou-Salon:**   Pretty, charcuterie-friendly reds; diffuse whites.

QUINCY

STATUS: *AOC 1936*
TYPES OF WINE: *Dry whites*
ZONE AND PRODUCTION: *From 5,000 to 8,000 hectoliters on 170 hectares of a possible 500 in the communes of Quincy and Brinay*
GRAPES: *Sauvignon Blanc*
SOILS: *Sand and gravel on layers of clay and chalk*
PRICE: *25ff*
BEST VINTAGES: *'95, '90*

Quincy was the second viticultural region in France to receive AOC status. (The first was Châteauneuf-du-Pape.) Its vines, which occupy a long plateau bordered by woods, above the left bank of the Cher, were cultivated by the Citeaux monks in the fourteenth century; its vintages were once considered "the wine of Bourges."

Quincy's vineyards almost disappeared after the Second World War, however, as its young moved to Paris and as old vignerons retired with no successors. (Quincy was considered a village of roofers.) But since the mid-eighties Quincy has been staging a comeback. Established vineyards are being taken over by newcomers—several, new not only to the region but to winemaking, "chose" the profession—and planting continues: The local *syndicat*, itself a recent development, predicts that the zone will soon have two hundred hectares in production.

The Quincy appellation applies only to white wines. On its hot, light soils, Sauvignon ripens a full week earlier than it does in Sancerre, easily reaching a potential of 13 percent alcohol, even 15 percent. Acids arc generally, and naturally, low, making Quincy the creamiest and softest of the Cher's Sauvignons. Old texts and old-timers talk about the elegance of Quincy Sauvignon, which often had residual sugar. But tastes have changed. Consumers want fresher, livelier, and drier whites. The Quincy vignerons oblige by picking grapes greener, then chaptalizing. Those I have tasted, however, seem caught between two worlds—the alcoholic, unaromatic, rustic, and perhaps slightly oxidized wines of grandfather and the fresh, clean, vibrantly fruity style favored today.

Quincy's robe is usually straw yellow; its aromas, vinous with banana and Muscat notes; its structure, rather soft. This unfocused style is not surprising given Quincy's late reawakening and hit-or-miss vinifications. Progress seems stalled by widespread, though not unendearing, amateurism. At this stage it's hard to discern why Quincy won such early AOC recognition or why it was considered one of the Loire's most elegant wines. But a couple of movers and shakers might turn things around, showing us gorgeous Quincys, amiable, creamy wines which reveal yet another facet of Sauvignon.

Several producers make reds and rosés from Pinot Noir and Gamay which may be sold as Vin de Pays du Cher et de l'Arnon. Thin, sometimes spicy, they sell out within three months of the harvest, mostly to local cafés.

❧ PRODUCER RATINGS ☙

HIGHLY RECOMMENDED
Domaine Mardon   Domaine Sorbe

BY THE GLASS
Domaine des Bruniers (Jérôme de la Chaise)
Claude Houssier   Denis et Nicole Jaumier

❧ ❧

HIGHLY RECOMMENDED

Domaine Mardon, Quincy: Under Pierre Mardon's stewardship, this thirteen-hectare *domaine* was the leading house for quality Quincy; its wines were on the lists of more than thirty Paris restaurants. Following his death in 1989, Pierre's widow and his brother Jean, a former roofer, took over. After a brief shakeout, the wines are once again ambassadors for the appellation. I'd be delighted to meet either the mineral-rich, lightly herbal '94 or the lively '93, a meatier and more serious Quincy, in a wine bar.

Domaine Sorbe (see Reuilly): On his two and a half hectares of Quincy, Jean-Michel Sorbe makes clean, commercial, New World–style Sauvignons: a meaty, apricot- and peach-scented '94; a pleasant, if overly oaky, barrel-fermented '93 that won a gold medal in Paris.

BY THE GLASS

Domaine des Bruniers (Jérôme de la Chaise), Quincy: This young electrician-turned-winemaker put together a ten-hectare *domaine* and built his own cellars. The Quincys need work but de la Chaise seems committed. To watch.

Claude Houssier, Quincy: Friends in Chinon love Houssier's Quincy, which they buy after gallery-museum trips to Bourges. The dedicated president of Quincy's growers' *syndicat*, Houssier makes soft, Muscat- and banana-flavored Sauvignons; somewhat amateurish, occasionally flawed, though not unpleasant.

Denis et Nicole Jaumier, Quincy: Jaumier is a Parisian who yearned to make wine. After studying in Bergerac and in Bordeaux's La Tour Blanche, he took over the *domaine* of an elderly vigneron in 1987. The wines show promise, particularly an ample '89 with Pinot Gris notes and a bitter almond finish; slightly off-dry because Jaumier likes to leave a bit of residual sugar. A '90, however, was flabby, simply alcoholic.

REUILLY

STATUS: *AOC 1937 (white); 1961 (red and rosé)*
TYPES OF WINE: *Dry whites, reds, and rosés*

ZONE AND PRODUCTION: *Roughly 7,000 hectoliters, made on 132 hectares within six communes, on hills overlooking the Arnon, a tributary of the Cher*
GRAPES: *Sauvignon Blanc, Pinot Gris, Pinot Noir*
SOILS: *The best sites are Kimmeridgian marl, like Sancerre.*
PRICE: *25 to 30ff*
BEST VINTAGES: *'95, '90*

Reuilly is an appellation to watch. Midway between the vineyards of Loir-et-Cher and those of Sancerre, it is an ancient viticultural region that seemed about to disappear until the mid-eighties, when it emerged as another Sauvignon satellite.

Its relatively hot, dry climate and its full, soft Sauvignons tend to resemble those of Quincy, ten kilometers to the east. Reuilly seems to be evolving more quickly, however, and its wine now comes in two styles. The first is rustic, rather neutral, creamy, and alcoholic. The second—generally from younger producers who rigorously decant the juices and use aromatic yeasts, tank fermentation, temperature controls, and other modern techniques—is fresher and more perfumed. White wines account for 60 percent of production.

Reuilly was once known for its *vin gris de pinot gris*, today 15 percent of production. A fragrant, vinous "rosé," the wines often have trace amounts of Pinot Noir blended in. Pinot Noir was first planted in the region in the sixties and is chiefly used for reds, accounting for 25 percent of production. The grapes generally vat for about a week in enameled tanks, with some pumping over. Most do not age in barrel. The best are charming bistro Pinot Noirs, light, tart, and tasting of cherries and cherry pits.

About a dozen growers produce Reuilly in commercial quantities; most also cultivate cereal crops. There has been a great deal of progress since the mid-eighties and vineyard prices have doubled. Reuilly seems a generation ahead of Quincy.

⇜ PRODUCER RATINGS ⇝

LEADERS
Domaine Claude Lafond   Domaine Sorbe

RECOMMENDED
Didier Chassiot   Gérard Cordier   Guy Malbête

BY THE GLASS
René Ouvrat   Jean-Pierre Thiolat   Jacques Vincent

⇜ ⇝

LEADERS

***Domaine Claude Lafond,* Reuilly:**   The president of Reuilly's growers' *syndicat,* Claude Lafond is the appellation's most dynamic winemaker and its best. Constantly expanding, he works twenty-five hectares; he's formed a society with another vintner (Jacques Renaudat) to produce more wine; and he instigated the formation of an association of eight winemakers who shared the expense of building cooperative cellars—the Chai de Reuilly—equipping it and hiring a cellar master to make each grower's wine according to individual specifications (types of yeast and fermentation temperatures, for example).

Wines from Lafond's own *domaine* get better all the time. His marrowy '94 Reuilly blanc La Raie was truly fetching, an ample white with mineral and tropical-fruit notes. Lafond pampers his second Reuilly blanc, the single-vineyard Clos des Messieurs. Yields are lower, harvest is later, and the wines stay on their fine lees until June bottling, resulting in flavorful Sauvignons like the creamy, super-ripe '93. (I also love the label: silhouettes of Lord Peter Wimsey–ish *messieurs* in black tie, with cigars and wine.)

Lafond's attractive rosés of Pinot Gris, called La Grande Pièce, are fragrant and textured. His reds, called Les Grandes Vignes, would be excellent choices for ambitious wine bars. Lafond vats his red grapes longer than most—for nearly two weeks, in good years. The '94, with its clear Pinot Noir fruit, was a fine wine for the vintage. The well-focused '93 offered appealing Pinot fruit, accented with licorice and clove. (After tasting it, I thought I'd have a glass with broiled salmon and pasta—and ended up finishing the bottle!)

Domaine Sorbe, Preuilly: A law student who abandoned the bar in May 1968, Jean-Michel Sorbe is a vigneron on the move. He's doubled his acreage to nine hectares. His cellars—already relatively modern (temperature controlled, stainless steel tanks and new oak barrels)—will be rebuilt in 1997; he's president of an association for the development of Reuilly-Quincy; and he vinifies for *négociant* Alexander Mellot. His wines show improvement but still need work. A '94 Reuilly blanc was crisp, clean, and herbaceous. His barrel-fermented Sauvignon seemed a curious mix of the bland and the quirky. Flashes of pistachio and coffee mixed with oak and fruit enlivened an otherwise neutral '89. Sorbe's Pinot Noirs range from the tart, light '93 and '94, to the engaging '89, with pretty flavors of cherries and cherry pits.

RECOMMENDED

Didier Chassiot, La Ferté: Aggressive Sauvignons and very nice, light Pinot Noirs; clear, supple, and appetizing with light orange-zest notes.

Gérard Cordier, La Ferté: Pinot Gris is the only wine Cordier cellars and it's the best wine he makes. An attractive coral, it's a clean, almondy wine, both flowery and vinous. Cordier sells a lot of it to La Mère Poulard in Mont-Saint-Michel.

Guy Malbête, Bois Saint-Denis: Pleasant wine-bar Reuillys across the board: ripe Sauvignons; rough, cherryish Pinot Noirs; vinous, hard, dry Pinot Gris.

BY THE GLASS

René Ouvrat, La Ferté: Rough-hewn, bouillony Pinot Noirs; woody Sauvignons and Pinot Gris. Ouvrat likes the latter as a dessert wine, with cake.

Jean-Pierre Thiolat, Diou: Rustic, juicy Pinot Noirs and raw Sauvignons.

Jacques Vincent, Lazenay: Aromatic, new-generation Reuillys to drink fresh from the fermentation tank.

CHATEAUMEILLANT

STATUS: *VDQS 1965*
TYPES OF WINE: *Reds and rosés*
ZONE AND PRODUCTION: *1,700 hectoliters, made on 59 hectares in eight communes*
SOILS: *Sand and pebbles on a clay-silica base*
GRAPES: *Gamay, Pinot Noir*
PRICE: *25ff*
BEST VINTAGES: *'95, '90*

In the heart of George Sand country—a landscape of narrow rivers, of stone cottages, and of bourgeois villas once inhabited by this or that solicitor who somehow figured in Sand's life—are the low vine-covered plateaus producing VDQS Châteaumeillant.

Its most "traditional" wine is *vin gris*, made by a direct press of the harvest. Reds usually ferment in tank, vatting for a week. Flinty streaks in the soils can give the wines a steely character. And the fact that Châteaumeillant is halfway to Auvergne, with ruder weather than that of northern Berry, can in difficult years result in greenish wines. In good years the wines are spicy and kirsch-scented. Reds, as well as rosés, benefit from chilling; most are made to be drunk immediately, though reds can age for up to five years.

Aside from the co-op, Châteaumeillant has only a handful of active vignerons. But the wines sell out; growers are investing in their cellars, replanting and reclaiming abandoned lands. And Châteaumeillant has filed its demand to be upgraded to AOC. The producers listed below are all located in Châteaumeillant.

❧ PRODUCER RATINGS ❧

HIGHLY RECOMMENDED
Maurice et Patrick Lanoix

RECOMMENDED
Cave des Vins de Châteaumeillant   Domaine des Tanneries

HIGHLY RECOMMENDED

Maurice et Patrick Lanoix: The Lanoix work fourteen hectares and recently bought another five. They cultivate some cereal crops, and Mme. Lanoix makes Crottin-shaped chèvre the men like to serve with their version of a *kir*—iced Gamay laced with *crème de mûre* (blackberry). The wines are essentially the same, though Maurice's are bottled under Domaine du Feuillat and Patrick's under Cellier du Chêne Combeau. Gamay represents 75 percent. Maurice also makes pungent Sauvignon Blanc, a Vin de Pays. While the wines need work—adding less sulfur and less, or ideally no, tannins, for example—they are generally pleasant wine-bar reds and rosés, with pretty kirsch and cherry fruit. And there are some lovely surprises to be savored in Maurice's Cuvée Spéciale, from eighty- to one-hundred-year-old vines, aged in new Tronçais barrels and Patrick's Pinot Noir, a mineral, minty charmer.

RECOMMENDED

Cave des Vins de Châteaumeillant: Founded in 1965, this cooperative vinifies the entire harvest of its sixty members, making a *vin gris* of Gamay and Pinot Noir (fair and fruity, though oversulfured); a Gamay blended with Pinot Noir (supple and pleasant, with musky flavors recalling Cabernet Franc); and Domaine des Garennes, an easygoing red from a twelve-hectare property.

Domaine des Tanneries: From their ten hectares of vines, Henri Raffinat and sons Jean-Luc (Amboise) and Eric make pleasant spice- and cherry-flavored wine-bar reds and rosés, each with equal portions of Gamay and Pinot Noir.

COTEAUX DU GIENNOIS

STATUS: *VDQS 1954*

TYPES OF WINE: *Dry white, red, and rosé*

ZONE AND PRODUCTION: *Roughly 6,500 hectoliters, made on 128 hectares spread out over fifteen communes in the Loiret and the Nièvre*

GRAPES: *Sauvignon, Gamay, Pinot Noir. As of 1995, reds must be a blend of Pinot Noir and Gamay.*

SOILS: *The principal zones are high, arching hillsides of clay and silex or sandy, gravelly terraces around Bonny-sur-Loire on the left bank of the river and slopes and plateaus, around Gien and Cosne on the right.*

PRICE: *15 to 25ff*
BEST VINTAGES: '95, '90, '89

The vineyards straddling both banks of the Loire from Sancerre and Pouilly, extending north to the pottery city of Gien, date back to the Gallo-Roman period. In 27 B.C. Emperor Augustus authorized the planting of vines in Cosne and until World War II the area had close to 4,000 hectares of vines.

Today the Coteaux du Giennois seems a footnote to Loire wines. Yet I love some of its light reds. They are elegant, sturdy, and specific to a *terroir*, often tastier and more exciting than reds from Sancerre or Beaujolais. But the appellation is a long way away from realizing its potential, and quality is too uneven to come to any solid conclusions about what types of wine the region should be making and from which grapes. Many put their faith in Sauvignon, pointing out that their vineyards are kissing cousins of Sancerre and Pouilly. The success that at least one producer, Alain Paulat, has had with Pinot Noir and Gamay, however, reminds one that the Nièvre is, indeed, in Burgundy. Paulat bottles each separately. But as of the 1995 harvest, the law, in its infinite wisdom, obliges vintners to blend the two.

Most of the appellation's vines, as well as its producers, are located around Cosne. Many years ago they applied, unsuccessfully, for their own appellation. The INAO also refused to include them in Pouilly, grouping them instead with the Giennois. But they are entitled to add "Cosne-sur-Loire" to "Gien" (or "Giennois") on their labels.

The majority of the Giennois's dozen or so producers also cultivate grain and seed-oil crops. One, Langlois, produces rather intense *cassis* from its own plants. Several are major players in other appellations.

PRODUCER RATINGS

OUTSTANDING
Alain Paulat

RECOMMENDED
Balland-Chapuis   Hubert Veneau

BY THE GLASS
Caves de Pouilly-sur-Loire   Langlois Père et Fils
Poupat Père et Fils

OUTSTANDING

Alain Paulat, Villemoison-Saint-Père: I love Paulat's wines. A fortyish rebel and motocross biker with punky black hair and a single earring, Paulat marches to the beat of a different drum. He has five and a quarter hectares of Gamay (60 percent), Pinot Noir, and a bit of Sauvignon Blanc on the chalky soils of south-facing slopes. He practices organic viticulture and hand harvests in small cases. Destemming is not systematic. No yeasts are added. He refuses to doctor a weak vintage with sugar. Vatting lasts about fifteen days. Wines that ferment in stainless steel tanks are pumped over; those in open cement tanks are punched down. The wines age a year in tank and up to seven months in old oak *demi-muids*, which is where the impressive '92s were resting during my last visit in November 1993.

Paulat loves the "virility" of Gamay and makes his for cellaring. I have often mistaken the superb '89 and '90 for Pinot Noir. Supple, smooth, with full, persistent fruit, I am still savoring them in 1995. Paulat's Pinot Noirs are no less impressive, all fine-grained with succulent fruit, and the rosés are firm and fragrant.

Of his style, Paulat says, "I'm against the trend toward finesse. I'm seeking character and rusticity in my wines." But his wines have finesse to spare—along with guts and character.

RECOMMENDED

Balland-Chapuis, Bué: Joseph Balland's family has been making wine in the Sancerrois since 1650. He has eighteen hectares in that appellation; from his wife's family (Chapuis), he got a couple of parcels in Bonny-sur-Loire in the Giennois which he built up to sixteen hectares. I find Balland's Giennois more interesting than his Sancerres. The whites and rosés (Gamay) often have an intriguing basil-mint-fennel character; the Pinot Noir–based reds are sometimes accented with orange and tangerine zests. But Balland could make better wine in both appellations if he were more rigorous about tried-and-true methods of viticulture and vinification (lower yields, for example) rather than infatuated with trends—as evidenced by the late-harvest Sauvignon he makes from his Bonny vineyards in great vintages like '89 and '90. Fermented and aged in new oak, it is off-dry (4 grams residual sugar), ripe, and honeyed, with flavors of hay, fruit, toast, and coffee beans. Interesting, if a bit heavy-handed.

Hubert Veneau, Saint-Père: Veneau, a man's man, is a good ol' boy with twenty-two hectares of vines in Pouilly, twelve on south-facing slopes and plateaus in the Giennois, and another seventy-five devoted to grain crops. He makes average wines in each appellation. The most interesting are his Giennois Pinot Noirs. Partially aged in newish oak, they are not big wines, but they have charming cherry-vanilla flavors. Chilled, they'd be pleasant company in a wine bar.

BY THE GLASS

Caves de Pouilly-sur-Loire (Pouilly): Light but pleasant Giennois wines.

Langlois Père et Fils, Pougny: Full-flavored Giennois wines with some rough edges. Intense *crème de cassis*.

Poupat Père et Fils, Gien: The only producers in Gien—and downtown Gien, at that. The wines are rather diluted.

VINS DE L'ORLEANAIS

STATUS: *VDQS 1951*
TYPES OF WINE: *White, red, and rosé*
ZONE AND PRODUCTION: *3,000 to 7,000 hectoliters, made on 146 hectares spanning thirty communes*
GRAPES: *Pinot Meunier (here Gris Meunier); Pinot Noir and Chardonnay (here Auvernat Noir and Blanc); Cabernet Franc*
SOILS: *A mix of clay and sand, gravel, or flint, with outcroppings of chalk*
PRICE: *15 to 17ff*
BEST VINTAGES: *'95, '90*

Situated at the bend of the Loire, as the river curves from its north-south axis to an east-west orientation, Orléans was a major shipping port in the days of transport by river. Conveniently close to Paris, the city was favored by the Capetian kings who used it as a base. And over the course of nearly twelve hundred years, its wines furnished the royal tables as well as those of the bourgeois and the workingman from the Beauce to the Ile-de-France.

Already important in the sixth century, the Orléanais vineyards continued to expand throughout the Middle Ages. Rabelais rated the wines as highly as the *crus* of Beaune. Olivier de Serres placed its "delicious and pleasant" reds among the best in the realm. And in the seventeenth century, notes Roger Dion, the Orléanais vineyard was comparable in power and wealth to contemporary Bordeaux. Before the advent of railroads enabled the shipping of wines from the Midi and Algeria to Paris, and before its vineyards were attacked by phylloxera, the Orléanais had some 20,000 hectares of vines. The expansion of the city of Orléans ate up more vineyards; still others, with colder soils, were turned to cereal crops. Today the VDQS area is a thin, sheltered band—three or four kilometers wide—extending along the banks of the Loire for some sixty kilometers, alternating with market gardens, asparagus patches, and orchards.

In their golden age, the wines of the Orléanais were made from Auvernat Noir—Pinot Noir—which was replaced by Pinot Meunier (Gris Meunier in the region), as well as lesser, higher-yielding grapes, when vignerons sought more productive varieties to meet the demands of Paris's burgeoning need for cheap wines. Gris Meunier is still the appellation's leader. Cabernet Franc places a close second, followed by Auvernat Blanc (Chardonnay) and Auvernat Noir.

Both Gris Meunier and Auvernat Noir can make delicious and characterful light reds. Later-maturing Cabernet Franc, even in ripe years, comes across as lean and bell-peppery—though vignerons like working with it as it is less fragile than the Pinots and more structured and tannic. (A separate appellation, Orléans-Cléry, which will apply only to reds made from Cabernet Franc made within five communes south of the Loire, is in the works.)

Gris Meunier and Pinot Noir tend to vat less than a week; Cabernet, slightly longer. Rosés are made by bleeding the Gris Meunier vats. For me, the Orléanais is about one wine, Gris Meunier, which I love for its sprightliness, its juicy flavors, its uniqueness. The INAO, however, has been encouraging (mandating) blends of Gris Meunier and Pinot Noir. They're not bad at all; they're even fleshier than pure Gris Meunier and probably more commercial. They're just slightly more banal than the varietal versions.

All of the region's growers are farmers who cultivate fruit trees, vegetables, and grain crops as well as vines. Two cooperatives, Les Vignerons de la Grand'Maison and Covifruit, make 80 percent of Orléanais wine.

✧ PRODUCER RATINGS ✧

HIGHLY RECOMMENDED
Clos de Saint-Fiacre   Jacky Legroux

TASTED IN PASSING WITH PLEASURE
Javoy Père et Fils

BY THE GLASS
Covifruit   Lucien Harnois   Les Vignerons de la Grand'Maison

✧ ✧

HIGHLY RECOMMENDED

Clos de Saint-Fiacre, Mareau-aux-Prés: When I arrived for our interview, Daniel Montigny, the president of the growers' *syndicat* and its leading producer, was harvesting root celery. Its aroma filled the barn. Crates of apples were stacked at the entry. Most of his revenue, however, comes from seventeen hectares of vines. And investments in the cellar—machine harvester, stainless steel tanks—show it.

Montigny's most attractive wines are the light reds from Gris Meunier and Auvernat Noir—or, increasingly, a blend of the two. The blends are seductive light bistro reds, mostly expressive of the Meunier in their makeup. With their lively cherry and cherry pit fruit, they are perfect for wine-bar lunches, picnics, fresh goat cheese. The Auvernat Blanc is a pleasant, light Chardonnay. The Cabernet is too bell-peppery for me.

Jacky Legroux, Mareau-aux-Près: Down the road a piece from Daniel Montigny (with whom he shares equipment), Jacky Legroux has nine and a half hectares of vines within four communes. We tasted amid crates of potatoes, apples, and bottles of Legroux's apple juice (rather like *premier cru* Mott's). I love the Gris Meunier and I admire the kirschy Pinot Noir (though the Meunier was more delicate, finer). The other wines are acceptable; more interesting is an experimental fruit juice of Cabernet.

TASTED IN PASSING WITH PLEASURE

Javoy Père et Fils, Mézières-lez-Cléry: Dependably delicious Orléanais wines in all three colors.

BY THE GLASS

Covifruit, Olivet: The *eau-de-vie de poire* is quite tasty; the Orléanais wines are fair.

Lucien Harnois, Cléry-Saint-André: Somewhat rustic though interesting Orléanais wines.

Les Vignerons de la Grand'Maison, Mareau-aux-Prés: Respectable, if somewhat bland, Orléanais wines.

THE SANCERRE TABLE

"One doesn't dine more luxuriously in Berry than one does in Paris, but one dines better," said Honoré de Balzac. Indeed, the hearty, frank cooking—the long-simmered stews, the succulent game, the abundance of wild mushrooms, the stick-to-the-ribs potato pies and caramelized-apple tarts—makes Berry and neighboring Sologne my favorite gastronomic region in the Loire.

Sologne links the Orléanais and Beauce (France's granary) with Berry, which, in turn, is the doorway to Limousin and Auvergne. Gone are the soft skies, the gentle hills, and the poplar-lined routes of Touraine. The landscape here is grayer, sadder, more haunting. The cooking is heavier and more rustic. The two most emblematic dishes—Sologne's *civet de lièvre*, a rich hare stew, and Berry's *poulet en barbouille*, an equally rich chicken dish—resemble the blood-thickened stews of Touraine but are, for no readily apparent reason, more filling. The word *barbouille*, perhaps, reveals the Berrichon spirit: It implies that the dish is so delicious that eaters make messes of themselves by going at it with all fingers—a distinctly un-French thing to do!

Other classic dishes are simply and clearly heavier. *Boulettes*, Berry's little hand grenades for the stomach, are essentially well-seasoned meatballs of ground pork, veal, and beef; potatoes; and egg. Local carp is traditionally stuffed with sausage, carp roe, bread crumbs soaked in milk, hard-boiled eggs, potatoes, shallots, mushrooms, onions, and herbs. The fish is sewn up, placed on a bed of mushrooms (or carrots) and onions, and doused with wine and butter and cooked for an hour and a half.

Finally, there's the ubiquitous potato pie. Never a major player in the western Loire, the potato begins to move center stage in Berry, foreshadowing the role it will have in Auvergne. And the most popular of Berry's many potato dishes is the *pâté* (or *galette*) *de pommes de terre*. This is usually a large disk-shaped, double-crusted pie made of puff pastry or short-crust pastry encasing well-seasoned potatoes, often blended with *fromage blanc*. After the pie is taken from the oven, crème fraîche is poured through the hole in the center of the crust. The recipe can be altered by kneading together the filling and the dough, and many cooks add ham or bacon, though purists claim that turns the dish into a *tourte*.

The potato pie touches on two other themes in local cooking. Cream is used with more abandon here than in Touraine—it is poured into most pies—and there is a large variety of *galettes*, *tourtes*, and *tartes*, both savory and sweet. *Citrouillat*, or *pâté à la citrouille*, is a savory pumpkin pie made like the potato version. (Sologne is an important pumpkin-growing region.) The pumpkin meat is diced and left to macerate overnight with chopped onions, parsley, and garlic. *Chaussons* (turnovers) or *galettes* filled with chèvre are also popular.

A bit north of the wine route is the town of Pithiviers from which hails the dessert *galette* of the same name, a sandwich of puff pastry, this one filled with almond frangipane. Encasing terrines *en croûte*—particularly terrines made of game—is a specialty of the Orléanais that drifts into Berry as well. *Pâté de Pâques* is also called *pâté à la oeu* (with eggs): A lard-based pastry encloses a terrine of pork, veal, kid, and hard-boiled eggs. A lighter version uses a butter-based crust or may omit the crust entirely. *Tourte Berrichonne* is made with potatoes, onions, and eggs; another local *tourte* uses mushrooms, cream, and ham. Sweet pies are made with pumpkin, pear, plum, and apple. The most famous, *tarte Tatin*, specifies Orléans's *reinette* apples.

The ponds of Sologne and the streams of Berry teem with freshwater fish—carp, pike, eel, lamprey. These are essentially prepared as they are in the rest of the Loire, with occasional regional variations. Pike *à l'Orléanaise*, for example, is seasoned with vinegar, recalling that city's days as a vinegar capital.

Carp seems to inspire more recipes than any other local fish. It is grilled, braised in red wine, encased in aspic, poached and served with mayonnaise while still hot; it's sliced, floured, and fried, or it's cut into steaks and sauced with red wine. Often it is stuffed, its filling some variation on the recipe described above. But perhaps the most historic stuffed carp recipe is *carpe à la Chambord*, which probably dates from the time of François Ier.

An avid hunter, François built the Château of Chambord in an iso-lated, marshy area typical of Sologne. Its only charm was its plentiful game. The dish—which called for stuffing the fish with sweetbreads and tiny game birds, cooking it for two hours in white wine, and serving it surrounded by woodcock, partridge, and quail—celebrates a return from the hunt.

Sologne's game forests cover 40 percent of the region and are among the best in France. In addition to serving as a base for terrines, wine-laced stews, and civets, the catch may be baked, grilled, or roasted. It may be stuffed with chestnuts or walnuts or garnished with cabbage. Small birds, like woodcocks, are larded, roasted, then stuffed with mashed livers, crème fraîche, and *eau-de-vie*, and cooked again.

Berry also leads France's regions in the cultivation of lentils as well as seed-oil crops; Sologne leads in asparagus production and is also known for strawberries and *cornichons*. The latter are added to pork cutlets cooked with red wine and *eau-de-vie*, as well as to beef tongue cooked with tomato, red wine, and cloves. Berrichons once raised sheep for their wool. The meat seems to have been appreciated, too; no longer wool producers, Berrichons still enjoy *gigot à la sept heures* (lamb cooked slowly for seven hours), lamb with white beans, and a variety of lamb stews. The pig is eaten with equal enthusiasm: *saupiquet* is braised ham in a shallot, tar-ragon, white wine, and cream sauce; *crépinettes* (sausage patties enveloped in caul fat) are cooked with wine, cream, onions, garlic, and herbs; *sanguettes* resemble *boudins noirs*. *Andouillettes* are usually grilled but may also be served with a sauce of crème fraîche, mustard, shallots, and local white wine or *eau-de-vie*.

Local fruit dominates the dessert repertory. *Cotignac* is a paste of quince made with or without apples; it is eaten on its own or with fresh cheese. *Poirat* is a covered pie filled with pears, seasoned with pear *eau-de-vie*, sugar, cinnamon, and pepper, and doused with cream. Aside from *tarte Tatin*, Orléans's *reinette* apples are also made into cakes, *beignets* or *beugnons*, cooked in a thick crêpe batter. Berry borders on Limousin and desserts such as *gouère* (made with *reinettes*) and *millat de Levroux* (with black cherries) are basically *clafouti*. *Sanciaux* are thick crêpes served at Mardi Gras—or any-time, in my experience.

Honey from the Gatinais (in the Orléanais) is incorporated into many confections, and there are several indigenous candies. A confectioner from Issoudun, frequented by Balzac, introduced local marzipan to Parisians in 1884. The town of Montargis, slightly off the wine route, is the birthplace of the *praline*, or *prasline*, an almond coated in caramelized sugar. The recipe, which dates from 1630, comes from the chef of the Comte de Plessis-Praslin. So successful were the candies that the cook left the count's kitchens and opened a shop nearby, in the center of Montargis, called Maison de la Prasline, which still exists today.

Cheese is generally featured in contemporary meals. Several interesting sheep's- and cow's-milk cheeses are made in the region, but the Sancerrois is truly chèvre country. It gives the Loire its most famous goat cheese of all, the pungent small drum called Crottin de Chavignol.

According to producers, hot *chèvre*—with or without a salad—is not traditional; it was "invented" in Paris in the 1970s, but most Sancerrois restaurants now serve it. *Fromagée*, however, is traditional: A popular appetizer or snack, it is fresh cheese (usually goat) mixed with chives and shallots or garlic. It goes very nicely with a glass of fresh Sancerre (in any color) or Chasselas. And every single one of the local wines—but particularly the region's best Sauvignons—goes sublimely well with a chunk of nicely aged farmhouse Crottin.

Crottin de Chavignol and Company

Records show that goats have grazed the chalky hills and plains around Chavignol since the sixteenth century (though they are believed to have been present here much longer). Since 1829 the cheese they produce has been called Crottin de Chavignol. Officials say the name comes from a terra-cotta oil lamp that had the same form as the mold used for making the cheese. A more popular theory says that it comes from the word for horse or mule dung, *crotte*, which corresponds to the way the cheese originally looked and tasted: The shape of a bullet, it was black, hard, and barely edible.

Today's Crottin de Chavignol is a small, flat drum that weighs about 60 grams (2 ounces). The *appellation contrôlée*, which dates from 1976, extended the original cheesemaking area to include most of the Cher department as well as parts of the Loiret and the Nièvre. Crottin de Chavignol must be made of whole goat's milk (frozen curds are permitted but Crottins made from them may not be labeled "Fermier"). Some producers drain the curds on cloth before ladling it into molds, a practice unique to this region. By law, Crottin de Chavignol must age for at least ten days, but it is at its most classic at twenty to twenty-five days when its crust is nicely bluish. (Younger chèvres used to go by the name Sancerrois, but the INAO now forbids the use of other place names for chèvres made in the Crottin de Chavignol area.)

Another traditional way of serving Crottin is *repassé:* Dry cheeses are piled one on top of another in an earthenware or glass jar for a month or longer until they look humid and squishy. Their flavor is almost too pungent for wine; a marc might be more appropriate.

Crottins originally were made by wives of farmers or vignerons who used the cheese from their small herds of three to twenty goats to help sell their wine. Today 15 percent (up from 5 percent in 1990) of the appellation's twenty million cheeses is sold by the person who made them. Another 55 percent is sold by large dairies like Triballat, and 30 percent by *affineurs* who collect fresh cheeses from producers, and then salt, mold, and ripen them for at least a week.

HIGHLY RECOMMENDED LARGE PRODUCERS AND *AFFINEURS*

Claude Crochet, Bué: Laurent Crochet, sixth-generation *affineur*, collects fresh cheeses from some thirty farmers and turns out one million Crottins de Chavignol a year. I've tasted all stages and found them all extremely good. Crochet also has a boutique on a side street in Sancerre.

Dubois-Bouley, Chavignol: Gilles Dubois's grandmother made Crottins to sell with her husband's wine. Sales were so good that she started collecting cheeses from others. Now Gilles works with eighty suppliers. At his modern plant, eight women salt the newly arrived cheeses; others staff the pleasant shop in which Crottins at all stages of *affinage* are displayed. A *repassé*, aged for several months, has a texture reminiscent of Brie and a strong, rich flavor. An ultra-sec, also aged for several months, is powerful and nutty. My favorite was the classic three-week-old Crottin, which was delicious.

Domaine du Port Aubry, Cosne: Emmanuel Melet has four hundred goats, a well-equipped, modern dairy, and thirty hectares of clover and alfafa. His Crottins are fruity, acidulated, and tasty—and they often win awards. Melet also makes a wonderful Tomme de Chèvre, a large, fresh cheese which he sells by the slice; terrific year-old Crottins steeped in a blend of walnut and soy oils with a branch of thyme; and very old, very strong *terrine de fromage* or *fromage du diable* in the style of cheeses his grandmother made from chèvres that were flawed or over-the-hill.

Michel Chamaillard, Santranges: A friendly cheesemonger at Gien's Saturday market and Cosne's Sunday market, Chamaillard has funky Crottins of all ages. Young ones taste farmy and grassy. Some old orange-tinged versions were too hard and reeky for me. Chamaillard also carries a local cow's-milk cheese that he names after his town, Santranges. It is fresh and mellow.

HIGHLY RECOMMENDED SMALL PRODUCERS

Domaine des Rouches, Saint-Bouize: Xavier Maîtrepierre lets his goats pasture in the open air. He delivers most cheeses to Dubois but ages 5 to 10 percent himself. They're terrific.

Jacques Dépigny, Nérondes: This youngish producer is a favorite of the enthusiastic new director of the Crottin *syndicat*.

Gilbert Houzier, Ménétréol: Creamy, flavory Crottins, sometimes too salty but usually with fine lemon and hazelnut notes.

Philippe Jay, Jars: Dependable, award-winning Crottins.

Edgar Roger, Neuvy-Deux-Clochers: Milky, soothing Crottins with green-olive notes.

Annie Samson, Veaugues: The favorite of most local Crottin buffs.

OTHER

Michel Denizot, Chavignol: Unfortunately, the first Crottin shop you see on entering Chavignol is Denizot's. In 1990 he was convicted of fraud for selling Crottins made from foreign milk as Crottin de Chavinol.

Fromagerie des Pelets, Morogues: Not a favorite of mine, but several knowledgeable cheesemongers swear by it.

From the Orléanais comes Olivet, a cow's-milk cheese shaped like a large Camembert, as well as two sheep's-milk cheeses, Capécieux and Blason d'Orléans. And at markets throughout the region, there are goat's- and cow's-milk cheeses bearing whatever name the vendor desires.

Olivet takes its name from the town in whose tuffeau caves the cheeses were matured. Traditionally the cheeses were covered with ash, or placed on hay, or wrapped in plane tree leaves for aging, giving rise to the Olivet sub-types *cendré, au foin,* or *bleu.* Increasingly, Olivets have the bloomy white rind of Camembert, the ash, hay, or leaves having become mainly decorative.

M. Lavarenne, Orléans: A reputable *affineur* with excellent artisanal Olivets—supple, straw yellow, lightly pungent with fruity, nutty flavors.

Elevage de Maison Neuve, Châtillon-sur-Loire: A producer of two interesting sheep's-milk cheeses, Capécieux, a pungent, nicely sharp cheese shaped like a long roll and aged for two months, and Blason d'Orléans, a washed-rind cheese shaped like a square with rounded edges, that is unctuous, ripe, and supple.

Vinegar

When the Loire was a main commercial artery between Nantes and Paris, boats unloaded their goods at Orléans, the port closest to the capital. Wines represented a good part of any shipment, and those that had turned during the journey were left on the docks. As early as the fourteenth century the Orléanais began transforming the soured wine into vinegar. The advent of railroads and Pasteur's experiments with vinegar, which led to methods of speeding production as well as the ability to manufacture in bulk, nearly annihilated the local craft. At the turn of the century the city had two hundred artisanal vinegar makers. Today there is only one, Martin-Pouret.

The company, founded by Emile Pouret in 1797, is run by great-grandson Jean-François Martin. Martin-Pouret's vinegar starts with good wine from small *domaines* in Chinon and Bourgueil in the Loire as well as Bordeaux and Champagne. It takes three weeks for the wine to be transformed into vinegar, which will then age for another six months in larger oak barrels to develop its aromas and round off its rough edges. The firm turns out fifty liters of vinegar every three weeks. Companies using industrial methods can produce 30,000 liters in two days.

Oak age also lowers the vinegar's acidity. A Martin-Pouret vinegar is 7 percent acetic acid compared with the normal 6 percent. Martin explains that large companies often reduce acidity by adding water to the vinegar (making it blander) and that even at one degree higher, his vinegar tastes smoother, less raw, because the flavors of oak and old wine dominate—which is true.

VIII

The Auvergne

Wₑ have traveled a long way from the *douceur* of archetypal Loire to the rugged terrain of a more insular Loire. Paralleling the Saône and the Rhône rivers, this Loire takes us across mountain ranges and extinct volcanoes to spas and hot springs, through the forests of Allier and Tronçais, past fields of wheat and lentils and pastures where France's famous Charollais cattle graze. It is a land of a thousand potato dishes, of hard sausages and strong mountain cheeses.

Left off the official Loire wine map (which stops after the Sancerrois), the wines of this region resemble those of Beaujolais. Gamay is the principal grape, and the wines it makes here are hearty, easygoing, fruity, and occasionally more.

There are four wine zones: Saint-Pourçain is in the Allier department (hard by the source of oak for the world's most sought-after barrels). Due south is Côtes d'Auvergne in the Puy-de-Dôme department. The Côte Roannaise (in the backyard of restaurant Troisgros whose chef-owner has invested in a two-hectare vineyard) and the Côtes du Forez (outside Montbrison) are in the department of the Loire. The Côte Roannaise, formerly VDQS, received AOC in 1994; the others are still VDQS, though each has applied for similar upgrading to AOC.

Obscure, confidential, each was once a thriving wine region. In the Middle Ages, the wines of Saint-Pourçain were as prestigious as those of Beaune. They traveled by the Allier and the Loire to Paris. The wines of Forez and those of Auvergne flourished when the mountains were densely populated. As transport of goods by river declined, Saint-Pourçain's star faded. And when children left the mountains for cities, the little wines lost their built-in markets.

If latitude were all, the four might still prosper as they did in the nineteenth century. Saint-Pourçain and the Côte Roannaise are roughly due west of Macon; the Côtes d'Auvergne and the Côtes du Forez look east to Lyons. Altitude, however, exacerbates the severity of Burgundy's rigorous continental climate; winters are rude, summers short, rainfall abundant, and frost a constant threat. Appellations, therefore, are designated almost slope by slope, parcel by parcel, demarcating alluvial terraces and sunny, sheltered hillsides with well-drained soils, generally granitic or volcanic in origin.

In addition to Gamay, the region's wines are made principally from Pinot Noir and Chardonnay. There are small amounts of Sauvignon Blanc and Aligoté, generally used for blending, and a smattering of local varieties of which Tressallier, cultivated in Saint-Pourçain, is the only one of any continuing importance. All of the above varieties, as well as Viognier, may also be used in regional Vins de Pays. Those made in the Loire department are called Vin de Pays d'Urfé, named after the writer Honoré d'Urfé.

Today all four regions are witnessing something of a rebirth. In Saint-Pourçain and the Côtes d'Auvergne, sons are returning to the family property after having studied viticulture and enology at Beaune. They invest in cellars, buy new equipment, and are intent on making serious wine. The Côtes du Forez, where the co-op produces nearly all the appellation's wine, appears the least dynamic. The most exciting for me is the Côte Roannaise, which seems the most blessed by nature to produce world-class wine. The Gamays from this region—which could, and surely will, be a lot better—are already silky and fine-grained, mouth-watering blends of fruit and minerals.

COTES D'AUVERGNE

STATUS: *VDQS 1977*
TYPES OF WINE: *Red, white, and rosé*
ZONE AND PRODUCTION: *20,630 hectoliters, made on 420 hectares within*

54 communes from Clermont-Ferrand to Issoire, mostly on south-facing slopes between 350 and 400 meters high. Most is red.
GRAPES: *Whites—Chardonnay; reds and rosés—Gamay, Pinot Noir*
SOILS: *A variety, including sand, granite, chalk, marl, and decomposed volcanic rock, primarily basalt*
PRICES: *22 to 35ff*
BEST VINTAGES: *'95, '90, some '94s*

Posters of Auvergne rarely show its vineyards, opting instead for apocalyptic vistas of the extinct volcanoes of the Massif Central; *Sound of Music* landscapes of cows grazing on green mountain pastures; clear, deep mountain lakes; or the eerie, explicit sculptures of its isolated Romanesque churches. Indeed, it is surprising to find vines in such a rugged environment. Yet wrought-iron balconies on town houses in Clermont-Ferrand bear witness to the region's once-lucrative wine trade, when 50,000 hectares of vines covered its slopes.

The wine industry in Auvergne today is in the early stages of rebirth, but progress is constant and encouraging. When I first visited the Côtes d'Auvergne in 1990, I left feeling that, despite anecdotal exceptions, the findings of an earlier government study still hit the mark: "They [Auvergne wines] are traditionally deeply colored, meaty, and robust. Their rusticity well matches the nature of the men, the landscape, and the cooking."

Since that time, however, I've witnessed a rapid evolution in quality as well as significant investments in vineyards and cellars—as evidenced by the cooperative. The wines, quickly losing their rusticity, are becoming, if anything, too modern—crisp, fragrant, New World varietals, perhaps scented with notes of new oak. (This, too, will pass, as vintners find their own styles.)

Most of the wines are reds based on Gamay. They are usually made by semi-carbonic maceration, vatting for four or five days, or more, in all manner of tanks. They often have a bit of carbon dioxide—because the vignerons want it that way. Pinot Noir and Chardonnay are often aged in new Tronçais barrels.

A number of the best communes—including Boudes, Corent, Châteaugay, and Chanturgue—may add their names to that of Côtes d'Auvergne on the label. And indeed, wines from these areas are among the most impressive, particularly the fragrant rosés from the clay-chalk soils of Corent and the juicy, structured reds from the volcanic soils of Châteaugay and clay-

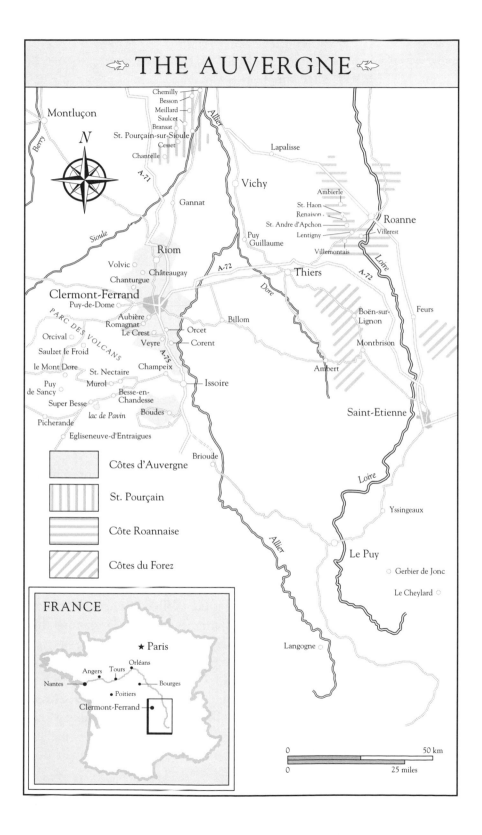

THE AUVERGNE

Montluçon

N

Chemilly
Besson
Meillard
Saulcet
Bransat
St. Pourçain-sur-Sioule
Cesset
Chantelle

Allier

Lapalisse

Vichy

A-71

Gannat

Ambierle
St. Haon
Renaison
St. Andre d'Apchon
Lentigny

Roanne
Villerest

Sioule

Puy
Guillaume

Villemontais

Loire

Riom

A-72

Thiers

A-72

Volvic
Chanturgue

Châteaugay

Dore

Boën-sur-
Lignon

Feurs

Clermont-Ferrand
Puy-de-Dome

Billom

PARC DES VOLCANS

Aubière
Romagnat
Le Crest
Veyre

Orcet

Corent

Montbrison

Orcival

Saulzet le Froid

le Mont Dore

Champeix

A-75

St. Nectaire

Ambert

Puy
de Sancy

Murol

Issoire

Besse-en-
Chandesse

Saint-Etienne

Super Besse

lac de Pavin

Boudes

Picherande

Egliseneuve-d'Entraigues

Brioude

Côtes d'Auvergne

St. Pourçain

Côte Roannaise

Côtes du Forez

Loire

Yssingeaux

Allier

Le Puy

Gerbier de Jonc

Le Cheylard

Langogne

FRANCE

★ Paris

Orléans

Angers
Tours

Nantes

Bourges

Poitiers

Clermont-Ferrand

0   50 km

0   25 miles

chalk soils of Chanturgue. I put Madargues in this category, too, though I'm not sure whether it's a question of *terroir* (Madargues's soils are a crazy quilt of Puy-de-Dôme sedimentation) or of a particularly good vigneron, in this case Bernard Boulin.

⊰ PRODUCER RATINGS ⊱

LEADER
Michel Bellard

EXCELLENT
Boulin-Constant

TO WATCH
Cave Saint-Verny   Domaine Sauvat   Pierre Goigoux

HIGHLY RECOMMENDED
Domaine de Sous-Tournoël

⊰ ⊱

LEADER

Michel Bellard, **Romagnat:** If you want local color, show up here for the Saturday-morning open house. Bellard, who looks like a boozy Philippe Noiret, holds court behind the tasting bar. Bellied up when I visited were a solicitor, a psychologist, the local Dom Ruinart rep, and a rugby director, all downing glass after glass while cutting into rounds of Saint-Nectaire, sausages, and country bread.

Bellard is nobody's fool. With fifty hectares spread over ten communes, as well as a seven-hectare vineyard in Saint-Pourçain, he's the Auvergne's biggest private producer and its most visible. While his wines can taste watery in difficult vintages like '94, most are pleasant quaffers, among them a generic Côtes d'Auvergne (a light, kirschy red with licorice notes); Chanturgue (soft, beefy, and chewy, with flavors of kirsch and cherries, fine for a noisy bistro); Châteaugay (red and white); Corent rosé (vinous, with hints of candied orange peel); Sauvignon Blanc (thin and rough); a *mousseux* and several proprietary *cuvées*, including a late-harvest white, a blend of Muscat and Chasselas. His most unusual wine is his *vin de paille,* a Gamay picked a month after the normal harvest, dried for two weeks on straw mats in an attic, and pressed at around 15 percent potential alcohol. The alcohol is raised to 17 percent with sugar. Lightly sweet, it's medicinal, nutty, rather strange and original. Bellard thinks he can get an appellation for it because the wine was served with dessert at the baptism of Napoléon III.

EXCELLENT

Boulin-Constant, **Riom:** Bernard Boulin, a beefy Clermont native with the up-front manner of a New York bartender, is a former Michelin worker who, for pleasure, drank Burgundy and read the works of respected Bordeaux enologists Ribéreau-Gayon and Emile Peynaud. In 1976 he found some vines and a decrepit cellar, quit his job, and now makes powerful yet fine-grained Madargues Gamays and Pinot Noirs. Grapes from his eight and a half hectares are hand harvested and vat for twenty-one days. Pinot Noir ages for eight months in new Tronçais barrels. The lightly tart '94 Cuvée des Grandes Heures, an exceedingly agreeable blend of plum, cherry, and oak, may not be Romanée-Conti but it's real nice drinking. Richer vintages, like '89 and '90, are even better.

TO WATCH

Cave Saint-Verny, **Veyre-Monton:** The co-op, founded in 1950, has 308 members and produces about half the wine in the Côtes d'Auvergne. In 1991 it became part of Limagrain, Europe's largest seed specialist, who invested fifteen million francs to rebuild the cellars and equip them with computer-controlled stainless steel tanks and pneumatic presses. There's a new outlook, too, and it's a good one: Lower yields are mandated, and higher pay is given for ripe, healthy grapes.

In the summer of 1995, the Cave was selling '92s and '93s. The '93 white Première Cuvée was a perfect example of the new style of wine. A sleek, appley Chardonnay, it was crisp, clean, and attractive. The '92 red Première Cuvée was suave, light, with attractive cherry, tobacco, and spice flavors. My only disappointment was the '93 Corent rosé, which was floral but a bit neutral. The co-op, situated at the base of the Corent hills, produces nearly all of that commune's wines. I preferred the characterful, fragrant rosés of its previous incarnation.

Domaine Sauvat, **Boudes:** Thirtysomething Claude and Annie Sauvat are ambitious and conscientious. Their winery, created in 1987, consists of nine hectares of vines, predominantly Gamay. The Sauvats harvest by *tri*, then cull the best from that selection on a sorting table. The wines ferment in stainless steel tanks; the Chardonnay and some of the Pinot Noir age in oak barrels. The wines are tasty and will surely improve as the Sauvats refine their craft. The oak was a bit too pronounced in the otherwise impressive '93 Boudes, a clean, tasty Chardonnay. The '93 red, also slightly oaky, was fetching and could give many a Sancerre rouge a run for the money.

Pierre Goigoux, Châteaugay: This spirited twenty-eight-year-old studied in Mâcon and Beaune, then created an eight-hectare *domaine*, starting with the family garden. He's sure of Auvergne's potential and sure he can meet the challenge. Goigoux makes both Châteaugay and Chanturgue, red and white. I prefer his gutsy, pretty reds and have a weakness for the Châteaugay: The '94 was vibrant, with focused blackberry, blueberry flavors. An '89 was jammy and rich, with flavors of cherry, cherry pits, and kirsch.

HIGHLY RECOMMENDED

Domaine de Sous-Tournoël, Volvic: Jean Gaudet, who works with son Alain, is elegant and sentimental. He speaks of the days when the thirst of Volvic's lava workers made wine a profitable local industry. He makes wine the old-fashioned way, harvesting in old buckets, using a gentle old screw press, and vinifying in old barrels. His apricot- and nut-flavored rosés and supple, kirschy reds are rustic, but charming and personal.

COTES DU FOREZ

STATUS: *VDQS 1956*
TYPES OF WINE: *Red and rosé*
ZONE AND PRODUCTION: *Approaching near-term goal of 10,000 hectoliters, from 200 hectares within twenty-one communes around Montbrison, occupying east- or southeast-facing slopes at altitudes of between 400 to 600 meters*
GRAPES: *Gamay*
SOILS: *Decomposed granite, with outcroppings of volcanic rocks such as basalt*
PRICE: *12 to 25ff*
BEST VINTAGES: *'95*

Urbanization has eaten up some of the Côtes du Forez's best slopes, particularly in communes such as Boën-sur-Lignon, which is considered the capital of Forez wine. Essentially, this is dairy country. During lunch at the Auberge de Trelins, around the corner and up the hill from the co-op (which produces nearly all of the appellation's wine), the talk at other tables was of cows—of milk, of dairies, and of dairy cooperatives.

Côtes du Forez wines are Beaujolais-style Gamays. They are pleasant to drink young and fresh. In very ripe years, locals say you can taste the sun of the Midi.

Les Vignerons Foreziens, Trelins: The cooperative, which released its first wine in 1962, makes 98 percent of Côtes du Forez wines and 60 percent of the Vin du Pays d'Urfé. Nearly all of its two hundred members deliver their entire harvest. Gamay is elaborated in several styles: a rosé; a rather cheesy sparkling wine; and at least four *cuvées* of red, from *primeur* to a richer bottling from volcanic soils. Additionally, the CEO of Le Train Bleu in the Gare de Lyon is a Forezian who serves Forez wines in his restaurant and comes to select his own *cuvée*, which represents 10 percent of the co-op's volume. At their best, the wines are lean and pleasant, though they are sometimes diffuse and watery.

COTE ROANNAISE

STATUS: *AOC 1994*
TYPES OF WINE: *Red and rosé*
ZONE AND PRODUCTION: *Roughly 7,000 hectoliters, made on 150 hectares within twenty-six communes on the outskirts of Roanne, mostly on east- and southeast-facing hillsides. The heart of the zone is around Renaison and Ambierle.*
GRAPES: *Gamay*
SOILS: *Granitic*
PRICES: *15 to 30ff*
BEST VINTAGES: *'95, '93, '90*

Visually, the Côte Roannaise has more in common with Tuscany than with Touraine. It presents a landscape of hilltop villages, of shady church squares and ochre stone houses with terra-cotta tiled roofs and backyards edged with cypresses and bay laurel. Vineyards slope down mountainsides, meeting pine forests and fields of grazing sheep and cattle.

Viticulturally, the Côte Roannaise has much in common with Beaujolais, which lies roughly due east. Its vineyards, some as high as 500 meters, are higher than those of Beaujolais, however, and harvest is a week later—though Gamay seems riper here than in Saint-Pourçain, the Côtes d'Auvergne, or the Côtes du Forez.

Grapes are hand harvested. The hills are too steep for machines, the wineries too small, and the method of vinification—for the most part semi-carbonic—is best done with handpicked grapes placed uncrushed into tanks or wood vats. Vatting lasts from four to ten days.

I find Côte Roannaise wines more beguiling than many Beaujolais. For one, they are handcrafted, not industrial or generic, as many Beaujolais seem to have become. (Over the past five years, however, some Roannaise producers seem to be following the industrial Beaujolais lead.) The aromas of the best Côte Roannaise wines are true to the varietal, not to yeast strains. The style is that of a lovely light red, lean but supple, with fine, precise fruit and an easy elegance.

That said, I find it troubling, at the very least, that the INAO has prohibited the use of grapes other than Gamay. Before Côte Roannaise received its *appellation contrôlée* status, some winemakers habitually blended substantial proportions of Pinot Noir with their Gamay. It is misguided, at best, that the INAO now requires that Côte Roannaise be made solely from Gamay. (One doubts the bona fides behind this condition when, at the same time, the INAO mandates blends of two or three grape varieties for wines classically made from a single grape type—as it is doing in Touraine-Mesland, in the Giennois, and in the Orléanais.) The new law forces some of the best producers to change their way of making wine or to forgo the appellation.

PRODUCER RATINGS

EXCELLENT
Alain Demon

HIGHLY RECOMMENDED
Domaine des Millets   Domaine du Pavillon   Paul Lapandéry

RECOMMENDED
Michel Desormières   Jean-François Pras
Robert Sérol   Philippe et Marcel Vial

BY THE GLASS
Simon Hawkins   Antoine Néron

EXCELLENT

Alain Demon, **Ambierle:** A former factory worker who switched to wine when his company closed, Demon makes fine-grained, succulent Roannaise wines. Every vintage from '88 to '94 is recommended, in both the normal bottling and the richer Réserve made from fifty- to one-hundred-year-old vines. I opt for the '93 over the '94 because the latter exhibited minor traces of earthiness under lush plum and cherry-vanilla fruit, while the suave '93 was all focused fruit flavors with the slightly acidulated finish typical of that vintage. Demon also makes charming mint- and apricot-scented rosés and another serious red. This, from old vines on a parcel excluded from the Roannaise appellation in a recent redelimitation of the zone, ages for six months in oak barrels and is sold as Vin de Pays d'Urfé. The '93 was a satisfying blend of licorice, mint, and spice. Both it and the more vibrantly fruity Réserve Roannaise are light-years away from industrial Gamay.

HIGHLY RECOMMENDED

Domaine des Millets, **Lentigny:** Pierre Gaume, bowing to client demand, produces an increasing amount of Chardonnay (Vin de Pays d'Urfé) of which the '94 offered pleasant, mineral, apple-pineapple flavors and a smidgeon of *terroir*. His Côte Roannaise is far more interesting though, and he makes several *cuvées* of it, each one prettier than the last. The normal bottling of '94 displayed attractive plummy fruit but was somewhat undermined by a hint of earthiness. In richer years, like '89 and '90, I loved the silky, fine-grained Arris, with its clear cherry fruit mingled with spice, musk, and minerals, and the deeper Les Millets. Two serious Gamays.

Domaine du Pavillon, **Ambierle:** Maurice Lutz makes charming, lean reds from his five hectares of vines. But the stars here are the serious rosés. Ambierle was once known for its *vin gris*, and Lutz's versions show why. Macerated for six to eight hours, they are deep, structured, and packed with kirsch and cherry fruit. Wonderful. Even the '94 was rich, firm with fragrant peach notes. Unfortunately, because clients won't buy Roannaise rosés, Lutz is making less and less of this very special wine.

Paul Lapandéry, **Saint-Haon-le-Vieux:** Lapandéry, in his seventies, is a born raconteur who singlehandedly wants to preserve the ancient *paysan* (peasant) traditions of France. In his straw hat and wood sabots, he pulls out the thick dossiers he submitted to the INAO, claiming not only AOC status for Roannaise wines but *cru* status for his own parcel, an eight-hectare vineyard on a hillside above Saint-Haon. Called La Rousselière, it is pitched at a seventy-two-degree angle, too steep for any machine to maneuver.

Because Lapandéry's Côte Roannaise usually consisted of more than 30 percent Pinot Noir and up to 3 percent Chardonnay (which Lapandéry feels refines the wine), the new appellation (which he lobbied so long to win) is, in his words, "a *catastrophe*." He'll obey, but doesn't know what he'll do with his other grapes. (I think they'd sell like hotcakes as Vin de Pays.)

Lapandéry works with son Francisque (Beaune), and even when the Roannaise are pure Gamay, their wines are like no other in the appellation. Yields are as low as those of first-growth Bordeaux, i.e., 25 to 30 hectoliters per hectare. No carbonic maceration here: Lapandéry punches down the cap twice daily during the ten-day vatting. The wines age a year or more in old oak barrels. Lapandéry fines with egg white and does not filter.

It's true that many tasters would find the '93 and one bottle of '88 I tasted too dried out. But another '88, though rustic, was curiously elegant, with clear cherry flavors mixed with oak, spice, and apricot pits. The mellow '94 was a soft weave of dried cherry, caramel, and tobacco; '89 was a velvety blend of wood, cherry, spice, and orange zest. Even when they miss the mark, Lapandéry's wines are honest, specific, and personal. Wines to think about, to chew over.

RECOMMENDED

Michel Desormières, Renaison: In rich vintages, this *domaine*'s best *cuvée*, which comes from the granitic slopes of the Coteau de Montolivet, is truly mouth-watering, with exuberant strawberry and raspberry flavors, plus hints of violet. A great bistro wine.

Jean-François Pras, Saint-Haon-le-Vieux: Young Pras created his four-hectare estate in 1988. Both his '92 and '93 show promise, particularly the latter, a lightly tart Gamay with juicy plum flavors.

Robert Sérol, Renaison: The busy, chatty president of the Côte Roannaise growers' *syndicat*, Sérol has two separate estates. The first, his own, consists of eight hectares of vines. The second, a partnership with restaurateur Pierre Troisgros, consists of two hectares of a slope called Les Blondins, which gives the Sérol-Troisgros collaboration its name. Sérol also bottles a special Vieilles Vignes *cuvée* for Troisgros. Sérol's wines, among the lightest I tasted in the appellation, are sometimes silky and perfumed but otherwise ordinary. The '94s—both Les Blondins and the Cuvée Troisgros—revealed the bright, banana-scented Gamay fruit often associated with Beaujolais Nouveau.

Philippe et Marcel Vial, Saint-André-d'Apchon: The Vial brothers, who recently took over their grandfather's eight and a half hectares, make floral rosés and one particularly attractive *cuvée* of Côte Roannaise, Boutheran, from seventy-year-old vines on a well-exposed slope.

BY THE GLASS

Simon Hawkins, Villemontais: A newcomer with light, pleasant '93s and watery '92s.

Antoine Néron, Villemontais: The Coteau de Rochette bottling is worth trying.

SAINT-POURÇAIN

STATUS: *VDQS 1951*
TYPES OF WINE: *Red, white, and rosé*
ZONE AND PRODUCTION: *Roughly 20,000 hectoliters, made on 506 hectares in twenty communes running along the right bank of the Allier until Saint-Pourçain, then along the Sioule and its tributary the Bouble. Most is red.*
GRAPES: *Reds and rosés—Gamay, Pinot Noir; whites—Chardonnay, Sauvignon, Tressallier (50 percent maximum), Aligoté*
SOILS: *Sand, gravel, chalk, granite, with layers of clay*
PRICE: *15 to 40ff*
BEST VINTAGES: *'95, '90, some '94s*

In the Middle Ages, Saint-Pourçain wines were among the most prestigious in France. Chiefly pale reds with a brownish tinge called *oeil de perdrix* (eye of the partridge) as well as some delicate whites, Saint-Pourçain wines were shipped up the Allier and Loire rivers to Paris, where they furnished the royal table. Philippe le Bel was a particular admirer and his enthusiasm made the wines a must among the nobility. A classification of wines sold in Paris in 1360 placed Saint-Pourçain and Beaune at the top. Nobles settled debts with exclusive merchants by paying with Saint-

Pourçain wines instead of cash. Traveling south, Saint-Pourçain wines furnished the papal cellars; they were poured at the most sacred ceremonies or when the pope received princes or great gentlemen.

While it is unlikely that Saint-Pourçain will ever regain its former glory, the atmosphere here is very much one of renewal. As specialized farming replaces polyculture, Saint-Pourçain's sons get degrees from the Lycée de Beaune and work harvests in California; as cellars are renovated and equipment updated—with new tanks, temperature controls, and, inevitably, machine harvesters (which are now the rule)—the wines have shown progress.

In general, the whites are aromatic and pleasant; some have oxidized notes and very raspy finishes, which are appealing in an Old World sense. They may be made from a single grape variety or, increasingly, from a blend of Chardonnay and Tressallier, and often, Sauvignon Blanc. (Tressallier, also known as Sacy, easily reaches high alcohol levels but often tastes green and is not particularly aromatic. Pure, it tastes something like Sauvignon but is rawer and more aggressive. Its acreage is diminishing in favor of Chardonnay.) Producers generally offer two *cuvées* of Gamay: a light version, with a Beaujolais-style semi-carbonic maceration, and a richer one, which, like the region's Pinot Noir, vats for a week to ten days. (Experiments with aging in new Tronçais barrels are done with Chardonnay and Pinot Noir.) While producers favor their whites, I prefer the sassy, personalized Gamays; the light Pinot Noirs with mellow spices and the gentle approach of country reds that wrap the tongue like a favorite blanket.

⤙ PRODUCER RATINGS ⤚

LEADERS
Domaine de Bellevue   Jean et François Ray
Union des Vignerons de Saint-Pourçain-sur-Sioule

TO WATCH
Domaine de Chassignolles   Joseph et Jean-Pierre Laurent

⤙ ⤚

LEADERS

Domaine de Bellevue, Meillard: The Pétillat family, with seventeen hectares of vines and a firm track record, is one of the pillars of the Saint-

Pourçain wine community. Their wines are served in Paris's Ambassade d'Auvergne as well as the Musée d'Orsay.

Not everything is a winner, but all are solid wine-bar finds. I have particularly liked both the '89 and the '93 Grande Réserve white, with their pronounced Sauvignon notes; the '94 Grande Réserve Pinot Noir, with its pleasant cherry pit flavors; and two different *cuvées* of the '88 Grande Réserve Pinot Noir: the first, silky and pretty, the second, lean and varietal, rather like a very, very light Côte Chalonnaise.

Jean et François Ray, Saulcet: This sixteen-hectare family winery is one of the oldest and most respected in the appellation—and a popular choice among local students for wine apprenticeships. Its white Saint-Pourçains include vinous, nutty blends of Tressallier, Chardonnay, and Sauvignon Blanc which, in the '93 vintage, came across thinner and rawer than the creamy Le Coquillard, made from pure Chardonnay. Ray's Saint-Pourçain rosés (all Gamay) are always pretty; the fragrant '94, with flavors of apricot, is a case in point. Red Saint-Pourçains include light, strawberry-scented Gamays; silkier, more concentrated Gamays from granitic soils, bottled as Cuvée des Gaumes (the '94 offered lots of cherry pit and sour cherry flavors); and a blend of Pinot Noir with one-third Gamay, called La Font Gervin.

Coquillon Vendanges d'Eté is the name the Rays have given to their New World hydromel: Chardonnay grapes whose fermentation has been stopped with honey (from the Rays' production). Interesting, but it's not about to upstage the Gamays.

Union des Vignerons de Saint-Pourçain-sur-Sioule: If you have tasted one Saint-Pourçain wine it is probably the co-op's well-traveled Ficelle. Inspired by a legendary sixteenth-century barkeeper who sold wine in pitchers, the Ficelle's bottle is etched with folkloric depictions of wine-imbibing. When the time came to pay, the barman fixed the price by dipping a multi-knotted string in the pitcher to determine how much had been consumed. The current wine, a Gamay, is made to fit that image of a knock-back light red. It undergoes a three-day vatting and is meant to be served well chilled. Always a good quaffer, the wine was understandably richer in '89 and '90 than it was from '91 to '94, but it is always within the chipper "hi-bye" red wine family.

Founded in 1950, the co-op produces 60 to 65 percent of Saint-Pourçain's wine. Its 160 members bring their entire crop. A new lab and reception room were added in 1994–95, and a new estate, Domaine de Chinière, joined the co-op's extensive portfolio of wines.

The lineup includes a vinous *vin gris* of Gamay; a supple, fruity Réserve Spéciale Gamay; a light, spicy, and sometimes rather elegant Pinot Noir; a gingery, very dry Réserve Spéciale (predominantly Tressallier); several floral "seasonal" whites, such as a Mise de Décembre and a Cuvée Printanière; and two *domaines*, Domaine de Chinière and Domaine de la Croix d'Or, which is my favorite. Each *domaine* produces a red (predominantly Gamay) and a white. Chinière's '94 was thin but had pleasant sour cherry fruit. Croix d'Or was, as usual, richer and more tannic than the co-op's other reds. Whites from Chinière are Chardonnay-Tressallier blends. The '94 was crisp and effective, with fragrant apricot notes and appealing texture. Croix d'Or, which adds Sauvignon and Aligoté to the mix, is often among the best in the appellation; ample, with clean, clear flavors of grapefruit, pineapple, hay, and grass.

TO WATCH

Domaine de Chassignolles, Besson: On their twenty hectares, Bernard Gardien and sons Olivier and Christophe (both Beaune grads) make fresh, vinous blends of Sauvignon and Tressallier and supple bistro Gamays. Olivier, who worked at Mondavi and Iron Horse, ages his Pinot Noir Réserve des Châteaux in new *barriques*. The '94 was engaging, a light, fine-grained red, perfect for a wine-bar lunch or snack.

Joseph et Jean-Pierre Laurent, Saulcet: Jean-Pierre studied at Beaune and did *stages* with Bachelet in Chassagne and Ray in Saint-Pourçain. He's convinced that local wines can age and is orienting production in that direction, fermenting selected *cuvées* of white and aging his best *cuvées* of red in new or newish oak barrels, and releasing them several years after the vintage. In the summer of 1995, the Laurents were selling their best '92s. The white Cuvée Prestige, pure Chardonnay, offered ripe fruit and massive oak flavors. The Laurents recommend drinking it with a strong-flavored cheese, a pairing that might balance the oak. The Gamay, kirschy and tannic, was a good wine-bar red. The Laurents also make ultra-dry, nutty white blends and spicy Pinot Noirs, also aged in oak.

THE AUVERGNE TABLE

My first night in Saint-Pourçain I wandered into a bistro on the river Sioule. A cozy place filled with locals, it fed cheaply but honestly. My appetizer, a *feuilleté au jambon,* was a perfect introduction to the region's hearty fare. In Touraine such a description would surely bring a puff pastry sandwich encasing a shaving of ham and a whisper of hollandaise. At the gateway to Auvergne, however, it consisted of a hash of ham and floury béchamel in a thick crust. I had driven all day; the onset of autumn chilled the September air; the bulky pie was like a big old quilt.

Stick-to-the-ribs cooking is required in Auvergne. Drive from Saint-Pourçain up Le Mont Dore, or from Montbrison up the Monts du Forez, and you feel as if you're climbing to the top of the world. Light shifts dramatically, casting great shadows across a landscape of forests, of isolated villages with astonishing Romanesque churches, of cows herded to summer pastures in the high mountains. Lush green meadows, called *puys,* were formed by extinct volcanoes whose eruptions left deep mountain lakes and whose black lava, used as local building material, gives a rude beauty to market towns such as Besse-en-Chandesse.

Although some sort of public cuisine developed for visitors who came to take cures at spas like Vichy, local cooking here is basic, copious, and hearty, based on potato, pig, and cabbage as well as on bread and cream. It has filtered into mainstream French life, too: At the turn of the century, Auvergnats fled the deprivation and isolation of the mountains and moved to Paris, where they sold coal, wood, and wine and opened cafés. They brought with them not only their mountain cheese and charcuterie but soul food like *aligot* and *potée:* The first is one of the world's great potato dishes; the second is a heartwarming, all-pig variation on pot-au-feu.

One of the more lovable aspects of Auvergnat cooking is the high regard in which it holds the potato. By me, there's nothing you can do wrong to a potato—provided you add enough fat. The potato exists, in large part, to inspire the fat in question to strut its stuff—much the way Peter Martins partnered Suzanne Farrell. In this respect the Auvergnat repertory does not disappoint.

Aligot, mashed potatoes beaten over a flame with fresh cheese (Cantal or Laguiole), butter, and cream until the cheese melts into long strands, is suave, lightly granular, with a light tang of young cheese. Always memorable. More typical of the Cantal region than of the Mont Dore, it is nevertheless eaten throughout Auvergne, as is the Berrichon *pâté de pommes de terre.* While Le Mont Dore does have its own variation on the *aligot* theme—mound the mixture into a dome and gratinée it—its kitchens more typically offer *truffade.* To some, this is merely another form of *aligot.* The *truffades* I've eaten, however, are hash brown–like cakes made of finely sliced potatoes cooked with fresh cheese (usually Cantal), bits of ham, lard, or bacon, perhaps shallots, and salt and pepper; panfried, then flipped like a crêpe; and served accompanied either by a slice of mountain ham or a dandelion salad. A similar dish, *gratin* or *patcha Forezien*, is said to have originated in *jasseries*, the huts in which shepherds made cheese during the summer when the cows grazed the mountain meadows. The Auvergnat *rapée de pommes de terre* recalls a *rösti*—grated potatoes mixed with eggs and browned until a crust forms on each side. Potatoes are also roasted, sautéed in lard, baked in crusts, put in soups and omelets, stuffed with seasoned pork, or mixed with pork and made into sausages. The only plain boiled potatoes I have ever encountered in Auvergne were those accompanying *potée*.

Potée—literally any dish cooked in an earthenware pot—exists in some form or other in many regions. In Auvergne, however, it is something like a national dish. The most stolid version might be Marissou Tourret's, in *La Cuisine Auvergnate*, in which a half dozen parts of the pig—ribs, shank, leg, and so forth—simmer with beans, carrots, celeriac, onion, cabbage, and potato. The meat is served on a platter surrounded by the vegetables. *Potée* can also be soupier—the Auvergnats are major soup eaters—in which case it approaches another Auvergnat classic, *soupe aux choux* (cabbage soup), which inevitably includes either bacon or salt-cured pork called *petit salé*. The latter, served with Puy lentils, is yet another Auvergnat contribution to classic bistro fare.

Pork was the major source of protein in Auvergne, and until recently, each family killed one or two pigs a year. The slaughter was the occasion for *grillades* and a feast of *boudins* and *gogues* while work continued on the serious business of preparing the hard, dry sausages and the hams that are the glory of Auvergnat pig cookery.

Auvergne's *saucissons de montagne* (by law, made above 600 meters) are a mix of pure pork, roughly three parts lean meat to one part fat, plus salt and garlic. Other spices are optional. (Some producers add a glass of red wine.) The sausage dries in well-ventilated rooms for one to five months. (Times vary according to the thickness of the casing, the altitude of the farm, and the nature of the drying room.) *Jambon cru d'Auvergne* benefits from a Label Rouge. In general, the haunch is rubbed with salt (some also use pepper, and some saltpeter) and then spends thirty to fifty days in a salting tub. The salt is knocked off and the ham is put in a drying shed or an attic to dry for roughly five months. At this point it may be eaten, though many producers go one step further, burying the ham in wood ash and aging it in a cool cellar for up to two years. The ash protects the ham from air and pests and adds a smoky nuance to the flavor. A particularly delicious variation on this theme ends the process by cooking the ham in hay for three hours.

Often the butt of French jokes about avarice, Auvergnats use every last bit of leftovers as well as every last scrap of the pig. Remains of the *potée* are used to stuff cabbage and form the base of *le Pounti*, a kind of meat loaf, with Swiss chard, milk, onion, parsley, prunes, eggs, and herbs. Pâté de foie employs a third each of lard, liver, and leftover meat. *Grattons* (cracklings) may be baked into brioches or mounded into a block to form a type of rillettes. The snout might be cooked and served on lentils; the ear, made into a "*fromage*," particularly around Ambert. In the Saint-Etienne area, the heart, lungs, skin, kidneys, lard, and stomach of the pig—liberally seasoned with cayenne and garlic—are made into a potent sausage called *sabardin* or *Saint-Bardin* or *sac boudin* or any variation thereon. *Boudin d'herbes*, from the Boën area, is made with cabbage, chives, parsley, leeks, blood, and fat enveloped in a small casing and cooked for two hours. ("Very heavy and hard to digest," say locals.)

The most famous of the Auvergnat dishes making use of a variety of meats of other animals is *tripoux*, packages of sheep's tripe, smoked bacon, ham, chitterlings, parsley, garlic, and spices, cooked for eight hours or more in white wine. Better cuts of meat were reserved for feasts. *Gigot brayaude*, one such dish, is lamb, traditionally cooked in the oven of the village baker. While the Saint-Pourçain area and the Côte Roannaise raise Charollais cows, beef dishes are few: Beef cattle went to market; others were raised for the milk which would be transformed into one of Auvergne's many cheeses.

The Auvergnat cheese platter is rich, varied, and delicious. It ranges from small disks of herby mountain goat, to chevrotons, to flat *briques*—half goat, half cow's-milk—to spicy, dome-shaped Gaperons, to the ewe's-milk Le Lavort, to Pavin, to a passel of *appellation contrôlée* cheeses made of cow's-milk: Fourme d'Ambert and de Montbrison (both blues), Saint-Nectaire, Bleu d'Auvergne (each of which will be discussed individually), to Cantal, Salers, and Laguiole, somewhat beyond our wine route.

Fresh cheeses are used to enrich egg and potato dishes or they are baked in brioches. Aside from the brioche—and the *fouasse* of the Cantal area— Auvergne's traditional breads tend to be rustic, based on buckwheat and rye. The frugal Auvergnat put stale bread to good use in *brézou*, a soup of hard bread soaked in milk or wine. And one finds a precursor to *aligot* in *patranque*, stale bread soaked with milk and stirred over the fire, with fresh cheese, garlic, and herbs. Most of the region's cakes are derived from its breads. *Pompes* or *bourriols* and *mattefaims*, large crêpes, are made from yeast batter and can be either sweet or savory (though *pompe* might also signify a brioche or a puff pastry tart). A *millard* is a cherry clafouti. Fruit tarts are made with a yeast dough or pâte brisée. Sweet brioches are often filled with preserved fruits.

In the mountains, the fruits are likely to be those that can be gathered wild—bilberry, blackberry, raspberries, sloe. Cherries, peaches, apples, pears, strawberries, and almonds flourish on the Limagne, the fertile plains surrounding Clermont-Ferrand. *Pâtes de fruits* and candied fruits are a specialty here. Before its hillsides were given over to housing, Clermont-Ferrand was known for its apricots. Angelica, another local crop, is used by many local chefs to make *nougat glacé*. From the Velay comes verbena, made into a liqueur called Verveine by the Pagès company.

Walnuts are a frequent garnish and walnut oil was traditionally used to dress salads as well as in cooking. Chestnuts appear in sausage stuffings and soups and also garnish roast ham and turkey, particularly in Clermont-Ferrand. The green lentils grown above Le Puy-en-Velay are used in salads and are the traditional accompaniment for *petit salé* and pig snout.

Among the region's other resources are a number of France's premier mineral waters—Vichy, Volvic, and Royat, for example. Wild mushrooms like *girolles, cèpes, pieds de mouton, trompettes de la mort, mousserons,* and *coulemelles* are all gathered in Auvergne's forests. They are sautéed, made into soups, or added to omelets. Delicate *omble-chevalier* (similar to salmon trout), trout, and carp are fished from mountain lakes, and the Allier still provides some salmon. Lake and river fish inspire some of Auvergne's most restrained cooking—*truite aux lardons* (trout with bacon) and trout cooked in Saint-Pourçain blanc. *Truite au bleu* (in which the fish is gutted minutes before being cooked in vinegar-laced court bouillon or water) was purportedly created in the region in the fifth century by the then bishop of Clermont, Sidoine Apollinaire. Auvergnats claim authorship of coq au vin, too, saying it was originally made with Chanturgue wine. This proposition is supported by Philippe Couderc in his *Les Plats Qui Ont Fait la France* (Editions Julliard: Paris, 1995).

And if such a gastronomically endowed region needs another contribution to the world of food and wine, it has one: About a twenty-minute drive northwest of the vineyards of Saint-Pourçain is the Tronçais Forest, a ten-thousand-acre preserve of century-old oak trees from which are made the Rolls-Royces of wine barrels.

Cheese

The cheeses found along the wine route include the Fourmes (d'Ambert and de Montbrison), Saint-Nectaire—all AOC—and countless nonappellation cheeses. Cantal, Salers, and Laguiole, and to some extent Bleu d'Auvergne, are essentially cheeses from the Cantal department and thus beyond the scope of the wine route.

Like many of the noble cheeses in France, Auvergne's are in danger. Great ones can be found, but not without searching. Every aspect of production is changing and has been for some time. Regrettably, the changes indicate standardization. The mountains are emptying out as sons and daughters move to the plains for work in industry. The Ferrandaise and the Salers cows, rustic breeds well adapted to mountain life, are increasingly replaced with Frisonnes and other breeds whose yields are higher but whose milk is thinner and blander. Large companies are swallowing small farms. Industrial dairies are gobbling up the family-owned as proposed EEC regulations require expansion that, for many, would effectively mean starting from scratch.

Each cheese has its own story, however. And within each appellation there are still breathtaking examples of the cheeses that are so integral to the glory that is France.

FOURME DE MONTBRISON AND D'AMBERT

Madame Michelle Taillandier lives in a stone house on the top of a pine-covered mountain. On her twenty-hectare farm she tends six milk cows. She makes one Fourme a day, sometimes two; it takes twenty-five liters of milk to make the two-kilo cheese. Mme. Taillandier adds the evening milk to the morning milk, heats it to 30 degrees Celsius, adds a soupspoon of rennet, and lets the mixture sit. After two and a half hours, curds have formed. Mme. Taillandier cuts through them to drain the whey (or *petit lait*), then molds the cheese, layering in a coffee cup of salt with the coagulating curds. She places the mold on a wood rack or ledge for a day, piercing the cheese to aid drainage. She will turn the cheese twice a day for twelve days and heat the room to 18 degrees Celsius. At the end of this time the cheese has formed a light crust. Mme. Taillandier moves it to a cellar behind her kitchen where the cheese will age for four or five months. She pierces the cheese so that air can penetrate and encourage development of Fourme's characteristic blue mold. During this time its crust will thicken, becoming speckled with a bloom of gray-white mold, later splotches of yellow or red-orange mold, as aging continues.

Mme. Taillandier makes Fourme de Montbrison, the lesser-known kin of Fourme d'Ambert. Essentially the same cheese—a tall cylindrical cow's-milk cheese marbled with blue mold—both are *appellation contrôlée*. They are made on either side of Monts du Forez throughout the departments of the Loire, Puy-de-Dôme, and in sections of Cantal, around Saint-Flour. Ambert is a sizeable provincial town on the west slope of the Monts du Forez; Montbrison, on the east. By tradition, west-slope producers make Fourme d'Ambert; those on the east, like Madame Taillandier, Fourme de Montbrison. But they are entitled to make either or both. (Discussions are underway to separate the two, however.)

Fourmes are ancient cheeses, believed to have been made in the Pays des Arvernes (from which comes the name "Auvergne") before Caesar. The word *fourme* comes from *forme*, the mold containing the curds, whence *fromage*. Fourme is a typical mountain cheese, the production of which occurred in the summer when shepherds herded the cattle up the mountain to pasture. The rhythm of the seasons and the Forez's cold, humid climate determined the nature of the cheese. Fourme is tall, 19 centimeters high and 13 centimeters in diameter. It is rich (by law a minimum of 50 percent fatty matter), buttery, a bit salty, and very fruity.

At its best, Fourme d'Ambert or de Montbrison is a noble cheese, among the greatest of the blues. Such examples are not easy to find, however, and they are rapidly becoming an endangered species. The Mme. Taillandiers are as much a part of Auvergne folklore as shepherds cooking *patcha* in their *jasseries*. Virtually all of today's Fourme d'Ambert or de Montbrison (more than 5,000 metric tons yearly) is made by dairies. The milk is almost always pasteurized, making it necessary to add industrial starters. Industrial strains of Roquefort penicillium are introduced to develop the blue mold. The cheese may be sold less than a month after it was made. Adding insult to injury, Fourmes are generally wrapped in foil to prevent moisture (and weight) loss, a practice that also hinders flavor development as well as the development of a firm, thick crust, mottled with yellow and red molds: Foil-wrapped Fourmes all have clammy, greasy crusts.

Worse, the trend is toward consolidation. Many of the dairies are being eaten up by big companies like Triballat—though the cheese may still be sold under the name of the smaller dairy. Finally, the producer's union,

CIFAM (Comité Interprofessional et Interdépartemental de la Fourme d'Ambert ou Fourme de Montbrison), has this misguided philosophy as one of its goals: "To make a product that is uniform from house to house."

Mme. Taillandier was the only producer of farmhouse Fourme I found. (One young man has begun working near Ambert but his cheeses are not yet ready for prime time.) The industrial Fourmes could have been made in Lille—or in Brooklyn. The Fourme from L'Essor/Balbigny, for example, was bland and rubbery—and Balbigny, already in the Triballat stable, is one of the most respected of the dairies. In response to consumer interest, two large dairies—Tarit and Forez-Fourmes in Tauves—have added rather bland raw-milk versions. A stellar small dairy, *Fromagerie de la Genette* was sold in 1993; the Fourmes it currently produces can no longer be recommended. The only Fourme left to recommend is:

Fromagerie du Grand Passeloup, Liergues: This small family dairy is in the hills of Beaujolais, no longer within the Loire or the Fourmes d'Ambert or de Montbrison appellation. But the Lapierres make very good Fourme. A key difference is that the Lapierres thermize their milk. (Gentler than pasteurization, thermizing involves heating the milk to 65 to 70 degrees Celsius rather than to the 95 degrees of pasteurization.) This is the Fourme on the cheese tray at Troisgros. It becomes buttery, *moelleux*, rich, and savory when aged for several months by Hubert Mons, a colorful *affineur* with a shop in Roanne and cellars in the Côte Roannaise.

Mme. Michelle Taillandier, La Chamba: Mme. Taillandier makes Fourme because she can't be bothered schlepping her milk down the mountain twice a day to the cooperative. Her kids all abandoned the hills for work in factories on the plains. When I visited on a September morning, Mme. Taillandier was out of mature cheeses. I tasted a month-old version that had only just begun to marble. It was chalky and creamy, with a mild flavor like slightly pungent butter.

SAINT-NECTAIRE

Saint-Nectaire is one of the last great farmhouse cheeses left in Auvergne and, for many, one of the finest cheeses in France. Made in seventy-two communes, mostly within a fifty-kilometer radius of Clermont-Ferrand, at altitudes ranging from 750 to 1,300 meters, it is a cow's-milk cheese shaped into an eight-inch by one-and-a-half-to-two-inch disk. Its rind may be tinged orange and covered with a white and gray bloom, or a dusty gray speckled with yellow and red mold. A well-matured Saint-Nectaire is straw yellow, supple, and unctuous; its rich, complex flavor is fruity, at times nutty, with the moldy-mushroomy smell of wine cellars.

The cheese takes its name from Henri de la Ferté-Sennecterre, duc and maréchal, who was tireless in his efforts to promote it. He presented the cheese to Louis XIV, who thereafter sought it for his table. Saint-Nectaire became an *appellation contrôlée* in 1973, though the particularities of its production have been protected by judicial decree since 1955.

Besse-en-Chandesse is at the heart of the production zone. From there you climb narrow mountain roads ever higher into the slopes of Le Mont Dore, to windswept farms looking down on Lac Pavin, to villages where old women push wheelbarrows stacked with Saint-Nectaires to aging cellars. The rude climate discourages any type of agriculture besides cattle raising; the volcanic soils and the abundant and varied flora make for a rich pasturage. In *The French Cheese Book*, author Patrick Rance observes of Saint-Nectaire, "The esters from pasture plants of exceptional variety and sweetness give the interior a bouquet unrivalled by any other cheese I can think of."

At more than 12,000 metric tons a year, Saint-Nectaire is the fourth most important AOC cow's-milk cheese in France and it ranks first in farmhouse production of such cheeses. Poised at 45 percent farmhouse, 55 percent industrial, production is sliding toward consolidation: The number of farmers shrinks annually, with six hundred in 1990, four hundred in 1995, and the number expected to decrease to two hundred within the next couple of years, though the acreage will remain the same.

Saint-Nectaire is made twice a day, after the morning and evening milking. (It takes roughly fifteen liters of milk to make a Saint-Nectaire.) The milk, kept at around 30 degrees Celsius, is poured into a vat (either a wood *baste* or a plastic or stainless steel tub). Rennet is added, and some add commercial starters as well. After an hour the curd has formed and the mass is cut into pea-sized grains to aid draining. Later the curds are heaped into a block. Then the cheese is pressed to remove most of the whey. It is left to drain again, divided into cubes, and put in wood, aluminum, or plastic molds, 21 centimeters round and 5 centimeters high, and is gently pressed. Once unmolded, it is stamped (a green oval if farmhouse, square if dairy), salted, put back in the mold (wrapped, preferably, in cloth), and pressed again—this time for twenty-four hours during which it is turned once. The cheese is then unmolded, wiped or washed, put to dry, and later taken to a cellar for aging. While maturing the cheese, the *affineur* (or farmer who ages his own Saint-Nectaire) must turn it and wipe or wash the rind regularly—first with brine, then with water. (Many add iron oxide, which gives an ochre cast to the rind.) Some wipe the rind with the hand or a rag. This results in a thick, dusty, gray rind which, after two months, becomes speckled with yellow and orange mold. That's when the cheese is ripe for eating.

Saint-Nectaire risked going the way of Fourme. Its best breed of cow, the Salers, is disappearing, replaced with the higher-yielding Montbéliard and Frissonne. And ancestral methods of fabrication—such as the use of wood *bastes* for making the cheese and mats made of rye straw for aging them—were in the process of being forbidden under EEC regulations. At this writing, however, Saint-Nectaire seems to have taken major steps to protect its traditionally made artisanal cheeses.

For centuries the warm, fresh milk has been poured into wood *bastes*. There was no need to add anything to start the "fermentation." The *baste* developed its own starters—as many as forty different strains—and these strains, unique to each farm, gave an inimitable specificity to each cheese. Plastic and stainless steel vats don't have indigenous yeasts, so producers using them must add industrial starters, making their Saint-Nectaires that much more identical to the Saint-Nectaire of the neighboring farm. Additionally, Saint-Nectaire was traditionally aged in naturally vaulted caves carved in volcanic rock, posed on mats made of rye straw. EEC regulations would have put an end to that practice, too, mandating climatized rooms and stainless steel racks.

In an effort to save these ancestral methods, Saint-Nectaire producers filed a *dossier de dérogation*, a request for a special dispensation. The decision has not yet been rendered but it is expected to be favorable, which will permit producers to continue making their Saint-Nectaires in wood *bastes* and aging them on rye straw mats. These are the ones to look for.

By law, Saint-Nectaire may be sold after twenty-one days. Only 5 percent of Saint-Nectaire's producers age their own cheeses. Most sell *en blanc*, at between two to fifteen days, to *affineurs* or to *courtiers en blanc* (cheese brokers) who further age them in their cellars.

The best Saint-Nectaires are made from milk of either the spring pasturage (March through June) or the second fall growth (September and October). Count six weeks if you like a blander—though still characterful—Saint-Nectaire, and two to three, even four months, if you prefer the full-blown variety.

EXCELLENT

Nicole and Bernard Charbonnier (Ferme des Ribages), Besse-en-Chandesse: This young couple was ready to take on the whole system to fight for traditional Saint-Nectaire (Cantal, too, as they produce a bit of that). The Charbonniers have Salers cows, use wood *bastes*, and age all of their cheeses, placing them in natural caves and turning and wiping them every two or three days. Well made, layered with rich flavors, the cheeses are superb.

HIGHLY RECOMMENDED

Pascal Trapenat: At 1,203 meters above sea level, this farm between Besse and Super-Besse is the highest in the Puy-de-Dôme. M. Trapenat tends to adhere to traditional methods of production. Most of his herd is Salers. He sells the majority of his cheese to *affineurs* but ages some in his own cellars. The forty-five-day-old cheese available when I visited was too young to savor. Judging it was like pronouncing on a young wine; it was mild, lactic, fresh, and promising. The Trapenats also make tasty, lightly sweet *brioche de tôme*.

Mme. Janine Roux, Beaune-le-Froid: Good butter and full-flavored Saint-Nectaires.

Jean Verdier et Fils, La Godivelle: A farm at the end of the world, making mostly Cantal as well as some funky Saint-Nectaires with hard rinds, dimpled with craters like the surface of the moon and splotched with yellow and orange mold. A two-month-old cheese was nutty, winy, and strong; you really knew it was there.

See also the *affineurs* and *crémeries* below.

OTHER CHEESES

Saint-Nectaire derivatives: Murol, a bland cow's-milk cheese with a hole in the center; Pavin, created by the *affineur* Guillaume (*see below*), resembles Murol, without the hole; Savaron, a neutral, pasteurized cheese, aged in Auvergne, was invented by *affineurs* and is often passed off as Saint-Nectaire.

Bleu d'Auvergne: An *appellation contrôlée*, this cheese is made principally in the mountains of Cantal and in parts of the Puy-de-Dôme as well. It was invented in 1850 by an Auvergnat farmer who decided to mix curds with a moldy chunk of rye bread. Now made entirely by dairies—with penicillium injected to encourage mold development—it is chalkier and more acidic than Fourme. A company called Reynal et Varagne, a dairy in Trizac, however, makes a superb raw-milk version.

Gaperon: A hard, spicy, dome-shaped cheese flavored with garlic, salt, and pepper, it was made on farms from buttermilk (*gape* in patois) or *petit lait* (whey). Locals say it was hung to drain in women's stockings, then molded, tied, and aged for three months, giving the cheese its characteristic form. Its traditional zone of production was around Thiers and Billom, pink garlic–growing regions. Now made by dairies, its production is dominated by Laiterie Garmy. Two other producers are recommended: *Fromagerie R. Quillier* (*see below*) and *Gapéron du Père Daroit, Le Mas d'Argnat,* in Sayat, who makes a tasty, fresh, and spreadable Gaperon from curds (which seems a contradiction in terms).

Le Lavort: When cheesemonger Michel Abbonenc and I were lamenting the death of farmhouse Fourme d'Ambert, Abbonenc tried to look on the bright side. Citing a new sheep's-milk cheese made near Ambert, he said, "One tradition dies, but it's replaced by another." The name of this "new" tradition is Le Lavort, from the Fromagerie du Terre Dieu in Puy-Guillaume. It's made by Patrick Baumont, a former agricultural adviser, who wanted to make cheese the old-fashioned way. As *brebis* (sheep's-milk cheese) had never been made in Auvergne, Baumont spent time with producers in Spain and returned with the tube pan–like molds that give the cheese its distinctive form. Baumont's Le Lavort is a raw-milk, lightly pressed *brebis* with 65 to 75 percent fat, aged for seven months. (Abbonenc ages it longer, saying it ends up looking like a stone from an old château.) Pungent but not sharp, it is now on the cheese trays of chefs like Michel Bras. Some pundits are saying Le Lavort is the best thing to happen to the dairy industry since Marie Harel invented Camembert.

The region's goat cheeses usually have no name—other than *briques*, chèvre, *chèvroton, cabricou, cabécou*—but can be quite tasty. Usually dry, the older ones are sometimes aged in vine leaves.

In local markets and shops in towns like Ambert, Issoire, and Montbrison, you'll find Briques (flat, rectangular cheeses, often a blend of goat and cow's-milk) and Vachards (sometimes called Tome d'Auvergne or Le Montagne), made from leftover curds of Fourmes or Saint-Nectaire. These should be eaten fully ripe when the rinds are thick and—as many old-timers prefer them—crawling with mites called *artisons*.

AFFINEURS AND CHEESE SHOPS

Michel Abbonenc, Ambert: A small boutique with delicious hams, local candies, wine, and above all, cheese. Abbonenc ages some himself—including super Saint-Nectaire, a spectacular year and a half old Cantal, and Le Lavort.

L'Auvergnat, Renaison and Roanne markets and Les Halles Diderot in Roanne: Hubert Mons, a garrulous Auvergnat with an elaborate mustache, has wonderful Saint-Nectaire and scrumptious Fourme from Fromagerie du Grand Passeloup in the Beaujolais, which he ages until it's *moelleux*.

Marcel Barbat, Besse-en-Chandesse: A tiny shop with attractive displays of cheese, eggs, and wood molds. The Barbat family has been aging regional cheeses since 1900, *and* works with twenty suppliers. Cheeses are matured in caves, on mats of rye straw. Martine Barbat, who runs the shop, is kind and helpful. Everything is excellent—from butter and fresh Tome to the delicious, winy Salers, the spicy Gaperon, and the richly nuanced two-and-a-half-month-old Saint-Nectaires. Don't miss the Trizac Bleu d'Auvergne.

Fromagerie Marcel Guillaume, Montaigut-le-Blanc: *Affineurs* of Saint-Nectaire (good, seven weeks old), Cantal, and so forth, the Guillaumes are principally known for Pavin, a cheese created by the family and on which they have a trademark. In the style of Murol but without the hole, it is a supple, lightly pungent cheese made by a dairy in Cantal.

Maison Dorlac, Clermont-Ferrand: A *crémerie* specializing in Saint-Nectaire, Cantal, and butter, owned by a veritable cheese-lover who ages his Saint-Nectaire for a minimum of two months. It is super.

ALSO RECOMMENDED

Chèvrerie de Pierrefitte, Ambierle: Herby, tasty chèvres from the Côte Roannaise area (*see* Charcuterie).

Fromagerie R. Quillier, Bergonne: One of the best Gaperons I tasted comes from this producer.

François Vazeilles, Marché Saint-Pierre (Les Halles): Excellent four-month-old Saint-Nectaire covered with dots of yellow mold.

Les Produits de la Ferme and a Friday market for organic produce, both in Clermont.

Puy Lentils

The fields of Landos are just above Puy-en-Velay. In the city, it was another sweltering, sunny September afternoon. The plateau, however, looked like the Yorkshire moors; dark clouds hung low in the sky, wind battered stands of hay. Using a bale as a windbreak, Norbert Palisse invited me to share his thermos of coffee and to talk farming in general and Puy lentils in particular.

Typical of the region's farmers, Palisse has fifty-six hectares in the environs of Costaros, the heart of Puy lentil production. He raises dairy and beef cattle, cereal crops, and lentils, which cover four to six hectares. When the green lentil starts to be shot with blue, it is ready for harvest, which generally starts in mid-August and can last until October. Most were already in, though Norbert still had a patch to pick.

Archeological finds indicate that lentils were cultivated in the region in Gallo-Roman times. Climate and variety of lentil explain why Puy harvests what are considered the aristocrat of lentils. The *lentille verte de Puy* cooks quickly. It has a fine skin; a delicate, mineral flavor; and is not mealy. At the end of 1995 Puy lentils will receive an *appellation contrôlée*.

Anicia, the seed variety, was developed from the original Puy lentil and takes its name from Anicium, the ancient name of Puy-en-Velay. Within each grain's yellow covering is anthocyanin, a natural pigment which gives cornflowers and blueberries their color. Mixed with yellow, it produces a green skin; as it is not uniformly distributed, a marbling effect is created. Berry also grows green lentils, at least twice as much as Puy, but they have no appellation.

The climate, not the region's volcanic soils, defines the *terroir*. The lentil suffers in the Velay as grapevines do on some of the most privileged vineyard sites. On the plateaus surrounding le Puy, from 600 to 1,000 meters above sea level, winters and springs are long and rigorous. Even in summer the weather is not warm enough for the lentils to fully ripen—which explains the fine skin and the low starch-content characteristic of Puy lentils.

Like most of Velay's five hundred lentil growers, Norbert Palisse does not sell his crop directly. Most goes to the cooperative; some to middlemen who collect, sort, clean, and package the lentils, which they sell to companies like Maison Sabarot and Basmaison. Palisse notes that Puy lentils don't need presoaking and that, when fully cooked, they're never mushy. He likes his lentils with tomatoes, grilled sausages, and wine.

APPENDIX A

Wining, Dining, and Touring

RESTAURANTS

During my Loire travels I've eaten in hundreds of restaurants. In this guide I've tried to limit myself to my favorites and to offer a range of possibilities from simple cafés, with only a plat du jour at lunch, to celebrated temples of gastronomy. From time to time, I mention a restaurant I don't like because its high profile will mean its name is familiar.

Restaurants and hotels are grouped according to the viticultural region to which they are attached. Note, however, that many straddle two zones: Both Le Lion d'Or in Romorantin-Lanthenay and L'Hostellerie le Relais in Bracieux, for example, are midway between eastern Touraine and the Sancerrois. La Licorne, in Fontevraud, is included in Anjou because it is in the Maine-et-Loire, but it is closer to Chinon than it is to the Layon.

The Relais & Châteaux (R&C) chain has members throughout the Loire. With the exception of those known for their kitchens, like Jean Bardet in Tours, Le Lion d'Or, and Le Relais, the hotel restaurants are not reviewed separately. In general, I find the food well-mannered but undersexed.

Prices are based on a meal for two, wine included: $ represents under $40; $$, under $80; $$$, up to $150; $$$$, above $150. When I include ($) it means that the restaurant might jump to the next price range if you order a particularly expensive dish or wine.

OVERNIGHT

The power of suggestion being what it is, most Loire voyagers want to spend at least one night in a castle. Happily, an ever-increasing number of the region's most impressive châteaux—many of them classified monuments—are being turned into hotels (many are R&Cs) and *chambres d'hôtes* (bed-and-breakfasts—B&Bs).

The key difference between a hotel and a B&B is personal contact. In a B&B, which usually has between two and twelve rooms, you really are being received into someone's home—whether it's a château or a farm. You're often invited to join your hosts for tea or an aperitif, and many offer a *table d'hôte* dinner. You should expect this welcome. A *chambre d'hôte* should be a sort of entry into local life. The prices often compete with those of full-scale hotels that routinely offer amenities—TVs, phones, pools, tennis—not necessarily available in *chambres d'hôtes*. (And rooms in *chambres d'hôtes* often don't have keys.)

Expect to pay from $150 to $500 a night in a Relais & Châteaux; from $80 to $500 in a B&B. In addition to rooms in "historic monuments," I've also included simple or simply convenient hotels in which prices range from $40 to $100.

REGIONAL SPECIALTIES

Producers and shops offering local specialties are recommended for each region. First, I list the producers described in the food essays of individual chapters. (For more information, see the chapter in question.) Then I include a roundup of other specialties.

MARKETS

Unless otherwise specified, markets are only in the morning.

FAIRS

Every year, it seems, the fairs and festivals in the Loire grow in quality and quantity. The most serious wine fairs are held from late January or early February—when the Salon des Vins de Loire takes place in Angers—to the beginning of April. The season for local fairs starts at Easter, picks up steam through the summer, and slows down in the fall, but it doesn't end until All Saints' Day. That said, you can usually find a wine fair, or convocation of a local wine society, or some such event. To keep abreast, call the nearest Syndicat d'Initiative.

THE NANTAIS

RESTAURANTS

Auberge de la Source, La Chapelle-du-Genêt: Yves Beneteau worked at Boyer in Reims and at Jeanne de Laval in Les-Rosiers-sur-Loire before opening this auberge in his native Mauges. He mines its fields and farms for free-range fowl, mushrooms, and foie gras, comfortably blending the urbane (marinated salmon and coriander) and the down-home (rabbit on a bed of *girolles*). $$$

La Bonne Auberge, Clisson: An airy, contemporary country auberge with a mouth-watering menu and a talented chef, Serge Poiron, who could make Spam taste delicious. There is authority and a sure sense of flavor in the salt cod topped with salmon; the tart layered with sautéed *cèpes* and local foie gras; the exquisite squab and the profiteroles. It's not "new" food but it's delicious food, well conceived and reasonably priced. $$$

La Châtaigneraie, Sucé-sur-Erdre: The Discreet Charm of the Bourgeoisie at its most appealing: a park bordering the river Erdre; prim dining rooms out of *The Importance of Being Earnest;* and the Delphin family's textbook *haute bourgeoise* cuisine, of which Loire classics like river fish in *beurre blanc* and frogs' legs in *sauce poulette* are particularly tasty. $$$($)

Cheval Blanc, Saint-Laurent-des-Autels: Jean-Baptiste Solignac, who cooked for Mmes. Pompidou and Barre at the Hôtel Matignon, took over his in-laws' little hotel and brought Big City Gastronomy—expertly sautéed foie gras and sliced peaches on a tarragon-scented veal glaze—to its dining rooms. $$$

La Cigale, Nantes: A classified monument, La Cigale's interior hasn't changed since the brasserie opened in 1895. Jacques Demy filmed *Lola* here, and it's fun just sitting in its giddy overkill of stained glass, mosaics, and melodramatic statues of Pierrot and Colombine. The food, delivered faster than you can say *plateau de fruits de mer,* is no better than it needs to be. $$($)

Crêperie Saint-Croix, Nantes: A cheerful, efficient spot for parchment-thin, hot, buttery crêpes. $

Hostellerie le Domaine d'Orvault, northwest of Nantes: Solid fifties corporate comfort: big leather armchairs; blond wood; easy-listening music; thick slabs of John Dory; full-flavored partridge; and a terrific cheese selection. $$$($)

Les Jardins de la Forge, Champtoceaux: Paul Pauvert converted his father's forge into a sun-flooded restaurant. The Loire fish (notably salmon) couldn't be more skillfully prepared. Pauvert's vegetable or fish mousses are as pretty, as suave, and as finely flavored as his petit fours. His elegant cakes are the stuff of childhood fantasies. Excellent service and good Loire wines. $$$($)

Manoir de la Comète, Saint-Sébastien-sur-Loire: High-concept, tasty food and high-concept decor undermined by the icy reception. $$$($)

***Mon Rêve,* Basse-Goulaine:** In an Art Deco villa with a luxuriantly offhand garden, Gérard Ryngel offers addictive tuna tartare, succulent rabbit stew, and the world's juiciest frogs' legs, bathed in a terrific sauce with lots of shallots, parsley, Muscadet, and crème fraîche. Ryngel's extraordinary wine list numbers no fewer than sixty Muscadets. $$$

***Le Navarin,* Les Sables d'Olonne:** The salad of Breton lobster with sautéed *girolles* and pigeon with foie gras, paired with a chilled red from nearby Mareuil, make for a perfect lunch on the promenade overlooking the sea, in one of France's most popular beach resorts. $$($)

***La Pipette,* Vertou:** A century ago, cityfolk strolled along the banks of the Loire on Sundays, visited wine cellars, and stopped here for sausages grilled over vine cuttings. Today the menu has expanded but the best choices remain the grilled *saucisses aux Muscadet,* fat *boudins,* and potatoes baked in embers. $$

***(Rendez-vous) Café des Pêcheurs,* La Chevrolière:** The bar's a hangout for Lac de Grand Lieu fishermen whose catch is served in the upstairs dining room. Frogs' legs or eels are panfried and sauced with garlic, parsley, and butter; pike or *sandre* come with a tart *beurre blanc.* Paired with a cold Grolleau Gris, a meal here makes for a true and delicious taste of this little-known region of still waters, marshes, and vineyards. $($)

***Le Saint-Fiacre,* Saint-Fiacre-sur-Maine:** A friendly bistro behind the village church, with a 55ff menu and one hundred Muscadets. $

***Torigai,* Ile-de-Versailles, Nantes:** This stylish restaurant on the banks of the river Erdre looks like I. M. Pei's pyramid set on a marina, but it's a lovely showcase for Shigao (Tony) Torigai. The Tokyo-born chef mastered classic French cuisine in the kitchens of Paris's Hotel Bristol, then rose through the ranks of Nouvelle with Alain Senderens and Michel Guérard. His expertly rendered French fare often has Asian accents: roast squab (marinated with honey, lemon zest, ginger, wine, soy, and sake); ravioli of sweetbreads and foie gras in a rich wild-mushroom broth. $$$

***Les Voyageurs,* Vallet:** Nantais wine honchos "do" lunch here over *sandre* with *beurre blanc* and *frites.* Lunch only. $$

WHERE TO STAY

***Château de la Jaillière,* La Chapelle Saint-Saveur:** Though expensive for what it is, this B&B in the middle of a farming hamlet is one of the pleasantest places to stay in the Nantes-Anjou area. The nineteenth-century château looks more like a public school than a castle. Its four guest rooms are simply but nicely decorated with antiques and bric-a-brac. The little pool seems permanently filled with the grandchildren of the castle's owner, the Comtesse d'Anthenaise, who simultaneously stirs cocktails, tends to dinner, recounts local lore, and draws out clients. $$$

Hostellerie le Domaine d'Orvault (R&C; *see* **Restaurants**): A reliable choice. A bit out of the way but set in an attractive park. Tennis courts, spacious rooms, and thoughtful amenities. $$$ ($)

L'Hôtel, **Nantes:** A popular small hotel across from the château and near the railroad station, its small rooms are decorated in a subdued modern style. Rather pricey for what it is. $$$

WHERE TO FIND NANTAIS SPECIALTIES

BAKED GOODS

Au Plaisir des Gourmets, **Nantes:** Since the Dollet family of La Haie-Fouassière went out of business at the end of 1992, the only satisfying Nantais *fouasse* I've found comes from this neighborhood baker.

Maligorne, **Mareuil-sur-Lay:** Honest-to-god *gâche Vendéenne,* buttery, chewy, and lightly perfumed. Other traditional baked goods include *échaudés* and *gâteaux minutes.*

Petit Mouzillon, **Le Pallet:** Most local shops carry these handmade cookies (that look as if they're packaged by Stella D'Oro).

Préault, **Sigournais:** Artisanal *brioche Vendéenne* baked on the farm.

BUTTER

Pascal Beillevaire, **Machecoul, Nantes, and Sables d'Olonne:** The world's best butter (it's unpasteurized), drop-dead crème fraîche, and Old-World preparations like the milky dessert *caillebottes.* Beillevaire also sells terrific cheese.

CANDIES (*BERLINGOTS, RIGOLETTES,* ETC.)

Bonté Confiserie, Confiserie Gourmandine, and *Gauthier-Debotte,* all in Nantes: The latter worth a visit if only for its vintage decor.

CHEESE (CURE NANTAIS)

Laiterie Saint-Père (Alexandre et Joan Jamin), **Saint-Père-en-Retz.** Available in many supermarkets and cheese shops.

DUCKS

Gilbert Burgaud, **Challans.** Burgaud sells his special ducks to La Tour d'Argent and to other top restaurants. In the Nantais, he supplies Mon Rêve and Torigai, among others.

Jean-Michel Soulard, **Les Herbiers:** Excellent birds, favored by Serge Poiron of La Bonne Auberge.

SAUCISSES AU MUSCADET

La Pipette, **Vertou** (*see* **Restaurants**).

Tertrou, **Vallet:** Juicy *saucisses au Muscadet,* also good garlic sausage, *jambon blanc,* and *boudins.*

PRODUCE

At markets, look for members of *Terroir 44,* a grouping of producers from the Loire-Atlantique. They will also welcome you at the farm.

SPIRITS

Distillerie Seguin, **Machecoul:** Now part of Rémy Martin, this firm produces *eaux-de-vie de vin* (or de marc) des Coteaux de la Loire (also known as *fine Bretagne*) made from Muscadet and Gros Plant.

Société Vrignaud Fils, **Luçon:** The inventor and sole producer of Kamok, a coffee liqueur created by the firm's founder in 1860.

WINESHOPS

The Loire's two best are in the Nantais:

Les Amis du Vin, **Saint-Nazaire and La Baule:** Serge Batard offers a wide selection of wines and whiskies. The excellent Loire choices include his own Muscadet.

Fief de Vigne, **Nantes:** The fief of Jean-François Dubreuil, it's full of his finds from all over France, with a great roundup of what he likes in the Loire.

MARKETS

Tuesday: Challans; *Thursday:* Ancenis; *Friday:* Ancenis, Clisson; *Sunday:* Vallet; *Every day:* Nantes (Talensac is the best. Also, on Saturday, Petit Holland).

OTHER THINGS TO SEE AND DO

Beaches: West of Nantes: La Baule (the most stylish), Le Croisic. South of Nantes: Pornic, Saint-Gilles-Croix-de-Vie; the island of Noirmoutier.

Clisson: A picturesque town on the confluence of the Sèvre and Moine rivers. Its fifteenth-century market hall, surrounded by several steep cobbled streets, survived the ravages of the Vendée Wars. Much of the town did not, however; it was rebuilt at the beginning of the nineteenth century in an Italianate style.

Guérande Peninsula: Breton sea salt is "harvested" in the salt pans of villages like Batz-sur-Mer and Guérande, west of Nantes.

Nantes: Places of particular interest include the Cathedral of Saint Peter and Saint Paul, with its Flamboyant Gothic nave; the castle, begun by Duke François II in 1466 and continued by his daughter, Duchess Anne (later, queen of France); the eighteenth-century city, centered around two graceful squares (the Place Graslin and the Place Royale) and the Passage Pommeraye (a lovely nineteenth-century shopping arcade, also featured in Demy's *Lola*). The Musée des Beaux-Arts often has compelling exhibits.

Puy du Fou: Right-wing politician Philippe de Villiers put together this open-air spectacle in which 1,500 locals reenact the history of Vendée, from pre-Revolution to counterrevolution and beyond. Performed on weekend nights, the show includes horses, fireworks, and living dioramas.

FAIRS AND FESTIVALS

The largest wine fair is held in Vallet the third weekend of March. In Challans, a *Foire à l'Ancienne* the last two Thursdays of July and the first two Thursdays of August. On August 15 and the following Sunday, *Fête des Poissons* (Fish Festival) or *Fête du Lac de Grand Lieu*. It's the one time of the year nonfishermen can visit the lake, which is the largest plains lake in France. As part of the festivities, the men who have the right to fish here row visitors to the middle of the lake for a *coup de seine:* They throw out long nets, then position themselves on all sides to bring the haul to shore. (A *coup* [throw] lasts a half-hour to an hour.)

SUGGESTED ITINERARY

Morning: a) Domaine de l'Ecu (Le Landreau) or Domaine Pierre Luneau-Papin
    (Le Landreau)
       b) Château du Cléray (Vallet)
Lunch: La Pipette (Vertou) or Le Saint-Fiacre
Afternoon: c) Château de Chasseloir (Saint-Fiacre)
       d) Domaine de la Louvetrie (La Haie-Fouassière)
Dinner: Mon Rêve (Basse-Goulaine), La Bonne Auberge (Clisson), or Les Jardins
    de la Forge (Champtoceaux)

ANJOU-SAUMUR

RESTAURANTS

A La Ferme, **Angers:** Nostalgia for the land draws an elbow-to-elbow lunch crowd to this restaurant behind the cathedral where a Brissac red paired with *poule au pot* make for a passable rendition of your basic harvest lunch. $$

L'Ancre de Marine, **Bouchemaine:** Decent food at rather decent prices, salmon *rillettes,* pike with *beurre blanc.* $$

Auberge de la Contrêche, **Champ-sur-Layon:** Reasonable prices, friendly service, tasty terrines, meats grilled over the hearth and Didier Richou's wine. What more could you want? $$

Auberge de la Corniche, **Chaudfondes:** A no-nonsense pit stop on a hairpin turn of the Corniche Angevine with a hard-to-beat $9 menu. $

Auberge de l'Eventard, **Angers:** "Park Avenue rustic" is the design theme of this restaurant north of Angers, on the highway to Paris: timbered ceilings, faux Henri II breakfronts, and ornate mirrors. The food is fussy but nicely rendered. Best bet: sumptuous wild duck surrounded by figs. It looks like a Dutch still life and tastes as good as it looks. $$$($)

Brasserie de la Gare, **Angers:** Convenient and popular, with a good selection of Aubance-area wines, but food and service leave much to be desired. $

Caves de Marson, **Rou-Marson:** Yes, there are tour buses, but this restaurant is no trap. In a labyrinthine cave in a country hamlet, a group of very gracious local women bake *fouasses* and *foués* over a wood fire, stuff them with *rillettes* and goat cheese, and, for $20 a person, feed you till you burst. A seasonal fruit crumble for dessert and as much Anjou blanc and rouge as you can drink. $

Clos Saint-Médard, **Thouars:** Creative cooking, nice Anjou wines, in the heart of the old section of town. $$($)

Le Dagoberte, **Doué-la-Fontaine:** The plat du jour costs $8, and Vignobles Touchais is up the street so there are vintage Layons at bargain prices. The hare was a bit dry and the sauce too vinegary—but so satisfyingly authentic. $($)

Ferme-Auberge le Chapy, **Allonnes:** Duck *rillettes,* quiche of white asparagus, grilled lamb, seasonal fruits and vegetables on a farm in the market garden district above Saumur. $($)

Grandgousier, **Angers:** A minuscule restaurant with a generous fixed-price menu featuring meats grilled over the hearth. A different local wine comes with each course. $

Jeanne de Laval, **Les Rosiers-sur-Loire:** My favorite restaurant for traditional Loire cooking. Michel Augereau, a gentle bear of a man, uses nothing out of season. Farmers and fishermen deliver produce to his door. Journalists dubbed Augereau's father "the king of *beurre blanc.*" Michel's is sublime. If you're lucky, it sauces fresh-from-the-river pike, *sandre* (the best I've ever eaten), or salmon (to die for). $$$($)

La Licorne, **Fontevraud:** Stylish setting and stylish cooking (couscous of lobster with fresh favas) in a romantic eighteenth-century town house. Good Loire wines. $$$

Le Quéré, **Angers:** Excellent food undermined by insolent service. $$$$

Relais d'Anjou, **Saint-Georges-sur-Loire:** After stints in top Paris restaurants, chef Patrick Claude would prefer never again to make the *beurre blanc* he learned from his mom. But with his light-as-air *sandre,* his phenomenal *beurre blanc* is a must. Also, sautéed foie gras on a Layon sauce (served with a glass of good Chaume), superb sorbets, and cloudlike cold soufflés. $$

Relais de Bonnezeaux, **Thouarcé:** This small restaurant in a converted railway station has carved a niche for itself in the local wine community, providing ambitious meals (eel braised in Bonnezeaux, *pintadeau* [young guinea fowl] in an Anjou rouge sauce) at reasonable prices and an extensive wine list that's strictly Angevin. $$

La Rivière, **Saint-Rémy-la-Varenne:** A casual restaurant on the banks of the Loire where, on summer nights, you can eat *fritures,* grilled rabbit, or pike with *beurre blanc,* on a terrace, drinking good local wines, as the sun sets on the river. $$

Le Salamandre, **Angers:** The restaurant of Hôtel Anjou features heavy Renaissance-inspired decor and heavy, elaborate dishes like filet of sole rolled around shrimp and mussels. $$$

Le Terminus, **Murs-Erigné:** Families and businessmen skip the gourmet fare, opting for the generous $10 menu featuring spicy *andouillettes* and fries. $

Les Tonnelles, **Béhuard:** If you visit the magical island of Béhuard you'll want to linger. And the terrace of this restaurant is the best place to do it. The well-conceived wine list offers lots of excellent choices to pair with langoustine-stuffed zucchini blossoms, Loire *sandre* in a lightly tart herb sauce, grilled salmon with *beurre blanc,* and fricassee of eels. The service may be slow, but who cares? Les Tonnelles is a festive island of activity on an island of total calm. $$

Le Toussaint, **Angers:** Michel Bignon, a talented chef, seemed in a slump since his move from a side street to a town house near the château. Signs are that he's refound his verve. Examples of what Bignon *can* do include delicate mushroom terrine, lovely local foie gras, and *crémets d'Anjou* garnished with fresh berries. $$$

Vigneron, le Clezio, **Saint-Aubin-de-Luigné:** Breathes there an Angevin who doesn't smile at the mention of this cozy place? On Sundays it's packed to its beamed ceilings, and everyone orders country terrine followed by whatever fish in *beurre blanc* or farmhouse chicken and garlicky sautéed mushrooms. $($)

WHERE TO STAY

Château de Noirieux, **Briollay:** A new member of the R&C chain, this gracious château is set in a pretty park north of Angers. The kitchen aims to please with dishes like lobster and wild mushrooms and saddle of rabbit with dried fruit. $$$$

Domaine de Mestré, **Fontevraud:** Owned by Fontevraud's mayor, Dominique Dauge, the *domaine*—today a working farm as well as a B&B—once belonged to the abbey. The rooms are spic-and-span and ornamented with a few good and useful things. The Dauges, an attractive, intelligent couple, seem to have made a "quality of life" decision to stay on the farm and make it viable. (Mme. Dauge, who cooks meals, also makes soap sold under the name Martin de Candres.) Most of the farm's produce ends up on the dinner table: rabbit terrine, roast veal, and fresh cow's-milk cheese (one of the best things I've ever tasted). There's a faint whiff of spiritual superiority, but the Dauges are gracious hosts with endless tips for finding the Loire's lesser-known treasures.

Hôtel Anjou, **Angers:** A fading grande dame, not without charm. Good central location. (*see* Restaurants) $$($)

Le Prieuré, **Chênehutte-les-Tuffeaux:** This former priory sits on a high bluff overlooking the Loire. There are forty rooms in the main house, parts of which date from the twelfth and the fifteenth centuries, and an additional twenty-five rooms in somewhat motelish bungalows. The hotel has a pool, tennis courts, a grand terrace for cocktails, a vast dining room (a bit cold but with great river views), and a competent kitchen which offers correct rather than exciting cooking. The staff is robotic. $$$$ (R&C)

WHERE TO FIND ANJOU'S SPECIALTIES

CHARCUTERIE

Rillettes, rillauds, gogues: *Serge Chauvin,* Les-Rosiers-sur-Loire; *Robert Gasté,* Rochefort-sur-Loire.

Foie gras

- *Jean-Marie Béduneau,* **La Jumellière:** When planning a special meal—one in which an old Layon will be highlighted—foie gras from Béduneau seems de rigueur in Anjou.
- *Mme. Camille Chabauty,* **Airvault:** A delightful woman who makes very good duck *rillettes* and foie gras.
- *Mme. Corabeuf,* **Vihiers:** An excellent producer who's completely smitten with her craft.

Gesiers, etc: *Les Colombiers de Maumusson,* Cléré-sur-Layon: Mireille and Pierre David, particularly known for their meaty birds (which are now sold by Fauchon), also make succulent *rillettes de pigeonneaux.* Their *gésiers* are perfect for salads or hors d'oeuvres.

CHEESE

Fromage Passion, **Angers:** Bernard Caron, the owner of this spic-and-span shop, is truly passionate about cheese. Every cheese is perfectly selected, perfectly cosseted, and brought to perfect ripeness in Caron's aging cellars beneath the shop. Trust him. You'll taste the real thing here. Caron also makes *crémets d'Anjou*.

Jacqueline Seigneuret, Airvault: Mme. Seigneuret brings her marvelous selection of Chabichous du Poitou and other Deux-Sèvres chèvres to the Saumur market every Saturday, to Thouars every Friday.

CHOCOLATIERS WHO USE ANJOU'S LIQUEURS AND SPIRITS

Galloyer is the most famous—and the chocolates are wonderful—but my favorite is *Les Délices de la Tour*. In the attic above his shop, Gilbert Benoit makes seventy types of chocolates—all sublime. When I visited, he was dipping Cointreau-filled truffles into melted white chocolate.

FRUITS AND VEGETABLES

Jean-Yves Péron's "new vegetables" are marketed by *Légumes Plaisir* in Mauves.

In addition to local markets, look for fruit and vegetable specialties at the sources listed below:

Patte-de-loup apples: *Domaine de la Borde*, Vergers-des-Mauges, Saint-Pierre-Montlimart.

Mushrooms

Musée du Champignon, Saint-Hilaire-Saint-Florent, just outside of Saumur.

Mary Yves, Saint-Rémy-en-Mauges, a small farmer who, among other things, cultivates sublime yellow *pleurottes*.

Fruit Preparations

You cannot find a better version of *pâté de prunes* than at *Allard*, Les-Ponts-de-Cé and Angers: from August to September, in the *reine-claude* season.

Troglo'tap, Turquant: Alain Lupin has resuscitated the lost art of making *pommes tapées*, a method of oven drying apples that was popular at the turn of the century. At the end of the tour he doles out lip-smacking samples of *pommes tapées* reheated with red wine, cinnamon, and sugar.

MARKETS

Wednesday: Angers; *Thursday:* Brissac; *Friday:* Thouars; *Saturday:* Angers, Saumur; *Sunday:* Montsoreau.

OTHER THINGS TO SEE AND DO

Béhuard: A magical island between Rochefort and Savennières with stone houses, tight streets, chickens pecking in yards, and an eerie fifteenth-century chapel which seems to grow from the rock on which it was built.

Cadre Noir, Saint-Hilaire-Saint-Florent: Awesome "ballets" on horseback performed by the elite corps of France's Ecole Nationale d'Equitation (National Riding Academy).

Châteaux and their settings:

- **Angers:** A lumbering fortress to visit for the must-see fourteenth-century Apocalypse Tapestries; also visit the old quarters of town.
- **Brissac:** Set in a dreamy park, it's an endearing architectural hodge-podge of fortressy fifteenth-century towers bracketing an ornate seventeenth-century central pavilion.
- **Montreuil-Bellay:** The mix of architectural styles reflects its transition from a defense-oriented medieval fortress to a Renaissance home; also, a fairy-tale setting on the river Thouet, and a beguiling town.
- **Montsoreau:** The fifteenth-century fortress sits stiffly on the quay like a proud old general still at attention; the town is charming and the Sunday market is fun.
- **Saumur:** A wonderful exterior; also visit the old quarters of town around the Place Saint-Pierre.

Cunault: Another enchanting riverside town. The church, an important Romanesque abbey, has 223 fabulous sculpted capitals. (On summer Sundays there are lovely chamber concerts.)

Fontevraud Abbey: Founded in the eleventh century, it is one of the largest groups of monastic buildings in Europe. Eleanor of Aquitaine, Henri II, and Richard the Lionhearted are buried here.

Troglodytes: The cliffs between Montsoreau and Saumur are riddled with caves called troglodytes. Inhabited until the 1930s, most have been abandoned, though some are used as wine or mushroom cellars. Northwest of Saumur, there are two interesting troglodyte settlements, La Fosse and Rochemenier.

Musée du Champignon: More *Phantom of the Opera* tuffeau caves carved into the hillside. In these caves, mushrooms are cultivated, and the various methods—beds, boxes, sacks—as well as different varieties—Paris, shitake, and *pleurotte*—are the subject of the tour.

FAIRS AND FESTIVALS

- Monday, Tuesday, and Wednesday at either the end of January or the beginning of February, Angers, *Salon des Vins de Loire*.
- Last weekend of May, Montreuil-Bellay, a different-themed fair each year, e.g., Medieval, Belle Epoque.
- First weekend of June, Tigné, *Fête des Vins Rosés* on the grounds of Gérard Départieu's château.
- First Sunday of July, Brissac, a *Rillaudée*.

- The weekend after July 14, Saint-Aubin-de-Luigné, *Fête des Vins Millésimés* (Vintage Wines) and *Foire aux Anguilles* (Eels).
- The second and third weekends in September, Chacé-Varrains, *Fête du Champigny*.
- The Saturday following Saint-Maurice (at the end of September), Brissac, an eight-hundred-year-old goose and garlic fair.
- October, Mouliherne, *Foire aux Pommes* (Apples); Martigné-Briand, *Vendange Belle Epoque;* Saint-Rémy-la-Varenne, *Foire aux Légumes Oubliés* (Festival of Forgotten Vegetables).

SUGGESTED ITINERARY (ONE AND A HALF DAYS)

DAY ONE
Morning: a) Claude Papin (Beaulieu-sur-Layon)
       b) Vincent Ogereau (Saint-Lambert-du-Lattay)
Lunch: Les Tonnelles (Béhuard) or Auberge de la Contrêche (Champ-sur-Layon)
Afternoon: c) Victor Lebreton (Juigné-sur-Loire), Didier Richou (Mozé-sur-
       Louet), or Christophe Daviau (Brissac)
       d) Mark Angeli (Thouarcé)
Dinner: Jeanne de Laval (Les Rosiers-sur-Loire)

DAY TWO
Morning: a) Bouvet Ladubay (Saint-Hilaire-Saint-Florent)
       b) Clos Rougéard (Foucault brothers) (Chacé)
Lunch: Caves de Marson (Rou-Marson)

TOURAINE

RESTAURANTS

Aigle Blanc, Azay-le-Rideau: Ambitious, nouvelle-ish fare. Good local wines. $($)

Auberge de la Brenne, Neuillé-le-Lierre: Ghislaine Sallé was born on the farm that today supplies her with the pigs for her tasty *rillettes*, herby pâtés, and smoky *andouillettes*, as well as the chicken and cream for her *fricassée de volaille au Vouvray* (an old family recipe for chicken stew). $$

Auberge de l'Hermitière, Le Grand Lucé: Deep in the Bercé forest, this Sarthoise chalet serves local guinea hen with wild berries and *girolles;* crêpes stuffed with sour cherries and vanilla ice cream; good Jasnières and Coteaux du Loir. $$($)

Auberge des Huiliers, Thizay: In what looks like a municipal meeting room, Mme. Faret serves authentic *matelotes d'anguille*, locally raised fowl, and so forth. For communions and anniversaries M. Faret serenades with his accordion. $

Auberge de Port Valière: Jean-Jacques Thomas, ex-sommelier chez Bardet, opened this country wine bar, stocked it with superb selections, and took over the cooking as well. A delicious salad, with mounds of sautéed *rillons*, is a meal in itself. Wonderful local cheese, *clafouti*, homemade preserves. $$

***Au Plaisir Gourmand*, Chinon:** In an eighteenth-century town house, Jean-Claude Rigollet turns out masterly renditions of French classics: cloud-light pike mousse, veal kidneys in a pungent mustard sauce, deeply flavored hare or oxtail stew. Good Chinons and Bourgueils. $$$

***Automat Gourmand*, Azay-le-Rideau:** A cozy place with cozy food: poached eggs with morels; *beuchelles*; oxtail and rabbit terrine. Poky service but nice local chèvres and wines. $$

***Le Balzac*, Saché:** Jahan's café serves ample lunches of omelets, *rillettes*, roast chicken, and Jahan wine. $

***La Caillère*, Candé-sur-Beuvron:** An honest restaurant with kind service. The dining room's a bit sad but the patio's a fine place to pair a Touraine-Mesland with pike in Bourgueil sauce. $($)

***La Chancelière*, Montbazon:** Dishes are gemlike miniatures: tiny rounds of lobster, in the shell, the tail meat removed and posed on a potato *galette*; vanilla soufflés cooked in eggshells, on an orange sauce which looks like yolks. $$$($)

***Chandelles Gourmandes*, Larçay:** A pretty setting overseen by a conscientious couple who seek out the best of everything—from foie gras to chèvre to Montlouis to tea. $$$

***Le Croissant*, Sainte-Maure-de-Touraine:** A tiny, cluttered hotel with homey quiches, roast pork, and potatoes. $

***L'Ecu*, Belâbre:** After a trip to the Romanesque abbey of Saint-Savin, sample chef Daniel Cotar's sensitive musings on the flavors of the land: Belâbre foie gras, carp soufflé in a Pinot Noir sauce, and local squab basted with local honey. $$$

***Ferme-Auberge Bouland*, Mareuil-sur-Cher:** Françoise and Frédéric Bouland make goat's- and sheep's-milk cheese and feed you as if they plan to turn you into foie gras. A meal includes herbed chèvre on toast, fritters filled with goat cheese, braised kid, and an assortment of cheeses from the farm (all wonderful). $$

***Ferme-Auberge des Grillons*, Limeray:** Rather than sell their poultry at the Amboise market, Gilbert and Nicole Guichard invite you to the farm. To the sound of quacking ducks, you eat smoked *magret* (duck breast) and roast chicken, local chèvre, and apricot tarts. $($)

***Jacky Dallais (La Promenade)*, Le Petit-Pressigny:** Touraine's best restaurant is tucked away in a tiny village surrounded by green valleys and stone farmhouses. Dallais, who worked with Joël Robuchon before taking over his mother's café, reveals his superb sense of flavor, texture, and proportion in dishes such as langoustines wrapped in leek, seasoned with marjoram; turbot topped with chopped truffles and artichoke hearts; roasted lobe of foie gras with braised endive;

sautéed mirabelles, laced with Poire and topped with Poire sorbet; chocolate puff pastry encasing a lava of chocolate sauce which flows around rich vanilla ice cream. Excellent Loire wines. $$$

Jean Bardet, Tours: Fancy French à la Jackie Collins. Bardet can turn out breathtakingly delicious food—river fish with a sauce based on Banyuls and crushed lobster shells, or salmon on a bed of leeks and *rillons*—but many conceits, like a combo of duck and calamari, don't work. There's an inexpensive (and inviting) *prix fixe* menu. Otherwise $$$$.

Maxime's, Poitiers: Christian Rougier, the young chef, takes orders, shows *Monsieur* the cigar selection, and turns out tasty, ambitious fare like warm lobster with sprouted lentils in a grapefruit-truffle vinaigrette. The local chèvres, served with homemade bacon and onion bread, are worth the detour. $$$($)

L'Odéon, Tours: Facing the train station is this very satisfying brasserie with delectable oxtail terrine, fricassee of frogs' legs with favas and bacon, great *andouillettes*, *crêpes Suzette*, and Claude Papin's Layons. $$

L'Oubliette, Rochecorbon: A pretty room in a troglodyte cave with winsome dishes like asparagus flan on watercress sauce and duck stew with a shallot confit. $$

Restaurant Charles Barrier, Tours: Forget the fussy decor and the nouvelle-isms. Go for the pig's foot which comes with an oniony *boudin noir* and a velvet purée of potato and butter. The *matelote d'anguille* and the juicy squab could have been prepared by a local grandmother. $$$$

Respectable, Pricey ($$$) Restaurants of No Particular Charm or Imagination:

- *Pierre Benoist*, Croutelle.
- *La Charmille*, Châtellerault.
- *Le Langeais*, Langeais.
- *Le Lys*, Tours.
- *La Roche le Roy*, Saint-Avertin.

WHERE TO STAY

The Relais & Châteaux chain has eight members in Touraine: Château d'Artigny (Montbazon), Château de Marçay (outside of Chinon), Château de Noizay (near Vouvray), Le Choiseul (Amboise), Domaine de Beauvois (Luynes), Domaine des Hautes de Loire (Onzain), and Les Hautes Roches (Rochecorbon), and the Hôtel d'Espagne in Valençay. All are $$$$.

Artigny, François Coty's stately pleasure dome, is the grandest. Its chef, Francis Maignaut, is ambitious and talented. (Ask to sit in the circular dining room.) Carved into the cliffs of Vouvray's "Première Côte," Hautes Roches is the most unusual, with its deluxe "troglodyte" rooms. Le Choiseul, overlooking Amboise, is perhaps the most beguiling—and the kitchen keeps improving. The family-owned Domaine des Hautes de Loire, an ivy-covered *gentilhommerie* (manor house), may be the most caring and personal—with one of the best kitchens. Artigny and Marçay have superb Loire wines.

Château de Montgouverne, Rochecorbon: Jacques and Christine Desvignes turned a pretty eighteenth-century château in the middle of Vouvray's vineyards into a gem of a B&B. The park, with its centuries-old sequoias and cedars, is a classified monument. Guest rooms (all have TVs and phones) and public rooms are bright, country-elegant, and cheerful. Christine makes stylish dinners— smoked salmon with herbed crème fraîche on potato pancakes; cabbage stuffed with duck with cherries and mushrooms. The wines could use work, but there's a heated pool. $$$($)

Château de Réaux, Chouzé-sur-Loire: Built principally in the fifteenth century, Réaux, a *monument historique*, is unique among Touraine's fairy-tale castles. Its facade of light-red brick and limestone gives it the look of a fantastical checkerboard. Réaux is owned by the dynamic Florence de Bouillé, who knows everyone, is full of good advice, and presides over dinner of white asparagus, poached salmon, chèvre, and fresh berries in her antique-filled dining room. $$$($)

Le Diderot, Chinon: A simple, moderately priced, charming hotel on a medieval street. Wood fires; homemade jams; bicycles; caring, knowledgeable service. $$

WHERE TO FIND TOURAINE'S FOOD SPECIALTIES

CHEESE

Pouligny-Saint-Pierre

- *Mme. Blondeau*, Pouligny-Saint-Pierre.
- *Courthial*, Pouligny-Saint-Pierre.
- *La Ferme des Ages*, Le Blanc.
- *Mme. Geffrault*, Mauvières.

Sainte-Maure-de-Touraine

- *Bacquart*, Braslou.
- *Lydie et Louis Bulté*, Saint-Epain.
- *Castelli*, Saint-Michel-sur-Loire.
- *Cuvier*, Vouvray.
- *Jacques et Catherine Descré*, Marcilly-sur-Maulne.
- *Jean-Luc Douet*, Bossée.
- *Fontaine*, Draché.
- *Guériteau*, Sainte-Catherine-de-Fierbois.
- *Héribert*, Pussigny.
- *Jérôme et Sylvie Huan*, Anché.
- *Jean Lepage*, Seuilly.

- M. *et Mme. Ondet*, Crissay-sur-Manse.
- *Rabusseau*, Panzoult.
- *Mme. Richard*, Tendu.

Supermarket Chèvres

- *Lamorinière*, Neuillé-Pont-Pierre.
- *Marie-Claire Meneau*, Avon-les-Roches.
- *Moreau*, Pontlevoy.
- *Vazereau*, La Roche-Clermault.

Selles-sur-Cher

- *Bouland*, Mareuil-sur-Cher.
- Christian Egreteau, Fougères-sur-Bièvre.
- *Gaillard*, Contres.
- *Jean-Pierre et Martine Moreau*, Pontlevoy.
- *Jean-Claude Rousseau*, Châtillon-sur-Cher.

Valençay

- *Jean-Michel Chambonneau*, Mazères.
- *Mme. Coetemerer*, Selles-sur-Nohant.
- *Ferme du Petit Bellevue*, Pruniers.
- *Mme. Richard*, Tendu.

Cheese from the Vendômois

- *La Chèvrerie d'Authon*, Authon.
- *Laiterie Taillard*, Villiers-sur-Loir.
- *Mme. Minier*, Lunay.

Other Cheeses

- *La Brosse Perusson*, Loches.
- The best shops for local cheese are *Au Parfum de Beurre* and *La Ferme des Vignes* in Tours.

Charcuterie

- *Didier Arnoult*, Ile Bouchard.
- *Jean-Jacques Bergère*, Vernou.
- *André Berrier*, Chinon.
- *Jacky Blateau*, Tours.
- *Michel Fuseau*, Restigné.
- *Hardouin*, Vouvray.
- *André Mamoux*, Vernou.
- *Perriot*, Montrichard.
- *Pierre le Gal*, La Ville-aux-Dames.

OTHER TOURAINE SPECIALTIES

Baked Goods

- *Jousseaume*, Roullet: This artisanal producer of *tourteau fromagé* is located in Charente, but his *tourteau* is sold at Au Parfum de Beurre in Tours.
- *Briocherie Lelong*, Tours: While not a specialty of Touraine, honest-to-God brioches are hard to find. This tiny shop across from the train station makes only brioches—rich, buttery, and real—in a number of sizes as well as in loaves. If they're warm from the oven, buy twice as much as you need. The aromas wafting from the wrappings will crack even the most iron-clad resolve.
- *Mahou*, Tours: In addition to contemporary loaves, Mahou offers a panoply of ancient regional breads, including his buttery, aromatic rendition of the *fouasse* described by Rabelais in *Gargantua*.

Confections: *Poirault*, Tours: A *confiserie* specializing in two ancient Touraine preparations, stuffed prunes and barley sugar.

Spirits

- *Cellier du Beaujardin*, Bléré: This cooperative cellar turns out a respectable commercial version of local *vin d'épine*, called Epine Noire de Touraine.
- *Claude Richard*, Marçon, La Chartre-sur-le-Loir: An artisanal distiller who makes raw but authentic Poire William, Golden Apple, and Cassis *eaux-de-vie*.
- *Société Chambord*, Huisseau-sur-Cosson: This deluxe liqueur takes its name from the famous château.

MARKETS

Monday: Lencloître, Richelieu; *Tuesday:* Bourgueil, Montbazon; *Wednesday:* Blois, Loches; *Thursday:* Châtillon-sur-Indre, Chinon; *Friday:* Montrichard, Richelieu, Vernou; *Saturday:* Le Blanc, Bourgueil, Saint-Aignan, Sainte-Maure-de-Touraine, Tours; *Sunday:* Amboise.

OTHER THINGS TO SEE AND DO

Candes-Saint-Martin: A beautiful village on the confluence of the Loire and the Vienne. Its church, built in the twelfth and thirteenth centuries on the spot where Saint Martin died, fits on its tiny square like a piece in a chess set. But step inside and the church seems to balloon up out of nowhere, as immense as a cathedral. Soaring columns with serene sculptures culminate in Angevin vaulting, a local variation on the Gothic theme.

Châteaux and their settings (a mere dozen out of hundreds):

- **Amboise:** The castle, which sits atop an inviting, strollable town, was begun in 1492. Nearby is Le Clos Lucé, where Leonardo da Vinci spent his last years.
- **Azay-le-Rideau:** Built in the early sixteenth century, this is a harmonious jewel of a château, set on the Indre river. The town is a jewel, too.
- **Blois:** Murder and intrigue unfolded in the halls of this important château, parts of which are feudal (thirteenth century); others, Renaissance (fifteenth); still others, from the seventeenth. The town, a major agricultural crossroads, is the fief of Jack Lang, the late President Mitterand's cultural affairs minister.
- **Chenonceau:** Perhaps the most famous and romantic Loire Valley château, Chenonceau, built in the sixteenth century, is a masterpiece of Renaissance architecture straddling the Cher river.
- **Cheverny:** A classic Renaissance château known for its symmetry and its sumptuous furnishings.
- **Chinon:** The ruins of the medieval château stretch across the top of the town, overlooking the river Vienne. A fairy-tale town, Chinon has well-preserved medieval areas and several interesting churches. The birthplace of François Rabelais, La Devinière, is nearby.
- **Langeais:** A fifteenth-century château whose period furnishings illuminate aristocratic life at the dawn of the Renaissance.
- **Loches:** A fortified village with a feudal fortress and fifteenth-century cages used by Louis XI as torture chambers.
- **Saché:** Honoré de Balzac and Alexander Calder were drawn to this serene village in the Indre Valley to live and work. A Calder mobile dominates the town square. Balzac set *Le Lys dans la Vallée* in its environs. The château, built between the sixteenth and eighteenth centuries, was a place of refuge for the writer, whose study, which remains much as it was when he wrote *Le Père Goriot*, is open for visits.
- **Ussé:** Supposedly the inspiration for "Sleeping Beauty."
- **Valençay:** The castle owes its celebrity to Talleyrand, who, at the behest of Napoleon, engaged in what was then a novel form of diplomacy: He entertained foreign dignitaries with sumptuous feasts— prepared by Antonin Carême.
- **Villandry:** The château's painstaking re-creations of sixteenth-century gardens are the interest here.

Saint-Savin: A Romanesque abbey with important art. Unfortunately, the crypt was recently closed, to preserve the abbey's most significant works from deterioration.

Tavant: A drab village with a wonderful Romanesque church, the crypt of which is a low, vaulted room, a forest of columns, every inch covered with frescoes—all painted eight hundred years ago by a lone monk who never imagined anyone would see his handiwork.

Tours: Vieux Tours is centered around the Place Plumereau, a maze of cobbled streets lined with fifteenth-century houses, and the cathedral district. Saint Gatien's cathedral (thirteenth to sixteenth centuries) is a fine example of French Gothic style. Nearby are the medieval château, several museums, and delightful pedestrian streets such as the rue de Scellerie, antique-dealers' row.

FAIRS AND FESTIVALS

- The Fondettes wine fair is the second weekend in February. On Easter, wine fairs in Amboise, Saint-Georges-sur-Cher, and Sazilly.
- The Sunday after Easter, a wine fair in Selles-sur-Cher. End of April, a wine fair in Jasnières.
- First weekend in May, Mennetou-sur-Cher, *Foire aux Andouillettes;* wine fair in Cravant-les-Coteaux.
- Last weekend in May, Fontaines-en-Sologne, a strawberry festival.
- At Pentecost (end of May), wine fairs in Meusnes and Montoire.
- First weekend in June, Sainte-Maure-de-Touraine, goat cheese fair (but the streets are lined with food stands of all sorts).
- July 26th (Saint Anne's Day), Tours, a garlic fair.
- Third Sunday in July, Bourgueil, basil and garlic fair.
- End of July, Saint-Aignan, *Journée du Vin.*
- First weekend in August: Chinon, medieval festival.
- Two weeks later, Saturday only, Chinon, *Foire à l'Ancienne.*
- Third weekend in November, Montrichard, *Vins Primeurs* (New Wines).
- October, Tranzoult, *Foire aux Légumes Oubliés.*

SUGGESTED ITINERARY (TWO DAYS)

DAY ONE—**Western Touraine**
Morning: a) Charles Joguet (Sazilly)
       b) Bernard Baudry (Cravant-les-Coteaux)
Lunch: Au Plaisir Gourmand (Chinon)
Afternoon: c) Marc Delaunay (Bourgueil) or Pierre Caslot (Restigné)
       d) Pierre-Jacques Druet (Benais)
Dinner: Auberge de Port Valière. (An alternative would be to switch the morning and afternoon visits and have dinner at Jacky Dallais in Le Petit-Pressigny, about an hour south of Chinon.)

DAY TWO—**Eastern Touraine**

Morning: a) Le Haut Lieu (Huet-Pinguet) or Clos Naudin (Foureau)

      b) Domaine des Aubuisières (Fouquet), Didier Champalou, all four in Vouvray

Lunch: Auberge de la Brenne (Neuillé-le-Lierre)

Afternoon: c) Caves de Oisly-Thésée (Oisly)

      d) Domaine de la Charmoise (Soings-en-Sologne)

Dinner: Grand Hôtel Lion d'Or (Romorantin-Lanthenay) or L'Hostellerie Le Relais (Bracieux). (Each of these recommendations is described in the Sancerrois restaurant section but each is as close to the vineyards of eastern Touraine as it is to those of the Center.)

SANCERROIS

RESTAURANTS

Auberge des Templiers, Les Bézards: This classic house of haute cuisine maintains its venerable reputation despite frequent turnover in the kitchen. $$$$

Auberge du Vigneron, Verdigny: Friendly prices and service, a good local wine list, and toothsome regional fare. $$

Au Fin Chavignol, Chavignol: Good omelets, chèvre tourtes, and hare stews. The Sancerres are just fine, particularly with Dubois's Crottins. $

Chez (Cheu) l'Zib, Menetou-Salon: Smells of winy stews, a cluttered room with a sagging timbered ceiling, a bottle of *cassis* passed from table to table to make *kirs* with Menetou. And no menu. A typical meal: terrine with home-pickled *cornichons*, pike in a soothing shallot cream sauce, lamb or garlicky sautéed rabbit, and chocolate charlotte. The restaurant generally serves only lunch—but you don't finish till five, by which time the hunters have come in for drinks accompanied by ladies in serious hats. At its best, Chez l'Zib is Pagnol. Loire soul food. $$

La Cognette, Issoudun: In a "Masterpiece Theatre does Balzac" setting, Alain Nonnet and his son-in-law cook Berrichon classics straight from the heart—lentil soup with truffles; Brenne carp stuffed with sausage—as well as more contemporary fare such as batter-fried packets of langoustines and shitakes. $$$

D'Antan Sancerrois, Bourges: A deservedly popular wine bar featuring all good things Sancerrois. $($)

L'Espérance, Pouilly-sur-Loire: At its best, the food is lovely: warm smoked salmon on sautéed *pleurottes* and *cèpes*; wild duck with honey and citrus zests; and gingerbread terrine, layered with cinnamon ice cream. $$$

L'Etoile, Saint-Thibault: *Grillades, fritures,* and good Loire selections on the banks of the river. $$

Grand Hôtel Lion d'Or, **Romorantin-Lanthenay:** This is the best restaurant in the Loire Valley. Didier Clément's menu is exciting—everything is finely conceived, finely tuned, masterly. One example: Saddle of hare in a sweet-sour sauce, garnished with root chervil and figs, was the finest game dish I've ever eaten. The flavor was haunting; Tuscan in balance, finesse, and modernity. With a bite of ripe fig, it was voluptuous and decadent, evoking ancient hunt scenes in châteaux. Excellent Loire (and other) wines. The deft service is overseen by Clément's mother-in-law and by his wife, who is also a cookbook author. $$$$

L'Hostellerie le Relais, **Bracieux:** Hard by the château of Chambord, Bernard Robin revives ancestral dishes such as *carpe à la Chambord,* a delicious blend of the region's history and its ingredients. Robin's more contemporary fare is delicious, too, and his *crème brûlée* is the one you first fell in love with. Good Loire wines. $$$$

Hôtel-Restaurant la Renaissance, **Magny-Cours:** Racing drivers order the *ficelle Nivernaise,* a crêpe filled with ham and cream, or slabs of Charollais beef bathed in a morel cream sauce. $$$$

Jacques Coeur, **Bourges:** A venerable bistro with perfectly rendered classics, such as flavorful mackerel in white wine, and Berrichon staples like chicken *en barbouille.* The waiters invented niceness: One saw us lusting after the hand-cut fries at another table and brought us our own platter. Then he furnished maps and pamphlets—again unsolicited. $$

Moulin de Chaméron, **Bannegon.** A romantic getaway in a restored mill with tasty, creative food (salad of langoustines and chicory, lamb in sage sauce, confit of radishes); excellent local chèvres; fine Loire wines; and a well-documented mill museum. $$$

Le Rivage, **Gien:** On the quay overlooking the Loire, a solid hotel-restaurant with kind service and complicated, not entirely successful dishes. $$$

La Solognote, **Brinon-sur-Sauldre:** A comfortable restaurant with delicious game: partridge with cabbage, pheasant sausage on a bed of chestnuts and endive, savory *cèpe* pie, and *civet de lièvre* as classic as it comes. Good Loire wines. $$$

La Tour, **Sancerre:** A favorite of many local vintners, it has an extensive wine list but the food is too fussy for me. $$

WHERE TO STAY

Auberge du Vigneron, **Verdigny:** Simple rooms in a typical Sancerrois village. (*see* Restaurants) $$

La Cognette, **Issoudun:** The hotel rooms (in an annex) and the breakfasts are among the nicest in the region. (*See* Restaurants) $$$

Grand Hôtel Lion d'Or, **Romorantin-Lanthenay:** The hotel has all the comforts of home, if home happens to be Trump Tower. (*see* Restaurants) $$$$ (R&C)

La Rêverie, **Pouilly-sur-Loire:** A pleasant B&B in "downtown" Pouilly. $$($)

La Solognote, **Brinon-sur-Sauldre:** Simple rooms attached to the restaurant. (*see* Restaurants) $$($)

La Verrerie, **Oizon, Aubigny-sur-Nère:** This magical private château, built in the fifteenth and sixteenth centuries by the Stuarts and set in a magnificent park with a tree-lined lake fed by the river Nère, is owned by the Comte and Comtesse de Voguë. Most of the guest rooms are on the second floor of the château and they are all beautifully decorated with antiques and rich fabrics. Do take the public tour, if only to see the fifteenth-century chapel and the salon with four statues made in 1450 called "*pleurants*," which come from the tomb of Duc Jean de Berry. You may arrange to dine with the de Voguës in the château. $$$$

WHERE TO FIND SANCERRE'S FOOD SPECIALTIES

Crottin de Chavignol

- *Michel Chamaillard*, Santranges (Gien's Saturday market and Cosne's Sunday market).
- *Claude Crochet*, Bué and Sancerre.
- *Jacques Dépigny*, Nérondes.
- *Domaine du Port Aubry*, Cosne.
- *Domaine des Rouches*, Saint-Bouize.
- *Dubois-Bouley*, Chavignol.
- *Gilbert Houzier*, Ménétréol.
- *Philippe Jay*, Jars.
- *Edgar Roger*, Neuvy-Deux-Clochers.
- *Annie Samson*, Veaugues.

Other Cheeses:

- *M. Lavarenne*, Orléans: Olivet.
- *Elevage de Maison Neuve*, Châtillon-sur-Loire: Sheep's-milk cheeses, Capécieux, and Blason d'Orléans.

Other Regional Specialties

- *Charcuterie Pierre Bigot*, Sancerre and Saint-Satur: Jambon de Sancerre smoked over vine cuttings is the delicious specialty of this artisanal charcutier.
- *Pâtisserie Raymond Carré*, Romorantin-Lanthenay: One of the best *tarte Tatins* you'll ever find—succulent, lip-smacking, with great sweet-to-acid balance. His other pies and cakes are wonderful, too.
- *Alain Bernard*, Verdigny: My preferred address for *pâté* (or *galette*) *de pommes de terre* is located in the wine hamlet of Chaudoux. Stuffed with a peppery mix of potatoes, ham, and crème fraîche, it's great soul food.
- *Denis Pajon*, Millançay: In his typical small-town bakery Pajon uses pumpkins from his parents' farm to make *citrouillat*—pumpkin, parsley,

and onions baked in a puff pastry crust. His *tartes Tatins* feature local apples; his quiches, Sologne's *girolles*.

VINEGAR

- *Martin-Pouret*, Orléans.

MARKETS

Wednesday: Bourges, Romorantin-Lanthenay; *Saturday:* Aubigny-sur-Nère, Bourges, Gien, Romorantin-Lanthenay; *Sunday:* Cosne, Meung.

OTHER THINGS TO SEE AND DO

La Borne: A community of potters who have settled here from all over the world. There is a permanent exhibition of the works of fifty local potters in what was formerly the village school.

Bourges: A delightful provincial city, with cobbled streets, good galleries, and several important sights. The Gothic cathedral Saint-Etienne is a must for its richly ornamented exterior and its soaring interior with magnificent stained glass windows dating from the thirteenth to the seventeenth centuries. Jacques Coeur's palace is a fifteenth-century mansion built by the merchant who, among other things, financed the campaigns of Jeanne d'Arc.

Chambord: The largest and most flamboyant of the Loire Valley châteaux, Chambord was built in the sixteenth century as a hunting lodge for François Ier. It has 440 rooms, thirteen major staircases (including the famous double-spiraled staircase), and seventy minor staircases. Its towers, turrets, and chimneys give it a skyline all its own. During Louis XIV's stay in Chambord, Molière staged *Le Bourgeois Gentilhomme*. (Smaller châteaux in the region include Meillant, Menetou-Salon, and La Verrerie.)

Gien: The premier attraction is the *Faïencerie de Gien*, a pottery factory with a museum and a "seconds" shop where the selection is broad and the prices half what you'll find in town.

Nevers: Known for its pale blue pottery. A leading manufacturer is *Montagnon*, a small, artisanal firm. Its beautiful faïence is always impeccable: The owner smashes anything that doesn't pass muster. The Municipal Museum, several blocks away, has an excellent collection of Nevers pottery. Also of interest are the ducal palace and the cathedral.

Nohant: George Sand spent her childhood in this picturesque village, returned often during her adult life, and died here in 1876. Sand evoked the Berrichon countryside in works such as *Petite Fadette*. Her home has been turned into a museum.

Pottery: In addition to having exceptional soils for wine, the Sancerrois has excellent soils for pottery. The zone extends in an arc from Gien to La Borne to Nevers.

FAIRS AND FESTIVALS

- The first of May or the following weekend, Sancerre, *Foire aux Fromages*.
- Pentecost, Sancerre, *Foire aux Vins*.
- Second Sunday of June, Jargeau, *Foire aux Andouillettes*.
- First weekend of July, Morogues, *Fête Internationale des Chieuves* (goat cheese).
- First Sunday in August, Bué, *Foire aux Sorciers* (Sorcerers).
- August 15, Quincy, *Grande Fête du Charbon de Bois* [coal] *à l'Ancienne*.
- Mid-August, Menetou-Salon, *Caves Ouvertes* (Winery Open Houses).
- Last weekend of August, Quincy, *Journées de l'Océan*, and Sancerre, *Foire aux Vins*.
- Last weekend of September, Millançay, *Foire à la Citrouille* (Pumpkin).
- Second Sunday in October, Tranzault, *Foire à la Citrouille et aux Légumes Oubliés*.
- Last weekend of October, Romorantin-Lanthenay, *Journées Gastronomiques*.

SUGGESTED ITINERARY (TWO DAYS)

Day One
Morning: a) Alphonse Mellot or Domaine Vacheron (Sancerre)
        b) Lucien Crochet or Vincent Pinard (Bué)
Lunch: Au Fin Chavignol (Chavignol) or Auberge du Vigneron (Verdigny)
Afternoon: c) Henri Bourgeois (Chavignol) or André Dezat (Verdigny);
        d) Francis Cotat (Chavignol)
Dinner: Le Solognote (Brinton-sur-Sauldre)

Day Two
Morning: a) Château du Nozet (Pouilly-sur-Loire)
        b) Didier Dagueneau (Saint-Andelain)
Lunch: Chez (Cheu) l'Zib (Menetou-Salon)
Afternoon: c) Domaine du Châtenoy (Menetou) or Henri Pellé (Morogues)
        d) Claude Lafond (Reuilly)
Dinner: La Cognette (Issoudun) or Grand Hôtel Lion d'Or (Romorantin-Lanthenay)

AUVERGNE

RESTAURANTS

Auberge des Cimes, **Saint-Bonnet-le-Froid:** Chef-owner Régis Marcon, winner of prestigious cooking awards such as the Bocuse d'Or and the Prix Taittinger, explores the flavors of the countryside. In fall, this might mean a mushroom festival: *cèpe* salad and foie gras; savory *tuiles* topped with *mousserons,* frogs' legs, and deep-fried leek; morels stuffed with crayfish. All perfect, as are the river fish, game, and desserts. $$$($)

Auberge des Massards, **Sury-le-Compte:** On Sundays this *ferme*-auberge outside Saint-Etienne is packed with families celebrating First Communions and anniversaries. Marcel (a one-man band) and Nicole Tissot raise crops and cattle. But their place is so popular it consumes most of the harvest of neighboring farms, too, and seems to employ the entire commune. The garlicky frogs' legs and the rösti-like *rapée* make for good, sloppy eating. $($)

Au Pont de Raffigny, **Saint-Anthème:** Alain Beaudoux, the young chef-owner, worked at Troisgros before returning home to transform this former disco into an ambitious restaurant. The new decor includes a fake burbling brook. But you want to like it because, like Beaudoux's cooking, it's from the heart. Clear, simple flavors characterize dishes like rockfish on puréed eggplant, rabbit stuffed with vegetables, and kidneys garnished with *rapée.* At lunch you can also opt for the plat du jour, a great favorite with local workers. $$($)

Bateau Ivre, **Puy-en-Velay:** A thoroughly satisfying restaurant run by a friendly couple who use regional produce to delicious effect: woodsy *mousseron* soup; Velay lamb with mashed potatoes and morels; lentils tossed with diced vegetables; good regional cheeses and wines. Desserts are both homey and glorious. $$

La Bergerie, **Super-Besse:** Before opening her own place (in a restored barn on a ski trail), Marie-José Verny worked for her uncle, Antoine Sachapt, the dean of Auvergnat cooking. Today she offers terrific renditions of *truffade, potée,* coq au vin, fruit tarts, and *clafoutis*—all based on local ingredients. $$

Chêne Vert, **Saint-Pourçain:** The best bet here is the potato pie, with ham and onions in a lard-based crust—a meal in itself. $$

Clos Saint-Pierre, **Clermont-Ferrand:** This friendly brasserie is Jean-Yves Bath in a more relaxed mood. An inviting spot with jokey waiters, crusty country bread, flavorful Saint-Nectaire, silky salmon smoked over a wood fire, and tasty lamb brochettes. $$

Gérard Anglard, **Clermont-Ferrand:** Imaginative cooking based on regional produce: rabbit in a creamy sauce infused with garlic from Billom; cinnamon ice cream with caramelized apples. $$($)

Gérard Truchetet, Clermont-Ferrand: In search of a fast-food restaurant in the industrial zone where Auvergne's enology labs are located, I fell upon this classic fifties-style restaurant. A classic fifties-style chef, Truchetet worked in hotels making international cuisine before opening this place—where he turns out deeply satisfying Auvergnat fare: salad of pigs' trotters on Puy lentils; ham with a creamy, lightly spicy wine sauce; nougat glacé with angelica from Issoire. $$($)

Jean-Yves Bath, Clermont-Ferrand: An engaging and dynamic chef, Bath "deconstructs" traditional Auvergnat dishes to make them contemporary and exciting: *potée* with duck and foie gras; salmon with bacon and truffles; ravioli bursting with Cantal cheese. Desserts include delicious warm fig tart and luscious banana whipped cream in puff pastry. Bath also makes his own aperitifs from Seville oranges, hawthorn, ginger, and dandelion. $$$$

Pierre Gagnaire, Saint-Etienne: If there are a thousand things you can do with a carrot, a slab of beef, and a cup of cream, Gagnaire will whip up number one thousand and one, perhaps adding cardamom, cockscombs, or chamomile. A high-profile chef who compares cooking to jazz and architecture, Gagnaire occupies a Gatsbyesque 1930s mansion. He has always drawn the cream of international society to this drab city, and you will have a better meal if you're one of them. $$$$

Troisgros, Roanne: Cool beige piped with burgundy, taupe leather chairs, and antique credenzas, Troisgros could be a Park Avenue law firm. Butter comes in little "Is it craft or is it art?" pots; the wine list in a heavy notebook. The food's just about perfect: shrimp, calamari, and vermicelli on an olive oil–based emulsion; frogs' legs in a truffle-infused cream sauce; sweet-sour slices of duck with lime-scented favas and fig. $$$$

WHERE TO STAY

Auberge des Cimes, Saint-Bonnet-le-Froid: When I made my pilgrimage to the source of the Loire, I stayed in one of the tasteful rooms above the restaurant. Breakfasts are splendid, including homemade *fromage blanc,* jams, granola, croissants, and fresh orange juice. (*see* Restaurants) $$($)

Au Pont de Raffigny, Saint-Anthème: Twelve simple and pleasant hotel rooms above the restaurant. A good base for touring the Ambert area. (*see* Restaurants) $$

Chêne Vert, Saint-Pourçain: A serviceable hotel. (*see* Restaurants) $$

WHERE TO FIND AUVERGNAT SPECIALTIES

CHEESE

Fourme

- *Fromagerie du Grand Passeloup,* Liergues.
- *Mme. Michelle Taillandier,* La Chamba.

Saint-Nectaire

- *Nicole and Bernard Charbonnier (Ferme des Ribages)*, Besse-en-Chandesse.
- *Pascal Trapenat*, between Besse and Super-Besse.
- *Mme. Janine Roux*, Beaune-le-Froid.
- *Jean Verdier et Fils*, La Godivelle.

Other Cheeses

- *Chèvrerie de Pierrefitte*, Ambierle: Goat cheeses.
- *Fromagerie R. Quillier*, Bergonne; Gaperon and other cheeses.
- *Gapéron du Père Daroit, Le Mas d'Argnat*, Sayat: Gaperon.
- *Fromagerie Marcel Guillaume*, Montaigut-le-Blanc: Le Pavin.
- *Fromagerie du Terre Dieu*, Puy-Guillaume: Le Lavort.

Cheese Shops and *Affineurs*

- *Michel Abbonenc*, Ambert.
- *L'Auvergnat*, Renaison and Roanne markets and Les Halles Diderot in Roanne.
- *Marcel Barbat*, Besse-en-Chandesse.
- *Fromagerie Marcel Guillaume*, Montaigut-le-Blanc.
- *Maison Dorlac*, Clermont-Ferrand.
- *Les Produits de la Ferme*, Clermont-Ferrand.
- *François Vazeilles*, Marché Saint-Pierre (Les Halles), Clermont-Ferrand.

OTHER AUVGERNAT SPECIALTIES

CHARCUTERIE

Baffaleuf, Montaigut-le-Blanc: Honest, high quality *jambon blanc*, sausages, and pâtés from an engaging and serious young couple. Muffin lovers shouldn't miss the brioche studded with ham and olives and spiked with cognac.

Berthelier, Ambierle: Free-range pigs provide the raw material for Berthelier's extraordinary hams, sausages, *andouilles*, and terrines. The must-taste is the ham cooked in hay, which takes two years to make. It is as rich and complex as a great wine.

Lassalas (Salaisons des Monts d'Auvergne), Clermont-Ferrand and Nebouzat: Grandfather Lassalas began by selling products from his farm at the local market. His son moved from farm to town, buying pigs and transforming them into delicious mountain hams, *saucissons, boudins*, and *petit salé*.

Maurice Pallut (Salaisons du Haut-Cantal), Chanterelle: Another village lost in the mountains but not just another charcuterie. The pigs are fed whey drained from the curds of Saint-Nectaire. Neither the hams nor the sausages have additives—nothing other than salt and, for the *saucissons*, garlic and pepper. The ham is fabulous, thick and meaty; the *saucisson*, rich, winy, meaty, and garlicky, a masterpiece.

Odile and Gérard Grange, Saint-Bonnet: Devoted to making artisanal charcuterie, the Granges turn out delicious Beaujolais-laced sausage; excellent ham; moist, rum-spiked terrine; and pungent Saint-Bardin which they bury in cinders to ripen its already ripe flavor.

La Sauvete, Saint-Martin-la-Sauvete: Deep in quiet farmland some 700 meters high, the Pallanche family turns out tasty hams; chewy, spicy *saucissons;* and flavorful *pâté de tête*. Most sells out at the Saturday Montbrison market.

OTHER REGIONAL PRODUCTS

Noël Cruzilles, Maître Confiseur, Clermont-Ferrand: An artisanal producer of *pâtes de fruits* and candied fruits. So good, the fruit tastes as if just picked.

L'Oubernia, Besse-en-Chandesse: M. Mercier carries *saucissons* from Maurice Pallut, a range of local wines and liqueurs, and good local cheeses.

Pagès, Puy-en-Velay: This lovely boutique hasn't changed since it opened in 1859. You can stock up on Auvergne's *pâte de fruits,* Pagès teas, Puy lentils, dried *girolles,* Marc d'Auvergne, *eaux-de-vie,* and Verveine du Velay, the house specialty. A liqueur made of thirty-three regional plants, macerated with *eau-de-vie* from Cognac, then distilled and blended with honey and sugar, it is served as a *digestif.*

Produits de la Ferme, Clermont-Ferrand: Some thirty farmers deliver their excellent cheeses, hams, sausages, honey, and so forth directly to the shop.

MARKETS

Monday: Besse-en-Chandesse, Billom; *Wednesday:* Clermont-Ferrand, Egliseneuve-d'Entraigues, Murol; *Thursday:* Ambert; *Friday:* Champeix, Clermont-Ferrand organic farmers' market; *Saturday:* Brioude, Montbrison, Puy-en-Velay.

OTHER THINGS TO SEE AND DO

Besse-en-Chandesse: A pretty Auvergnat town of fifteenth-century houses and shops made from gray-black volcanic rock.

Clermont-Ferrand: The home of the Michelin tire company is "worth a detour" for its churches—the Romanesque Notre Dame du Port and the Gothic cathedral Notre Dame de l'Assomption, made of black volcanic rock—and its old neighborhoods (behind the cathedral, near the market hall, and across town, in Montferrand).

Gerbier de Jonc: A trickle of water issuing from a spigot on desolate Mont Gerbier (1,551 meters high) in deepest Ardèche marks the spot widely accepted as being the source of the Loire.

Lac Pavin: The quintessential mountain lake—clear, cold, 92 meters deep, perfectly round. (A simple restaurant overlooking the lake used to be owned by a fisherman who supplied the kitchen with whatever he caught. Ownership has changed; the view hasn't.)

Le Parc des Volcans (Volcano Park): This is the largest national park in France, covering nearly 400,000 hectares from Clermont-Ferrand to Aurillac. The volcanoes that created Auvergne's hot springs, lakes, and emerald green peaks and craters are the unifying theme. The northern part encompasses the Chaîne des Puys (eighty in all, of which the most famous is the Puy-de-Dôme) and Le Mont Dore (including the Puy-de-Sancy, at 1,886 meters, the highest point in central France).

Puy-en-Velay: The indelible image of this ancient city is that of the eerie Rocher d'Aiguilhe, a needle-shaped boulder, topped by the tenth-century Chapelle Saint-Michel. Its inscrutable presence (as well as that of the Rocher Corneille) seems to explain why le Puy became an obligatory stop on the road to Compostela. Other worthy sights include the old city, the twelfth-century cathedral, and the collection of lace at the Musée Crozatier, a legacy of the days when the city was a center of lace making.

Romanesque churches: Auvergne's network of fabulous Romanesque churches bears witness to its role as a gathering point for pilgrimages to Compostela. The facades are squat and austere. Inside, however, the churches are richly ornamented with haunting sculptures of animals and biblical scenes. Some 250 buildings have preserved all or part of their Romanesque past. The major ones are Notre Dame du Port in Clermont, Saint-Austremoine in Issoire, Saint-Nectaire, and Notre Dame d'Orcival.

Tronçais Forest: The 10,594-hectare forest that provides the oak for the world's best wine barrels is also a beautiful, serene site to visit, with its ponds and . . . mighty oaks.

Vichy: The most famous (and infamous) of the region's hot springs and spas.

FAIRS AND FESTIVALS

- First weekend of April, Panissières, *Journées du Saucisson.*
- Second to last weekend of April, Roanne, *Foire aux Vins et aux Fromages.*
- End of June, Thiers, food festival.
- Last weekend of July, Besse-en-Chandesse, *Foire aux Vins et aux Fromages.*
- Last weekend of August or first weekend of September, Saint-Pourçain, *Foire aux Vins.*
- For a week in mid-September, Puy-en-Velay, *Fêtes Renaissance du Roi de l'Oiseau.*
- First weekend of October, Montbrison, *Journées de la Fourme.*

- Beginning of November, Saint-Haon-le-Vieux, *Foire aux Vins Bourrus* (New, Unfinished Wine)
- First Saturday in November, Saint-Bonnet-le-Froid, *Foire aux Cèpes*.
- November 11, Pelussin, *Journée de la Pomme*.

SUGGESTED ITINERARY (ONE AND A HALF DAYS)

Day One

Morning: Saint-Pourçain: Pétillat (Meillard) or Ray (Saint-Pourçain)
Lunch: La Bergerie (Super-Besse)
Afternoon: La Ferme des Ribages (above Besse-en-Chandesse); Caves de Verny (Corent) or Bernard Boulin (Madargues)
Dinner: Jean-Yves Bath (Clermont-Ferrand)

Day Two

Morning: a) Alain Demon (Ambierle)
        b) Paul Lapandéry (Saint-Haon-le-Vieux)
Lunch: Restaurant Troisgros (Roanne)

APPENDIX B

Glossary

GENERAL

AOC (Appellation d'Origine Contrôlée): An official designation for a product (wine, spirits, cheese, charcuterie, poultry, lentils, etc.) from a geographically limited zone that has been made or grown according to legal specifications. (For wines, regulations cover such factors as grape varieties, yields, ripeness, and alcohol levels.) A guarantee of authenticity.

Department: One of 95 French administrative units. Smaller than a state, larger than a county, it has no precise USA equivalent.

Douceur: A word frequently used when describing any and all aspects of the Loire—from its landscape and its light to its climate, wines, and foods—it means softness, smoothness, mildness, gentleness, sweetness.

Doux: Sweet, mild, tender.

Epicerie: Small grocery, general store.

Fermier: Farmer, farmhouse product.

INAO (Institut National des Appellations d'Origine): The government agency responsible for determining and regulating French appellations of origin, including AOC and VDQS wines and products such as cheese, butter, charcuterie, beef, and poultry.

***Lieu dit* (pl., *lieux dits*):** Literally "named place," it is the time-honored way of referring to a particular parcel which may or may not be a vineyard. It has no legal force.

Ligerian: Things or people from the Loire; Loire-like. (Cf. American, Venetian.)

Stage: A workshop, apprenticeship, or clinical studies lasting from several hours to several months.

Syndicat: An association, union, or syndicate: ——— d'Initiative, tourist office; ——— *de vignerons*, association of winegrowers.

Troglodyte: Cave dwellings, notably those dug into the tuffeau cliffs of Touraine and the Saumurois.

Tuffeau: Soft, chalky, sedimentary soils of the Paris Basin. The building stone of the châteaux, churches, homes, farms, and bridges of Touraine and the Saumurois. (Not to be confused with the volcanic "tuff.")

Vin d'honneur: The wine served to kick off a ceremony (e.g., weddings, local fairs).

WINE

Argilo-calcaire: A soil type consisting of clay and chalk.

Argilo-siliceux: A soil type consisting of clay and silica.

Assemblage: A blend of two or more wines (from the same or different grapes, according to the appellation) to arrive at one (or several) finished wine or wines.

Ban de vendange: The authorized date for the start of harvest.

Barrique: A Bordeaux barrel holding 225 liters.

Biodynamics: A philosophy of viticulture as set forth by Austrian philosopher Rudolf Steiner. Homeopathic vine treatments replace chemicals; planting, pruning, and other vineyard operations are scheduled by the positions of the planets. As Noël Pinguet of Vouvray describes biodynamics, "It's a synthesis of agriculture over the course of history, the observations of farmers throughout civilization."

Blanc de blancs: A white wine made of white grapes.

Blanc de noirs: A white or a pale pink wine made from red grapes that have been pressed immediately off their skins and vinified like white.

Bleeding: The drawing off of juice from a vat of red grapes. It is one method used to make rosé wines, as well as a technique some vintners use to make their reds more concentrated.

Botrytis (*Botrytis cinerea*): The name of a mold that, under certain conditions and with certain types of wine (notably Sauternes and the *moelleux* of the Loire), results in a shriveling of the grapes and a concentration of sugar and acid. These wines are characterized by aromas and flavors of honey and, often, a dense, layered, almost syrupy richness. Also called noble rot (*pourriture noble*).

Brassage à l'air comprimé: A method of stirring up the fermenting mass with filtered air injected from a canister used in the production of red wines.

Breton: Cabernet Franc.

Brut: This applies to "dry" sparkling wine with 0.8 to 1.5 percent sugar; and to an unfinished wine taken from a tank or barrel for sampling, as in *brut de cuve* (tank).

Carbonic maceration: A method of fermentation in which bunches of whole grapes are put into a tank filled with carbon dioxide. Fermentation starts within the individual berries. This method, which produces supple, early-drinking, very aromatic wines, is primarily used with Gamay, particularly in Beaujolais.

Cépage: Grape variety.

Chaptalization: The process of adding sugar to grape juice before fermentation in order to raise the degree of alcohol of the finished wine. French laws permit chaptalization to up to 2 percent alcohol.

Clone: A plant (e.g., a vine) reproduced asexually from a single parent.

Clos: A walled (or otherwise enclosed) vineyard.

Crémant: A sparkling wine with creamier, less forceful bubbles than Champagne.

Cru: The term is applied to a vineyard or a specific area of production, generally of superior quality; a growth. Bonnezeaux, Quarts-de-Chaume, Coulée de Serrant, and La Roche aux Moines are considered the *crus* of Anjou.

Cubitainer (cubi): A plastic jug, usually of 22- to 33-liter capacity, used for buying wine in bulk directly at the winery. Buyers generally bottle the wine at home.

Cuvaison: Refers to the making of red wine; specifically, the practice of fermenting the grape juice with the grape solids (skins, pips, etc.) in order to extract color, tannins, and aroma. Generally, the longer the *cuvaison* (or vatting), the deeper the color of the wine and the more tannic.

Cuve: A tank used for wine production. It may be made from stainless steel, plastic, cement, fiberglass, or other materials; ——— *à pigéage:* a stainless steel tank used in red wine production. The tank is equipped with a mechanism that breaks the cap of grape solids and stirs up the fermenting mass.

Cuvée: Derived from the word *cuve*, this usually applies to a specific blend or lot of wine, e.g., a reserve wine, a single vineyard, or a young- or old-vines bottling.

Débourbage: In white wine production, the practice of allowing the *bourbes* (solid matter such as pits, stems, seeds, and bits of pulp and skin) to settle out of the grape juice before fermentation begins.

Demi-muid: A barrel of 600-liter capacity.

Disgorging: Part of the process of champenization. (*see* Méthode champenoise)

Doux, vin: Sweet wine.

Fillette: In French, a young girl; in the Loire, the term is also used for a half (35-centiliter) bottle.

Filtration: The process of clarifying a wine before bottling to remove yeast cells and other matter, usually by passing the wine through filter pads or diatomaceous earth (kieselguhr).

Fining: A method of clarifying wine by adding various coagulants or clays (egg whites, isinglass, gelatin, bentonite). As these substances settle to the bottom of the tank or barrel, they draw impurities with them, leaving the wine clear.

Foudre: A large wood cask.

Grains Nobles, Sélection de: European law permits vintners in Layon, Bonnezeaux, Quarts-de-Chaume, and Aubance to label their *vin liquoreux* as "Grains Nobles." In 1993 producers from these appellations, in conjunction with the local branch of the INAO, wanted to go a step further. Inspired by existing legislation in Alsace, they adopted more stringent standards. Grapes must have a potential of 17.5 percent alcohol when picked (or a natural richness of 298 grams of sugar a liter). Often abbreviated as SGN or GN.

Gris, vin: A pale rosé made like a *blanc de noirs,* by a direct pressing of the red grapes.

Hectare: 2.47 acres.

Hectoliter: 100 liters or 26.5 gallons. One hectoliter produces eleven cases of wine. Yields are expressed as hectoliters per hectare.

Hybrid: In wine, a grape variety obtained by crossing varieties from different species (e.g., *vinifera* and *labrusca*).

ITV (Institut Technique de la Vigne et du Vin): A government-sponsored agency carrying out research and experiments in all aspects of wine production.

Lees: The deposit thrown by a young wine which settles to the bottom of the tank or barrel. (*see discussion in* Muscadet)

Liquoreux: A very lush sweet wine.

Maceration: (*see* cuvaison)

Malolactic fermentation: The transformation of sharp malic acid (as in apples) to creamier lactic acid (as in milk), which normally occurs after alcoholic fermentation and which results in a less acid wine. Loire reds generally undergo malolactic fermentation; the whites usually do not—although some producers are experimenting with partial or complete malolactic, particularly in very acid years. Also called secondary fermentation.

Méthode champenoise: A technique for making sparkling wine that follows the model of Champagne: A still wine is bottled with additional yeast and sugar. It undergoes a second fermentation or *prise de mousse* during which carbon dioxide is produced and trapped in the wine, begetting the bubbles. Sediment produced by this second fermentation is directed to the neck of the bottle, where it will rest against the cork, by a process called *riddling.* The bottle is tilted and twisted on specially designed A-frame racks called *pupitres* for several weeks until it is upside down. "Disgorging" is the name for the process by which the sediment is removed. EEC regulations now prohibit the use of the term on labels outside of Champagne; in the Loire it has been replaced with *méthode traditionnelle.*

Millésime: Vintage, vintage year.

Moelleux: 1) Refers to sweet wines of the Loire (*see discussions in* Anjou *and* Touraine); 2) literally, "marrowy," a wine with marrow, which can, and often does, include dry wines, particularly those which have aged *sur lie;* 3) mellow.

Mousseux: Sparkling wine.

Must: Unfermented grape juice.

Oeil de perdrix: Literally "partridge eye," it refers to pale, coppery rosés or *vin gris* made from black grapes.

O.N.I. VINS (Office National Interprofessionel des Vins): A government agency overseeing the production of *vins de table* as well as the marketing of all French wine.

Passerillé: A term describing raisined or shriveled grapes whose sugars have been concentrated as a result of loss of water.

Pétillant: A slightly sparkling wine (*see* Vouvray); also used to describe anything that sparkles: a wine, a woman, the atmosphere of a restaurant.

Phylloxera: A vine louse transported from America that ravaged the vineyards of France between 1860 and 1890.

Pièce: A Burgundy barrel with a 228-liter capacity.

Pineau de la Loire: Chenin blanc.

Pourriture noble: Noble rot (*See* Botrytis)

Presse, vin de (**press wine**): In red wine production, the term refers to the wine pressed from the grape solids after the free-run wine has been drawn off (devatted). More tannic than free-run wine, press wine may be blended into the *assemblage* (usually in small amounts) or kept apart.

Prise de mousse: (*See* Méthode champenoise)

Rack, racking: The siphoning of young wine from one tank (or barrel) to another in order to separate it from its lees.

Residual sugar: The sugar left in wine after fermentation has finished or been stopped.

Riddling: (*see* Méthode champenoise)

Sicarex: A research agency funded by the growers and *négociants* of the Nantais.

Skin contact: A method of obtaining richer flavors and texture in white wines by leaving the grapes in contact with their skins for anywhere from several hours to several days before pressing them off their skins for fermentation. (Red wines are made by fermenting the grapes with their skins.)

Sulfur: Used in the vineyard to combat various fungi, pests, and maladies; in the cellar, to clean barrels, prevent oxidation, stun indigenous yeasts, and stop fermentation of sweet wines. It is also added at bottling. Loire vintners have tended to sulfur with a heavy hand. (Overdoses of sulfur can cause a prickly sensation in the nose as well as massive headaches. Wines with too much sulfur often smell and taste reduced—unexpressive except for a vaguely dirty aroma—until they are sufficiently aerated. Decanting is advised.)

Sur lie: Literally, "on lees." 1) The maturing of white wine on its lees; 2) a method of bottling white wine in which the wine is drawn directly off its lees. (For amplification, *see discussion in* Muscadet)

Tannin: A substance found in grape skins and stems—as well as in oak barrels—which imparts flavor and structure to a wine. It is also an antioxidant and helps the wine age. Tannic wines often taste astringent when young—think of strong tea or underripe walnuts—but become softer and rounder as the tannin precipitates out as the wines age, forming part of a red wine's sediment.

Terroir: The concept of *terroir* unites the specifics of a vineyard site—its soils, subsoils, exposition, the opening of the countryside.

Thermoregulated: Temperature-controlled.

Tri (also spelled trie): In winemaking this has two meanings: 1) a labor-intensive method of harvesting by successive passes through the vineyard to pick selected bunches (or grapes) at each pass, rather than harvesting all the grapes at once; and 2) the sorting over of grapes once they have arrived at the winery, e.g., to discard those affected by rot. The table on which this second *tri* occurs is a *table de tri,* or sorting table.

VDQS (Vin Délimité de Qualité Supérieure): A rank between AOC and Vin de Pays, VDQS wine is produced within a delimited zone and according to laws regarding production similar to those governing AOC. Most VDQS wines have applied for promotion to AOC.

Vin de Pays: Loosely, country wine; a rank beneath VDQS, generally covering broad regions such as Jardin de la France.

VQPRD (Vin de Qualité Produit dans une Région Déterminée): EEC initialese for wines of quality above table wine. In France, this means all AOC and VDQS wines.

Wine thief (pipette): A hook-shaped tube with which vintners suction wine from a barrel for tastings.

CHEESE

Affinage: Maturing of cheeses.

Affiné: Aged.

Affineur: Someone who specializes in the aging (maturing) of cheeses.

Artisons: Patois for tiny cheese mites.

Baste: Vat traditionally used for cheesemaking in Saint-Nectaire.

Biologique: Organic.

Bleuté: Cheese developing a blue mold on its crust; or cheese at the stage when such a mold develops.

Brebis: Ewe; sheep's-milk cheese.

Brique: A low, flat, rectangular cheese.

Caillé: Curd.

Cendré: Cheese coated with ashes.

Crémerie: Cheese shop.

Croûte: Crust or rind of a cheese.

Cru: 1) Raw: *lait* ———, raw milk; 2) specific place or region (*see definition under* Wine).

Fromage blanc: Fresh cheese, with little or no salt.

Label Rouge: An official designation for agricultural and other food products (poultry, meat, charcuterie, dairy, fruits, vegetables, salt) made according to certain specifications.

Mold: 1) Container used in cheesemaking that determines the shape of the cheese; 2) the fungus developing on the surface or in the center of the cheese, either naturally acquired or induced with industrial bacteria.

Pasteurization: Heat treatment that destroys both good and bad microorganisms.

Pâte: Interior of cheese.

Petit lait: Whey.

Repassé: Overripe cheese. (*See discussion in* Crottin de Chavignol)

Thermisé, thermisation: A heat treatment of raw milk at lower temperatures than pasteurization.

Tonne: 1,000 kilograms.

Washed crust (or rind): A class of cheeses whose crusts are washed in brine, *eau-de-vie*, or marc as part of the maturation process, e.g., Livarot, Munster.

APPENDIX C

Suggested Temperatures for Serving Loire Wines

(Temperatures given here are Fahrenheit.)

WHITES

Muscadet: I like them really iced, to around 43 degrees. Those aged in oak should be served warmer, up to 55 degrees.

Chenin: Serve sec at 48 degrees, demi-sec at 46 degrees, and *moelleux* at 43 degrees. (*Note:* If prior experience leads you to believe the Chenin in question may have overdoses of sulfur, decant an hour in advance, and refrigerate. If you have not aerated the wine in advance, try pouring it from one decanter to another several times.)

Sancerre and Pouilly: Serve most around 48 degrees. Those aged in oak should be served between 55 and 58 degrees.

Sparkling wines: Serve between 41 and 45 degrees.

REDS

Lighter reds, including almost all those based on Gamay, most of those based on Pinot Noir, and young or young-vines style Cabernet Franc, should be chilled to between 55 and 58 degrees. Richer Cabernet and Sancerre rouge, as well as any aged reds, should be served cool but not cold, at between 59 and 62 degrees. If the wine is throwing sediment you should decant it. If it suffers from overdoses of sulfur, decant in advance or aerate by pouring from one decanter to another.

ROSES

Chill rosés as you would dry whites, 43 to 48 degrees.

APPENDIX D

Conversion Tables

YIELDS

One hectare equals 2.47 acres, which I have rounded off to 2.5 acres.

One hectoliter equals 100 liters, or 26.5 gallons.

Yields are expressed as hectoliters per hectare, and abbreviated as hl/ha.

Converting hl/ha to tons per acre or cases per acre must be approximate. The amount of wine made from a lot of grapes varies depending on the efficacy of the press and the style of wine (botrytized or shriveled grapes will produce less juice than normally ripe grapes). The conversions given below correspond to dry table wines, such as Chinon or Sancerre. A case is understood to comprise twelve full bottles of wine.

Hl/Ha	Tons/Acre	Cases/Acre
10	0.71	44.7
20	1.42	89.5
30	2.13	134.2
40	2.84	178.9
50	3.55	223.7
60	4.26	268.4
70	4.97	313.1
80	5.68	357.8
90	6.39	402.6
100	7.10	447.3

TEMPERATURES

°C (Celsius)	°F (Fahrenheit)
10	50
15	59
20	68
25	77
30	86
35	95
40	104
100	212

BIBLIOGRAPHY

In addition to the works listed below, I relied on reports by government agencies such as various Chambres d'Agriculture, FIVAL (Fédération Interprofessionnelle du Val de Loire), regional wine and food *syndicats*, CIDIL (Centre Interprofessionel de Documentation et d'Information Laitières), FROMAGORA, ITV, O.N.I.VINS, and regional meteorological services, as well as on the specific statutes promulgated by the INAO governing each appellation of origin (wine and food), VDQS, and Label Rouge. I also read local magazines such as *Touraine* and *Anjou* as well as yearly editions of the *Guide Hachette Vins*, Gault-Millau's *Le Vin*, and the green Michelin guides for each region of the Loire Basin.

Androuet, Pierre. *The Complete Encyclopedia of French Cheese*. New York: Harper's Magazine Press, 1973.

Asher, Gerald. *On Wine*. New York: Random House, 1982.

Bardon-Labarrière. *La Touraine à Table*. Mur de Sologne: Editions Dominique Labarrière, 1983.

Beaumord, Madeleine. *La Cuisine Traditionnelle Française: Recettes du Val de Loire*. Tours: La Nouvelle République, 1986.

Bespaloff, Alexis. *The New Frank Schoonmaker Encyclopedia of Wine*. New York: Morrow, 1988.

Blanchet, Suzanne. *Les Vins du Val de Loire*. Editions Jema, 1982.

Bois, D. *Les Plantes Alimentaires chez Tous les Peuples et à Travers les Ages*. Paris: Lechevallier, 1927.

Bonneton, Christine, ed. *Anjou*. Paris: Christine Bonneton, 1985.

———, ed. *Bourbonnais*. Paris: Christine Bonneton, 1984.

———, ed. *Touraine*. Paris: Christine Bonneton, 1989.

Bréjoux, Pierre. *Les Vins de Loire.* Paris: Compagnie Parisienne d'Editions Techniques et Commerciales, 1956.

Camiran, J. de. *Le Vignoble du Pays Nantais*. Nantes: Presse de l'Ouest, 1937.

Chast, Michel, and Henry Voy. *Le Livre de l'Amateur de Fromages*. Paris: Robert Laffont, 1984.

CNAC (Conseil National des Arts Culinaires). *L'Inventaire du Patrimoine Culinaire de la France: Pays de la Loire*. Paris: Albin Michel, 1993.

———. *L'Inventaire du Patrimoine Culinaire de la France: Poitou-Charentes*. Paris: Albin Michel, 1994.

Curnonsky (Maurice Sailland, Prince des Gastronomes). *Recettes des Provinces de France*. Paris: Productions de Paris, 1962.

Denoueix, Martine. *Les Pays de la Loire: A Gastronomic Heritage*. Laval: Siloe, 1993.

Dion, Roger. *Histoire de la Vigne et du Vin en France, des Origines aux XIXème Siècle*. Paris: Flammarion, 1959, 1977.

Duijcker, Hubrecht. *The Wines of the Loire, Alsace, and Champagne*. London: Mitchell Beazely, 1983.

Galet, Pierre. *Cépages et Vignobles de France*. Vol. 1, *Les Vignes Américaines*. Montpellier: Imprimerie Charles Dehan, 1988.

———. *Cépages et Vignobles de France*. Vols. 2 and 3. Montpellier: Galet, 1958 and 1962.

Gilbert, François, and Philippe Gaillard. *Pays de la Loire, des Côtes du Forez au Pays Nantais*. Guides des Vins Gilbert & Gaillard. Paris: Solar, 1991.

Grigson, Jane. *Jane Grigson's Fruit Book*. New York: Penguin, 1982.

———. *Jane Grigson's Vegetable Book*. New York: Atheneum, 1979.

Huguet, Jean. *Les Vins de Vendée, des Origines à Demain*. La Mothe-Achard: EFA, 1990.

Johnson, Hugh. *Modern Encyclopedia of Wine*. 3rd ed. New York: Simon & Schuster, 1991.

———. *Vintage: The Story of Wine*. New York: Simon & Schuster, 1989.

———. *Hugh Johnson's Modern Encyclopedia of Wine*. 3rd ed. New York: Simon & Schuster, 1991.

———. *World Atlas of Wine*. 3rd ed. New York: Simon & Schuster, 1985.

Lachiver, Marcel. *Vins, Vignes, et Vignerons*. Paris: Fayard, 1988.

Librairie Larousse. *Larousse Gastronomique*. Paris: Larousse, 1984.

Maisonneuve, Dr. *L'Anjou: Ses Vignes et Ses Vins*. Vol. 1. Angers: Imprimerie du Commerce, 1925.

Quittanson, Charles. *Connaissance des Vins et Eaux-de-Vie: Code Analytique des Vins et Eaux-de-Vie Français*. Paris: Publications Borelli, 1984.

Rabelais, François. *Gargantua*. Paris: Livre de Poche, 1994.

Rabelais, François. *Gargantua and Pantagruel*. Translated by J. M. Cohen. Middlesex, Eng.: Penguin, 1986.

Rance, Patrick. *French Cheese*. London: Macmillan, 1989.

Robinson, Jancis. *Vines, Grapes, and Wines*. New York: Knopf, 1986.

Root, Waverly. *The Food of France*. 1958. Reprint. New York: Knopf, 1977.

Sophos, O. *Les Nobles Vins de Touraine*. Tours: DK, 1937.

Spurrier, Stephen. *French Country Wines*. London: Willow Collins Books, 1984.

Tardif, Bernard and Nina, and Jean-Louis Boncoeur. *Cuisine et Vins en Berry*. Editions Horvath.

Tourret, Marissou. *La Cuisinière Auvergnate*. Nonette: Editions Créer, 1990.

VanDyke Price, Pamela. *The Penguin Book of Spirits and Liqueurs*. Harmondsworth, Middlesex: Penguin, 1980.

Vence, Céline, and Jean-Claude Frentz. *Tout est Bon dans le Cochon*. Paris: Robert Laffont, 1988.

Verroust, Jacques, Michel Pastoureau, and Raymond Buren. *Le Cochon: Historie, Symbolique, et Cuisine du Porc*. Paris: Editions Sang de la Terre, 1987.

Vigier, Philippe, ed. *Une Histoire de la Loire*. Paris: Editions Ramsay, 1986.

Wells, Patricia. *The Food Lover's Guide to France*. New York: Workman, 1987.

Willan, Anne. *French Regional Cookery*. New York: Morrow, 1981.

INDEX